The Art of Testing Network Systems

Robert Buchanan, Jr.

Wiley Computer Publishing

WILEY

John Wiley & Sons, Inc.

New York • Chichester • Brisbane • Toronto • Singapore

Publisher: Katherine Schowalter

Senior Editor: Marjorie Spencer

Managing Editor: Micheline Frederick

Text Design and Illustrations: Aesthetic License/Kristine Buchanan

Designations used by companies to distinguish their products are often claimed as trademarks. In all instances where John Wiley & Sons, Inc. is aware of a claim, the product names appear in initial capital or all capital letters. Readers, however, should contact the appropriate companies for more complete information regarding trademarks and registration.

This text is printed on acid-free paper.

This publication is designed to provide accurate and authoritative information in regard to the subject matter covered. It is sold with the understanding that the publisher is not engaged in rendering legal, accounting, or other professional service. If legal advice or other expert assistance is required, the services of a competent professional person should be sought.

Library of Congress Cataloging-in-Publication Data:

Buchanan, Robert W., 1947
    The art of testing network systems / Robert W. Buchanan, Jr.
      p.   cm.
    Includes bibliographical references and index.
    ISBN 0-471-13223-3 (cloth : alk. paper)
    1. Computer networks—Testing.   I. Title.
TK5105.5.B83 1996
'004.6'028'7—dc20   95-45445
                                                  CIP

Printed in the United States of America
10 9 8 7 6 5

Acknowledgments

Since the first objective of any book is to clearly communicate its contents, my thanks to Gretchen Banducci for dotting the I's, crossing the T's, and keeping most of my sentences to less than a paragraph in length.

Theory provides the structure, while practice develops procedures and measures the benefits. Chuck Luckaszewski, whose experience as a network consultant to corporations with large networks, several of which are pioneers in network testing, helped provide examples and insight which created balance between theory and practice. This, I believe makes the book equally valuable for the network manager in the trenches, the financial decision maker, and the applications developer/tester.

Thanks also to Bob Shervem whose suggestions on the benefits of testing presentation structure, layout, and figure content, help make Part I easier to understand for the manager and financial decision maker.

My thanks to both Rig Currie and Ron Kopeck for their confidence in me. Rig was the first person who encouraged me to write down my experiences and knowledge of network testing, while Ron gave me the hope to believe I could find a publisher for this book.

Very special thanks goes to my wife and friend, Kris. She helped in innumerable ways during the planning and writing of the book. In particular, Kris is the only one I know who could have developed my scribbles into the complex, interesting, and informative diagrams and figures that illustrate the book.

About the Author

Robert Buchanan, Jr. spent 4 years as Sr. Vice President and General Manager of LANQuest, a network consulting company and independent test lab. During his tenure at LANQuest, he developed many network testing procedures and several widely used testing utilities. Prior to LANQuest, he spent 7 years in product management at 3Com Corporation. Today, he is a network consultant working with both end users and product vendors. Mr. Buchanan has written many articles for networking journals including *LAN Magazine*, *Network World*, *CNEPA Journal* and *Network Expo* and has spoken at Interop, NetWorld, Network and PC Expos, and Comdex.

Preface

Network testing is time-consuming, often difficult, and, if done correctly, *extremely valuable in maintaining a reliable and high-performance network*. I have written this book in the hope that you, like the company examples described here, can use testing to improve your network's quality.

Networks are very complex systems and the only way to test them is to partition them into manageable layers and functions that can be analyzed. Doing this is truly an art, the **art** of testing. My original intent with *The Art of Testing Network Systems* was to provide a comprehensive guide that included step-by-step instructions for testing and using testing tools. As I wrote the book, however, I realized that step-by-step procedures encompassed too much detail to fit into a single book. Each of the three parts of this book could easily be a separate book.

In talking to many network managers and support people involved in testing today, I also realized that what they lacked in the beginning was not the detail of how to use tools, but guidance on the basic philosophy of what to test, the methodology of how to test, and the benefits they should expect from different types of testing. This is the information they really needed to make testing a beneficial and cost-effective tool.

Therefore, this book is focused on helping you understand the benefits of testing and getting you started on proactive (testing) that complements reactive (monitoring) management of your network. It provides guidelines on why to test, when to test, and how to structure testing to get relevant, reproducible, and accurate results.

This is the only book I know of dedicated to network testing. Hopefully, as the network market realizes the benefits of testing, more books will become available that continue the goal of *The Art of Testing Network Systems*; helping you keep your networks up and running.

Contents

Part IV

Introduction

Most network managers are very unhappy with their return on investment from network management products, which have not provided the information or tools necessary to help them meet the challenges of complex client-server applications, file service performance tuning, and internetworking services, such as electronic mail and groupware applications. While network management tools help network managers pinpoint problems more quickly, the basic problem is that they are not delivering on their promise of keeping the network from failing in the first place. Unfortunately, many network managers just continue in this stressful, reactive mode because they don't have the time, experience, or financial authority to evaluate or pursue other alternatives. Network managers who consider testing, often quickly dismiss it because they feel they don't have the resources or time to pursue what they believe will require a substantial investment.

The plain truth is that today's internetworks have enormous downtime rates. If senior management and network managers don't identify new alternatives to improve this problem, down sizing and deployment of client-server applications either aren't going to happen or aren't going to be successful.

Proactive system testing complements the existing investment in network management products and provides a proven approach for improving system and application quality. Proactive testing is an inexpensive approach for avoiding network slowdowns and failures, and it is just beginning to be employed by network professionals. Companies, such as American Express, Boeing, Motorola, Lehman Brothers, American Stores, MCI, American Airlines, Goldman Sachs, and Fingerhut, are beginning to use testing as a potent capability to improve network systems management and client-server application development. However, with all the potential benefits of proactive testing, most network planning and support organizations do not actively and methodically test their network and network applications. Testing is often an infrequent and poorly planned exercise, which returns significantly less value than it should. While some leading companies have learned to test through trial and error, the benefits of network testing for companies just starting to test are limited. They lack the experience, guidance, and information necessary to make testing valuable and cost-effective, and the learning curve is steep if they have to "learn as they go."

Information presented in The Art of Testing Network Systems can help you identify and implement proactive testing opportunities that will provide significant benefits in keeping your networks up and running. Example I.1 presents one case study on the benefits of proactive network testing.

Example I.1

A large financial securities company tests its production network every day to ensure uninterrupted up time for key users.

The company has developed several client-server applications for securities trading. Every day when the markets open, the system must be up, running, and ready for the traders. If the system isn't available, the downside can be quite expensive. If the system is slow, the downside can also be quite expensive. The staff found that the best way to guarantee system availability was to perform, in effect, a *regression test* (defined in Chapter 4) on the system every morning before the markets opened. Initially this was done by hand, but now the process is automated using Mercury Interactive's LoadRunner.

The automated process runs every morning. Problems that are identified are immediately sent to the network manager for resolution before the users arrive for work. This not only improves application availability, but frees critical resources from tedious, manual tasks. Return on investment in testing tools and resources is better system reliability and availability. This means lower support costs, higher user satisfaction, better use of critical resources, and potentially higher profit for the company.❑

While most testing is not done on production networks, this is a unique example of how proactive testing can be applied to reduce risk and improve quality. Other examples of production network testing are discussed in Part III.

Bringing together a testing philosophy and methodology that addresses the complex, heterogeneous nature of today's company-wide internetworks and client-server applications is *The Art of Testing Network Systems*. The book presents guidelines and procedures based on over nine years and thousands of hours of network product management, testing, consulting, and network administration by the author and associates at major network vendors, network consulting companies, large end users, and independent test labs.

HOW TO USE THIS BOOK

This book is divided into four parts:

- **Part I**, Chapters 1 to 8, is an introduction to the fundamentals of network testing Read this part to familiarize yourself with basic testing procedures, methodologies, and objectives. Part I also explains how to use testing as a complement to existing network management and troubleshooting tools and procedures.

- **Part II**, Chapters 9 to 17, provides detailed instructions and reference material for testing the network transport layers, routers, switches, hubs, and wide area network (WAN) links.

- **Part III**, Chapters 18 to 29, provides detailed instructions and reference material for testing the network application and presentation layers, including client-server applications, database servers, and graphical user interfaces (GUIs).

- **Part IV**, Chapter 30, provides a brief summary of products and tools available for network testing.

Target Reader/Responsibility	Pertinent Chapters
Network manager "Sign-off" responsibility for new systems Financial responsibility for new systems Responsible for implementing new systems	Introduction Part I
Network system design, modification, or support New technologies Network transport layers Telecommunications	Introduction Part I Part II
Design, implement, or support network applications Support the network operating system (NOS) Develop user interfaces Support the workstation's operating system Train network users	Introduction Part I Part III
Implement a network test lab Perform network product evaluations Improve the network's quality	Introduction Part I Part II Part III

Figure I.1   Recommended reading based on interest and area of responsibility.

Depending on individual interest and area of responsibility, some portions of the book are more pertinent than others. The following recommends various approaches to reading this book, as summarized in Figure I.1.

Everyone should read the Introduction and the first eight chapters. If you are a network manager, have "sign-off" responsibility for new systems, have financial responsibility for new systems, or are responsible for implementing new systems, pay particular attention to the special section on Acceptance Testing, Chapter 5.

If you are responsible for network system design, modification or support; new technologies; the network transport layers; or telecommunications, Part II provides detailed test objectives covering the network transport layers or infrastructure. Be sure to read the Introduction and Chapters 1 through 8 before embarking on Part II.

If you design, implement or support network applications; support the network operating system (NOS); develop user interfaces; support the workstation's operating system; or train network users, Chapters 1 through 8 and Part III provide information on testing client-server applications and presentation layers, such as Microsoft Windows.

If you are responsible for implementing a network test lab, performing network product or technology comparisons, or improving your network's quality, then you should read the *entire* book. Parts II, III, and IV can be used as reference guides as you undertake specific testing projects. Pay particular attention to Testing Philosophy and Methodology discussed in Chapter 6, and Test Configuration Alternatives presented in Chapter 7.

If you want to know about network testing tools, Part IV provides an overview of available test tool categories and individual products.

TESTING STANDARDS

One of the best things about networking standards is that there are so many of them. This allows everyone to accept one or more of the standards. The area of network management is no exception. Many companies originally developed proprietary protocols and monitoring techniques, and some still use them. However, one standard is becoming widely accepted. Simple Network Management Protocol (SNMP), and its extension for Remote Network Management (RMON), are now used by most major vendors and companies.

In the network testing market, there has not been a dominate organization that has been successful in creating standards. The Transaction Performance Council (TPC) has developed a series of transaction processing tests for databases. This has been used in the UNIX market, but TPC has never been widely accepted in the networking market. Several years ago, an industry group, called the Network Performance Alliance, attempted to establish benchmarking standards for networks. More recently, the Business Alliance Performance Company (BAPCO) has developed a series of application-based tests that measure network response time. These have been used widely, but are not fully accepted by several leading vendors. TPC and BAPCO address only performance.

A lack of network testing standards exists today, with no foreseeable resolution. Because of this, no one knows how his or her networks should perform, or how to accurately measure networks. Vendors don't have tests that buyers trust, and buyers don't know what to ask for or how to measure what they get. Test labs, testers, and test tool vendors do not have a consistent or documented terminology for describing their products or testing environments. To fill this void and help answer the above questions, The Art of Testing Network Systems *defines a terminology for describing the various elements of network testing and procedures for measuring network performance, reliability, and capacity. Throughout the book, terms are introduced, such as equivalent load, emulation, and load distribution, that will probably be new to you. Within the context of* The Art of Testing Network Systems, *each term has a well-defined meaning that is included in the text and then summarized in the Glossary.*

Since networks can be built with multiple, heterogeneous components from a huge selection of vendors, every network is essentially unique, and every network manager and application developer has site-dependent issues to deal with. Because there are many different network management products, network analyzers, and testing tools on the market, presenting a plethora of options and potential problems, the testing procedures described in this book focus on planning, process, data analysis, actionable results, and return on testing investment, rather than step-by-step instructions for using individual equipment or solving specific problems. This allows the test methodology to be employed across a broad range of projects. The book also helps to justify the cost and effort of proactive testing by illustrating the value of actionable test results, as illustrated in the previous example.

Part

I

Why Test?

KEEPING THE NETWORK UP AND RUNNING

Networks are becoming the platform of choice for many companies' mission-critical client-server applications, large electronic mail systems, and groupware programs. However, the rate at which client-server applications will be funded and deployed depends on the reliability and user acceptance of these systems. It is already evident that improved availability, reliability, and performance of both the network and network applications must be achieved to make these systems productive for the user and cost-effective for the company. Proactive testing is a proven approach for improving system availability, reliability, and performance.

This book is a guide to the philosophy, methodology, procedures, tools, and information that network managers need to keep their networks up and running. Generating accurate, reproducible, and relevant test results allows the network manager to measure the performance and reliability of the network and applications prior to deployment, when they are upgraded, and before they run out of capacity.

Network administrators and support personnel are constantly in a reactive, fire-fighting mode, struggling to maintain the uptime and performance of their networks. Traditionally, many organizations have just thrown some of their incredibly limited resources (money, people, and equipment) at solving network performance, reliability, and load problems. This never really worked, however, and it is becoming even less effective based on the nature of today's network environment. As illustrated in Figure 1.1, networks are being strained by:

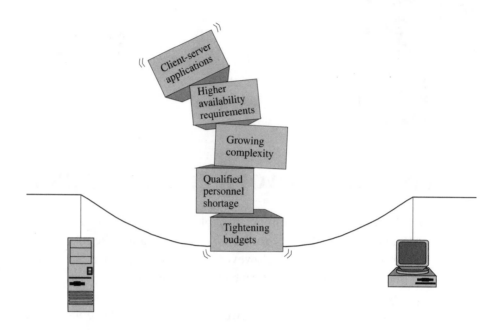

Figure 1.1   Causes of increasing strain on today's networks.

- **Client-server applications:** Client-server application users require a significantly higher degree of network availability, reliability, and responsiveness than productivity application users.

- **Higher availability requirements:** The user community requires mainframe-comparable system uptime, 24 hours a day, seven days a week.

- **Growing complexity:** Internetworks are growing larger and more complex both at the infrastructure and application layers.

- **Qualified personnel shortage:** Relative to the number of network installations, there is a declining proportion of qualified technical personnel.

- **Tightening budgets:** Budgetary resources available for network systems are declining relative to the increase in nodal connections.

Looking at this from the perspective of network applications, strain is increasing from:

- **Distributed core business applications:** As critical business applications are targeted toward networks rather than traditional mainframe (legacy) systems, new traffic loads and nonexistent or inadequate testing budgets and efforts are increasing network failure rates.

- **Distributed groupware applications:** The growing number of desktops running Lotus Notes and other collaborative software, whether off-the-shelf or developed in-house, is adding new servers and traffic loads.

- **Distributed management applications:** In some large networks, the legacy system dilemma of management overhead is rearing its ugly head. Management information flowing across the network is rising to volumes that are causing additional strain on the network. In large mainframe configurations, 30 to 40 percent of the system's capacity is often eaten up by management tasks. Network overhead is not to that level yet, but this is an area of growing network stress and concern.

Large networks have always had reliability problems, but outages are noticed even more now by users and management alike because more people than ever are using the network regularly, and a growing number of the users depend on the network for mission-critical applications.

In many ways, legacy systems are a wonderful role model of what to do and what not to do. While we can all argue that these systems often didn't meet user requirements for timely implementation of new applications and critical information access, the systems did provide exceptional uptime. For over 25 years, systems development, applications development, and operations support groups for mainframes and large minicomputers have used *monitoring and proactive testing* to help achieve the impressive uptime and reliability these legacy systems are known for. If network-based mission-critical systems are to achieve their true potential, they must be as reliable as existing legacy systems, while providing faster application development and deployment to better meet the accelerated pace of today's business.

Network monitoring has been used since the late 1980s, but missing is the proactive network testing. This is because few people have been able to figure out how to do it in an environment as complex as a large internetwork. However, the few companies who are doing proactive network testing are reaping big rewards, as shown in the following examples.

Example 1.1

A large retail chain that owns more than 1,000 stores is in the middle of a massive client-server application development project. The company, which like many has traditionally been IBM mainframe- and SNA-based, is doing *all* new application development on client-server platforms. It currently has several major applications under development, including payroll, purchasing, and other financial applications. It is using testing in the planning, design, purchase, and development of client-server applications, and to guarantee that it's existing network has the capacity to support the rollout of these new applications.

Based on its IBM mainframe performance experience, the company realized early that proactive network testing would be a major requirement in client-server development. Its efforts started over one year ago. It developed testing procedures from scratch because there were no guidelines, standards, or reference materials available. The process has been very difficult and much harder than its mainframe experiences because of the increased complexity of the network environment. But the hard work has paid big dividends already, and the company expects it to be critical to the successful deployment of its client-server applications. The test focus has been performance, capacity planning, and some acceptance testing.

Some of the issues the company has encountered include:

- Difficulty in identifying traditional workflow composition and transaction mix because the GUI allows the users to generate different sequences of events based on menu selections. Also, it has been time-consuming to equate business operations, such as retrieving a record (the simplest transaction), with network operation and traffic generation. For example, users found that one record access (a single transaction) generated 120 network requests/responses. They analyzed this using a new product from CoroNet, which captures application transactions similar to the way an analyzer captures network packets. They sent a specified set of transactions to the server and measured the associated network activity. This proved to be very manual and time-consuming, but the only way they found to characterize application traffic patterns.

- The basic network system is critical to the success of the client-server applications. Developers found that the network system has to be measured and understood early in the development cycle. Performance, capacity, and reliability problems at this level are often harder to fix, cost more, and require more lead time than comparable application-level problems. One key to successful client-server applications is a stable network platform.

- Client-server applications tend to be very integrated, therefore the applications need to be tested concurrently for interoperability. A problem in one can affect them all. Since these are mission-critical applications, users can't afford to have this happen.

Although this company had to learn these processes through trial and error, you can use the proven approaches for transaction load modeling, infrastructure testing, and other testing procedures presented in this book to accelerate the process and ensure a good return for your effort.

The effort to develop a proactive network testing capability has been difficult, but the return on the investment has been worth the effort:

- When the initial client-server application was tested, results were good for 20 concurrent users. When the load was increased to 30 users, the application crashed. This surprised them, but they were happy it happened during testing and not after deploying it on the production system.

- Using a product from Mercury Interactive called LoadRunner, loads were modeled that represented estimated equivalent production loads. Running these load/stress tests against the database server crashed the server almost daily over a one-month period. The company had to get the database vendor involved to improve the stability and capacity of the software to meet its needs.❏

- For some product purchases, the company included benchmarking as an acceptance criterion in the contract. This ensured that the system could meet its needs prior to purchase.

The benefits of proactive testing achieved by this company can also be applied to your network by following the philosophy and methodology outlined in this book.

Example 1.2

A large oil company proactively tests network upgrades for compatibility and interoperability. It found that many network problems were caused when upgrades, particularly software upgrades, were applied to the network. Since there were plans to significantly grow the number of network nodes, managers figured that if they couldn't resolve these upgrade issues, matters would only get worse as the number of users increased.

Today, they use a small test configuration and automated scripts of application commands to verify that an upgrade passes the same tests as the current version before deploying it across the production network. The cost for developing the tests and setting up the small test network was less than the price of many network analyzers. Since the tests are automated, running the tests takes minimum support staff time. This has reduced problems related to upgrades and improved network reliability.❏

Example 1.3

Examples 1.1 and 1.2 focus on application and client-server application testing. This example is about a major financial services company that used proactive network testing during the planning and design of a major new nationwide network installation. Testing was used to evaluate technologies, such as satellite links, frame relay, and switched lines to determine which provided the capacity and functionality required for the new system. This company was developing a new network infrastructure or baseline on which future applications would run. The fundamental challenges for the planning group were:

- Defining a test process.

- Developing testing tools (most of which were developed in-house).

- Building a test lab.

- Developing network traffic models for applications that would run on the network, but were not yet designed, built, or available.

Part II of *The Art of Testing Network Systems* answers most of the challenges this company faced. It discusses in detail how to test various network components and subsystems, such as routers, switches, hubs, and communication links. As a senior member of the company said, "We couldn't have done it without the lab." The lab provided several key technical and financial benefits, including:

- Technical benefits:

    Test input from the lab was used to plan and design the network based on individual component capacity.

    Lab tests determined that IPX protocol did not work well in a satellite transmission-centric environment. This eventually eliminated satellite (VSAT) as an option.

    Lab results were used to estimate the cost to grow capacity as the network grew.

    Test scripts developed in the lab are being used today to verify hardware and software changes and upgrades to the network. As one employee said, "Couldn't live without it."

The test lab came to be viewed as a learning center for the technical staff, who really enjoyed working in the lab. It became viewed as a "perk" to work there.

Application development began to use the lab, also.

- Management/Financial benefits:

    The lab provided senior management with a higher level of confidence based on hard test facts.

    Test data from the lab allowed the company to negotiate with vendors from a position of knowledge about product capabilities and problems.

    Using test data, the company established acceptance criteria and penalties that were included in agreements and contracts.

    Vendors contractually committed to fixes for product problems.❏

Testing both network applications and the network infrastructure or baseline is critical. If the baseline isn't solid, applications running on the network won't be responsive and reliable. If the baseline is solid, but the applications don't provide required performance and capacity, users will perceive the network as unavailable or unreliable. Both parts must work in unison. That is why Part II discusses testing the network infrastructure, and Part III discusses testing the application/presentation layers of the network.

Testing can be compared to inexpensive maintenance, like regularly changing your car's oil. Simple tests to verify product performance, compatibility, interoperability, and reliability prior to deployment on the production network can have significant payback, as illustrated by the previous examples and the next two sections.

The Art of Testing Network Systems *provides a philosophy and methodology that makes network testing a valuable, timely, and cost-effective part of network system development, implementation, and support. The capital cost of network testing is significantly less than for larger systems, and typically less than the reactive mode of troubleshooting most companies now employ. A production network can be emulated in a small lab environment for a fraction of the production network's cost; and, with care, testing can be done on the production network. By using a small portion of existing budgets for purchasing monitoring and troubleshooting tools, a company can perform proactive testing to get information that will keep the network up and running with less effort.*

THE COST OF SLOWDOWNS AND DOWNTIME

Considering the increasing demands companies are putting on their networks to support critical revenue-generating services (such as computerized telesales, securities trading, and customer support desks) and the growing technical complexity of the network system, it is not surprising that real dollar losses for network users are escalating due to network slowdowns and downtime, as illustrated in Figure 1.2.

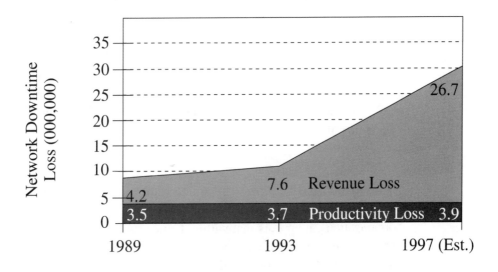

Figure 1.2 End-user network downtime costs.

Data available from Infonetics Research (8/1/94) shows that productivity loss based on local area network (LAN) and server outages has remained relatively constant, while revenue loss has risen dramatically for end users since 1989 and is expected to grow at an annualized rate of almost 60 percent from 1993 to 1997.

Since the early 1970s, proactive product/system evaluation, performance optimization, bottleneck analysis, and capacity planning have been employed successfully on large computer systems, by phone companies, and on America's space program to reduce downtime and improve performance of their systems. Proactive systems analysis of networks, however, has not been conducted by most companies. Network personnel are typically busy trying to resolve network outages and believe they lack the time, resources, experience, tools, and management support for proactive testing. In many cases, they are right! When asked about testing, network development and support groups often respond, "We don't have time for testing." The second most often heard response is, "Management won't pay for testing. It's easier to get approval to purchase another analyzer."

In most companies, it is much easier to get financial approval for a new analyzer or debugging tool than for testing software or lab equipment. But, if testing can reduce slowdowns and downtime by even a small percentage, the effort spent on avoiding problems (proactive testing) versus fixing problems (reactive troubleshooting) is worthwhile. First, companies need to surmount the initial hurdles (time and resources) to realize the benefits of testing. Chapters 6 and 7 outline methods to achieve success in your first testing project and show a valuable return for low up-front costs and effort.

Many of the largest, industry-leading companies are realizing that testing is a requirement they must support to achieve high-quality network systems. From an informal survey of Fortune 1000 companies and several government organizations, it appears that within the next two to three years, many of these groups will be conducting proactive testing to improve their network systems, and many will have established dedicated test labs.

It won't be surprising in the near future to hear company spokespeople say, "I can't afford not to be testing," based on:

- The increasing cost of slowdowns and downtime.

- The fact that reactive troubleshooting isn't providing required network reliability.

- The success of companies doing proactive testing.

Another benefit of testing is user satisfaction. If you ask support organizations how they detect network problems, the most common answer is that they hear about them from their users. LANQuest's network consulting group at one time supported about 20 end-user network sites. The group's experience showed that clients were heard from only when they had problems, which also meant that LANQuest knew there were problems only when they heard from a client.

Think back to the last time you spoke with your network users: wouldn't it have been nice to have solved a problem before the user experienced it? Wouldn't it have been well received if you had told them an impending problem was just detected and was being fixed? Proactive testing can help solve problems before they manifest, thereby improving overall user satisfaction and making the network support job easier.

THE COST-EFFECTIVENESS OF TESTING

Testing can be a very cost-effective approach to avoiding network problems. Let's consider a simple example of a mission-critical network system used for catalogue sales and to support a telesales organization. Customers call an 800 number to place orders. The software performs several basic functions through a series of menus and prompts based on a graphical user interface (GUI) under an operating system, such as Microsoft Windows. The telesales application:

1. Accesses a customer account by ID number, or captures the customer's name and address for a new account entry.

2. Verifies stock on hand for the requested items.

3. Validates the customer credit card number.

4. Places an order into the system.

5. Generates a packing and shipping slip.

6. Sends the order to the warehouse for fulfillment.

7. Interfaces with accounts receivable.

8. Updates inventory of the ordered items.

9. Enters a new account's customer name and ID into a mailing list.

If, for example, the company has 30 telesales representatives, each transaction takes two minutes, and each sale averages $50, the telesales department in one eight-hour day can process $360,000 in sales orders. If we assume that each sales rep is constantly busy and cannot handle additional customer calls, this sales rate generates approximately $94,000,000 in annual revenue. The telesales network configuration and current base revenue is shown in Figure 1.3.

Consider the company's potential loss if the system breaks down (network downtime). If the system becomes inoperable for only one hour, the company loses $45,000 in revenue, which it probably cannot recover, assuming that the call is lost and there is no excess telesales bandwidth to service more customers when the system comes back on-line. This is bad, but not horrible, as it represents approximately .04 percent of annual revenues. If the system experiences two failures, three failures, or monthly failures (one hour per failure), the financial impact on the company is less than .5 percent of annual sales. This is disturbing

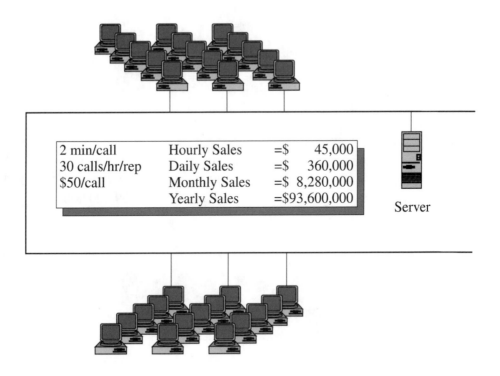

Figure 1.3 Telesales current base revenue with 30 sales representatives.

news, but the company will survive these crashes. Certainly, though, the problems would get the attention of upper management and be emotionally and physically draining on the network support staff. These are the type of outages Infonetics measured in their survey, and the scenario that most people fear and try to protect against with network management tools.

Now consider a second, an even more frightening scenario—a system slowdown. Why is this more frightening? Because a system slowdown can be significantly more expensive to the company than a system failure, and often the loss is less noticeable because it happens gradually. Assume that business is booming and the company adds five new telesales reps. If system performance is maintained so that each call can still be serviced in two minutes, the additional five sales reps can increase the yearly revenue to $109,200,000. The new target

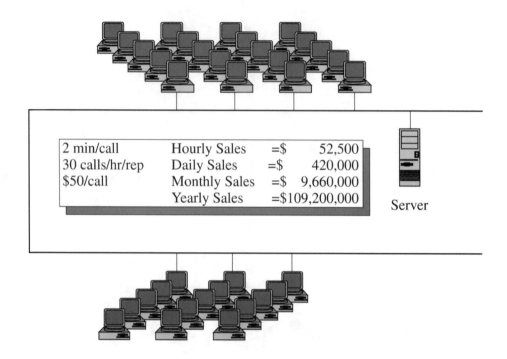

Figure 1.4   Telesales target sales rate with 35 sales representatives.

sales rate is shown in Figure 1.4. But what if system or application performance degrades due to the higher user load?

2 min 18 sec/call	Hourly Sales	=$	45,500
26 calls/hr/rep	Daily Sales	=$	364,000
$50/call	Monthly Sales	=$	8,372,000
	Yearly Sales	=$	94,649,000

Figure 1.5   Case I, telesales volume with 35 sales representatives and 15 percent system response degradation.

2 min 30 sec/call	Hourly Sales	=$ 42,000
24 calls/hr/rep	Daily Sales	=$ 336,000
$50/call	Monthly Sales	=$ 7,728,000
	Yearly Sales	=$87,360,000

Figure 1.6   Case II, telesales volume with 35 sales representatives and 25 percent system response degradation.

Case I: The additional load from the new sales reps slows system response time. The average transaction time increases 15 percent. Each transaction now takes two minutes and 18 seconds to complete, as shown in Figure 1.5.

If this persists, the company's ability to service sales calls and its annual revenue is basically unchanged whether the company has 30 or 35 reps. Therefore, the company has increased its overhead (additional salaries, benefits, capital costs) without being able to increase its revenue.

Case II: If performance degradation is slightly worse and reaches 25 percent, each call would take two minutes and 30 seconds to complete. The added sales representatives actually decrease the company's ability to service calls, as shown in Figure 1.6.

Because it takes an extra 30 seconds per call, the company actually falls short by 20 percent ($21,840,000) of the target sales rate in Figure 1.4. The new revenue estimate based on system degradation is actually $6,000,000 per year less than if the company had done nothing (current base revenue in Figure 1.3). This level of slowdown is a realistic example of what happens in many systems as load increases. Figure 1.7 summarizes the effect of system performance degradation on revenue potential.

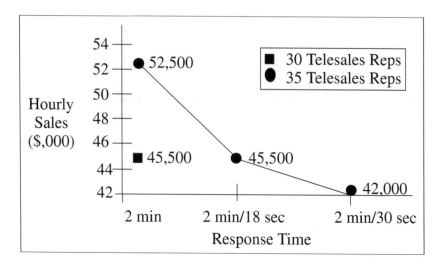

Figure 1.7   The cost to the company caused by system performance degradation.

When a network crashes, the typical recovery process is:

1.   Reboot the server.

2.   Briefly try to determine the problem cause.

3.   Verify the data integrity of the server and restore files, as required.

4.   Have the users log back on to the network.

5.   Continue network operations.

6.   Hope it doesn't happen again.

Slowdowns are also usually more difficult to resolve than a system crash. If the system slowdown persists for just two days, the revenue loss is equivalent to one hour of system downtime. In most companies, it would take more than two days to detect the slowdown. Then there is the inevitable scramble to get the system response time back to acceptable levels. If it takes one to four weeks to detect the degradation and improve performance to an acceptable level, the loss would range between $120,000 and $500,000, a substantial amount for any company to lose, and significantly higher than the loss due to multiple system crashes.

Slowdowns are more likely to occur than crashes, slowdowns can actually cost a company more money, and can be avoided by proactive testing for performance and capacity planning. Network management products can monitor production loads, but do not provide features that are effective for capacity planning, performance analysis, and bottleneck identification. These proactive steps can be accomplished only through a combination of system baseline characterization (monitoring) and proactive testing.

Avoiding downtime or slowdowns can mean significant savings for a company. Avoidance means knowing beforehand when and why a system slowdown will occur, planning for it, and upgrading the system before it occurs. The first step in avoiding problems is knowing what a system is capable of sustaining when it is installed (acceptance testing), and ensuring that as new software or hardware changes are made the system's capacity, performance and reliability are maintained or improved (regression testing). Acceptance testing is so important to the success of any system that a special section on acceptance testing is included in Chapter 5. Every department manager who signs on the dotted line for a new system should read and follow these guidelines to ensure that he or she "gets what he or she paid for!"

In the preceding example, two minutes was used as the baseline response time because that is how the existing system performed. A basic problem, however, is that no one really knows if two minutes is a good baseline number, or if it could have been reduced by tuning the application or configuring the server better. This example would have been completely different if application response time was 1 minute and 40 seconds to begin with, or could have been reduced from two minutes. In that case, new telesales reps would not have been needed to handle more calls, the system would not have degraded, and the company could have saved money by not hiring more reps. Answers to these

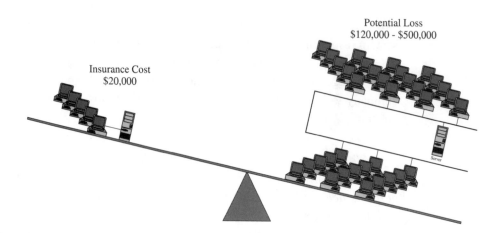

Figure 1.8   Proactive testing provides low-cost network insurance.

questions can be provided only through proactive testing and measurement of the system. See Chapter 22 on Configuration Sizing, Part III, for more information.

While the savings can be substantial, the cost of testing is typically low, as shown in Figure 1.8. Establishing a basic testing capability can actually cost less than a new network analyzer, and pay bigger dividends. For the telesales application example, a simple application response time test using a configuration of one server and three to four workstations could have predicted the response degradation. Total project cost for the first-time tester would have been approximately $20,000. This represents less than 10 percent of the potential revenue loss due to a slowdown. Proactive testing can provide very inexpensive insurance for the network, and the risk of not testing heavily outweighs the cost of testing.

THIRD-PARTY TESTING

You are probably familiar with network component testing, typically done by a trade journal or an independent test lab. Articles and reports that compare various servers, routers, adapters, and other network components can be very helpful, but they can also be misleading. For one thing, labs and publications don't want to be too harsh on vendors because vendors pay most of their bills through testing projects and advertising. The basic technical problem with these test results is that the test configuration doesn't reflect individual network environments, therefore the results may or may not be relevant to what you would measure if you were running a comparable test for your specific network configuration.

Further, if one adapter is reported as faster than another, does that mean users will see better network performance using the faster adapter? It may, but then again, it may not! Why? Because the adapter is only one component that influences system performance. What about the other components of the system? The network operating system (NOS)? The server? The application? The protocol stack? It is important to understand the difference between the capability of an individual component and collective component combinations. Chapter 6 discusses why subsystem and application testing are far more valuable and produce more actionable results than component testing.

Nevertheless, third-party test results can be helpful in making a first cut from a list of competing products. To understand how the products will work in your system, however, requires a more tailored analysis, one in which the test and loading represent your individual system and subsystem configurations.

PROACTIVE TESTING COMPLEMENTS OTHER TOOLS

Case studies measuring the satisfaction of new client-server applications show that the systems:

- were implemented much faster than comparable projects on mainframes or minicomputers

- provided higher initial customer satisfaction

- better met the information and timeliness requirements of their users

- were easier to use than previous systems

- provided less reliability than the system it replaced

- degraded more rapidly than anticipated as users were added

While the first four results are very positive, the last two indicate that these systems were not properly analyzed for reliability, performance, or capacity during design and development. There was probably little or incomplete multiuser application testing, capacity planning, and network infrastructure analysis performed prior to implementation. Proactive network testing could have avoided these problems.

Testing can help improve system availability, reliability, and performance, but it doesn't take the place of good monitoring and troubleshooting tools. Monitoring, troubleshooting, and testing have specific and individual capabilities. By using them to complement one another, client-server application developers, network managers, and support staff can achieve better network quality and higher network availability, reliability, and performance.

Today's network management products for troubleshooting and monitoring, and client-server application development tools don't provide the broad range of test suites needed to measure key aspects of the network system. These products do not include features for measuring performance, throughput, component sizing, response time, reliability, product comparison, and functionality. They do however, have capabilities that are useful for network testing. They can help baseline and characterize production network loads, collect nodal statistics that indicate how loads are affecting individual nodes, and help monitor the network during testing. Using these capabilities and a few specific network testing tools, you can accomplish the network test objectives discussed in Chapters 2, 3, and 4.

NETWORK TEST MANAGEMENT (NTM)

The Art of Testing Network Systems discusses the methodology of network test management (NTM). Network management addresses the many disciplines and tools for maintaining an operational network environment. NTM defines the process by which network, product, and application quality is verified before deployment and measured during operation through proactive testing.

Some people view NTM as a segment of network management; to others, it is a completely separate market segment. This distinction is not important. What is important is that today's network market, which is implementing client-server applications, leverage the value that proactive network testing offers. Network test management complements existing network management and application development tools, as shown in Figure 1.9. Testing provides a proactive and cohesive method of evaluating the quality, reliability, and availability of the network system infrastructure and its supported services and applications. Test data can also be used to establish realistic service thresholds that network management software monitor across the network.

The second half of the next chapter discusses how four distinct disciplines—client-server applications development, monitoring, troubleshooting, and testing—complement one another. By employing them correctly, the network

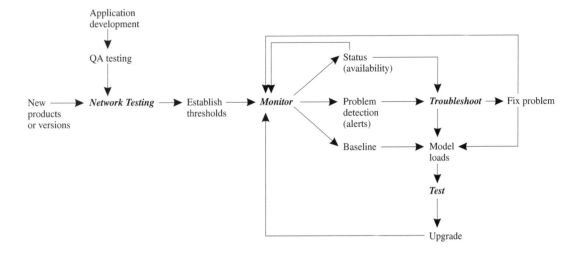

Figure 1.9   Network testing complements monitoring and troubleshooting.

manager can get the most from his or her network system. Chapter 2 begins the discussion by outlining how we have gotten where we are today, and how networks have become so complex and difficult to manage and troubleshoot.

Testing Complements Network Management

NETWORKING 101

The approach for monitoring, managing, and testing network systems is dependent on a good understanding of their architecture. Network systems perform four primary functions: storage, input/output (I/O), data transmission, and computation. Virtually every network is unique because of the vast array of multivendor products and configurations that can be deployed. These functions are implemented in different ways and on different hardware and software on different networks. Depending on the architecture of a specific network, these functions can be widely distributed or relatively centralized. The following discussion and Figures 2.1 through 2.7 provide a brief overview of key network terminology and architecture that significantly influence network management and testing considerations.

Networks have many more points of failure than the mainframes and minicomputers they are replacing which is why networking is so complex and the network manager's job is so hard. It is also the reason we cannot predict or estimate network operation. *Network monitoring tells what has happened. Network testing tells what will happen.*

Local area networks (LANs), as their name implies, developed as a file server and workstations located in close proximity to one another and connected with a high-speed link, as diagrammed in Figure 2.1. The file server runs a network operating system (NOS) that performs basic network functions, such as file storage, centralized printing, data transmission, and user security. The NOS, distributed between the workstations and server(s), in conjunction with the workstation operating system, manages data transmission and other communication between the server and workstations. Both the server and

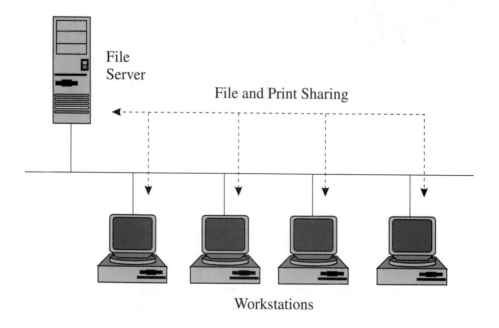

Figure 2.1   A basic local area network (LAN).

workstations perform computation. The server's CPU runs background network functions, and the workstation's CPU runs applications. The applications are stored either on the workstation or on the server hard disk. In this configuration, all communication is across a single path between the server and the workstations. Most basic LANs today are reliable and provide acceptable performance.

LANs generally evolve into larger, more complex networks with multiple file servers and special function servers, such as fax, backup, or mail servers. In larger networks, storage, input/output, and computational tasks are distributed across different servers, and data transmission between several nodes is often required for the simplest task. Transmission volume increases. As illustrated in Figure 2.2, sending a mail message can involve the file server, the mail server, the originating and destination workstation(s), and the fax server. This means that problems can now occur across a much broader range of network components and subsystems.   The job of managing and testing such a system grows exponentially in proportion to the size and services available on the network.

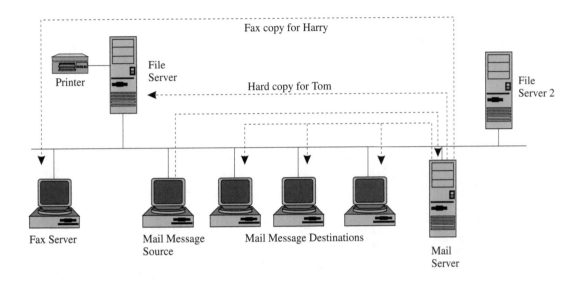

Figure 2.2   LAN complexity increased with more users, more services, and special function servers.

Testing the system requires measuring interactions between not only the workstations and file server, but between other nodes and services.

As the critical mass of LANs increased and their complexity grew, individual LANs, now referred to as network segments, were interconnected through local and wide area communication links to create large internetwork configurations.   With the addition of routers, switches, hubs, and multiple network topologies (Ethernet, Token Ring, FDDI, ATM, and so on), the number of things that could go wrong increased exponentially, and locating the source of a network problem became the tedious process we know today. Sending a mail message can now involve many more components, multiple segments, and timing considerations, as shown in Figure 2.3. Often, whole network segments can be viewed and managed only as a single component by network management software, thereby severely limiting the quality of network support. Testing complexity increases based on the breadth of configurations and hardware that must be assembled for a test project. Network loading becomes more complex,

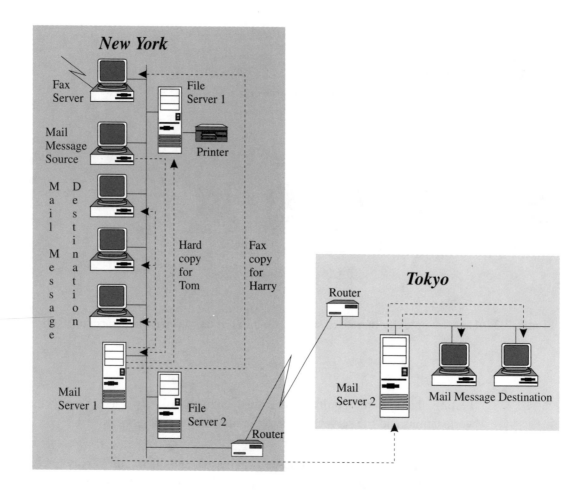

Figure 2.3   Internetworking adds more network complexity.

and communication link bandwidth and reliability can significantly affect test results.

In addition, as the community of remote network users grew, more dedicated communication servers were added to the network. Communication gateways to host computers and other information services expanded network complexity. Often, communication gateways do not provide good management capability but, instead, effectively shield information from the network manager. As application sharing increased, applications were moved from the file server to dedicated application servers to improve performance and management. The number of nodes that had to be monitored grew significantly along with the number of components involved in a single transaction, such as sending a mail message, as illustrated in Figure 2.4. Application loads and response times became critical network measurements, but existing network management software cannot measure these layers of the network. New workstation operating systems, such as Microsoft Windows, IBM's OS/2, and more graphically oriented applications and menu systems placed a greater load on the network, as shown

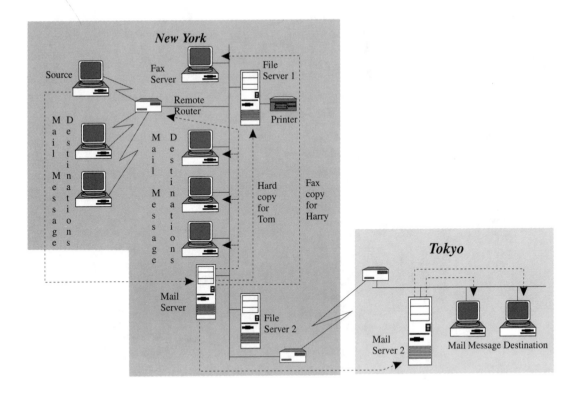

Figure 2.4   Networks add more applications, remote users, and communications gateways.

in Figure 2.5. Testing requirements increase for the application and presentation layers, since these layers now cause more network problems and performance issues.

Throughout the evolution of network systems, the network applications continued to run on the workstation, as shown in Figures 2.1 and 2.5. Whether the application was a productivity tool (such as a spreadsheet), database software (such as dBASE), or proprietary software, the data file was downloaded to the workstation and the application ran on the workstation. When the file operations were completed, the data file was written back to the server.

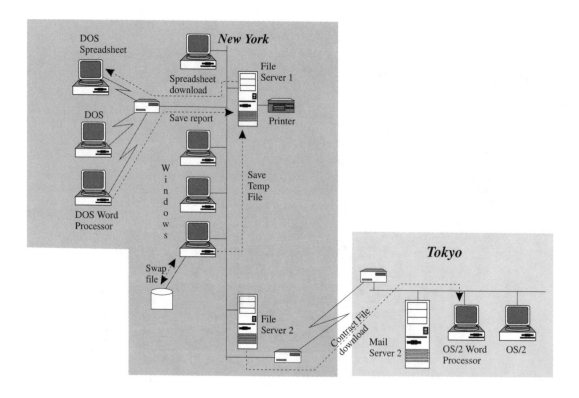

Figure 2.5 Application and presentation layer complexity increases network load and problems.

Today, new client-server applications using database software from companies including Oracle, Sybase, and Microsoft, are being implemented. These applications distribute processing across the database server and the workstations, as shown in Figure 2.6. The database server responds to transaction requests from the workstation side of the application. Files are no longer moved across the network, only transactions and responses (data records). Client-server applications fostered the development of quality assurance (QA) testing tools, most of which focus on GUI testing. Some of these tools actually improve the

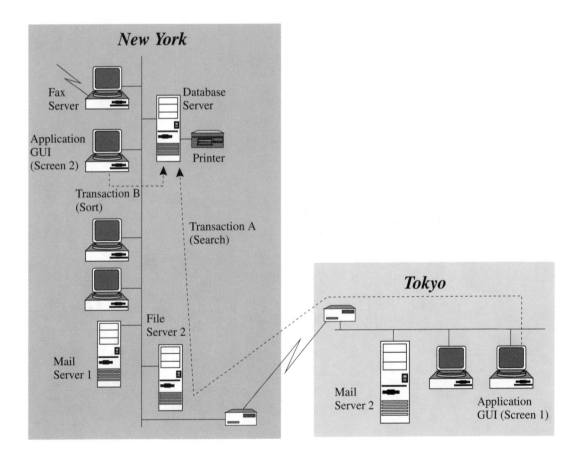

Figure 2.6 Client-server computing further distributes network functions.

ability to test the applications on the network, but most have a long way to go before they provide comprehensive network testing capability.

New graphical user interfaces for the workstations, such as Microsoft Windows and IBM's OS/2, provide an environment for complex application development, where single application requests generate multiple network requests, as shown in Figure 2.7. This increases the complexity of functional testing, performance tuning, and bottleneck isolation.

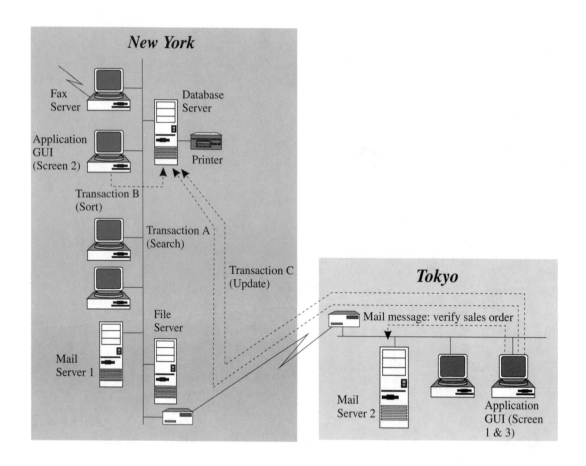

Figure 2.7   GUI interfaces and client-server applications expand network use.

Since network management products continue to monitor and collect statistics at the lower network layers, they have virtually no ability to provide useful management information for client-server and other application software. A few products are beginning to emerge that focus on application transaction monitoring, but these are in their infancy and do not provide sufficient detail to pinpoint bottlenecks and capacity problems. NTM is the only approach today that addresses this growing base of complex applications.

Today's networks are a heterogeneous assortment of various servers, communication links, and workstation environments. Often, multiple functions are supported on a single hardware platform in one network, while distributed across many platforms in another network. As illustrated in Figure 2.7, this flexibility of deployment increases the complexity of discussing, developing, managing, and testing network systems.

From a network support and management perspective, these rapidly growing networks:

- Created systems that are so complex that we cannot predict by experience, intuition, or existing network management products what will happen, when it will happen, or why it is happening. The only way to determine this information is through testing.

- Created products that are so complex that the vendors themselves have a difficult time testing, characterizing, and debugging them. Often, software and hardware bugs significantly influence the product's behavior, which can change from release to release. The only way to determine how a product will perform on your network is through testing the product in your environment.

- Created a market that is so competitive and dynamic that vendor claims are partly or completely inaccurate. The only way to verify that vendor claims are accurate and can be used in planning and design is through testing.

MANAGEMENT AND DEVELOPMENT TOOLS

Many tools, diagrammed in Figure 2.8, have been introduced into the market for network management and applications development. These include:

- Network analyzers, which collect and decode packet information on the network to assist in diagnosing network transport/protocol layer problems.

- Network management stations (NMS) using Simple Network Management Protocol (SNMP), such as HP's OpenView, Sun's NetManager and IBM's NetView/6000. These stations interact with SNMP agents residing on various network nodes to monitor network status. The stations collect and display nodal statistics; register alarms, such as high bandwidth utilization; and detect error conditions, such as a crashed router, on the production network. An extension to the SNMP standard that many vendors are now providing is the Remote Network Monitoring Management Information Base or RMON MIB.

- Resource management or software distribution applications that assist in configuring and reconfiguring network nodes, such as routers and downloading new software revisions.

- Network administration tools, such as Novell's FConsole, which allow the administrator to monitor and control system resources. These tools are typically NOS-dependent.

- Monitoring software, which resides on a specific network node, such as a server, and collects statistics about the performance and load on that node. Often, this software displays statistics locally and performs the function of an SNMP agent, which communicates to a central network management station.

- Database software, such as Oracle and SyBase, include tools for configuring and monitoring the performance and utilization of the database files, cache memory, and other resources on the server.

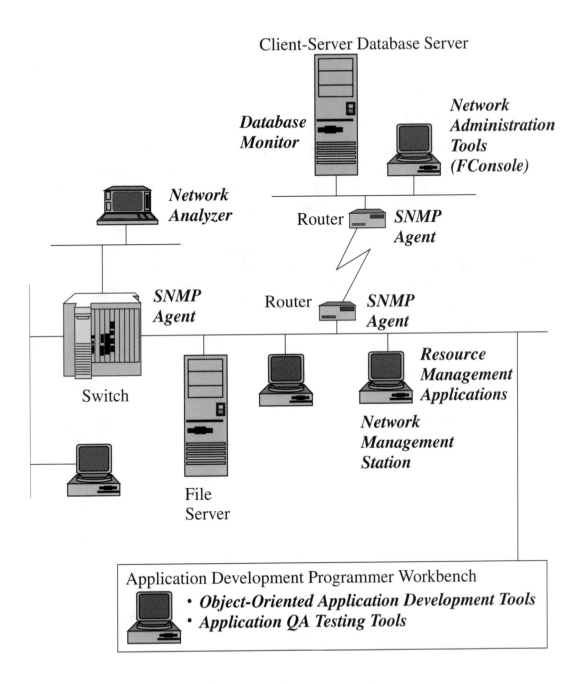

Figure 2.8   Network management and application development tools.

- Object-oriented application development or CASE tools, such as PowerSoft's PowerBuilder, provide software utilities and processes that improve application developer productivity and code manageability through features such as rules-based source code verification and revision control.

- Client-server application QA (Quality Assurance) testing tools, such as Microsoft Test or Mercury's XRunner, which provide an automated way of verifying or assuring the functional operation of the application and its graphical user interface (GUI).

Proactive testing tools, network management software, and application development tools must be used collectively to improve the network. Understanding how the latter tools work and the information they provide is fundamental to establishing network baselines and developing load models for testing.

Network Analyzers

Network analyzers capture packets or frames of information flowing through the network. A packet (or frame) typically includes three fundamental types of information: source and destination addresses, data, and control bits. Different network protocols, such as TCP/IP or Novell's IPX/SPX, have different packet formats. Analyzer features typically include:

- Packet capture, including address filtering, which ensures that only packets with specific source or destination addresses are captured.

- Packet decode, which is specific to each protocol. The level of decoding varies from simple decoding of packet type and address to sophisticated decoding, which interprets the data portion of the packet for commands, such as file open and file read.

- Packet playback or generation, which transmits packets from the analyzer onto the network.

- Other functions, such as graphical displays, current and trend statistics, and programmable operations, which assist the user in displaying and interpreting captured data.

Contrary to its name, a network analyzer does not actually perform analysis of the captured data. This is the task of the operator. A network support person, technician, or engineer uses the analyzer to capture, decode, and view packets from which information is collated and analyzed in order to detect problems, such as:

- Token Ring beaconing

- bad packets, such as runts on Ethernet and "soft errors" (e.g., frame-copied errors or receive-congestion errors) on Token Ring

- excessive broadcast packets (Broadcast Storm)

By analyzing captured network packets, the technician tries to detect anomalies and errors that point to the cause of the network problem. It is difficult to relate the flow of individual packets to application transactions, therefore, network analyzers do not provide application-level monitoring or data that can be related directly to specific application activity on the network.

A full discussion on the use of analyzers could easily comprise a book. For testing purposes, the primary functions of the analyzer are packet capture and packet generation. Capturing and analyzing packet traces can help in modeling test loads that are representative of the media level loads on the production network. Packet capture can also be used during testing to help detect network anomalies created by the test loads. Packet generation can be used to create loads on routers, switches, and other network components during testing. Analyzers are not directly used for application layer testing, but they are used during testing to passively monitor the test network for errors. Virtually every test lab and network support group uses network analyzers. You will need at least one and perhaps more, depending on your testing needs. Parts II and III discuss the use of analyzers based on the test objective and network configuration under test.

Network Management Stations

Network management stations provide extensive graphical representation of the network configuration and enable the network support organization to monitor the network and collect utilization statistics, alerts, and other pertinent information from many network nodes. Most network management stations are based on SNMP standards. SNMP agents running on various network nodes collect and summarize statistics that are sent to the management station management information base (MIB). This provides passive monitoring of the production network to detect network failures or alerts. Alerts arise when network or nodal thresholds set on the network management station are exceeded. These thresholds, such as network bandwidth utilization or dropped packets per second by a router, measure characteristics of the network that may indicate a potential problem.

Many vendors also offer "applications" for their network management platforms that provide resource management, such as software downloads and configuration changes across the network from a central network management station.

It is difficult to relate nodal statistics to application transactions, therefore, network management stations do not provide application-level monitoring or data that can be related directly to specific application activity on the network. Since most network testing is not done on production systems, network management stations are not typically used in network testing projects. Like the analyzer, management stations can be used to gather network statistics and load patterns, which can be helpful in generating load models for testing projects.

Resource Management or Software Distribution Applications

Resource management applications are available both from network management vendors and network operating system vendors. These programs can be very valuable during a testing project when test configurations must be changed across the network. For example, if the test network consists of 10 or more workstations and, during the test, the software configuration of the workstations must be changed, software that allows a single change to be downloaded to all workstations can both save time and reduce the possibility of error. Products, such as Novell's ManageWise and Microsoft's System's Management Server. fall into this category. If the testing is being done off-hours on the production network, this time savings can allow more extensive or timely testing to be accomplished. Similar products for changing router configurations across the network from a central workstation are available for network transport layer testing.

Network Administration Tools

These products provide a mix of monitoring and resource management features. All network operating systems (NOS) contain basic administration tools, such as NetWare's FConsole and LAN Server's NET ADMIN. These tools are used extensively in configuring test networks and can often assist in monitoring test conditions and collecting measurements on the production and test networks.

Monitoring Software

Monitoring software typically runs on an individual network node. Examples of monitoring products include Novell's ManageWise, IBM LAN Server's Performance Monitor/2, Saber's Server and LAN Workstation Managers, and Intrak's ServerTrak. Monitoring software collects intranodal information. On a network server, this would include, for example, cache hits, send/receive buffer utilization, memory utilization, and file opens/reads/writes.

During network testing, monitoring software can often provide extremely useful information in two ways. First, it can confirm that a baseline test load is representative of the production load (it creates the same level of activity for key system parameters) on a comparably configured node. Second, it can measure the impact on that particular node as the test load is increased to reflect more users or network activity.

A new category of monitoring software, represented by CoroNet's Management System (CMS) and Intel's LANDesk, monitors application sessions across the network. These products measure aggregate application loads and load per server or segment. This is useful information for identifying bottlenecks and overloaded servers, and can be used to establish load distributions for testing scenarios. Enhancements to the products are now providing some transaction-level information. This can help to define the transaction traffic for modeling loads on a test network.

Server-Based Databases

Most database products include features for monitoring the resource utilization of the database. Similar to monitoring software running on a server, database monitoring software collects statistics pertinent to the database, such as cache utilization, file reads/writes, connected users, average response time for database queries, and average record size.

During network testing, database monitoring software can be used similarly to server monitoring software just described.

Application Development or CASE Tools

Most companies developing client-server applications are using one of the various development systems on the market today. It is important, therefore, to understand that using such a development system does not ensure either the quality of the application or its behavior on the network. These tools are very beneficial in the application development stage. They provide rules-based checking of source code prior to compilation, to check for common programming errors. They also provide revision control and reusable objects for better software consistency and structure. They don't, however, provide testing capabilities. Before implementation, the application must be tested for features, functionality, performance, capacity, and interoperability. This testing requires tools that can replicate issues specific to the network, such as concurrent multiuser database access and application response time load curves as discussed shortly.

Application development tools are used by the application developer and contain many features to improve the developers' productivity and the manageability and reusability of the generated application code. These tools are not used directly in network testing.

Client-Server Application QA Testing Tools

These products provide scripting capabilities that allow the developer to prepare test scripts for the application, and they are particularly good for testing the GUI interface. The test scripts include actual application commands, such as keyboard input or mouse movement, and verification sequences to ensure the application responds correctly to the command. The scripts are generally used on a single station to verify application features by testing the various ways in which a user can invoke command sequences. This testing is necessary to safeguard that an application will work on the network. Passing the QA scripts on a single PC, however, is not sufficient to guarantee that the application works correctly in a network environment.

If the same scripts are run concurrently on multiple workstations, a test can be constructed to measure "network system" parameters, such as multiuser database access, response time load curves, reliability, and interoperability. These tools provide an efficient and automated, but not comprehensive, means of client-server application testing. Most of these tools have their foundation in GUI QA testing and do not yet provide the breadth of features needed for comprehensive network layer testing. They do, however, provide some good features and a starting point for proactive testing. Part III discuses how to use these tools to test not only applications, but:

presentation layers, such as Windows

NOSs

servers

workstations

In summary, network management tools provide three functions pertinent to proactive network testing:

Production network baseline input for modeling test loads.

Data collection during testing.

Load generation for testing.

Network management products, however, lack a major capability: They do not yet provide good information for application load modeling. This is an area where improvement is needed, and companies including CoroNet with its CMS product are leading the way.

As you read this and later chapters that describe the tool set needed for network testing, you will have to evaluate your current in-house inventory of programs to determine which capabilities are available and where you need to supplement them with additional products and tools. Part IV provides a summary of available test tools to assist you in evaluating and selecting them for your in-house testing needs.

NETWORK TEST MANAGEMENT TOOLKIT

The products just described provide valuable tools for improving the quality of the network and network applications. Considering the sequence of activities that take place in the development, implementation, and evolution of the network, try to visualize how each product contributes to network quality during the development and production phases.

Examine Figure 2.9. Network management tools and application development tools are virtually on opposite sides of the circle. Huge gaps in the development and production cycles exist where a variety of testing activities should occur, but these tools do not support proactive testing. To proactively test a network, you need a combination of the tools already discussed and selected network testing tools to:

Figure 2.9 Tool set for network development and production.

- Test the network as a system.

- Test individual network components for reliability and performance.

- Test the layers of software and hardware that make up an individual network node, such as a server or workstation.

- Test the network system infrastructure, including routers, switches, and WAN links.

- Test network applications as the users see them for responsiveness and reliability in a multiuser network environment.

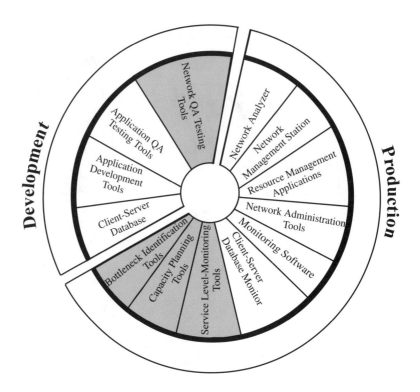

Figure 2.10   Supplemented tool set for proactive testing during network development and production.

- Monitor the network service level.

Figure 2.10 illustrates how specific tools for proactive network testing fill in the gaps of Figure 2.9 and create a complete *network test management toolkit*. Since most companies have some combination of network management and monitoring tools, the NTM toolkit is already partially complete. Putting together an effective test project requires a few specific testing tools and an understanding of what and how to test.

I just built a house and did some of the "raw" plumbing, which required joint soldering. Have you ever tried to solder a copper water pipe connection? If so, did you compare your completed soldered joint to that of a professional plumber? Did you notice any difference? Probably they both worked, but because of experience, the plumber's solder was smoother around the joint than yours, took about half the time to complete, and could be reproduced with accuracy time and time again to ensure that all fittings were watertight. Like soldering a pipe, applying network management tools to network testing improves with practice and experience. And, like plumbing, it is important that network testing is time-and cost-effective, consistent, and reproducible.

To analyze further, like a plumber, you will need a few specialized tools, beyond the general tools already discussed. We will call these tools *network test management tools*. They will make the job much easier and provide better results for less effort and time. Parts II, III, and IV discuss the tools needed for different types of network testing and the specific capabilities needed for each test.

To effectively communicate test results, graphs and diagrams are often very useful. A good spreadsheet, such as Microsoft Excel with appropriate data reduction and graphic templates, and a drawing package, such as Microsoft PowerPoint with appropriate network clip art, should be included in the NTM toolkit.

The toolkit, however, is just the beginning. Effective network testing must be based on a proven philosophy and methodology, as discussed in Chapter 6.

Making the Network Better

When was:

1. The last time you checked the oil in your car?

2. The last time you changed the oil in your car?

3. The last time you added water to the radiator?

4. The last time your car had an inspection and tune-up?

5. The last time you had the muffler inspected?

6. The last time your car broke down on the road?

The first three items represent proactive steps most people routinely take to prevent breakdowns and potential damage to their automobile. Many people also have routine inspections and tune-ups. Conversely, few people check the car's muffler unless they hear odd and loud noises coming from under the vehicle. Unfortunately, even the best-maintained car may break down now and then but, typically, the better it is maintained, the lower the probability of a problem.

This same logic also applies to networks. Slowdowns can be avoided, and failures that occur will be less frequent if you:

1. Check the key network components regularly for potential problems.

2. Replace components that fail tests.

3. Change/upgrade key components before they run out of steam.

4. Tune network components regularly before performance degrades.

5. Try to detect potential issues and avoid problems through proactive testing.

These five items are proactive steps that can be taken to improve network availability, reliability, and performance. To successfully accomplish items 1, 3, 4, and 5 requires a combination of network testing and network monitoring. Let's consider a few specific examples that illustrate how testing complements network management.

Example 2.1 Implementing a client-server database application.

Prior to deployment of the new application, response time tests are conducted and a load/response curve is created for 10, 20, 30, 40, and 50 user loads. At each test point, server and database monitors are used to capture information about the database server.

Test results indicate that for up to 30 users, response time is constant at an average 2.5 seconds per request. At 40 users, response time degrades slightly and increases to 2.65 seconds per request. The server monitor shows that the ratio of cache hits to requests decreases from 40 to 35 percent. If more memory is added and the cache hit ratio returns to 40 percent, performance is improved. Above 40 percent, however, no response time improvement is recorded.

At 50 users, performance degrades significantly. Each request now requires 2.8 seconds to complete. The cache hit ratio remains the same as for 40 users. However, the server packet receive error rate increases because of the additional load. Testing indicates that there is additional server capacity and, if a second adapter is added, the server receive error rate is reduced and performance improves to 2.55 seconds per request.

Since the initial number of users for the new application is 25, the system can safely be deployed because it is known that response time will be an average of 2.5 seconds per request. At the same time, thresholds can be set on the production system monitors to track the cache hit ratio and server adapter statistics, because it is known how changes in these can adversely affect performance.

This shows how testing and network management complement one another. Without testing, there would be no possible way of knowing the exact significance of the preceding parameters or how to set the alert thresholds on the production system.

Once the system is in production, there are many possible scenarios that may occur. The following are a few to consider:

1. Over several months, the number of users increases to 30. Based on test results, performance should remain unchanged. However, these new users are servicing a different customer base that uses different database records. The cache hit ratio decreases. This causes increased disk reads, increased overall server utilization, and decreased

performance. The predeployment testing, however, prepared the support group for this contingence. As the cache hit ratio began to decrease, the support group was alerted to the impending problem and took corrective action in the form of more cache memory or a faster disk to maintain the target 2.5 second response time.

2. The application performs very well and management decides to expand its use. Support is told that the number of users will increase to over 60 within the next six months. Based on test data, system performance will degrade significantly at 50 users; therefore, there will be a problem in supporting 60 users. Support can notify management immediately about this. Plans and budgets can be adjusted. Depending on further test results, several options are available. These could include:

    • **Very inexpensive solution:** Upgrade the server by adding a second adapter to increase network access capacity.

    • **More expensive solution:** Replace the server with a faster server or split the users between two servers, if the application/database supports such a configuration.

    • **More expensive solution that may impact the business's operation:** Delay the user increase until changes are made to accommodate the new load. This could include programming changes to allow the database to be distributed across servers, or database reorganization to speed access.

    The bottom line is that the predeployment testing alerted the company to a potential problem before it occurred.

3. The application works very well, except during specific times of the day. Nevertheless, the monitoring software indicates that all parameters are within their assigned thresholds. Therefore, support knows that the database server is performing properly and there must be another bottleneck on the production system that is causing the slowdown. While this does not pinpoint the problem, it does eliminate one area to look at.❑

Example 2.2 Router and wide area network (WAN) configuration.

Routers are to be installed in many remote branch offices that are currently connected with dial-up 14.4Kbps (Kilobits per second) lines to the main office. The routers provide an option for data compression. Prior to deployment, testing shows that for rates below 19.2Kbps, higher throughput is achieved using data compression. Between 19.2Kbps and 56Kbps, the throughput benefit using data compression varies. In some cases, it is actually lower because of processor overhead to perform data compression and decompression. Above 56Kbps, higher throughput is achieved without data compression. The trade-off is between the transmission rate and the router processor speed for performing the compression and decompression of the transmitted packet.

The routers are deployed and work very well; so well in fact that traffic between the home office and branch offices increases significantly, and the users begin to complain about system performance. Operations decides to upgrade all communication lines to 128Kbps using V.42bis modems. After the upgrade, performance decreases and user complaints increase. Monitoring the WAN transmission lines indicates there is available bandwidth, so why is performance lower? Someone remembers that testing results showed data compression doesn't always give the best performance. Operations dusts off the test results and turns off data compression in the routers. Performance improves and user satisfaction increases.❏

While the previous two examples illustrate how testing results gathered during development and deployment complement ongoing network management and troubleshooting, proactive testing can also provide significant benefits during all phases of a network's life. The next chapter explores the life (test) cycle of a network.

Life (Test) Cycle of a Network

CHANGING PERSPECTIVE

The life cycle of a network, shown in Figure 3.1, has five distinct phases: planning and design, development, deployment, production, and evolution. Network test management (NTM) can contribute to the quality and success of each phase of the network's life cycle. As discussed in previous examples, a large retailer is using NTM extensively in the development phase of client-server applications and in preparing the network for these new applications. A financial securities company is using NTM in the production phase to ensure system availability and reliability. An oil company is using NTM in the evolution phase to verify upgrades before deploying them across the network. And a major bank uses NTM in the planning phase for product evaluation. Each company has specific areas where proactive testing has provided distinct benefits.

The arrows in Figure 3.1 show the life cycle as a smooth, flowing activity, but most network managers and others in the trenches see it from a different perspective. Reality is that many LANs, networks, and internetworks were never planned, they were just deployed and grew up through a "grass roots" effect over

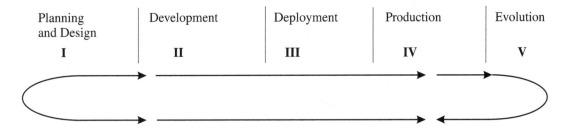

Figure 3.1   Five phases of the network life cycle.

the last 10 years. The network has almost always preceded mission-critical and client-server applications. If the network manager is lucky, he or she may have a little time for design and planning before deploying these new applications. Evolution usually is not the result of planned changes, but rather is the result of fixes for performance problems and service outages. The production phase for many networks may have never really been achieved. Production implies stability, and many of today's networks aren't, and have never been, stable.

This raises two basic questions:

1. What is the benefit of following the life cycle phasing? How will this change what the network manager does, and how will this improve the network?

2. How can an organization change from today's reactive mode to a more proactive and systematic approach, as outlined by the life cycle?

The first question is easier to answer than the second. In fact, this entire book is about answering the first question. In summary, following a systematic approach reduces risk of the unknown. Through testing, information can be gathered that eliminates the guesswork in predicting network problems caused by new applications or upgrades, low reliability, inadequate capacity, and degradation.

Moving from today's reactive environment to a more structured life cycle admittedly will take time and discipline. Most companies that are making the transition take one of three paths:

- **Slow migration:** This approach starts small and builds on success. The oil company discussed in Chapter 1 is a good example. By starting small, the cost in dollars and resources was low, and it was able to measure payback by comparing reduced support requirements to testing effort. With concrete data in hand, it is easier to advocate switching or spending dollars and effort on proactive versus reactive tasks. Often companies that have taken this route have used outside help to get started and accelerate the curve.

- **Project-related:** The retailer in the example in Chapter 1 has developed its proactive testing around specific client-server development projects. And once the capability is in place, it can expand proactive testing to other areas and projects.

- **Outside help:** Many companies turn initially to consultants or independent test labs to help them get started. This is a good approach, if a knowledgeable consultant can be found. The consultant should be able to help the company minimize cost while maximizing return for two or three initial test projects. At the end of the three projects, the company should have the facilities, experience, and tools to conduct testing, in which case the consultant would have paid for him- or herself through cost savings to the company.

FIVE PHASES OF A NETWORK'S LIFE CYCLE

Figure 3.1 illustrated the cyclical nature of the network's life cycle. Each of the phases includes various tasks or activities depending on the individual network:

- **Planning and Design:** This phase is a continuous effort for large complex networks. Whenever a new segment is added, an existing segment is modified, or services and applications are changed, planning and design activity, whether formal or informal, occurs. Activities such as defining requirement specifications, evaluating new products, designing the network topology, and simulation studies are included in this phase.

- **Development:** Based on planned network modifications, the development phase may be very long and complex, such as for a client-server application; or, it may not be required, when, for example, "off-the-shelf" hardware and software is purchased for the network.

- **Deployment:** This phase includes installation of new hardware, software, and services. Usually it is performed by the development organization, support group, or a systems integrator. Its length and complexity varies greatly. This phase should always include an *acceptance* test, as discussed in Chapter 5.

- **Production:** This is when the benefits of the network and its services are realized by the users. This is the network phase around which most network management and troubleshooting tools are oriented.

- **Evolution:** This phase represents network change and expansion or, more accurately, the realization that modification and expansion is required. Generally, before modification and expansion can be implemented, some elements of Phases I and II are required. Therefore, this phase is primarily an extension of the production phase. It includes regression testing, configuration sizing, and capacity planning activities.

Planning and Design

A wise colleague, Tom Peters, once said, "You can only manage what you can measure," and you cannot effectively measure anything without a goal or objective. Therefore, the first planning step is establishing a set of needs or requirements. The more specific the requirements, the better the measurements. For example,

- **Application requirements:** Five-second response time for accessing order entry status by account number. Eight seconds for accessing order entry status by surname.

- **Network Operating System requirements:** Ninety-seconds delay between spooling a print job to the printer and output beginning. Minimum file server sustained throughput of 500KB per second across each network interface, maximum of three interfaces.

- **Router requirements:** Sustained throughput of 40,000 packets per second across four ports.

Once defined, even if they are not complete, the *requirements specification* document is a starting point for the entire project or effort. (Chapter 6 discusses the *requirements specification* in more detail.) Undoubtedly, some requirements will change, some will be dropped, and some may be added as the project progresses. They form a living document that can be used to measure and track the objectives and success of the project.

Armed with the starting set of requirements, there are six distinct sources of input for planning, two of which are testing related. These are:

product collateral, such as data sheets, manuals, white papers, and evaluation software

trade publications and independent lab test results

recommendations from associates

product comparisons conducted in-house, including test results

simulations

experience

Let's forgo discussing four of the preceding six items and focus initially on testing related sources, items 2 and 4. During network planning and design, NTM can help properly size and configure servers, workstations, and other network components based on response and performance requirements using anticipated loads and load distributions. Testing results can be used to generate network-component characterizations as input to a simulation model. For example, router throughput varies significantly depending on the router configuration. Throughput can be affected by the number of segments, protocol combinations, filtering options, and network topology combinations. Generally, published test results are best case engineering maximums and may or may not be relevant to the specific router configuration you are considering for your network. Throughput rates based on your router configuration can help improve the accuracy of the simulation significantly. These can be obtained quickly and accurately through an in-house test project, as part of the overall planning effort.

NTM can be used in the planning stage to compare and evaluate alternative choices for network components and configurations. Measurements are made for performance (throughput), reliability, and interoperability under identical and ideal conditions. The relevance of the test results depends on how well the test models the production network. (Parts II and III explain how to ensure that your tests provide relevant results.) If an electronic mail system is planned to support 1,000 users, for instance, comparing two mail packages in a five-user test won't be representative of how either package will perform on the production network. Testing with a few users to compare product functionality works well, but for performance testing, an equivalent load of hundreds of users must be used to get relevant results. NTM provides methods of achieving this testing without having to set up a one-hundred-node network.

The bottom line is that NTM can help you answer many of the most baffling and risky decisions you face every time you have to grow or change the network. If you think about it, the buildings we work in, the roads we drive on, and the cars we use are all engineered to and tested against strict tolerances for safety, reliability, and ease of use. With NTM, you have the same power to ascertain that the products used in your network also meet strict tolerances for reliability, performance, and availability for a surprisingly small investment in dollars and effort.

Test results can be used in many different ways to address both technical and non technical issues. For example, test results can be used for:

Negotiating capital cost reduction: A large Southeastern bank used test results to negotiate better pricing when a higher-priced product was shown to perform only marginally better than a competitive product.

Proof of concept: A leading insurance company configured and evaluated a "typical" remote office network to ensure that the network services they required could be supported on a single server configuration as proposed by the vendor.

Interoperability verification: An aerospace engineering company was planning a network expansion. The company generally purchased all its computer equipment from a single vendor, but wanted to use less costly, third-party equipment. Test results were used to prove to upper management that the multivendor system was interoperable and reliable before budgeting for the lower-cost items.

Management education: While the development and support staffs realized which product was technically better, senior management of the government agency was leaning toward the better known of the two products. A network integrator sponsored an independent test of the competitive products. It used the testing project and results to educate the senior management.

Migration budgeting: A medium-size, Midwest manufacturer wanted to migrate its networks to a new network operating system. It used a test lab to perform migration testing to determine the most cost-effective and least disruptive method of upgrading workstations across the network. Based on test results it was able to assign a per-unit time and dollar cost for budgeting.

Conformance to vendor specifications: This has probably been the typical use of most test results, but as previously shown, it is not the limit of test results' usefulness.

As stated, other sources of test information include trade publications or independent lab reports. These can provide low-cost information for initial product screening. If you are evaluating new routers, a test report from Scott Bradner at Harvard, or an article in Data Communications, which compares six different products, may help you select two or three for in-house testing based on the configurations they support and their sustained throughput capacity. But first you should establish selection criteria in order to compare the test results with your needs (again the need for a requirements specification). Second, be sure you understand the conditions under which the tests were run to determine that the published results are relevant to your needs.

Simulation tools are also valuable for analyzing the throughput requirements of the transport layers and nodes, such as routers and switches. The difficulty with simulation is the time it takes to develop a model and the uncertainty in modeling the nodal characteristics. For example, which values should be used in the model for switch throughput characteristics? Throughput numbers available from the vendors are usually best case. Numbers in published reports may be highly dependent on the test configuration. If your switch configuration doesn't match the tested configuration in a report, or if vendor numbers are used for maximum switch throughput, the model's accuracy relative to your configuration is unknown. My experience indicates that throughput test results can vary by 50 percent between various configurations. In a complex model, individual nodal errors can be compounded geometrically or cancel one another out.

Currently, simulation tools do not provide the ability to model application loads in a workstation, server, or across the network, but simulation techniques continue to improve and they hold promise for the future. If you are conducting simulations, be sure to confirm basic assumptions and results through actual testing and monitoring of production environments. Simulation is only as good as its representation of the "real world." If actual and simulated results don't compare, question the simulation model, and adjust the simulation until it matches real-world results.

Development

During client-server application development, functionality and QA testing is performed by the software developer at his or her "workbench," which is typically a single workstation or a few-node network. Once the application is stable and working properly, NTM can be used for network level testing to measure and verify development objectives for:

multiuser file access

system loading and performance

application response time

reliability

final sizing and configuration of critical components, such as the database server

The requirements specification should include objectives for these network measurements. These requirements form the basis against which to measure the finished application before deployment. Results from this testing should be logged in a test journal for future use by network operations and support groups, as illustrated in the examples at the end of Chapter 2.

Continuous proactive network testing is very critical during development. After spending several years developing an application, one large transportation company discovered that the application couldn't support the anticipated transaction rate for 100 users. Testing exposed reliability and performance problems with the NOS. The company also discovered that it got very little guidance from the vendor on system-level tuning and capacity planning. The testing uncovered problems that delayed application deployment, but without it the company may have deployed the application only to learn about these performance problems in the field. This experience cost the company: It required installation of a new NOS and delayed the application by over a year.

If the company had more experience in network testing, it probably would have organized its testing to evaluate the baseline network earlier in the development cycle, and thus would have discovered the NOS problems sooner. Risk management in a development project starts with identifying unknowns as early as possible. This company believed vendor claims and made the assumption that the NOS was capable of supporting very high transaction rates. Luckily, it did have the good sense to verify the application performance and capacity before deploying it. In the future it will probably rely more on measured results than vendor claims.

Deployment

A well-known founder of a network analyzer company says, "The biggest cause of problems in most networks is the purchase order." Change causes uncertainty, and uncertainty can lead to potential problems. Adding a new application, more users, or new equipment to an existing network won't be successful if system reliability and performance isn't maintained. Therefore, it is very important to understand the impact of a change before deploying it across the production network. Before deploying a new client-server mission-critical application into an existing production environment, NTM can be used to measure the reliability and robustness of the current network infrastructure. NTM can measure the impact that new applications will have on the existing system by emulating the load that will be imposed on the network as the new applications are deployed.

If you estimate that planned expansion will add 10 to 15 percent additional load on the network transport layers and the equivalent of 15 concurrent users on the server, NTM can emulate these loads either in the lab or on the production network (for a short period) to measure their impact. It's best to detect performance problems before, not after deployment. As one user said, "If we were to do it again, we probably would do more user and volume testing before production."

For off-the-shelf products, testing prior to deployment can verify that the equipment meets vendor specifications and can reduce "infancy mortality rates" that is, failures that occur immediately after deployment of new equipment. This phase should always include an acceptance test process. The process may be complex or simple, depending on the products being deployed. By having an acceptance checklist and process, as outlined in Chapter 5, the chance for a successful, high-quality deployment will be greatly increased.

Production

On the production network, NTM can be used to proactively measure the availability and responsiveness of the system during operational hours. Using NTM application scripts and other tests run as a "ghost" user, response time and availability of network services and applications can be reported on a continuous basis. This is called service-level monitoring, and it is the single best measure of how the user perceives the production system.

Development testing tools can be used for service-level monitoring. The production scripts can usually be derived from those created during development. The incremental cost for this testing is very low. The operations or support group may even be able to get the development group to support and conduct this testing, as its results can provide beneficial input to future application revisions.

Most support groups use network monitoring and experience to isolate problems. Real-world testing techniques, discussed in Parts II and III, provide new capabilities for the support group to identify bottlenecks and isolate problems on the production network.

Evolution

NTM can be used to assist in ongoing network capacity planning and regression testing, using both emulation and real-world testing. Regression testing verifies that upgrades provide capabilities comparable to the current version. Capacity planning measures the network's ability to support more load without degradation. By accelerating network activity to emulate additional users, changes in network throughput, application response time and system reliability caused by additional loading can be measured before it impacts the production system. There is a simple method of implementing this testing, which is not intrusive to daily network operation and which does not require the production network to be shut down. It is discussed briefly in Chapter 7 and covered in more detail in Part III.

As new hardware and software product releases become available, regression testing ensures that upgrades to the production network will not disrupt the system. One large public utility company routinely tests all new releases before deploying them. An oil company recently set up a compatibility test lab because it believed that many of its network problems were caused from upgrades. The company plans on testing new product releases using a small lab and automated test scripts to assure compatibility and basic functionality of all upgrades.

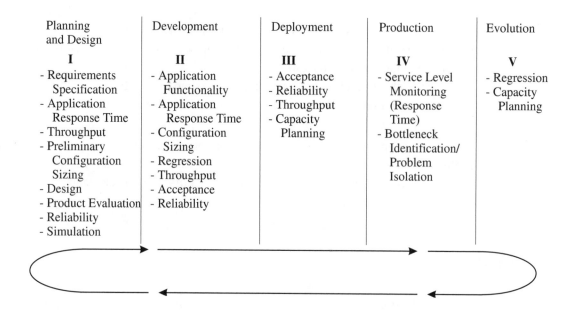

Figure 3.2   Testing is effective throughout the network life cycle.

Organizing Your Testing

Figure 3.2 shows the testing activities that apply to the various phases of the life (test) cycle of a network. The basis for all testing projects is a well-defined set of test objectives. Once the test objectives are established, other components of the test, including the network configuration, loading, and data collection can be defined. Chapter 4 describes 10 test objectives applicable to the various stages of the life (test) cycle of a network.

Ten Network Test Objectives

VIEWING THE NETWORK

The network can be viewed either from the bottom up or from the top down, depending on your perspective as a user, a network manager, support staff, or senior management. Historically, most network perspective has been from the bottom up. Initially, the most difficult task was to get a working and reliable network that moved packets of data from one node to another at high speed. The network hardware, transport layer protocols, and network operating system were the components the industry focused on when developing network management and troubleshooting products. These were also the components users focused on when selecting a network. If these components worked, the network provided the shared file storage and printing needed for productivity applications. This is the bottom-up view or the **network infrastructure** view.

Market maturity and the emergence of mission-critical, client-server applications, graphical user interfaces (GUI), and multitasking workstation operating systems have created a new level of network complexity. Today, these collectively create the major end-user and management perception of the network. No matter how well the network infrastructure works, the user equates the availability, reliability, and performance (response time) of the network with the quality of these layers. The following is the top-down view or the **application/presentation layers** view.

Comprehensive network testing must address both views, which are illustrated in Figure 4.1. Network support groups use the bottom-up view to ensure network reliability and throughput. Network users use the top-down view to measure network responsiveness and availability. While test objectives are

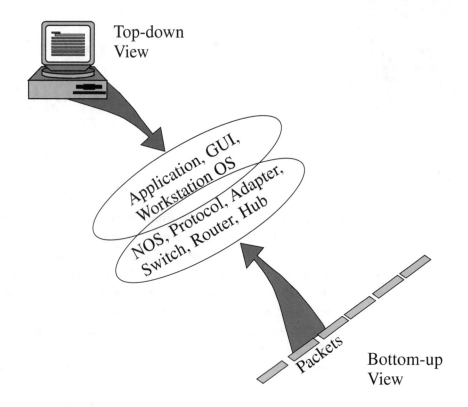

Figure 4.1   Bottom-up versus top-down network view.

similar, the testing methods and tools required for the two views differ. This chapter introduces 10 test objectives that span the network system layers. Part II applies these test objectives to the network infrastructure, and Part III applies them to the application/presentation layers.

Figure 4.2 illustrates a recommended approach for applying the test objectives to the five phases of the network life cycle. Based on my experience, this matrix covers the areas that provide the most return for the testing dollar. This matrix is only a guideline, however, and should be tailored to address specific issues of concern for your network.

		Planning	Development	Deployment	Production	Evolution
Network Application/ Presentation Layers	Application Response Time	X	X	X	X	
	Application Feature/ Functionality		X	X	X	
	Regression		X			X
	Throughput	X	X	X		
	Acceptance		X	X		
	Configuration Sizing		X			X
	Reliability	X	X			
	Product Evaluation	X				
	Capacity Planning			X		X
	Bottleneck Identification				X	
Network Infrastructure	Application Response Time					
	Application Feature/ Functionality					
	Regression		X			X
	Throughput	X	X	X		
	Acceptance		X	X		
	Configuration Sizing	X	X			X
	Reliability	X	X			
	Product Evaluation	X				
	Capacity Planning			X		X
	Bottleneck Identification				X	

Figure 4.2   Test objectives across the network life (test) cycle.

TEN TEST OBJECTIVES

Experience demonstrates that most testing projects have two things in common:

1. The actual time spent testing and analyzing the test data is short (15 to 25 percent) relative to the time required to complete the whole project, including planning, record keeping, managing, and reporting.

2. Successful projects are those that have a defined objective and test plan, and provide actionable results and conclusions. Projects should have

one or, at the most, two test objectives. More than two objectives dilutes the effort and makes developing a representative test environment virtually impossible. The importance of actionable results is discussed more in the Data Presentation section of Chapter 6.

Planning, load modeling, data reduction, and data interpretation are areas in which many test projects go astray, but these are the parts of a project that if done correctly, can be reused. As you perform test projects, the time to complete each can be reduced by developing procedures, and tools and gaining experience that allows for more productive testing. Planning starts with a well-defined test objective, as discussed shortly. An overview of data reduction and interpretation techniques is presented in Chapter 6 and discussed further in Parts II and III. Load modeling is discussed in Chapter 7, and Parts II and III for specific network layers under test.

There are 10 primary test objectives for a network system. Each objective has a specific methodology and approach. The following is a short overview of each objective with a discussion of how it is used during the different phases of the network life cycle.

1. Application Response Time Testing

This test measures how long it takes an application to complete a series of tasks, and best represents the user's perception of the network system (application, NOS, and network components). For a presentation layer, such as Microsoft Windows, the test measures how long it takes to switch between different desktop tasks or load new overlays. Running the test at various loads, number of real or emulated users, creates a load versus response time curve for each application tested, as shown in Figure 4.3.

For application tests, a series of commands that execute typical network activity, such as file opens, reads, writes, searches, and closes provide the best load model. The time it takes to complete commands is measured in seconds for each workstation running the test.

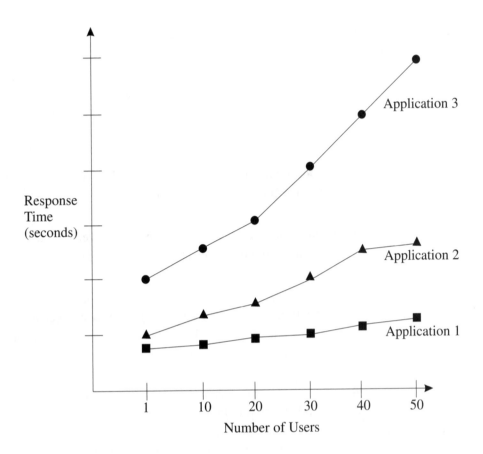

Figure 4.3   Load versus response time curve.

Presentation layer tests include response time measurements for switching between screens or loading a new application or overlay. This is particularly critical when the software is downloaded from a file or application server, as this can create a "hidden" load on the server and network. In GUI and multitasking environments, response times are very important, because of the overhead often associated with context or overlay "switching" operations. For on-line systems, such as a telesales application or securities trading desk, response delays can translate directly to more customer time on the phone (lower customer satisfaction) and to fewer customers serviced (lower revenue).

Response time testing is applicable throughout most phases of the network's life cycle:

- **Planning:** This testing can be emulated with an application prototype to measure acceptable network service levels for the requirements specification.

- **Development:** This testing can be used to verify that network service levels in requirements specification are being achieved.

- **Deployment:** This testing can be used to verify that network service levels in the requirements specification are met before acceptance and deployment.

- **Production:** This testing can be used to measure network service-level baselines and changes. This is probably the best measure of system quality and user perception.

Response time testing should always include monitoring the system for reliability. A reliability problem, such as a high number of dropped packets at a router or server, or a high number of bad packets because of a malfunctioning network component, can significantly impact response time measurements. Network analyzers should be used to monitor the system for errors during all testing.

2. Application Feature/Functional Testing

Feature testing verifies individual commands and capabilities of the application. It is usually conducted with minimal to light loads. It is focused on the user interface and application operations or transactions invoked by the user. Feature testing is typically done by the developer on his or her workbench and in QA on a small network configuration.

Functional testing is network-oriented. It verifies that the application's multiuser characteristics and background functions work correctly under heavy loads. It focuses on the network and file system or database server interaction when multiple users are running the application. Functional testing requires a network configuration and loading that closely models the production environment. This testing may be done in application QA or in a separate network lab. It is used only during three network phases:

- **Development:** This testing can be used to verify that the application performs as specified in a multiuser environment under anticipated production loads.

- **Deployment:** This testing is conducted separately or as part of an acceptance test to verify that the application performs as specified before deployment under anticipated production loads.

- **Production:** If problems are encountered on the production system, this testing can be used to verify that the application is working or not working as originally deployed.

3. Regression Testing

Regression tests compare the performance, reliability, and functionality of a new release of hardware or software to the current release. It assures that product upgrades will not impact the production network. Regression test projects are a combination of selected tests from the other test objectives. The key to regression testing is to ensure that the testbed and test cases represent critical components and risks that may be encountered on the production network.

This testing does not address new features in the upgrade. New features should be tested prior to regression testing as part of application feature/ functional testing. Although new product releases generally fix bugs in the current version, they often introduce new bugs that did not previously exist. These can cause serious problems if they occur in a key feature or capability of the product. Regression testing cannot test all features, but should be designed to verify that the key capabilities on which network users depend are working properly. This testing is performed in the development and evolution phases:

- **Development:** This testing can be used to verify that product upgrades work as specified and meet performance, interoperability, and reliability specifications.

- **Evolution:** This testing can be used to verify that product upgrades meet performance, interoperability, and reliability criteria comparable to the current version before deployment.

4. Throughput

Throughput testing is similar to application response time testing, but measures kilobytes per second (KBps) or packets per second (PPS) of data transferred, instead of measuring response time in seconds. This test is used to measure servers, disk subsystems, adapter/driver combinations, bridges, routers, hubs, switches, and communication links. Throughput testing is used to measure performance, find bottlenecks, compare different products, and size individual components of the network.

Throughput testing does not use application scripts. Depending on the network unit under test, this testing requires test software that performs server file input/output (I/O), generates transactions against a database server, or sends specific packets or frames on the network. Such testing is applicable throughout several phases of the network's life cycle:

- **Planning:** This testing can be used to compare products, generate nodal characterization for simulation models, and provide input to the requirements specification.

- **Development:** This testing can be used to verify that component and network throughput levels in the requirements specification are being achieved.

- **Deployment:** This testing is conducted separately or as part of an acceptance test to verify that component and network throughput levels in the requirements specification are met before deployment.

5. Acceptance

Acceptance testing is a "shakedown" of the system prior to deploying it into production. It is an excellent method of ensuring that the new system will be stable and provide acceptable performance in its initial release. Similar to regression tests, an acceptance test plan is really a combination of selected test objectives, such as response time, reliability, and feature/functionality.

Acceptance testing is employed in numerous other fields. Planes and ships always have shakedown flights or cruises before their maiden voyages. House buyers typically do a walk-through of a new home, testing light switches, appliances, and plumbing before they close escrow. Network acceptance testing is an often overlooked step in installing or upgrading a network, but it can provide both financial and technical peace of mind for the network buyer. Defense contracting is one industry that often requires "proof of performance," essentially an acceptance test, prior to authorizing payment for products, including networks.

An acceptance test can be used to receive final approval to go into production, and for payment for services by a system integrator or installer. Acceptance testing may be done on just the "new" piece, or the load model may emulate existing loads plus anticipated loads generated by the new application or component. Chapter 5 discusses the business issues and procedures for successful acceptance testing. Parts II and III discuss the technical issues of acceptance testing. This test is used during:

- **Development:** This testing should be conducted periodically during development ot verify that system requirements are being achieved.

- **Deployment:** This testing should be conducted to ensure that the system meets all requirements before it is accepted into production by the users.

6. Configuration Sizing

Results from *application response* or *throughput* tests can be used to size network components. Based on the test results and the tester's knowledge of the system's architecture and operation, specific system configurations or components are modified and the tests are rerun to measure performance differences. This is done

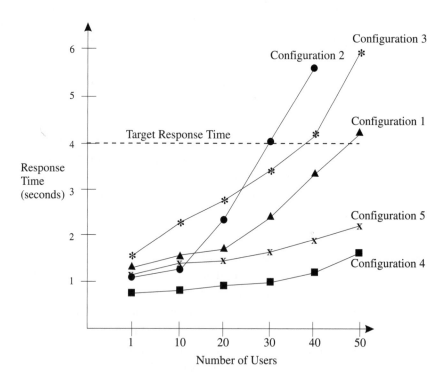

Figure 4.4   Load versus response time curves used for *configuration sizing*.

recursively until the desired performance level is achieved, as illustrated in Figure 4.4. For Configuration 2, there is no test point at 50 users because the system failed to complete the test.

Figure 4.4 illustrates how plotting load versus response time curves for alternative configurations can provide relevant information in making configuration and cost decisions if the objective for the new client-server application is a four-second response time for up to 50 users and 10,000 transactions per hour.

This testing is used during:

- **Planning:** This testing can be used to estimate system requirements for cost analysis and budgeting.

- **Development:** This testing can be conducted during development to determine system requirements to meet specific response or throughput goals.

- **Evolution:** This testing is used to resize components when system response time or throughput degrades.

7. Reliability

The network is run for an extended time period, typically 24 to 72 hours, under medium to heavy load. It is monitored for errors and failures. A reliability test can be part of an acceptance test; it can be used as a comparative measurement during product evaluation testing; or it can be part of a regression test run against a product upgrade. The more complex and "realworld" the load model, the better the test will measure the network system's reliability. Again, network analyzers are important for monitoring the system for errors during reliability testing.

Experience has shown that network systems have varying levels of survivability over a given duration and loading. All reliability tests will fail if run long and hard enough. The important information is when and how the failure(s) occur. Parts II and III discuss how to interpret reliability test results and apply them to the production network. Reliability tests are used during:

- **Planning:** This can be used as part of a product evaluation test to compare different products or establish requirement specifications. It can also be used to improve network infrastructure stability in preparation for client-server applications.

- **Development:** This testing can be used to verify that system requirements are being achieved.

- **Deployment:** This testing can be used as part of an acceptance test to verify that system requirements are met before deployment.

8. Product Evaluation

Traditionally, product evaluation has been focused on comparing individual products, such as servers, operating systems, or applications. In these tests, all network conditions are held constant except for the products being compared. The product evaluation perspectives of many companies are expanding to include **technology evaluation** and **subsystem evaluation**. In technology evaluation, two or more competing technologies are compared. This may be different wide-area communication capabilities or high-speed network media. In subsystem evaluations, combined hardware and software platforms are compared. Examples include database server configurations and groupware systems. Figure 4.5 illustrates these three levels of evaluation.

Like acceptance and reliability testing, product evaluation testing may include application response, throughput, and reliability measurements to determine the effect on the network when one unit under test is replaced by another. Product evaluation testing is primarily used in the planning phase of the network's life cycle to compare competitive products.

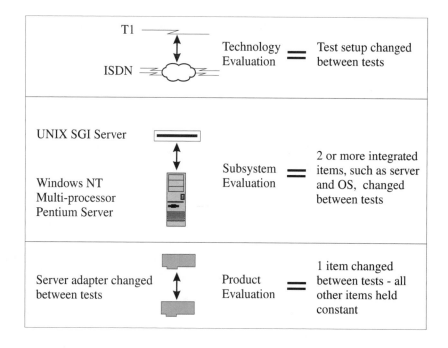

Figure 4.5 Product evaluation has taken on a broader scope that includes technology and subsystem comparisons.

9. Capacity Planning

This test measures how much excess capacity exists on the network. It determines at what point network resources need to be increased to support additional demand before significant degradation in performance or throughput occurs. Capacity assessment produces load versus response time data for the current user base and determines the user load at which unacceptable degradation occurs. This is called the knee in the load versus response time curve.

Testing is conducted with increasingly higher loads until performance reaches an unacceptable level or throughput cannot be sustained. The difference between the production network loads and the maximum sustainable throughput represents the system's excess capacity. Test objective 10 discusses the second step in capacity planning, bottleneck identification.

Capacity planning is typically used during the deployment and evolution phases:

- **Deployment:** This testing is used to determine the system's initial excess capacity. A load versus response curve is created that shows the number of additional users that can be added before degradation occurs. Additionally, it can be used to identify individual component capacity and determine where initial bottlenecks will occur as users are added.

- **Evolution:** This testing can be used to determine the current excess capacity of the production system and create a load versus response curve showing the number of additional users that can be added before degradation occurs. Additionally, it can be used to identify individual component capacity and determine where bottlenecks will occur as users are added.

10. Bottleneck Identification and Problem Isolation

Bottleneck identification indicates where bottlenecks and capacity limitations exist in the network which result in degraded system performance. To accomplish this, the maximum sustainable throughput on each system component is measured or calculated. Tests are then conducted on individual components to determine their capacity limits. The differences between the maximum capacity of individual components and the maximum sustainable throughput of the system determines where system bottlenecks and excess capacity exist.

The first step in troubleshooting is to determine where problems exist. Bottleneck identification and problem isolation testing point to the component in the network system that is overloaded or exhibiting some form of problem for the particular test case. The bottleneck may vary between test cases. For example, a client-server application test may show that the server is the bottleneck. An electronic mail system test may show that the wide area network

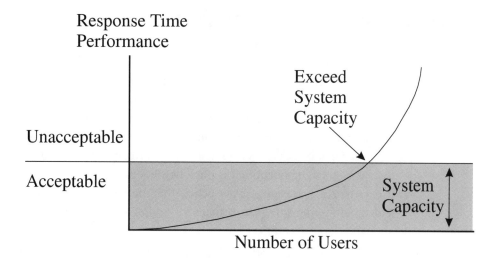

Figure 4.6 Capacity versus performance.

(WAN) link is the limiting factor. This testing can be used to determine which component must be upgraded to support additional network loads. Test results can help isolate a problem on the production network if the symptomatic load causing the problem can be reproduced. This is used during:

- **Deployment:** This testing can be used to help determine bottlenecks that impact performance and response time as a part of capacity planning.

- **Production:** This testing can be used to help determine bottlenecks that impact performance and response time or cause system problems as part of troubleshooting.

(Note: Isolation and diagnosis of load-dependent problems can be achieved if the symptomatic load can be re-created. Unfortunately, this is a difficult exercise, and today's NTM products do not provide comprehensive capabilities to assist in this analysis. Approaches for conducting this testing are discussed in Parts II and III.)

CAPACITY VERSUS PERFORMANCE

Capacity and performance, diagrammed in Figure 4.6, are requirements that network planners, developers, and support organizations must deal with; the two however, are often confused. Capacity is the ability to add more workload without decreasing performance to an unacceptable level. Capacity measurement determines how many more users or how much additional workload can be added before degrading performance. Although adding more resource to a component that is not a bottleneck does not increase performance, it may increase capacity. Any action that allows more workload (users) to be added before impacting performance is adding capacity to the system.

A performance bottleneck is any condition that impacts network response time or throughput. Network performance typically has high visibility in a company, consequently, capacity and performance must be balanced to meet today's network demands while planning for change and growth for tomorrow.

RANKING THE TEST OBJECTIVES

Most companies cannot and will not test for all 10 objectives just described. Based on the network's life cycle phase and perceived risks, a company should establish a testing program that addresses its major issues. The testing will be different from phase to phase of the network's life cycle, and test programs should change to reflect new areas of concern as the network grows and evolves. Often, the testing requirements vary across different network segments within the same company. Developing a test philosophy, as discussed in Chapter 6, that balances the risk of network problems versus the cost of testing provides a value statement that can help focus and direct the right amount of testing for your company.

Ranking the 10 test objectives is imprecise at best. Ask five people, and you will get five different answers. Three of the test objectives, however, are particularly important:

Application Response Time: As mentioned, this is the single best measurement of how the user perceives the network and a good historical

Acceptance Testing

A CONTACT BETWEEN THE NETWORK USER AND PROVIDER

As introduced in Chapter 4, *acceptance testing* is a shakedown of the system prior to deploying it into production. It is an excellent method of guaranteeing that the new system will be stable and provide acceptable performance in its initial release. *In a broader sense, acceptance testing is a contract between the provider (developer or integrator) of the network system and the buyer (network user).* It is a way of verifying the key capabilities, functionality, performance, and reliability of the system before it becomes productional and before it is fully paid for. Defining acceptance test criteria is also an excellent method of focusing the development or integration effort by identifying key system deliverables at the beginning of the project.

Acceptance testing is appropriate for any system installation or upgrade, but it is particularly important for client-server applications, complex network topologies, new technologies, mission-critical applications, and company-wide network services, such as Lotus Notes and electronic mail.

Acceptance test criteria and conditions should be formally defined at the beginning of the project. If the system or application provider is a system integrator or other outside organization, acceptance test criteria and conditions should be included in the contract, agreement, or statement of work. If the work is being done by an in-house organization, such as information technology (IT), then acceptance test criteria and conditions can be documented in an interoffice memo, statement of work, or other document. In either case, acceptance test criteria and conditions must be:

- Documented and agreed to by the parties at the beginning of the project.

- Included in requirement or design specifications.

- Measured throughout the project to ensure that the system is meeting its acceptance criteria.

- Verified in a final acceptance test, prior to deployment.

Even though acceptance criteria has been documented, the buyer or user of the system should be aware of two pitfalls that can occur during the project:

1. If the defined and agreed to acceptance criteria is not regularly measured during the project, there is little chance that it will be achieved during the final acceptance test. It is important that acceptance test milestones be included in the development or integration schedule to measure the system's progress toward meeting acceptance criteria. Progress payments can also be tied to the successful completion of these milestones.

   Another approach is prototyping key system components to verify that the acceptance criteria is achievable as early in the project as possible. A recent article in the trade press mentioned a company that spent several person-years developing a client-server application before it realized that the underlying network operating system could not sustain the anticipated load. Project risk and cost can be substantially reduced by prioritizing key objectives and verifying that they can be met as early as possible in the project.

2. If the final acceptance test is not conducted on the complete and final system, it is not a valid test. Often "minor" changes in the last few days of a project can have unexpected impact. Many examples are available that illustrate how last-minute changes caused performance degradation and impacted system reliability. If changes are made after the acceptance test, insist that the test be rerun to verify that the changes have no negative effect.

In most cases, the acceptance test process will be developed and run by the system provider. Nevertheless, the buyer (user, network manager, or senior management) must be involved in the acceptance test to check that all conditions and intent are met. The buyer must determine that the testing approach and test cases accurately measure the acceptance test criteria. Often, this is difficult for buyers to accomplish because they do not have the technical background to evaluate the testing procedures. Buyers may understand functionally what the system provides, but they probably won't understand how to verify its operation in an acceptance test. Using an independent consultant or network testing lab to review the proposed test methodology and test cases is an inexpensive way of validating the value of the acceptance test.

DEFINING ACCEPTANCE TEST CRITERIA

In defining acceptance test criteria, you should focus on three main areas:

performance or response time

functionality

reliability

Of course, each system, application, and buyer will have individual requirements, but a few rules of thumb should be followed in identifying specific acceptance test criteria:

- **Base the criteria on business or technical requirements:** This enables you to get to the heart of why you are implementing the new capability. For a new client-server application, don't try to establish criteria to test each and every command or option; instead, define criteria that measure a major application function or key technical attribute. For example:

    Creating a new purchase order, including cross-reference checks for credit history; assigning a unique reference number; and creating a packing slip in five seconds, is a business requirement that translates into measurable test criteria.

Testing the hardware reliability of a new Token Ring segment, to prevent soft or hard errors when the ring is heavily loaded is a key technical measurement that can be accomplished by loading the segment to between two and three times the anticipated load and monitoring soft and hard errors over a 24- to 72-hour period.

- **Be selective in defining the criteria:** Acceptance testing does *not* include testing the whole system for every bell and whistle. The intent of acceptance testing is to verify that critical, high-risk, and complex capabilities of the application or system are working. Therefore, limit the set of test cases: one or two cases covering performance, two to five cases covering functionality, and one test case covering reliability is a good acceptance mix. This totals between four and eight cases for the acceptance test.

- **State the criteria in measurable terms:** There is nothing worse than completing an acceptance test and then disagreeing on whether or not the system passed. State the test objectives in easily measurable terms. For example:

  The application will provide an average of three seconds response for 25 concurrent users when running a specific sequence of application commands defined in the requirement specification.

  The system will run for 72 hours at 50 percent load (as measured by the CPU utilization of the server) without any fatal errors. A fatal error is defined as a unrecoverable error that halts system activity or makes a key system feature unavailable.

  The system will perform the following functions and command sequences without error. For each function, the exact before and after condition of the system (for example, the content of screen fields) should be specified in sufficient detail to determine that the test completed successfully and without error.

CONDUCTING THE ACCEPTANCE TEST

Milestone acceptance testing should be conducted during development, and final acceptance testing should be conducted just prior to deployment. As an application or system evolves during development, functionality, then reliability, and finally performance is achieved. Therefore, acceptance test milestones must also follow this progression, or the testing will not provide relevant results for measuring progress toward acceptance. There are exceptions to this approach when reliability or performance criteria are of extreme importance, or there are perceived risks to meeting those goals. In such cases, early prototyping can help both clarify the risk and provide design input for the development effort. Milestone tests are not conducted on the target network, but are run in the test lab. Confirm that the test lab emulates the critical network components to make the test results as relevant as possible.

An often overlooked component of acceptance testing is the existing or baseline network that will support the new application or system. This can often be tested early in the project and can eliminate problems such as those noted in the trade press article and case studies mentioned previously.

The acceptance test agreement should clearly document where and when the final test will be run. Test labs are the worst place to conduct an acceptance test, because they are not the target environment. The best way to conduct the final acceptance test is with the final hardware and software fully installed and ready for production. If a new network is being installed or a segment is being added to an existing network, then it is practical to conduct the final acceptance test on the target hardware. Chapter 7 discusses ways of testing a predeployed system.

For client-server applications or other services that are being added to an existing network, it is also possible to conduct the acceptance test on the target network. The new application, service, or hardware is loaded on the production network, and a few workstations are used to create the test load. Chapter 7 and Part III discuss how to test on the production network without disrupting or significantly degrading the production environment.

IF THE ACCEPTANCE TEST FAILS

The acceptance test agreement must include a section on nonperformance, or what to do when the test fails. Any test that fails should be rerun up to three times to verify that the results (test failure) are reproducible. If the failure continues, the test environment should be baselined *without* the new components or applications to verify that the basic system is reliable and provides adequate performance. If the test environment fails, then the problem must be resolved and the acceptance test rerun on a stable environment.

If the test environment is stable and the acceptance test continues to fail, there are three possible alternatives:

1. Allow time for problem resolution and rerun the acceptance test.

2. Accept all or part of the new system or application as is.

3. Reject the new system or application.

The third alternative is self-explanatory, so let's discuss the first two alternatives in more detail.

Alternative 1

A problem resolution process should be included in the acceptance test agreement. The agreement should include a specified duration for resolving any problem encountered in the final acceptance test, and the number of retests allowed before the provider is in default of the agreement. The duration for problem resolution should be 10 to 30 days after a problem is identified. One or two retests of the final acceptance test are typically allowed.

If the system fails most or all of the acceptance test, it is a good indication that the objectives were not targeted or measured during development or integration. The test failures therefore probably indicate inherent system problems, and the system should be rejected. Deploying a system that does not meet baseline requirements is only asking for more trouble down the road.

Alternative 2

Accepting a system that does not pass part of the acceptance test may be a viable alternative depending on the severity of the failure. You may be able to accept the parts of the system that pass, or accept the whole system with concessions such as a reduction in price or free upgrades to resolve the problems. This is highly dependent on the type of failure and the interrelationship and dependencies between the various system parts. The best way to handle this contingency is to anticipate up front which alternatives are practical, and then structure the testing, acceptance criteria, and financial arrangements appropriately.

CHECKLIST

The following checklist will help in developing an acceptance test that works.

1. When planning the new system, identify the key criteria for its success.

2. Define specific, measurable acceptance criteria in the requirements specification. Communicate these clearly to the developers and buyers, to be sure that all parties "buy-in."

3. Include test milestones in the development schedule.

4. Define exact configurations and functions to be tested well before the first test milestone.

5. Include tasks and time in the development schedule for developing test cases, running the tests, and debugging problems.

6. Do not delay or overlook test milestones.

7. Evaluate all test data, including failures. Often a failure is more enlightening than a successful run because it detects underlying problems or issues that need to be addressed.

8. Identify specific tasks based on improving test results where meeting acceptance criteria appears risky or *no* improvement is seen between successive test milestones.

9. Rerun tests that fail or fall below expectations as soon as fixes are available.

10. Keep good records of all test results so that progress can be tracked.

11. Use item 10 to verify that test results are approaching acceptance goals.

12. Continually communicate status and expectations between the development team and the buyers of the system.

Philosophy and Methodology of Testing

WHERE TO START

A *test philosophy* establishes what should be tested and why. *Test methodology* defines how, or the process and procedures, of network testing. Develop a test philosophy and test methodology that address the critical aspects of your network system.

No organization can test its entire network and every component in it. What it can and must do is establish a test philosophy that covers critical aspects of the network. This chapter outlines a generic test philosophy and details the elements of a test methodology. To develop a workable test philosophy, it is recommended that you adapt the information in this chapter to your network and needs. To tailor these to your unique network installation, consider:

1. Where your network has historically been most vulnerable.

2. Your plans for network growth and new client-server or other applications.

3. How many resources (people, equipment, and dollars) can be applied to testing. Consider your initial investment and the obstacles you may have to overcome to get management approval. Often, it is best to start small and grow the effort based on measurable results.

4. Maintain flexibility to act on test results. Focus early on regression, performance, and acceptance testing, as these provide more measurable and noticeable results. Start by testing what you have installed with an emphasis on improving it. Often, product evaluation testing is where many people start, but unless it is part of a project that includes a major

purchase decision, it is difficult to show substantial return on investment.

Test philosophy identifies which key network subsystems should be tested and which of the 10 test objectives discussed in Chapter 4 and listed again here, provide the best return for the time, cost, and effort expended.

Application response time

Feature/functionality

Product regression

Throughput

Acceptance

Configuration sizing

Reliability

Product evaluation

Capacity planning

Bottleneck identification and problem isolation

Test methodology is an orderly system of procedures that, when applied to a project, ensures that the test results meet the test objective, and that the results are accurate, reproducible, and relevant. Each of the 10 test objectives requires a slightly different test methodology, although there are many similarities in the procedures. The test methodology includes six components:

• Planning

- Load modeling

- Test configuration

- Data collection

- Data interpretation

- Data presentation

Planning, record keeping, data collection, and data presentation are well-defined step-by-step procedures. They are the process part or science of network testing.

The "art of network testing" is in load modeling, test configuration, and data interpretation; they cannot be strictly defined in procedures. The test configuration must emulate critical network components. The load model must create traffic that generates results pertinent to the test objective. Data interpretation must analyze the test data to verify that the test truly measured its objective and that there are no secondary effects that make the test data invalid. If not done properly, any one of these steps can lead to erroneous conclusions.

As a simple illustration, let's consider using Novell's Perform3 testing tool to measure adapter throughput. This tool is used by many network vendors and test labs to compare adapter and adapter driver throughput. Perform3 measures adapter throughput by reading block size files, such as 64, 512, and 1024 byte blocks, from the server's cache, as shown in Figure 6.1. It performs the read operation for a specified number of seconds and then calculates the throughput in kilobytes per second based on the number of kilobytes of data read in the specified time. If more than one workstation is used, Perform3 coordinates the start of each test (block size) through one workstation that becomes the "master" so that all workstations start at the same time. It collects all test data at the end of the run and generates an aggregate throughput number in kilobytes per second for the test.

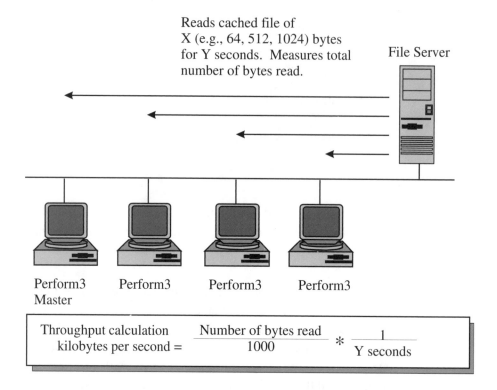

Figure 6.1 Novell's Perform3 performs cached reads from the file server for server adapter performance testing.

Two examples are presented next that illustrate the importance of correlating the basic operating principles of a network and the operation of the testing tool (in this case, Perform3).

Example 6.1 Server adapter throughput testing.

For a server adapter throughput test, four to six workstations run Perform3 against a single file server with a high-performance Ethernet adapter, as shown in Figure 6.1. When the results of one adapter test were collected and plotted, the server adapter's throughput was slightly greater than 10Mbps. Since Ethernet is a

10Mbps network, the results are obviously wrong, but why? The test setup was examined for possible hardware or software problems. There were none. Perform3 is a widely used tool. The probability of it incorrectly measuring kilobytes of read data and calculating throughput incorrectly was not likely. In addition, Perform3 results for other adapter tests using the same testbed appeared reasonable. The problem was not apparent.

When problems like this occur in a test project, the first diagnostic step is to instrument the test configuration so that secondary, independent measurements can be captured. Perform3 calculates throughput based on the total bytes transferred in a specified time. Therefore, the test network was expanded to include a network analyzer to measure total kilobytes transmitted during the test and a stopwatch to measure elapsed time for the workstations. When the test was rerun, the test duration time on the individual workstations did not compare with the stopwatch. The workstation clock was slower than the stopwatch.

Perform3's throughput calculation used the correct amount of data, but a shorter elapsed time, which resulted in a higher throughput rate than was physically possible. Calculating throughput using the stopwatch-elapsed time produced results that were within Ethernet's bandwidth. The workstation's adapter driver software was "hogging" CPU cycles, which impacted clock ticks or updates, thereby slowing down the workstation clock during the test. This example actually occurred during a test project at a well-known independent network test lab.❏

Example 6.2 Workstation adapter throughput testing.

Perform3 can be used to measure throughput of both the server and workstation adapter. The test configuration for a server test, as described in the previous example, is used by most test labs. For testing workstation adapter throughput, however, testing organizations have used different test configurations with varying results.

Some organizations use the same configuration for workstation adapter testing as for server adapter testing, and on the surface, this may seem reasonable.

Multiple workstations, however, can generate substantially more requests for cached file reads than a server can handle. Using this configuration, test results indicate that all adapters are roughly equal because the bottleneck is at the server, not at the workstation's adapter, which is the objective of the test. The server adapter in all the tests is the same, and the test is actually measuring server adapter throughput. Several well-known labs and trade publications have published such misleading adapter results.

The correct test configuration for measuring individual workstation adapter throughput, shown in Figure 6.2, is a very fast server and server adapter connected to a single workstation. As long as the server is faster than the workstation, the bottleneck will be at the workstation adapter. Perform3 is run only on the single

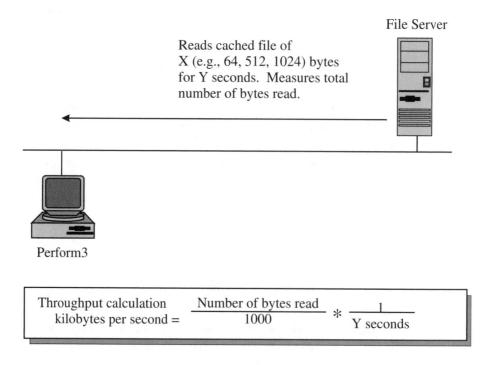

Figure 6.2   Correct test configuration for Perform3 workstation adapter performance testing.

workstation, and calculated throughput measures that workstation adapter's capacity to sustain throughput to the server. Using this test procedure, different adapters show different throughput measurements relative to their capability.❑

WHERE, WHY, AND HOW PROBLEMS OCCUR

The real-world networks that administrators must address are not nearly as structured as the test lab. Real-world networks are heterogeneous with varying loads throughout the day. Comparing the effect different products have on the network, tuning for performance, and identifying bottlenecks on a production network is much more difficult than testing in a lab. On a real-world network, there are complex hardware and software interactions that change second by second. These affect the performance, reliability, and availability of the network system. Since it is virtually impossible to accurately re-create this in a test environment, the challenge is to determine which interactions are critical to the test and to re-create their impact as accurately as possible during the test. Additionally, it is important to understand which interactions can be disruptive to the test by masking or influencing important test data, as illustrated in the previous examples.

If the test objective is to maximize the performance of a file server, there are many components in the server that contribute to its overall throughput. Figure 6.3 lists hardware and software components that influence the performance of a file server.

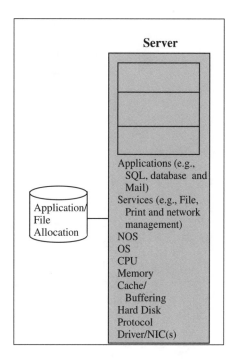

Figure 6.3   Many components influence file server performance.

Replacing a poorly performing component with a very high-performance component may eliminate one bottleneck, only to create a new bottleneck at another location in the server. Adding a second network interface card (NIC) to the server may eliminate the bottleneck caused by single NIC access to the LAN. However, this change may create a bottleneck in the server's cache or buffer handling because of the increased number of requests that can now reach the server through the two NICs. Resolving one component-level problem may not resolve a performance bottleneck, and may cause a worse condition elsewhere in the server.

The basic issues of what to test and how to test to achieve the objective comprise the "art" of testing. Testing on the network can be conducted at the component, subsystem, or system level. As illustrated in Figure 6.4, a network can be viewed as:

- hundreds to thousands of network components, such as adapters, hard disks, applications, and WAN links

- tens to hundreds of network subsystems, such as servers, routers, work-stations, and individual network segments

- one network or internetwork system

Each piece of the network system, as shown in Figure 6.4, can influence overall reliability and performance. For a complex network system, there is a fine line between components and subsystems. In fact, based on an individual test project, many network parts can be viewed as either a single component or a subsystem. For example, consider a router; for testing purposes, the router can be tested as a single node on the network, or it can be viewed as being composed of an operating system, individual boards supporting different network topologies and network applications, such as network management.

Some network parts can also be classified as components or subsystems of either the application/presentation layer or the network infrastructure. Adapter

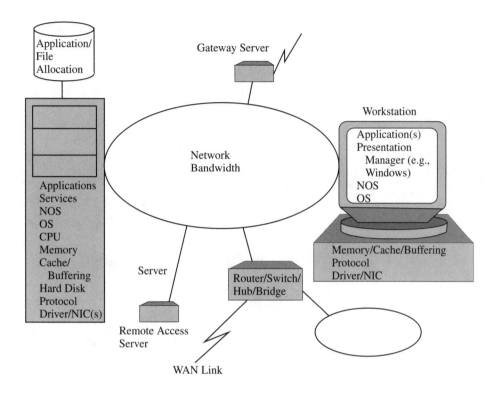

Figure 6.4 Network systems are a complex combination of multivendor products.

drivers and protocol software provide network transport capability and are often considered part of the network infrastructure. Most drivers and protocol stacks are very NOS-dependent, therefore they can also be considered part of the NOS. Should the NOS be considered a component or subsystem of the network? This may seem confusing, but working through these considerations is an essential part of developing the right test philosophy for the network environment. Figure 6.5 and the following discussion provide an introduction to the rationale behind the test philosophy explored in the upcoming sections.

NETWORK COMPONENTS AND SUBSYSTEMS

From a testing perspective, Figure 6.5 divides the network into components and subsystems that can be individually or collectively tested. Some parts, such as an

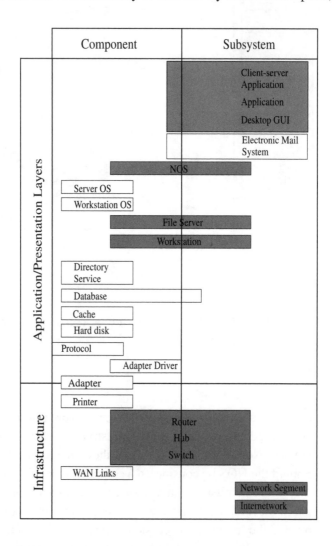

Figure 6.5 Classifying network system components and subsystems for testing.

adapter, are easy to classify as a component. Others, such as the NOS or a router, can be classified either as a component or a subsystem. Network planning, development, and support organizations will achieve a greater return on their testing efforts if they concentrate on testing at the network subsystem level. The reasons behind this include:

- Component-level testing does not generally provide sufficient information on which to base actionable decisions for the production system. Knowing which hard disk is faster does not translate into knowing whether the faster one will provide better systems performance or price/performance in the server configuration.

- Many companies have already standardized on network components, and issues such as support, spares, and unit price may vastly overshadow slight technical differences between the products.

- Component-level testing can always be done if subsystem test results are inconclusive.

Although most testing should be done on network subsystems, component testing provides benefit during:

- **Planning and design:** If a major product selection is being made, such as a new-generation adapter card, server, or workstation that will be standardized across the company, extensive component testing is justified. Test results may be used to select the most appropriate product, negotiate better pricing, establish spares requirements, or budget for installation and migration costs.

- **Isolation of bottlenecks and faults:** This testing must be done on the production system. Tools available today allow testing to be conducted, but require significant "hand-holding" by the tester. However, results are often worth the effort because they provide data that is impossible to acquire by any other means. Chapter 7 discusses testing on a production network.

During deployment, system-level *acceptance* and *reliability* testing can provide significant benefits. But because it is difficult to emulate an entire network system or use the production system for extensive testing, system-level testing is not typically feasible during most phases. There are always exceptions to any guideline. Recall the case study of the financial services company that tests its production network every day. The message is that testing is another tool to improve the network, but it is up to you to determine how best to employ it for your specific and unique needs. And, generally this takes some experimentation.

Subsystem testing is the best compromise. It provides the best return for the investment, it can be achieved either in a test lab or on a production network, and it generates actionable results relevant to the production environment. It is the first and last step of analyzing component-level problems, so it is the logical place to start.

PHILOSOPHY OF TESTING (SEVEN SUBSYSTEM TESTS)

There are seven subsystems that represent the minimum number of areas in which testing should be conducted. The philosophy behind choosing these seven subsystems is that they represent the most fundamental network system services, including:

basic network connectivity and data transport

file service

applications

user interface

During the testing in these areas, other components and subsystems of the network are also exercised. Therefore, if the other areas have symptomatic problems, their failure will be detected by these subsystem tests. Unfortunately, if these seven subsystem tests pass, it does not guarantee that all other network areas are working perfectly. My experience is that if these seven subsystems are appropriately covered, the testing effort will significantly improve the quality and reliability of the network.

When considering the seven subsystems for testing, be aware that not all 10 network test objectives outlined in Chapter 4 can or should be applied, because trying to do so creates a huge test matrix. Most companies would not have the time and resources to complete the test matrix. This problem is similar to the QA testing dilemma most network product vendors experience. There are too many test combinations to support. Over the years, most vendors have, through experience, narrowed testing to a limited number of configurations that uncover the most serious problems. This is what the seven subsystem tests are designed to accomplish for your network.

A large test matrix probably won't provide good return on your test investment. As in most endeavors, testing can reach overkill. Each company needs to determine the right mix of subsystems and test objectives that provide the highest payback. Guidelines and information included in this chapter and Chapter 7 will help in that decision.

Referring to Figure 6.5, the gray boxes show how the seven subsystems described here are classified, versus the other parts of the network. Figure 6.6 presents a test matrix of subsystems versus test objectives. It is obvious, as illustrated in the matrix, some test objectives just don't apply to a particular subsystem. For example, application response time is not a valid router test. This is a good starting point for test planning. It provides comprehensive coverage of key requirements for performance, reliability, and interoperability.

The seven subsystems are:

File server (S1): This testing is focused on the server hardware and NOS. Capacity planning and configuration sizing require that applications and services be installed on the test network. If servers are standardized across the network, product evaluation testing of competitive models should be conducted.

Network Subsystem \ Test Objectives	Acceptance	Performance	Reliability	Response Time	Capacity Planning	Functionality	Regression	Configuration	Product Evaluation	Bottleneck ID
1. File Server		X		X				X	X	X
2. Workstation		X						X		
3. NOS		X	X		X	X				
4. Application Client Server Database	X	X	X	X	X	X	X	X	X	X
5. Router/Hub/ Switch/Bridge		X	X		X	X	X		X	X
6. Network Segment	X	X	X		X					X
7. Internetwork	X	X	X		X					X

Figure 6.6   Recommended test objectives for the seven network subsystems.

Workstation (S2): Testing the workstation may not seem important, until you consider how much of the perceived network performance is attributed to the adapter, protocol, buffering, video refresh, and desktop management of the workstation. Like server testing, workstation configuration sizing and throughput testing should be conducted in conjunction with application and NOS testing so that the results are actionable relative to the production system.

Network Operating System (S3): There are many parts of the NOS that can be tested, but unless you are evaluating a new NOS, the only actionable test data concerns regression, reliability, and throughput results. The first two are important tests for a new release of the NOS to ensure that the software is stable and functional prior to deployment. Throughput testing is used to tune the NOS for improved performance.

For testing purposes, the NOS, file server, and workstations create the network platform on which applications and other services run. These are effectively tested as one subsystem, as discussed in Part III.

Application, Client-Server Database, and Workstation Desktop Software (S4): Testing these areas measures how the user will "see" the network. When implementing client-server applications, the five test objectives identified in Figure 6.6 (reliability, response time, capacity, functionality, and regression) are important. For productivity applications, the primary focus is regression testing and capacity planning. Desktop and GUI testing is similar to application testing.

Collectively, these software components are called the application layer, and are usually tested together, as discussed in Part III.

Routers, Hubs, Switches, and Bridges (S5): For testing purposes, the hardware and software of the product are considered a subsystem. Regression testing should be conducted before a new release is deployed. Similar to NOS testing, this testing validates the product is stable and functional (based on production network traffic requirements) prior to deployment. Since these products have many possible configurations, it is important to test the key configurations used on the production network. For example, one configuration may have Ethernet and FDDI segments supporting IP, SPX/IPX, and DECNet protocols with address-level filtering. Another configuration may have Ethernet and 56Kbps WAN links, such as a remote router, with only IP protocol. Both configurations must be tested. It is possible—and likely—that one combination will work while the other will encounter problems.

Reliability, functionality, and product evaluation should also be conducted when new product models are being considered or a significant new capability is added to the system. For example, if filtering, protocol encapsulation, or data compression are implemented for a router, functionality and reliability testing can uncover problems that may exist in these features.

The distinction between these products is becoming blurred, as routers take on switch characteristics and switches add routing to the capabilities. From a test orientation, these products are basically treated the same, as discussed in Part II.

Network Segment (S6): Once subsystems have been individually tested, they can be tested in a combined configuration that is representative of a "typical" network segment. This may actually require several test configurations depending on how diverse segment topologies are on the production network. Generally any existing segment (in a test lab or on a company network) that is known to work properly can be used as the baseline. The new subsystem is included in the baseline segment and tested to determine if any failures occur. The segment is tested for performance, reliability, and functionality.

Internetwork (S7): Once the subsystem works in the network segment, it should be tested in an internetwork configuration, if appropriate. This may entail connecting two small segment configurations and rerunning the tests used for item 6. This testing is important to establish that internetwork issues such as time-outs, directory service access and updates, network login, and access rights are operating properly.

My experience has shown that it is more cost-effective to forgo segment testing and concentrate on critical point-to-point paths through the internetwork, as discussed in Part II.

To reduce the cost and time of testing, Figure 6.7 shows how coverage of the seven subsystems can be achieved by focusing testing on four major areas:

Network Platform: NOS, file server, and workstations

Application Layer: GUI, desktop, application front end, workstation OS, and database software

Critical Internetwork Nodes: routers, hubs, switches, and bridges

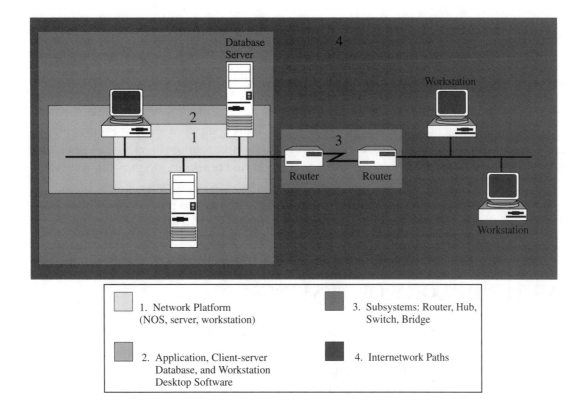

Figure 6.7 Four tests that provide comprehensive network test coverage.

Internetwork Paths: Critical point-to-point paths through the network system

Figures 6.6 and 6.7 define a test philosophy that encompasses seven major network subsystems, focuses on four major test environments, and measures network performance, reliability, and interoperability. You can use this test philosophy or, better yet, tailor it to meet your budget, resources, and existing network problems and concerns.

One large petroleum company has initially concentrated on regression testing network applications for compatibility. It configured a small test network (one server and a few workstations) and assigned one person half-time to conduct the testing. It plans on expanding into other areas, such as performance testing, as it becomes more familiar and comfortable with network testing procedures. In contrast, a major airline has a very large network testing lab that conducts testing in all seven of the areas listed. Many companies today are somewhere in between these two. The importance of testing is the return on investment—improved network quality, higher user satisfaction, and fewer fires to put out. As greater return is realized, greater investments in time and resources can be justified. To see the best return in the shortest time, you have to know how to effectively manage and run tests. A proven test methodology will get you started on the right track.

METHODOLOGY OF TESTING

The following sections outline the processes and procedures it is recommended you implement to ensure that each test accurately addresses the test objective; produces reliable, relevant, and actionable results; and is accomplished in the shortest time with minimal resources. The methodology of testing covers six areas:

Planning

Load modeling

Test configuration

Data collection

Data interpretation

Data presentation

Planning

Successful testing can never be haphazard; it must be planned, organized, documented, and communicated. Developing a plan and recording each step of the project is the key to success. It is important to record the test objective, test configuration information, problems, test data, intermediate conclusions, and virtually all details of the project. It is amazing how quickly test results can become unreproducible because of little elements that change in the test configuration or procedures; therefore maintaining a log is critical for every serious tester who wants to have relevant and reproducible results.

Test projects can quickly fill many journals spanning thousands of hours of network system testing and hundreds of test cases. Although a hard-bound lab book is sufficient, electronic logs make the recording process easier and provide better reference material for future projects. Be sure to backup the journal every day. An electronic journal makes it easy for the tester to reference past information, problems, and issues in planning new test series. Automated data collection and analysis tools can also be reused across projects. If properly documented, completed projects provide experience, data, and tools that make future projects easier, faster, less costly, and more valuable. In a moment, we'll itemize the benefits of an electronic journal.

Regardless of the method, every test project should be documented in a test journal, in which the test objective, test plan, test configuration, test data, and conclusions are recorded. Then any questions concerning the project or results can be addressed based on detailed information collected at the time it happened. At the conclusion of the testing, the test journal becomes a historical reference document that can be used in the planning of future projects and to re-create the test conditions.

A computerized version of the test journal is preferred because it:

- Makes integrating, manipulating, and combining text, raw data, spread-sheets, and graphic output easier.

- Becomes a permanent record that is easily reproduced and distributed to others for review.

- Provides a centralized repository for all test scripts.

- Is an excellent source of data for a formal test report or presentation, as required.

- Can be easily leveraged for future projects.

Test Plan

The test plan is the blueprint for the test project. While its format is not important (use whatever works best for the organization), it should cover the following material and be a "living" document that chronicles the progress of and changes to the project throughout its life. A good test plan includes:

- One-or two-sentence description of the test objective.

- Names of test personnel and technical support contacts for the project. Each test project should have a project manager, who is usually not the person doing the tests. The project manager is responsible for coordinating all project requirements and monitoring project progress. This person, therefore, needs both technical and managerial skills.

- Diagram of the test configuration and load model for the project.

- Versions of all hardware and software that will be used in the test project. It is very important to factor in sufficient lead time to collect and configure the necessary equipment. This detailed information enables the test configuration to be re-created, or to determine how a later test configuration differs from an earlier version.

- Number of test points per test script. This is important because it affects the duration of the testing portion of the project and the amount of data that must be analyzed. For some tests, the load points must be incremented until maximum values, such as throughput, are measured.

No.	Task	Task Assigned to	Start Date	Complete Date	Status
1.	Establish test objective				
2.	Assign project manager				
3.	Start test journal				
4.	Start test plan				
5.	Define test configuration				
6.	Start daily activity log				
7.	Start load model definition				
8.	Identify resources (people, H/W, S/W)				
9.	Start resource acquisition, as required				
10.	Define test points and test data collection				
11.	Outline test report				
12.	Identify data reduction Requirements				
13.	All resources for first test case available				
14.	Complete test configuration				
15.	Complete test load model				
16.	Start testing				
17.	Complete data reduction				
18.	Reduce first test case data				
19.	Review/evaluate results				
Repeat steps 13-19 for additional test cases					
20.	Complete all testing				
21.	Complete all data reduction				
22.	Analyze combined results				
23.	Begin test configuration teardown				
24.	Prepare report				
25.	Return/release resources				
26.	Archive test journal				
27.	File test scripts and problem resolution notes (to central location for reuse on other projects)				
28.	Project postpartum (what went right, what needs improvement)				
29.	End project				

Figure 6.8   Typical task milestone schedule.

- List of test measurements for each load point, such as response time in seconds, number of nodes, throughput in Kilobytes per second, and network errors recorded by a network analyzer.

- Definition of test scripts, load models, load generation software, and so on that must be developed for the project.

- Outline of the test report or other presentation materials that will be deliverables from the project.

- Project time line or schedule milestones. This will be refined as the project progresses, but can be used initially to establish deadlines and project scope. The most important issue during planning is to compile a list of tasks and task assignments for the project, as shown in Figure 6.8. Dates can be filled in later.

When estimating task duration, remember that it takes time to log test actions, results, and configuration information. For example, an installation of software that normally requires 1 hour, may require 1.5 hours or more because of the time required to log configuration options and installation results. For installations and configurations, a good rule of thumb is to multiply task times by a factor of 1.5 to 2 to include all documentation overhead. For a test that takes 30 seconds to run, it may take several minutes to record test results. Data recording time is dependent on the automation level of the test software. The best way to estimate recording time is to run practice tests and measure the time it takes to record data and setup for the next test run.

The time required for documentation may seem excessive, but thousands of hours of experience have shown that good documentation is invaluable for resolving any issues that may occur during or after testing is complete.

Daily Activity Log

The daily activity log provides a centralized, chronological history of the project. The purpose of this log is to document:

- Steps that were taken.

- Theories proposed as to what went wrong during installations or tests.

- Test data collected during the project.

- Any other pertinent project information.

The log should also be used to record ideas and paths taken that didn't lead to answers. Later on, when looking over the notes, something that was missed earlier may provide important information for resolving a problem.

Although project activities occur chronologically, tasks may not be completed in a chronological fashion. Often tasks are started, then interrupted or delayed for some reason while another task is begun. For example, the tester may:

- Set up one configuration, but have technical problems.

- Set up a second configuration.

- Receive a call with information for debugging the first configuration's problem.

- Start testing and collect test data for the second configuration.

- Collect test data for the first configuration.

- Add a third configuration.

The easiest way to cross reference this project information is to have it listed in the table of contents of the daily activity log. As a new topic is entered, whether it's setup information, troubleshooting, or test data, it should be listed in the table of contents immediately; do not wait until the end of the project, because the information may need to be referenced during the project.

As shown in Figure 6.9, information entered previously into the log is referenced on the top of the new page, with a *From Page ___ line*. For example, updated setup information, changes to the .INI file, and new AUTOEXEC batch files, should be referenced to the pages on installation at the beginning of the

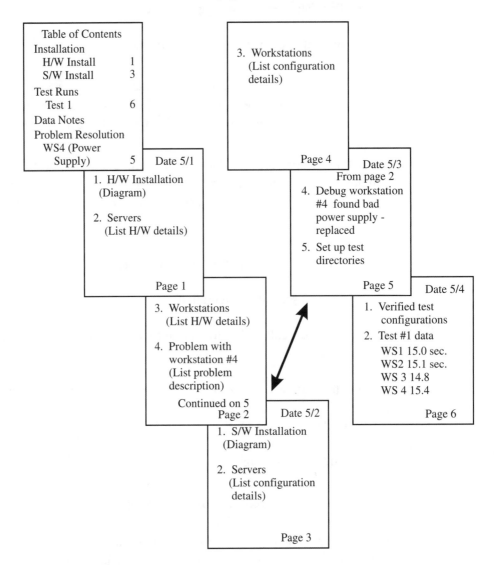

Figure 6.9 Sample daily activity log pages.

project. Another example is when hardware configuration changes are made to the original documented test configuration. Be sure also to reference the preceding pages; add a *Continued on* line at the bottom right of each page, as shown in Figure 6.9.

If the daily activity log is in electronic form, it can easily be referenced and updated during the project. At the end of the project, pertinent information (such as troubleshooting tips) can be extracted for future use. When using a hard copy log, write legibly! Others may need to reference the work or to pick up where you left off.

Project review is important on an ongoing basis. The tester and project manager should review results and progress on a regular basis. The daily activity log is an excellent tool for this, as it can be used to summarize progress to date, as well as to plan for upcoming project tasks.

Test Configuration Log

The test configuration log may be part of the daily activity log or maintained as a separate document or subdirectory. This log contains information regarding the hardware and software configuration of the test environment, and includes a diagram of the test configuration and all installation and configuration details. The test configuration log documents:

test bed equipment

software and applications

configuration information

This information provides a "paper trail" that may be used for future analysis when resolving test data inconsistencies and errors, or verifying unexpected results. It is not uncommon that a particular NIC may be causing bad packets; a combination of a particular vendors' machine and a certain NIC may be causing network errors; or mixed software versions may cause intermittent problems or performance degradation on the network. By having individual components logged, a problem can be traced to see if it follows a particular piece of hardware, or to confirm that correct software versions were used throughout the test configuration.

It is a good idea to draw a diagram of the network configuration, including the name, designation, or address of each component. Be sure to label all network segments and wide area communication links with their speed, the protocol used, and subnet addresses. For a hard-bound log, draw the configuration in the log following the table of contents. For an electronic log, use an application such as Microsoft's PowerPoint to create the diagram.

Assign names to servers and workstations in the test (such as Station1, Station2, or Station1-1, Station2-1, Station1-2, Station2-2) so each node can be uniquely identified. Record the following information for each node:

- Manufacturer and model number.

- Processor type and speed.

- System RAM.

- NIC card manufacturer, model, serial number, address, and jumper or software configuration settings. (**Note:** It may be useful to "code" each board with an identifier such as a colored sticker and an identifier [NIC A, NIC B, NIC C] that corresponds to the information logged for each of these types of components. In the event components are swapped from machine to machine, an entry can be made in the log book that "NIC A was installed in Station 5.")

- NIC software driver configuration settings.

- Option boards installed in the machine.

- Disk controller type, manufacturer, and model number.

- A printout of the EISA Configuration or Setup Configuration for EISA and micro channel machines.

For example, when testing the effect of various NIC combinations on server throughput, log a printout of the EISA configuration for each NIC tested in the server. For other components, such as routers and switches, log:

- manufacturer and model number

- software version number

- processor type and speed

- system RAM

- board revision level, model, serial number, and address

- printout of any configuration information

- network subnet address per port

For the network operating system (NOS), record the following information, as appropriate:

- For NetWare, record:

    server STARTUP.NCF (from DOS partition)

    server AUTOEXEC.NCF (from SYS:\SYSTEM)

    server system login script NET$LOG.DAT (from SYS:\SYSTEM)

- For other network operating systems, record comparable information as listed for NetWare.

- For the workstations, record CONFIG.SYS, AUTOEXEC.BAT, and INI files. If all stations are the same, only one copy is needed. If there are various types of machines, a record of each configuration is required.

For application software, record:

- version number

- file date and size

- application INI files or modified Windows INI file

- the drive mappings used for the software installation

It is best to use printouts provided by the various components and save them as files in the test configuration log or print them and paste them into the hard-bound test journal. When defaults are used, it is not necessary to document every setting; rather, document any installation options selected. If changes occur during the test, mark the changes either directly on the hard copy (use a different color ink) and note the date of the change, or generate new files with the date of the change.

Test Scripts (Subdirectory of Test Scripts)

This subdirectory includes all software needed to re-create the load model with a file-naming nomenclature that is easily understood. Figure 6.10 shows two sample configurations and a corresponding directory structure and file-naming convention for the test and loading. The file names describe pertinent information about the test. The key information includes a file ID number, number of workstations, and type of load represented by the file. This is particularly important for regression, response time, performance, and reliability testing where the tests may be rerun periodically to verify product upgrades.

At the conclusion of the project, this subdirectory should be moved into a test script archive directory for use by other test projects. This is one way of leveraging work from project to project to reduce the cost of testing.

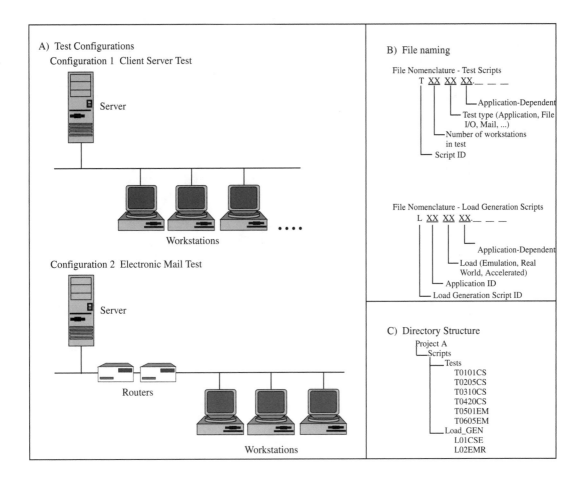

Figure 6.10   Example test script subdirectory organization B and file naming convention C for test configuration shown in A.

Problem Resolution Log

As problems are uncovered and resolved, information should be recorded in the daily activity log. Experience has shown that such information can easily get buried in the project notes, and thereby lost for future reference. It is worth the time to create a problem report in a problem resolution log so that information is captured in a single place. The problem report number should be recorded in the

Problem Report

Number_____
Date_____

Status

Reported_____ Date_____ Tester_____
Fixed_____ Date_____ Tester_____

Key Work References:

Problem Description:

Resolution:

Figure 6.11 Example problem report format.

daily activity log for cross-reference. By the end of most projects, there will be a valuable collection of tips, problem resolutions, and general technical information in the problem resolution log.

This log can be a simple text document in which there is one page per problem, or it can be a database that enables easier cross-referencing of material. The example shown in Figure 6.11 is a simple format that works and takes little time to create and use, but use whatever format you like, to make sure this valuable information doesn't "fall through the cracks."

At the conclusion of the project, this log should be moved into a historical log for use by other test projects and support organizations. This is another way of leveraging work done from project to project to reduce the cost of testing and network support.

Test Data (Subdirectory of Spreadsheets)

Collect all files containing test data, all data reduction programs and spreadsheets, and all graphs in one subdirectory. Since there will be "identical" files created from multiple test runs, it is very important to create a naming convention for these files and a subdirectory structure, as shown in Figure 6.12. Using this naming convention, note how easy it is to detect that results from run number 3 are missing from both the client-server and mail tests. (Parts II and III provide additional information on data reduction spreadsheets and formulas specific to the test cases described in those sections.)

Test Report

The test report format should be outlined prior to beginning the project to ensure that all information pertinent to the report is collected during the testing. The section on Data Presentation discusses the test report format and contents in more detail.

Load Modeling

Models used in network systems testing must provide complex loading to accurately represent the production network. Load models include a description of the:

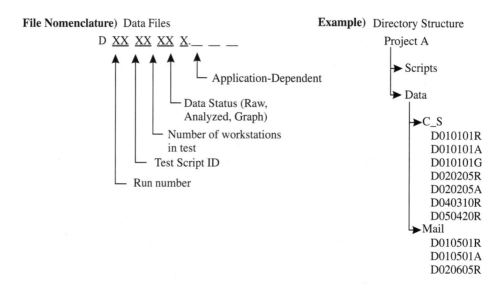

Figure 6.12   Example of test data file-name format and subdirectory structure.

- test software packages that will be used to produce the network load,

- amount and increments of each load type required.

One test may require network load as a sequence of IP packets with a distribution of 40 percent 64-byte packets, 45 percent 1024-byte packets, and 15 percent 512-byte packets. The amount and increment of network load could be defined as 40, 60, and 80 percent of bandwidth. Another test may define network traffic as a client-server application with a series of 10 transactions, including file open, search, update, merge, delete, sort, and close. The amount and increment of network load could be defined as the equivalent of 1, 5, 10, 20, 40, 60, 80, and 100 users.

Test software can take several forms:

- a proprietary client-server application run under control of a mouse or keyboard input macro,

- a productivity application run under control of a mouse or keyboard input macro,

- a test utility that generates prescribed activity, such as sequential reads, random writes, or

- a packet generator that inserts packets (for IP or other protocols), frames (such as Token Ring Source Routing) or cells (for ATM) onto the network.

Assume the test objective is to measure application response time and generate a 1 to 50 user load versus response time curve for a new client-server application. The application will be run by the users from a file server on one segment and access a centralized database that resides on another network segment, as shown in Figure 6.13.

The test traffic might include the following critical activities which affect system response:

- Windows-based client-server application test script that executes the top 5 to 10 transactions that are network- and SQL server-intensive, and represent the most critical response time conditions for the system.

- Application test scripts representing the current productivity applications run on the network, including both DOS and Windows applications. It is important to determine whether there is degradation to existing users of the file server, and degradation to the users of the shared database application that resides on the file server.

- DECNet and IP packet traffic that model background network load through the router between the client-server nodes and the database server. It is important to determine whether the existing router load plus the new client-server transaction load will degrade the router.

- File reads and writes that model electronic mail and other activity on the file server housing the shared client-server application overlays and

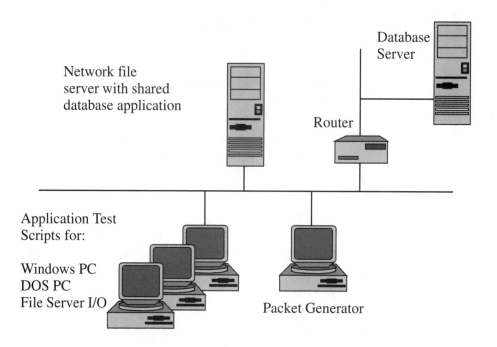

Network file
server with shared
database application

Database
Server

Router

Application Test
Scripts for:

Windows PC
DOS PC
File Server I/O

Packet Generator

Figure 6.13   Client-server application test configuration with test scripts for a
new client-server application and existing network activity.

temporary files. This extends the accuracy of the existing system loads
and is coupled with the second in modeling the real-world load on the
file server.

To generate the preceding loads requires four different load capabilities:

DOS-based productivity applications

Windows-based client-server and productivity applications

packet generation software

file I/O software

Don't create one monolithic test, and don't expect that one pass through the test suite will work. One test won't provide all the data needed; in fact, the opposite is more likely. Most tests require multiple runs, and problems are typically found in a few portions of the overall test. Therefore, tests should be segmented into logical groupings that can be run separately, concurrently, or serially. This provides the greatest freedom for configuring specific test cases, and allows significant portions of the tests to be reused in other test projects, thereby improving overall test productivity and reducing test preparation time.

Test Configuration

Testing can be conducted in one of three places:

- on a test network

- on a production network at off-hours

- on a production network during normal hours

Regression, configuration, product evaluation, throughput, and reliability testing for the network infrastructure is best done on a test network. A few infrastructure tests, as discussed in Part II, can be conducted on a production network. The application/presentation layer testing can be conducted either on a test network or on the production network under controlled conditions. Acceptance testing should always be done on the target network, never on a test network. Bottleneck identification and problem isolation should be done on the production network, unless a very well-defined test network is available that exhibits comparable symptoms.

Testing on the production network can be very cost-effective; unfortunately, existing network testing tools do not provide capabilities that support this well. The key steps to production network testing are:

1. Run multiple, short (less than two-minute) tests. Most users will not be significantly impacted by a short period of system degradation if they

are informed prior to the testing and recognize the potential value of the effort. Short test runs do not permanently increase the network baseline load.

2. Create a test script that initially produces small incremental loads and increases the load during each test run. By monitoring results, tests can be stopped when the objective is reached or before the production network is severely impacted or caused to fail. Using this approach, the test loads will not severely impact or disrupt the production environment.

Next we'll briefly discuss two ways of emulating the test configuration. The first approach provides faster payback and little up-front cost. The emulation is confined to a single PC and the use of the production network. It is a quick, but limited method for application regression and response time testing on the production network. The second approach is to use a network test lab. This is more costly, but provides a much broader range of testing capability. If your organization is considering testing, but wants to do a pilot project, the first method is certainly more cost-effective, but more companies are taking the second approach, and some are coupling both approaches for broader testing capability. Often, companies hire consultants to define and set up the lab, define test procedures, and help them get started. To get you started, Chapter 7 provides detailed information on production network testing and establishing a network test lab.

As illustrated in Example 6.2, page 94, defining the test configuration must be done very carefully to insure that the test actually measures the test objective. Parts II and III outline specific test configurations and requirements for the four areas of testing identified in the Network Test Philosophy section.

Data Collection (Reproducible Results)

Collecting the right test measurements and interpreting results based on those measurements is critically important to the success of the test project. For example, the same test software and network configuration can be used to do both performance and reliability testing. For performance, test data measures response time or data throughput; for reliability, test duration is important, but network and component loads, dropped packets, lost sessions, retries, and throughput are also critical to understanding failures. Network reliability data is important in performance testing too, but often overlooked. A failing component can grossly distort test results and lead to erroneous conclusions.

Figure 6.14 shows network throughput utilization percentages and network errors collected by a network analyzer for an Ethernet configuration. There are 112 total errors recorded with a peak error rate of 10 per second. Of the 112 errors recorded, 97 are CRC/alignment errors, and 15 are packet fragment errors. Ethernet packet fragments, the result of network collisions, are typical on Ethernet because of the Carrier Sense Multiple Access/Collision Detection (CSMA/CD) negotiation scheme used among the network nodes. One collision per second is

Utilization %	40
Peak Utilization %	50
Peak Error Rate	10
Total Errors	112
Total CRC/Alignment Errors	97
Total Oversize Errors	0
Total Undersize Errors	0
Total Fragments	15
Total Jabber Errors	0

Figure 6.14   Example of data collection using a network analyzer.

not unreasonable. CRC/alignment errors, however, are not considered normal. A high number of these errors indicates a problem with the cabling or a network adapter. This problem would affect performance data and give misleading results, therefore, it should be corrected and the test rerun to get accurate performance results.

Good data collection procedures start with documenting all hardware and software configuration settings, and continue during testing with:

1. Collecting all test data, including runs that fail and test configuration verification runs. If problems or issues occur later in the project, this data may help isolate the problem.

2. Documenting measurements from other tools, such as a network analyzer or a server CPU monitor that may be relevant to the test.

3. Taking multiple measurements at selected test points (typically the extremes) to verify the margin of error between runs. (Note: If identical test run results differ by more than a few percentage points, there is reason to suspect that the test configuration is not stable and further investigation is required to determine why.)

Data Interpretation (Relevant Results)

As this book's title highlights, network systems testing is not an exact science, but very much an art, particularly when it comes to interpreting test data. Test data is either easy to understand, such as response time in seconds, or very difficult to analyze, such as when a regression test fails on one platform, but passes on another. Data interpretation improves with testing experience and often relies on an in-depth understanding of how network subsystems and components interact.

Three procedures that help interpret test data are *data reduction, forecasting,* and *intermediate verification*, described in more detail in the next subsections.

Data Reduction

Before beginning the test, develop a data collection and reduction model. Often this is a spreadsheet and graphics, as described in Parts II and III. Sometimes, a small program may be required to consolidate large volumes of data into a manageable set of consolidated results. If the model is not developed before the test begins, it is very difficult to ascertain whether the tests are producing relevant results throughout the project.

In Figure 6.15, individual workstation response times are entered for each test run. The spreadsheet calculates average response time per run, average response time across runs, standard deviation between individual run averages, and a margin of error that is the percent difference between successive runs. A margin of error greater than 4 percent means that the test environment is not

Test Configuration ID - Test Journal page #____
Tester Name:

Workstation #	Run 1	Run 2	Run 3
Average per run			
Average across runs			
Standard Deviation			
Margin of Error			

Figure 6.15   Example data reduction spreadsheet for application response time tests.

stable, and it should be investigated to determine the cause before proceeding with the testing. Parts II and III include many other data reduction examples.

For tests such as reliability or configuration sizing, define the measurement criteria and develop a consistent, easy-to-read chart that plots the pertinent data for each run. For configuration sizing, this may include response time, number of load points, and various component sizes, such as cache size, number of buffers, and disk transfer rate.

Forecasting

Before starting a test, testers often have assumptions as to which settings will provide the best performance or what the test results will show. These can be used as a "reasonability" gauge of the test data. However, be careful not to let assumptions influence the final data reduction process; often, the assumptions will be wrong. They should be regarded only as a guide during the testing process.

Intermediate Verification

Data reduction and analysis should not be put off until all the tests are completed. It is best to complete these tasks as soon as possible after completing a test, and certainly before the test configuration is changed. This will uncover data inconsistencies or problems so that they may be addressed in the most effective and least costly manner. If the test procedures have to be modified because the results indicate a problem, it is better to do this for only one test case and not the entire project. Spending time verifying intermediate results takes discipline, especially under a time constraint, but many test projects run into trouble because they omit this step.

Be cautious before releasing or distributing intermediate test results. These are primarily for the benefit of the tester and project manager, and often, intermediate results change because of problems or new information that require test cases to be rerun. Once data is released, expectations are set, and it then becomes more difficult to communicate new, "contradictory" information. When this occurs, confidence in the project may deteriorate, and the accuracy of all test results will be questioned. The best advice is to be conservative about releasing results, until you are confident in their accuracy. (Data interpretation is very dependent on the test objective and subsystem under test. Spreadsheets, graphics, and tips on data interpretation are discussed in detail in Parts II and III.)

Data Presentation (Actionable Results)

The final step in the test project is to summarize and present test results in a project or test report. This report represents the primary deliverable of the project, and overall project perception is often based on its quality and clarity. Independent test labs and trade publications usually summarize test data and provide a ranking of the products tested, based on the results. In contrast, in-house test projects, are rarely tasked with drawing such simple conclusions. The 10 test objectives require that the project develop specific actionable conclusions from the results.

Most people don't want to read a long report on a test project; they want it as verification that the results are accurate and reliable. Based on hundreds of testing projects and reports, the following information should be included in any test report or presentation:

1. **Test objective:** One or two sentences explaining the purpose of the test effort.

2. **Conclusions:** The information and recommended actions obtained from the testing.

3. **Summary of test results:** The data on which the conclusions are based.

4. **Test philosophy and methodology:** A brief description of how the test was conducted. It should include the loading, test scripts, and data collection methods used, and an explanation of how the test methodology provided relevant and reproducible results.

5. **Test Configuration:** Diagram of network test configuration.

The report format can be a presentation, an executive summary (two to four pages), or a longer document (5 to 20 pages). An executive summary works the best for tests from which the results can be summarized in a graphical fashion, such as application response time, throughput, reliability, or product evaluation. Regression, configuration sizing, and application feature/functional testing require more written information be included. For these reports, include a one to two page executive summary covering the test objective, test configuration, and conclusions. Test results summarized in tables or brief descriptive paragraphs effectively organize and communicate supporting information in the body of the report.

On rare occasions, very detailed test reports of over 50 pages may be necessary. These often include chronological activity of the project from beginning to end or very detailed information on error conditions and error resolution. In all cases, an executive summary is essential, because a long report is rarely read from cover to cover. Usually, only a few people, such as the individual responsible for the project, his or her manager, and one or two others, will read the full report; the majority will read only the executive summary. Therefore, the guidelines just listed for content apply: Communicate all pertinent project information and conclusions in the executive summary, and all support information in the body of the report. By doing this, readers can quickly determine the value of the project and the potential payback for the costs incurred.

The best way of achieving an organized data presentation is to start it during project planning. During test planning, develop a description or outline of the project report. This is important for two reasons:

- **Data collection:** If the project report format is defined, the project manager can guarantee that all information is logged in the test journal in a manner that facilitates its inclusion in the report. Additionally, the report can be drafted and formatted during the project, thereby helping address the second item.

- **Time allocation:** Report writing is the second major cause for failing to meet the schedule on a test project. Can you guess the first cause? Preparing a report may take longer than a short presentation, but often an executive summary is the most difficult to write. Being concise and including all key information in a few words isn't easy. Therefore don't underestimate the time it takes. A rule of thumb is: allocate one week of report preparation for each month of project duration.

Note: Based on over 30,000 hours of testing experience, the number one cause for unexpected project delay is actually a tie between delays in collecting or acquiring the software and hardware for the test configuration, and having to rerun tests at the end of the project because the test data was not analyzed in an ongoing fashion throughout the project.

Be sure also to allocate time for reviews and edits. If possible, have at least two people review the report before distributing it. Allow at least one week for reviews and edits. Most reviewers, even those with the best intentions, usually have to be "encouraged" to get the review done, and usually it will take several days to get their input. Have the reviewers concentrate on the clarity of the message. Test results and conclusions will be perceived as accurate if the project is well understood and the readers have confidence in the fairness of the testing approach. Often, people have expectations that are different from what the test results actually show; therefore, the report must provide sufficient information to establish a level of confidence in the test conclusions.

Test projects often provide insight into many aspects of the network not previously analyzed in depth. However, it is also important to realize which insights are actionable and which are not. For example, if test results indicate a router model is not performing well under certain conditions, a project conclusion to replace all such routers probably wouldn't be actionable because of the cost involved. An actionable result may be to change the router configuration for better performance, or contact the router vendor to explore fixes for the problem. Often the "perceived" success of a test project is based as much on how the information is presented as what the information contains.

ALMOST READY TO START TESTING

The six processes described in this chapter form the foundation for the network test methodology. Parts II and III describe how to test for different test objectives using these processes as the foundation for the project. The last aspects to discuss about testing are where and how to test. Chapter 7 explains how to select the best test configuration and loading for a test project. The alternatives include using a test lab, using the production network, and using emulated loads versus real-world loads.

Most testers feel more comfortable in a test lab, but there are opportunities to reduce costs and achieve unique results by testing on the production network, and some large companies are already doing production network testing. Each installation will have to make its own decision on when to use a lab versus the production network. Chapter 7 provides information to help in reaching that decision.

Network Test Environment Alternatives

TWO DIMENSIONS

There are two dimensions to the test environment: The first is the network configuration; the second is the network load. As shown in Figure 7.1, combinations of emulated and real-world network loads and network test configurations can be mixed to accomplish the test objectives listed in Chapter 4. The upper left-hand quadrant, however, is not a practical combination as you will understand shortly.

Real-world load Emulated network	Real-world load Real-world network
Emulated load Emulated network	Emulated load Real-world network

Network Load

Test Network Configuration

Figure 7.1   Test environment dimensions.

TERMINOLOGY

Network test management (NTM) is not yet a widely used discipline, therefore, testing labs, testers, and test tool vendors do not have a consistent terminology for describing the test environment. The following terms define a nomenclature for the test environment that is used throughout Parts II and III.

- Emulation

- Real-world

- Test network configuration

- Load model

- Load distribution

- Load generator

- Load generator script

- Test script

- Actual-user load

- Equivalent-user load

- Accelerated load

As in any profession, testers enjoy having their own unique vocabulary, which sets them apart from others. Additionally, using this terminology will help you understand the various aspects of test planning and concisely communicate the test plan to others in the profession. The following sections define each of these terms and describe their relationship to one another.

Emulation versus Real-World

Mr. Webster defines emulate as "to imitate with effort to equal or surpass." The objective in emulation is to get as close as possible to real-world test results, while achieving the benefits of emulation—reduced resources—that make testing practical. As shown in Figure 7.2, the primary benefits of emulating network configurations and loads are reduced cost and time. There are two types of emulation relevant to network testing. The network test configuration and the network load can be emulated.

Emulating the production system requires that a test configuration be created that allows critical production system components and topology to be tested. An emulated network test configuration requires significantly fewer nodes and other network hardware than its real-world equivalent. Emulating the network load simply means that a "load generator" is used to create network

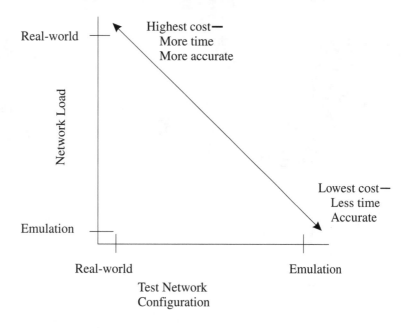

Figure 7.2   Benefits of emulation include lower cost and reduced time.

loading equivalent to the actual or anticipated production load. An emulated load can be created by a simple program doing file reads and writes to the server, or it can be a packet generator sending out specific packet patterns and rates on the network. Network load can also be emulated by running applications under the control of a script where each workstation generates the equivalent load of many actual users.

Real-world testing is what its name implies. The network topology used is the production network, a portion of it, or an exact lab duplicate. Network

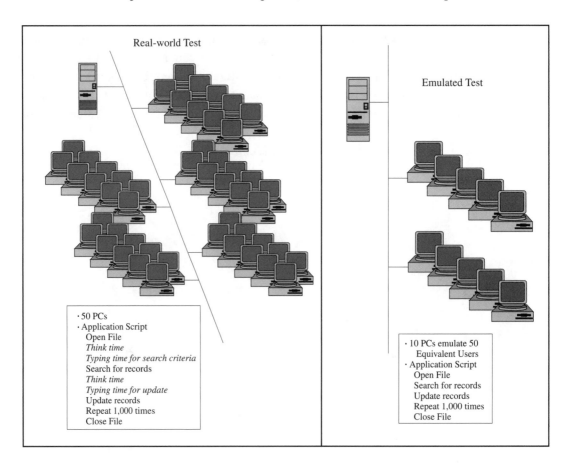

Figure 7.3   Emulation versus real-world test configuration.

loading is created using the actual number of users and the software that is running on the production system, rather than equivalent loading techniques. The loads can still be created through automated scripts, but these scripts, unlike the equivalent load scripts just mentioned, include pauses for user think time, character input at equivalent typing speed, and mouse movement delays that represent user interaction with the application.

The differences between emulation and real-world testing can be summarized in the simple application test environment shown in Figure 7.3. While the emulated test requires only 10 PCs, the real-world test requires 50 PCs. Therefore, set-up time and capital cost of the real-world test is significantly higher than the emulated testing and will provide only marginally better results. Also note the differences in the application scripts for the two test cases.

LOAD MODELING

The **load model** for a test project defines how much and what type of loading is required to achieve the test objective. Figure 7.4 outlines the decisions and details that go into developing the load model. The terminology shown in Figure 7.4 is discussed next.

The **load distribution** determines whether the loads will be emulated (*equivalent user load* or *accelerated load*), or real-world (*actual user load*). It defines the amount of each type of load required for the test. The load distribution influences the number of PCs and network configuration required to conduct the test. In Figure 7.3 the load distribution for the emulated test has each PC generating the equivalent-user load of five users. For the real-world test, each

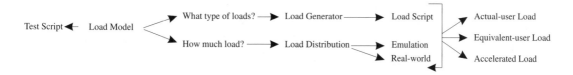

Figure 7.4   The load model decision process includes defining the type and amount of each load.

PC generates the load of one user (actual user load). It is easy to see the difference this makes in the required test configuration.

The load model identifies which load generator and load script will be run on each workstation in the test. The **load generator** is the software that creates the network load. This can be an application, test utility, or a batch file. The **load generator script** or **script** (for short) is the keyboard macro file, parameters, or

Load Model (LM)
    Load Generator = Application A
    Test Loads = 5, 10, 15 users

Load Distribution (LD)
    Equivalent User Load (5 users/workstation)

Load Generator Script (LGS)
    Series of application commands emulating transaction
        rate (I/O) of 5 typical users

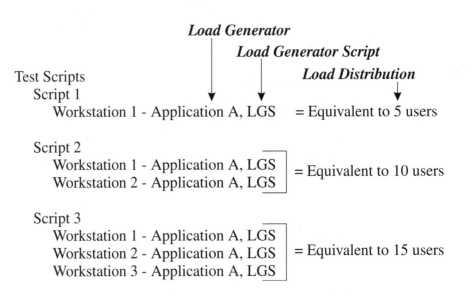

Figure 7.5   Example of a simple load model and test script.

commands that are input to the load generator; they describe the output to be generated.

The **test script** defines the implementation details for the load model. It lists which load generator and script will be run on each node during the test. A typical test project will have many test scripts. Figure 7.5 defines a simple load model and lists the resulting test scripts for three tests that have equivalent user loading of 5, 10, and 15 users.

In defining the load model, consideration must be given to whether **equivalent-user loading** will be used where each workstation creates a load of N "equivalent" users, or whether **actual-user loading** that replicates typical user pauses will be modeled. There are advantages and disadvantages to using both, but in most test projects, equivalent-user loading is the best compromise between cost and benefit.

Referring to the example on testing a new client-server application in Chapter 6, the load model for that test would be defined as:

1. Load generator is client-server application. Test load is 15 users.

2. Load generator is productivity application. Test load is 30 users.

3. Load generator is packet generator. Test load is 15 percent network load using combination of DECNet and IP packets.

4. Load generator is C program sending and receiving one 1,900 word mail message every 60 seconds. Test load is 25 concurrent mail users.

The load is defined in item 1 for the client-server application-under-test. The other load model components create a representative background load that emulates the existing production system. The loading requirements can be satisfied either by emulated or real-world loads. Depending on which alternative is chosen, the load distribution, load generator scripts, and test script will be very different. Let's consider how each would be defined.

Emulated Loading

In this case, the following would be the definition of the load model and test script:

1. *Load generator is a Windows client-server application.* Load distribution is equivalent user loading of five users per workstation. Load generator script commands are transactions one to five with no pauses. Script ID is T0105CS. Translated this means that three workstations execute the Windows-based client-server application. Each station generates the equivalent user load of five typical application users. The load generator is the actual application. The load generator script is keyboard and mouse input to generate required transactions against the database server. Since the script is emulating the load of five users per workstation, there are no pauses in the script for think time or typing rate.

2. *Load generator is a DOS word processing application.* Load distribution is equivalent user loading of 10 users per workstation. Script commands are file open, file read, edit, spell check, file write, and file close repeated 100 times with no pauses between commands. Script ID is T0210WP. Translated this means that three workstations execute a word processor application under DOS where each station generates the equivalent user load of 10 typical network users. The load generator is the DOS application. The load generator script is a series of keystrokes to invoke the required file I/O against the file server. Since the script is emulating the load of 10 users per workstation, there are no pauses in the script for think time or typing rate.

3. *Load generator is a network analyzer.* Load distribution is equivalent network load of 15 percent bandwidth. Packet sequence is captured trace file. Packet rate is 2,928 packets per second. Script (trace file) ID is T0415PG. One network analyzer generates Ethernet packets that model DECNet and IP packet traffic through the router at an equivalent network load of 15 percent. The load generator could be a network analyzer or a packet generator running on a PC. The load generator script is the series of commands that define the packet contents and rate per second to create the prescribed loads.

4. *Load generator is a C application.* Load distribution is equivalent user loading of 25 users per workstation. Script commands are file open, file read, send mail message, and read waiting mail message (messages sent in prior test) repeated 25 times with no pauses between commands. Script ID is T0325EM. One workstation runs a utility that performs file reads and writes to model electronic mail and other activity on the file server with an equivalent user load of 25 mail users. The load generator is a C program that writes and reads files. The load generator script contains program parameters that define the file size and number of writes and reads per minute that is equivalent to 25 active mail users.

The test script for the preceding test is:

1. **Workstations 1, 2, and 3:** Client-sever application - script T0105CS.

2. **Workstations 4, 5, and 6:** Word processing application - script T0210WP.

3. **Workstation 7:** C program - script T0325EM.

4. **Network analyzer:** Trace file - script T0415PG.

Figure 7.6 illustrates the test scripts and network configuration for the emulated loading. In emulating each of these four distinct loads, the test developer must understand the actual loading well enough to emulate it. Parts II and III discuss how to analyze application/presentation layer and infrastructure loads.

Real-World Loading

For the client-server application test, the following would be the definition of the load model and test script:

1. *Load generator is a Windows client-server application.* Load distribution is actual user loading of one user per workstation. Load generator script commands are transactions one through five with think

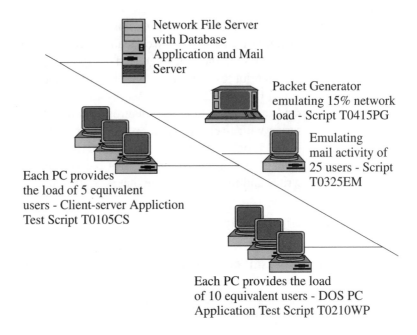

Figure 7.6   Load model using emulated loading.

time and typing pauses. Script ID is T0501CS. Translated this means 15 workstations execute the Windows-based client-server application. Each station generates the actual user load of one typical application user. The load generator is the actual application. The load generator script is keyboard and mouse input to generate the required transactions against the database server. Since the script is emulating the load of one user per workstation, there are pauses in the script for think time and typing rate.

2. *Load generator is a DOS word processing application.* Load distribution is actual user loading of one user per workstation. Script commands are file open, file read, edit, spell check, file write, and file close repeated once with pauses between commands. Script ID is T0601WP. Translated this means 30 workstations execute a word processor application under DOS where each station generates the actual user load of one typical network user. The load generator is the DOS application. The load generator script is a series of keystrokes to

invoke the required file I/O against the file server. Since the script is emulating the load of one user per workstation, there are pauses in the script for think time and typing rate.

3. *Load generator is a network analyzer.* Load distribution is the equivalent network load of 15 percent bandwidth. Packet sequence is captured trace file. Packet rate is 2,928 packets per second. Script ID is T0415PG. This is not changed from the emulated case. One network analyzer generates Ethernet packets that model DECNet and IP packet traffic through the router at an equivalent network load of 15 percent. The load generator could be a network analyzer or a packet generator running on a PC. The load generator script is the series of commands that define the packet contents and rate per second to create the prescribed loads.

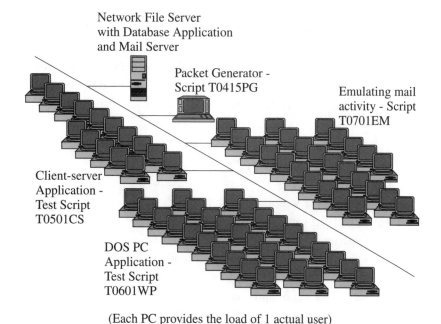

Network File Server
with Database Application
and Mail Server

Packet Generator -
Script T0415PG

Emulating mail
activity - Script
T0701EM

Client-server
Application -
Test Script
T0501CS

DOS PC
Application -
Test Script
T0601WP

(Each PC provides the load of 1 actual user)

Figure 7.7   Real-world loading example.

4. *The load generator is the mail application.* Load distribution is actual user loading of one user per workstation. Load generator script commands are file open, file read, send mail message, and read waiting mail message (sent in prior test). Repeat sequence one time with pauses between commands. Script ID is T0701EM. The load generator is the mail user program. The load generator script is keyboard or mouse point-and-click movements to compose, send, and receive mail.

The test script for the preceding test is:

1. **Workstations 1-15:** Client-sever application with script T0501CS.

2. **Workstations 16-46:** Word processing application with script T0601WP.

3. **Workstations 47-72:** Mail program with script T0701EM.

4. **Network analyzer:** Trace file as script T0415PG.

Figure 7.7 illustrates the test scripts and network configuration for real-world loading. Compared to equivalent user loading, real-world loading requires over 10 times the number of PCs.

Mixed-Case Loading

Real-world loading as shown in the previous example requires significantly more hardware. In most cases, it is cost prohibitive to conduct such testing. My experience in hundreds of test cases indicates that real-world test results are not much better than an emulated loading approach for the 10 test objectives. In practice, many tests use a combined loading approach. In the previous example, since loads 2, 3, and 4 are designed as background loading, it may work well to emulate them and only use real-world loading for the new client-server application, as illustrated in Figure 7.8. This approach requires a 20-node network, which is significantly smaller than the real-world case, and only slightly larger than the fully emulated case. This is an excellent compromise that will

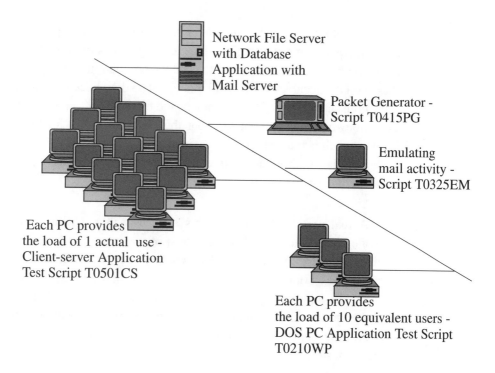

Network File Server
with Database
Application with
Mail Server

Packet Generator -
Script T0415PG

Emulating
mail activity -
Script T0325EM

Each PC provides
the load of 1 actual use -
Client-server Application
Test Script T0501CS

Each PC provides
the load of 10 equivalent users -
DOS PC Application Test Script
T0210WP

Figure 7.8   Less expensive, more practical mixed loading test alternative.

provide very representative response time measurements for the new client-server application.

Summary of Load Modeling

Experience shows that test results using equivalent user loading approximate real-world loading for most test cases. However, it is a good idea to do a few projects using both to build confidence that equivalent user loading provides good results. Equivalent user loading provides representative results for performance, response time, product evaluation, and interoperability testing. It also minimizes the overall time, resources, and capital costs associated with testing.

Actual user loading requires that the test network and production network have an equal number of nodes. This loading places more real-world loads on the server because it is very close to what the production network will experience (based on the accuracy of the load model). The drawback to actual user loading is the high capital cost of the equipment and increased set-up time. Although test execution time can be kept to about the same for either loading, actual user loading requires more setup and tear-down time, and usually requires more data collection and interpretation time simply because of the increased number of nodes in the test.

Actual user loading exercises system aspects not addressed robustly by equivalent user loading. However, most of these have to do with network and product boundary conditions, such as whether a network operating system (NOS) corrupts stack pointers when 1,000 users are actually logged in to the system. Such results may be important to a small minority of users, but in most cases, users are not pushing system boundary conditions on production networks. If they are, they have more problems than can be resolved by the addition of proactive testing.

There are various methods for determining the load distribution, all of which yield a load model that approximates activity on the production network. The key is realizing that the load model will never be completely accurate. The best way to test is to measure a range of scenarios, thereby providing several representative load curves that bracket performance or bound other test objectives. As NTM products become more sophisticated in translating monitored network traffic into load models, this process will be more accurate and require fewer test runs to achieve relevant results.

Accelerated Loading

The third type of loading, called **accelerated loading**, is used primarily for reliability testing. Accelerated loading attempts to compress into a few hours the type and levels of loads a system may experience over many months in the field. For example, a network typically runs at 15 to 40 percent capacity. In a reliability test, the objective may be to accelerate the load to 65 or 90 percent of capacity and maintain it for 12 to 72 hours. In this time, the system will execute the same number of operations, receive the same stress, and experience the same number of load peaks that would occur over many months in the field. Accelerated loading is a form of equivalent user loading where the number of workstations or other load-generating nodes are increased until the required aggregate load on the network, a server, or other component is achieved.

With load emulation, an equivalent or accelerated load can be created with less equipment and faster than a comparable real-world test. The test envelope shown in Figure 7.9 relates test objectives to test environment alternatives. Like the load model, the test configuration also has alternatives. These are discussed in an upcoming section, Test Network Configuration Options. Emulated loading, however, cannot always exercise specific aspects of the system that may be important to the test. Parts II and III discuss when and how to use emulated loading versus real-world loading for various tests.

It should now be clear why the upper left-hand quadrant of the test environment dimensions, shown in Figure 7.1 cannot be a representative test configuration. Applying a real-world load scenario (load generator and script) to an emulated network topology will not create sufficient network activity (there are too few nodes running the software) to generate a representative load.

NETWORK SIMULATION

Many people confuse the basic premises and differences between emulation and simulation. Emulation attempts to replicate production network response through proactive, hands-on testing of representative hardware and software. Simulation attempts to do the same through computer-aided modeling; it does not involve or require an actual network. Simulations are run on a single station, as shown in Figure 7.10, and do not require a network configuration.

Simulation is the process of using a computer program (simulator) to model the actions and responses of a network under load. The software is often run on

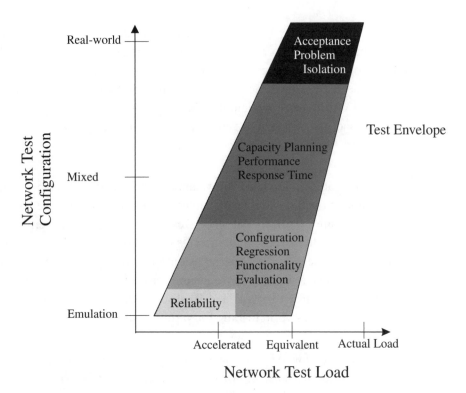

Figure 7.9 Relating test objectives to testing alternatives.

an engineering workstation, such as a Sun SPARC, or on a high-end PC. Product vendors include MAKE Systems, Optimal Networks, CACI Products, and Systems & Networks. A model is created that includes:

- **Network topology:** The network segments (Ethernet, Token Ring, FDDI, 10Base-T, WAN links, and so on) and interconnections (routers, switches, and so on) are defined in a model. The simulator provides libraries of various components and characteristics to choose from. This produces a network topology map that represents the network system to be simulated. Network nodes, such as routers and switches, are modeled using test results from various sources. The node is typically rated for maximum sustainable throughput or other throughput criteria provided by the simulation software vendor or the hardware vendor. Other nodes,

Simulation

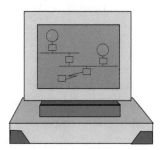

Sun SPARCstation 4

No actual network
involved in simulation.

Figure 7.10   Computer-aided network simulation runs on a single workstation or PC.

such as servers and workstations, may or may not be modeled based on the
simulation capabilities and the complexity of the model being developed.

- **Traffic Generation:** Input to the model in the form of a network load
  (for example, in packets per second) is used to represent the anticipated
  network load of the production system. Captured packet traces from a
  network analyzer or a statistical distribution of bursty traffic representing
  network activity are often used.

The simulation is run to determine where performance degradation or
bottlenecks may occur in the network due to the component placement and
modeled load. Once the model is developed, simulations are very useful for
"what-if" games, where the network topology, components, and loads can be
changed and the simulation rerun to determine the effect of the changes.
Additionally, a simulation can represent a very large network, typically much
larger than can be reasonably tested.

The drawback with simulation is that results are only as good as the model.
If simulation results are not correlated to actual test results from a test or

production system, then the level of accuracy and relevance of the simulation results cannot be ascertained. Always insist that simulation results be correlated to known values for a few basic configurations before relying on their accuracy for a large configuration model.

Using real-world or emulated testing provides correlation data to validate simulation results for basic configurations, such as router throughput or client-server application response. Proactive testing and simulation are complementary and together provide greater value than if used independently.

TEST NETWORK CONFIGURATION OPTIONS

There are two primary choices for the test configuration: the production network or a test lab. Each has advantages and disadvantages as discussed.

Production Network Testing

Figure 7.11 shows that there are three opportunities to test on the production network:

- **Predeployment:** This occurs when a new network or a new segment on an existing network is installed. Before deployment, the network or segment can be used as a large test lab, including measuring interaction with the production network.

- **Off-hours:** Off-hours testing is what most people typically think of when they talk about using the production system for testing. Off-hours testing is how many mainframe system groups have conducted testing for over 30 years. Many organizations use their networks 24 hours a day and do not have the ability to shut down the network or segments for testing. Although it works, it can be very time-consuming, requiring late nights and weekends for the support staff. This is not the preferred method of network testing.

- **Prime time:** Most testers fear that crashing the production network, while testing, can mean a lack of job security! While there is always the possibility that a network may crash, there are ways to minimize the risk. These are discussed under the section, Prime Time Testing. On the other hand, there are two benefits that cannot be overlooked. First, this is a very inexpensive way to test, as there is little or no additional capital expense. Second, because the testing is done on the production network, load conditions are very representative and test results are extremely relevant.

Predeployment Testing

A large paper products company installed two new Token Rings of several hundred nodes each. Its system integrator ran a reliability test on the rings as part

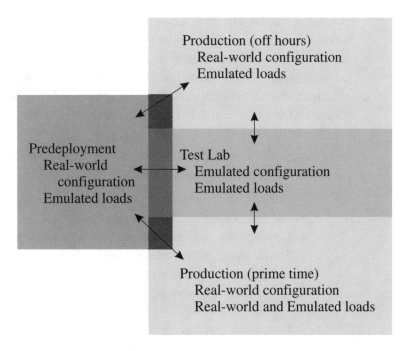

Figure 7.11 Leveraging the production network for proactive testing.

of the acceptance test. One ring encountered no errors over a 24-hour period. The other ring encountered a high number of token ring soft errors. These results lead to the discovery of a marginal adapter card in one workstation. This is a simple example of the benefit derived from predeployment testing. These results could not have been achieved in a test lab.

Predeployment testing can focus on on-segment, off-segment, to-segment, or combined testing. Each type of testing has a different objective and requires a different load model.

Example 7.1 How to test on the production network.

Let's assume that Company A's sales department has historically been on a minicomputer, and that it is being replaced with an Ethernet network and PCs. The new sales segment will be connected to other networks that exist in marketing, manufacturing, and engineering. All the groups will be using a common electronic mail system and product forecasting spreadsheets. Sales will use a new network-based order entry application that interfaces directly with manufacturing. Since the sales group is as large as the other three groups combined, the network support group is concerned with potential network load caused by increased mail activity and the new spreadsheet activity.

Once the new network segment and PCs are installed, four possible test scenarios can be conducted prior to deployment:

- **On-segment testing:** As shown in Figure 7.12, a load model is created to represent the mail and spreadsheet activity expected against the file and mail server on the sales network. Tests are run for response time, configuration sizing, throughput, and reliability. The testing ensures that the new segment is working properly: It is confined to the new segment.

- **Off-segment testing:** A load model is created to represent the mail, forecasting, and order entry activity from the sales segment to other network segments, as diagrammed in Figure 7.13. Using monitors, the other network segments are baselined for throughput and response time.

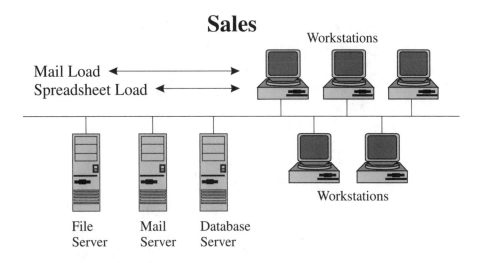

Figure 7.12 Load model for sales segment file I/O and mail activity.

Tests are run and the other segments are monitored to determine the degradation caused by the additional load from the sales segment. This testing measures the impact on the existing network. Since the loads are placed on the existing network during production hours, there is a possibility that they can cause problems or a failure. Therefore, test scripts are designed to create a series of increasing loads. The sustainability of these loads and their effect is measured on the other segments. This allows the load to be increased in steps, which prevents the potential of overloading the production network.

- **To-segment:** The load model from off-segment testing is modified to represent the mail and spreadsheet activity from the other segments to the sales segment, illustrated in Figure 7.14. By itself, this loading is not overly interesting, but coupled with on-segment loading, this represents the best approximation of the overall loading on the sales segment. For to-segment loading, if the test is designed to measure degradation or impact on the intersegment links, such as the routers and communication lines, nodes are required on the other segments for load generation. The involvement and measurement of the intersegment links can be elimi-

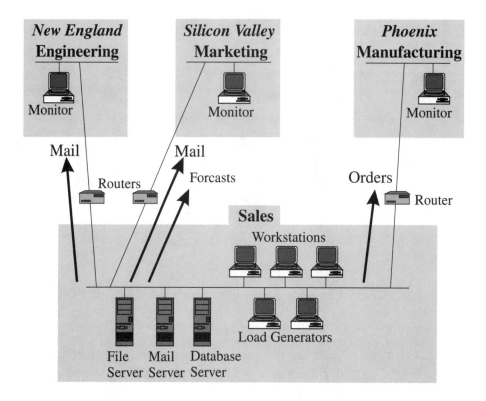

Figure 7.13   Load model for forecasting and mail activity from sales to other segments.

nated by using nodes on the sales segment as representative load generators for the other segments.

- **Combined testing:** As the name implies, this combines the load models for on-segment, to-segment, and off-segment into one test script. This test, shown in Figure 7.15, represents the best approximation of the real-world load the new segment will impose on its own resources, as well as the existing segments in marketing, manufacturing, and engineering. This is a good example of why several small test scripts rather than one large monolithic script should be created. The smaller scripts provide flexibility for designing different test scenarios without devel-

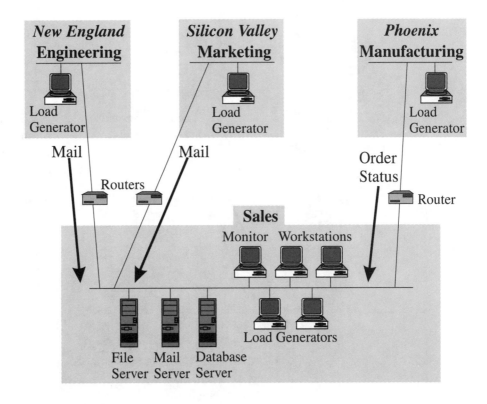

Figure 7.14   Load model for forecasting and mail activity from other segments to the sales segment.

oping new test scripts. Also, it is easier to develop and debug small test scripts. Once they are working, they can be combined into a larger test scenario.❑

Off-Hours Testing

This is a special case of predeployment testing. On-segment, to-segment, off-segment, and combined loading scenarios apply, with the caveat that the latter two only give relevant results if there are representative loads on the production segments during the test.

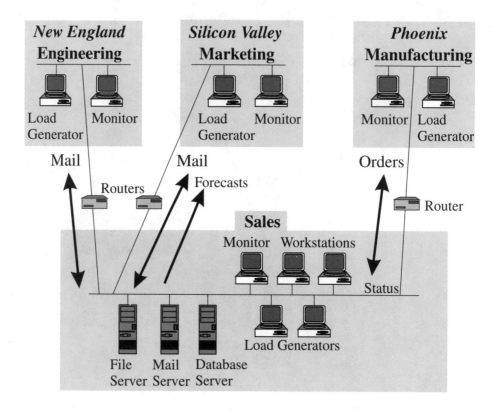

Figure 7.15 Load model for bidirectional forecasting and mail activity between sales and other segments.

This testing requires that the production network be modified to provide load generators and then be returned to its original condition prior to the segment returning to production status. This process is time-consuming and error-prone. With new products for network configuration management that provide automated software distribution and configuration for the workstations and servers, errors and time can be reduced. However, off-hours testing is still not the best choice for a network test.

Prime Time Testing

Prime time testing works well when new components or applications are planned for the production system. Figure 7.16 shows how a new remote access server environment (gray box) can be tested on the production network during prime time. Both the production network (a control group discussed in Part III) and the remote users are monitored for performance and degradation. The test uses the production network load as a background load while the new component or application is tested. To prevent disruption of the production network, load on the new component is added gradually. By monitoring both the production system and the item under test, impact to the production system and test data on the new network component or application can be collected in one test.

Since prime time testing does not require significant capital expense or set-up time, it is a very cost-effective method of starting proactive testing at a company. Some examples of tests that can be run inexpensively and with very little production system impact are:

- New services or applications, such as shown in Figure 7.16.

- Regression testing a new application. A number of test workstations access the new application while the production network continues running the current version.

- Product evaluation testing of certain components, such as adapters and drivers, where the new product is installed and tested by a small user group.

- Workstation testing where a new or upgraded version is used by selected users on the production network.

- Configuration sizing and tuning of workstations and servers where changes are made during off-hours and measurements are collected during normal use.

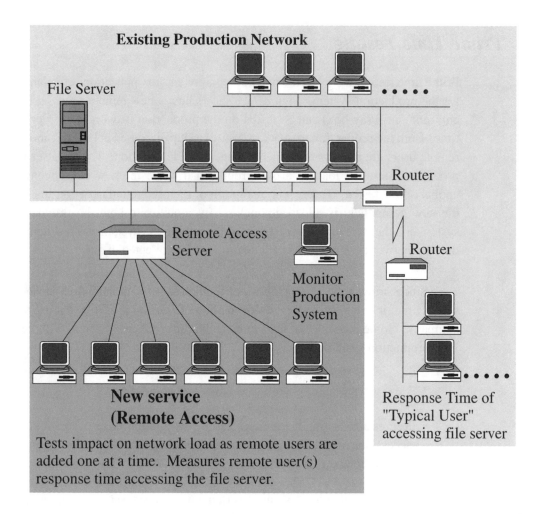

Figure 7.16   Example of prime time testing.

Figure 7.17 depicts how production network performance (either response time or throughput) and remote user response time are measured and graphed to compare impact as the remote user load increases. The graph shows that the production response time degrades marginally, but remote access degrades significantly when more than three users are active.

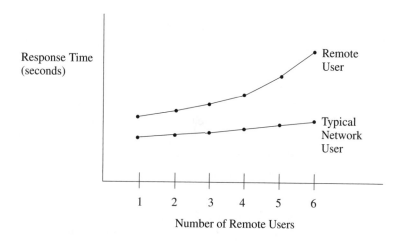

Figure 7.17 Graphing test data and production system response versus test load.

Production network testing can provide early test success at minimum cost and risk. Parts II and III discuss how to conduct prime time testing for various test objectives and network subsystems.

NETWORK TEST LAB

Most organizations that are committed to testing will eventually establish a network test lab. While there are many opinions on how a great lab should be organized, the simple truth is that the best lab is one that allows test objectives to be met at minimum cost while providing flexibility to meet changing company needs. This can be achieved by following a four-step approach to establishing your lab:

1. **Test Philosophy:** The basic reason for having the lab is to support the test philosophy, which defines the subsystems and test objectives that the lab must support, as discussed in Chapter 6. Don't establish a physical lab before defining the test philosophy. If a lab already exists,

but no test philosophy is in place, define one independent of the lab and then evaluate the lab to see how well it can support it.

2. **Test Network:** Identify the critical hardware and software components and configurations needed in the lab to duplicate the production network subsystems in the test philosophy. In setting up the lab, start slowly and learn from experience, or use the services of a consultant to get started. Parts II and III list specific configuration requirements for each test objective discussed.

3. **Version Control:** The test lab must support three versions of each subsystem. The current version, the previous version, and the next upgrade, as it becomes available. This provides the flexibility to:

    • Reproduce current problems or issues.

    • Verify whether production network problems were present in the previous version or introduced with the latest code. This can help in diagnosing the problem or rolling back to the previous version while the problem is being fixed.

    • Test new versions before they are deployed on the production system.

4. **Simplicity:** To be effective, a lab doesn't have to be like Novell's "super lab," which includes over a thousand PCs, or American Airlines lab that occupies thousands of square feet of floor space, or PC Labs' multitier test benches with stacks of PCs and neon lights. Many labs are not much bigger than a closet, and provide significant test results. One lab at a large oil company has only one server and a few PCs, yet it provides critical compatibility testing for a large network. Another lab has only one PC, yet it is able to measure critical response time for loading different applications on a securities trading desk. In network testing, good labs can come in small packages. While LANQuest Labs has thousands of square feet of space, an individual test project typically occupies only a few hundred square feet of floor space and includes fewer than 25 pieces of equipment.

A test lab for a large company will often include several individual test networks or configurations. For some tests, these may be connected to form a representative internetworked system. For other test objectives, they are used independently. Examples of how individual networks can be merged to create larger test scenarios are discussed in the following section, Test Environment Examples.

Facility Requirements

As just noted, significant testing can be done in a very small space, particularly if movable shelves are used to create a tiered lab environment. In a tiered lab, eight to nine workstations can be configured in roughly 16 square feet of floor space, versus 50 square feet in a conventional table-top-based lab. Figure 7.18 illustrates three alternative test bench configurations.

Configuration A is a tiered lab without movable shelves. For a tiered lab without movable shelves, allocate 32 square feet of space for nine workstations, servers, or small nodes. Space is required behind the shelves to allow access for cabling and changes. For large routers or other equipment, allocate five square feet per box. Allocate roughly 150 square feet of work and storage space for each 50 square feet of equipment space.

Configuration B is a tiered lab with movable shelves. For this configuration, allocate 16 square feet of space for nine workstations, servers, or small nodes. For large routers or other equipment, allocate five square feet per box. Allocate approximately 150 square feet of total work and storage space for each 50 square feet of equipment space.

For a nontiered lab using tables as in Configuration C, estimate 96 square feet of space for nine workstations, servers, or small nodes and 5 square feet for each large node, such as a router. Allocate 100 or more square feet of work and storage space for each 100 square feet of equipment space.

While network test labs for some trade publications have very expensive and fancy cabling configurations, keeping it simple can save money and be just

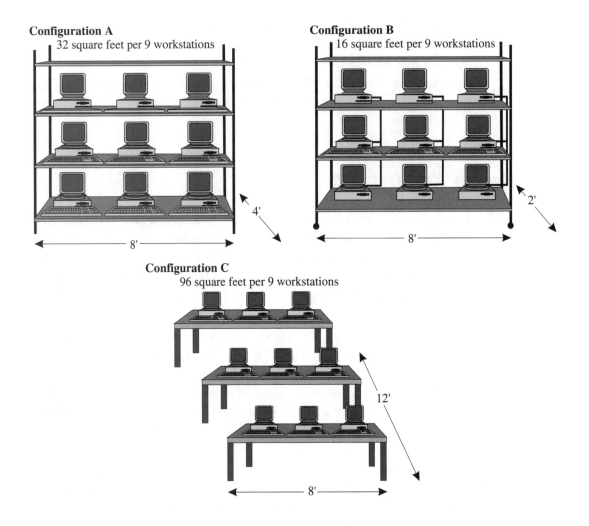

Figure 7.18   Different lab equipment configurations require various amounts of floor space.

as effective. If you have to test more than one cabling configuration, the key is easy access to the network nodes for swapping adapter boards and connections. The tiered lab configuration makes this an easy chore. Cabling can be strapped to the shelves, as shown in Figure 7.19. This configuration can be easily switched from Ethernet to Token Ring and provides ample power supply for the nine nodes.

Always confirm that the lab has additional cabling and connectors available, as these are often the cause of minor problems during testing.

Other equipment, such as routers, bridges, hubs and many switches, are often small enough to fit on the same shelves as the PCs. This equipment can also be stacked so that 3 or 4 boxes take up no more space than a single PC with a monitor. Large equipment can usually be placed in a corner of the lab, or even outside the lab, and cabled to the workstations located on the shelves.

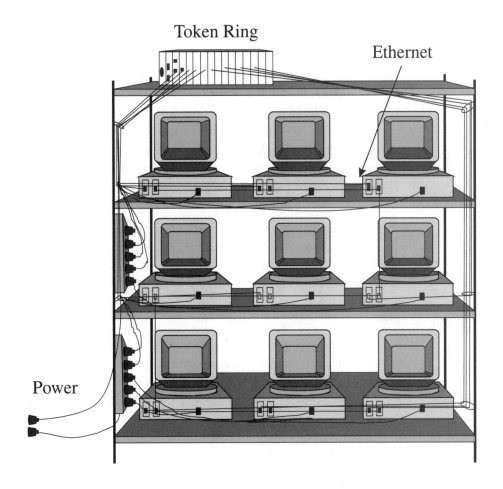

Figure 7.19   Tiered lab cabling is simple and accessible.

Power, cooling, and lighting requirements are often overlooked in configuring a test lab. As a rule of thumb, a standard 20-amp circuit is capable of handling 12 to 16 workstations with monitors. While a workstation/monitor combination may be rated at over 3 amps, measurements show that typical monitors and workstations pull less than 1 amp when running. When powering up, a unit may draw more amperage, therefore, make sure to turn on systems one at a time, so there isn't a large power draw per circuit. Larger systems, such as routers (for example, Cisco AGS), switches (for example, FORE Systems), and hubs (3Com 3GH) may require as much as 7 amps constant load, so keep them on separate power circuits.

Air conditioning in a typical office environment will generally handle the needs of a network test lab. If the room has a door, make sure there is both an air conditioning duct and a return duct in the room. If the room doesn't have good air conditioning, shutting the door will decrease ventilation and the lab may experience heat problems. When building a room for the lab, take the time to factor in both an air conditioning and a return duct. The few extra dollars it may cost are well worth it. It also pays to have a few extra electrical circuits installed. There can never be too many electrical circuits in a lab.

In the tiered lab configuration, lighting may be reduced in some portions of the room because of the tiers of machines. Make sure to add additional overhead lights for area lighting. Also plan for spot lighting, such as a swivel light attached to the test bench, to help in configuring and reconfiguring hardware within the network nodes.

Since test accuracy and reproducibility rely on control of the total environment, it is best to have separate copies of everything used in the lab, including current and previous revisions of all software and hardware. To accommodate the need for privacy, use lockable filing and storage cabinets for the lab.

Last, but not least, include a desk area in the lab and a workstation connected to the company network. These can be used while tests are running to keep up with other activities, record test journal information, reduce test data, and play solitaire as time allows between tests.

Figure 7.20 shows three different lab configurations. The smallest lab is only 208 square feet, while the largest measures a little over 600 square feet. Each lab has 27 nodes, a storage cabinet, as desk, and reasonable floor space for equipment access. Other approaches use equipment in cubicles that is connected to create test configurations as needed. Dedicated equipment is best, but just because a company can't afford that luxury doesn't mean it can't do effective testing.

The following examples illustrate how simple configurations can be used to accomplish many test objectives and how simple configurations can be combined easily to meet other test objectives. All the equipment requirements for these examples can fit into any of the three lab configurations illustrated.

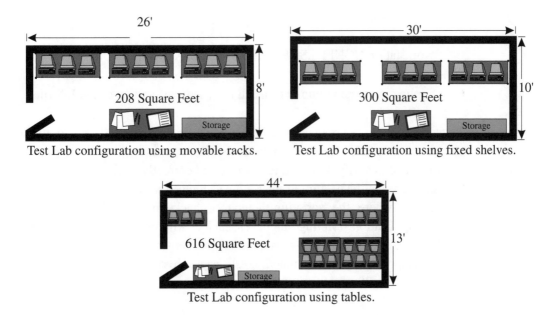

Test Lab configuration using movable racks.   Test Lab configuration using fixed shelves.

Test Lab configuration using tables.

Figure 7.20   Alternative lab configurations.

TEST ENVIRONMENT EXAMPLES

Example 7.2 Application Regression Testing.

If the test objective is to verify that client-server application upgrades maintain current functionality and performance, the network emulation may be as simple as a server and the number of workstations required to create a representative load. In this case, the test network emulates the critical components of the production network, specifically the database server, workstations, and application.

The test configuration documentation should include:

hardware configuration for the server and each workstation

NOS configuration files

workstation CONFIG.SYS, AUTOEXEC.BAT, and INI file

application version number, installation settings, and modified INI files

Test scripts include application commands that generate network activity, as shown in Figure 7.21. Test data includes the time it takes each station to perform the script and to verify that each test performed correctly. Test verification can be a simple visual inspection of the screen as images scroll by, or a more robust verification where the scripting language checks individual field content. Existing application scripting languages, such as Microsoft Test and Mercury's WinRunner, allow responses to requests to be verified. For each test run, an average response time is calculated. Test scripts are run for several load points, such as 1, 5, 10, 20, and 30 users.❑

Example 7.3 ATM Switch Testing.

If the objective is to test an ATM switch for cell loss and reliability, the test network topology will not resemble the production network. A test configuration

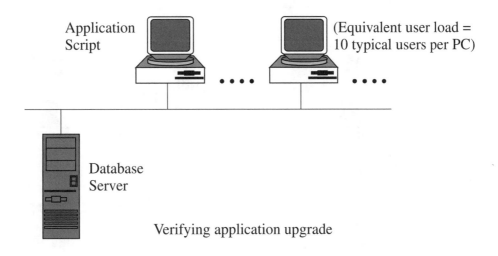

Application Script

(Equivalent user load = 10 typical users per PC)

Database Server

Verifying application upgrade

Figure 7.21   Client-server load and test bed emulation.

of input and output segments connected to the ATM switch is all that is required. There is no need for servers or workstations to be included in the test configuration. The emulated network isn't a network at all; it is simply the switch and cabling, as shown in Figure 7.22. The emulation, however, would allow testing to be done that represents various production network and switch configurations.

The test configuration documentation should include the ATM switch:

    manufacturer and model number

    software version number

    processor type and speed

    system buffer sizes

    board revision level, model number, serial number, and address

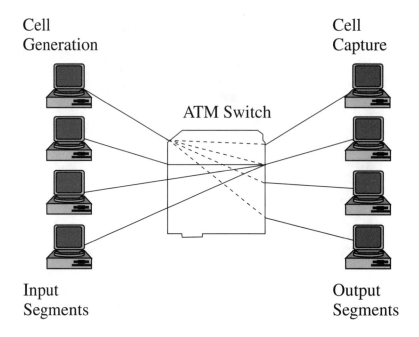

Figure 7.22   ATM switch load and test configuration emulation.

printout of configuration information

The testing requires load generators and monitors connected to each cable, as shown in Figure 7.22, to produce cell activity against the switch, and measure throughput and cell loss.❏

Example 7.4 Network Directory Service Administration.

Consider a network operating system or a large electronic mail system with a widely distributed directory or name service. The test objective is to verify that new releases of the directory service software propagate name changes throughout the multiple directory servers in a timely manner. To emulate this requires a network composed of many nodes acting as directory servers, with various interconnecting links, such as routers and wide area network (WAN) links of various speeds. No actual file servers or workstations are needed for the emulation. Figure 7.23 is a six-segment internetwork configuration that allows bidirectional and concurrent name update scenarios to be tested.

The load model generates directory updates as if they are entered from multiple segments concurrently. The updates must be synchronized, broadcast, and verified for correctness on each directory server. This can be done manually, but it may be more effective to write a program to verify the updates. Figure 7.23 has a single administrative console that can log in to all the directory servers and enter multiple name changes in a complex fashion.❏

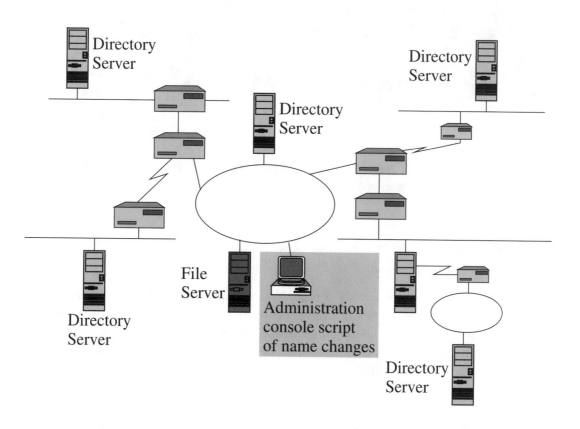

Figure 7.23 Multipurpose internetwork test bed emulation.

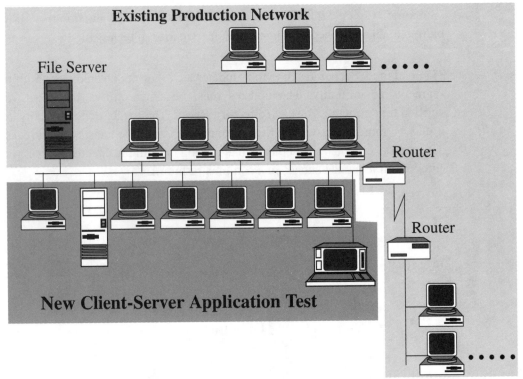

Figure 7.24 Adding hardware to the production network for prime time testing of a new client-server application.

Example 7.5 Client-Server Response Time Test.

The last example uses the production network to test the performance and configuration sizing of a new client-server application. The server and a few workstations are added to the existing network, as shown in Figure 7.24, and load versus response time tests are run using equivalent-user loading, diagrammed in Figure 7.25. Both the new client-server application and the production network are monitored.

Test data measure the time it takes each station to perform the load script, the kilobytes-per-second load on the production network, and throughput changes on the production file server. For each test run, an average response time is calculated for the client-server application. Test scripts are run for several load points, such as 1, 10, 20, 40, and 80 users. Either configuration settings or hardware for the server and workstations are modified. The tests are rerun during a period when the production load on the network is comparable to the last test session (often during the same time of day). Response time is compared, and the process is reiterated until the desired response time is achieved or configuration changes are exhausted.❏

Examples 7.2, 7.4, and 7.5 can be integrated into one "system" test that emulates the company's production network so that existing applications, the new

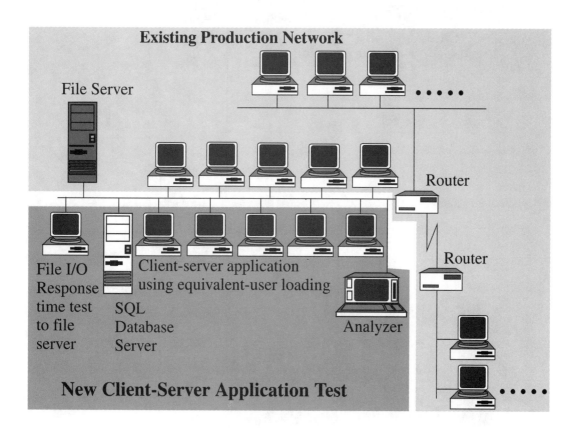

Figure 7.25 Prime time testing of new client-server application for response time and configuration.

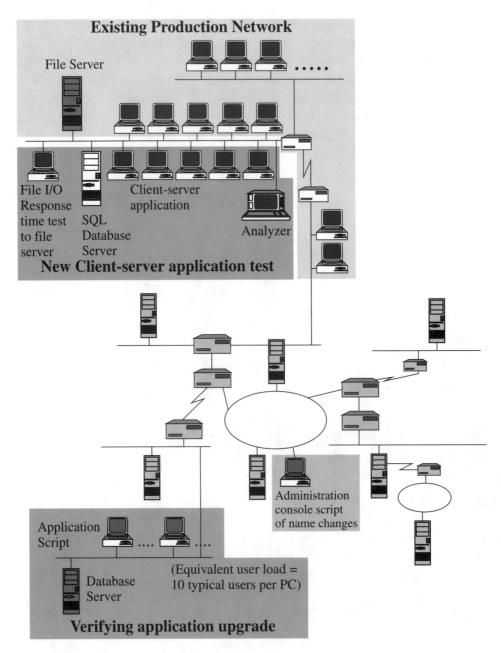

Figure 7.26 Complex test configuration composed of several simpler test scenarios.

client-server application, and other network loads (name updates) can be tested across an emulated internetwork between the home office and regional offices. Figure 7.26 illustrates the network for the system level test. This configuration, excluding the company network, can be configured in the 200 square feet test lab previously discussed.

Part I Summary

POCKET GUIDE TO NETWORK TESTING

The previous chapters introduced and discussed a set of guidelines for network testing which include: 10 network test objectives, a test philosophy, a test methodology, and testing terminology. Part I discussed the following test objectives and how they should be used throughout the network life cycle, as listed in Figure 8.1, to make the network manager's job easier and the network system and applications better.

- Application response time

- Feature/functionality

- Product regression

- Throughput

- Acceptance

- Configuration sizing

- Reliability

- Product evaluation

- Capacity planning

- Bottleneck identification and problem isolation

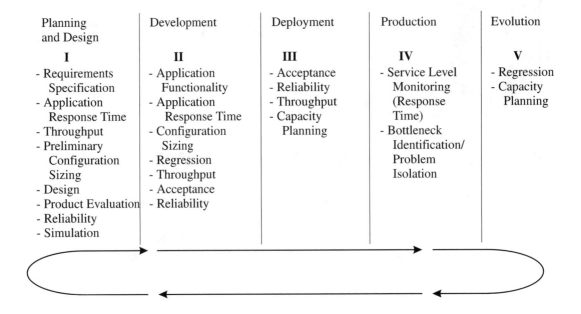

Figure 8.1   Test objectives throughout the network life cycle.

A test philosophy defines seven subsystems and four areas of concentration for testing. It maps appropriate test objectives to each subsystem, as shown in Figure 8.2.

The test methodology defines an orderly system of procedures that, when applied to each project, ensure that the test results address the test objective, and that the results are accurate, reproducible, and relevant. The test methodology includes:

- Planning

- Load modeling

- Test configuration

		Planning	Development	Deployment	Production	Evolution
Network Application/ Presentation Layers	Application Response Time	X	X	X	X	
	Application Feature/ Functionality		X	X	X	
	Regression		X			X
	Throughput	X	X	X		
	Acceptance		X	X		
	Configuration Sizing		X			X
	Reliability	X	X			
	Product Evaluation	X				
	Capacity Planning			X		X
	Bottleneck Identification				X	
Network Infrastructure	Application Response Time					
	Application Feature/ Functionality					
	Regression		X			X
	Throughput	X	X	X		
	Acceptance		X	X		
	Configuration Sizing	X	X			X
	Reliability	X	X			
	Product Evaluation	X				
	Capacity Planning			X		X
	Bottleneck Identification				X	

Figure 8.2   Recommended test objectives for the seven network subsystems.

- Data collection

- Data interpretation

- Data presentation

Testing terminology provides a concise nomenclature for defining the various load and test models:

- Emulation

- Real-world

- Test network configuration

- Load model

- Load distribution

- Load generator

- Load generator script

- Test script

- Actual-user load

- Equivalent-user load

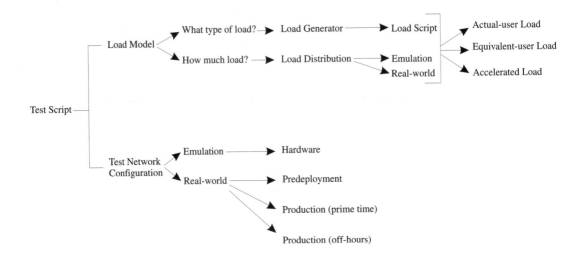

Figure 8.3   Load modeling and network test configuration definition includes type of load, amount of load, and testbed environment.

- Accelerated load

Also presented is a process for selecting and defining the best alternatives for the loading and test configuration, as summarized in Figure 8.3.

APPLYING THE NETWORK TESTING GUIDELINES

Parts II and III provide instructions on how to apply the above guidelines to network infrastructure and application/presentation layer testing. Test planning starts by identifying the subsystem to be tested and the test objective to be achieved. The first and most important decision is to configure the best test environment (network configuration and loading). Terms and concepts covering network test configurations and loading were introduced in the previous chapters and are discussed more fully in Parts II and III for each test case. Once these decisions are made, following the defined test methodology will ensure proper management of the test project.

The second and most important aspect of testing is data collection, reduction, interpretation, and presentation. Parts II and III include techniques and tips on analysis and interpretation. Parts II and III also cover typical test objectives for four areas of test concentration. To conduct testing not specifically covered in these parts, you can apply the approaches and techniques presented in the book to any component or subsystem of the network. For example:

- Response time tests are usually associated with applications. To conduct a response time test on the NOS, apply the same process and principles to creating a load model and defining a network configuration as for any other application response time test. This could be used to measure logon time for 100 concurrent users or printing time for a heavily loaded spooler.

- The same process for identifying bottlenecks on a server can be used to identify a bottleneck on a workstation.

- Acceptance testing for any subsystem can be conducted by following the same procedures as for application or network segment testing.

- Adapters, fax servers, and other components can be evaluated using the same process as for file server product evaluation. All aspects of the test network are held constant except for the product or component under test. For each competitive product, tests are run and the results are compared to determine the best (based on the evaluation criteria) product.

TESTING VALUE STATEMENT

Typically, most people carry medical insurance, home insurance, life insurance, and automobile insurance to cover themselves, their families, and their key possessions. This is analogous to having backup software on the network. It provides basic coverage that everyone hopes will never be used, and usually costs pennies on the dollar.

Some people have more insurance, for example, extended liability coverage, several life insurance policies, earthquake or flood insurance, coverage on a boat or recreational vehicle, and disability insurance. This is comparable to having network management products for the network. While there are added expenses, maybe another 1 or 2 percent of the covered amount per year, the additional coverage or protection provides a higher level of confidence that if something happens, they will be covered. Others go further still and take proactive steps to reduce their reliance on insurance coverage. These people take up exercise, quit smoking, lose weight to improve their health, buy safer cars with air bags, and take classes in boating safety. The additional cost of these proactive steps in many cases is very small relative to the potential return on investment.

Network testing is like taking proactive steps to reduce reliance on insurance measures. It is a proactive effort to reduce existing and future network problems. It costs very little compared to its potential savings. The following formula is a method of weighing the cost versus potential benefit of testing.

Recall the telesales example in Chapter 1, where network downtime and slowdown costs included lost sales, lower productivity of the users, the cost of the support group to resolve the problem, and potentially the cost of new network hardware and software. To be sure, these costs are often hard to measure exactly, but the following formula can help you estimate their past and potential dollar impact to your company.

Downtime

Productivity loss = hours the system was down x number of people affected x average hourly wage x percent impact on productivity.

Support cost = hours the system was down x number of support people involved x average hourly wage + prorated cost of debugging tools + delays to other projects (such as network upgrades).

Lost sales = hours system was down x sales per hour.

Network changes = product costs to repair the network.

Slowdowns

Productivity loss = number of people affected x average hourly wage x percent impact on productivity x hours (days, weeks, or months) the slowdown went unresolved.

Support cost = hours spent resolving slowdown x number of support people involved x average hourly wage + prorated cost of debugging tools + delays of other projects (such as network upgrades) + cost of resolving the slowdown (hardware + software).

Lost sales = percent system degradation x sales per hour x hours (days, weeks, or months) the slowdown went unresolved.

Network changes = product costs to upgrade the network.

Testing Costs

Facilities cost = hardware + software + test equipment + space allocation + desk + shelves + storage cabinet.

Personnel cost = number of people involved x average hourly wage x percent of time supporting testing.

In calculating downtime and slowdown costs, it is necessary to consider not only what problems have happened in the past, but what the exposure for failures and associated cost is in the future as the network becomes more complex in supporting mission-critical, client-server applications. The value of testing is in minimizing both the risk and the cost. The risk is the total potential loss due to slowdowns and downtime. The cost is the time and effort to conduct proactive testing. *Thus, the value of testing = risk versus cost.* In the telesales example, the risk versus cost was between a 5:1 and 25:1 margin. You have to calculate what you think it will be for your network and company. Try to be as objective and accurate as possible. You may be surprised to find that the value of testing for you will be much closer to the 25:1 than a 5:1 ratio.

Using the information provided in Part I, estimate the potential value and cost of network testing for your environment. Then use the guidelines and information in Parts II and III to make testing a productive part of your overall network systems management plan.

Part

II

Testing the Network Infrastructure

PART II INTRODUCTION

Try repeating 10 times: "If Peter Piper picked a peck of pickled peppers, how many pickled peppers did Peter Piper pick?" Then try repeating 10 times: "How much wood would a woodchuck chuck, if a woodchuck could chuck wood?" Network infrastructure testing asks the same two questions: "how many and how much," and it is just as difficult to get perfect as saying the above verses.

The network infrastructure is critical to the success of client-server applications, but often overlooked. A problem at this level is often harder to fix, requires more lead time, and can cost more than problems at the application/presentation layers.

Network infrastructure testing verifies that the network provides a stable, high-performance platform capable of supporting client-server applications and company-wide services, such as electronic mail and Lotus Notes. If the network infrastructure isn't fast and reliable, network services and applications won't be fast and reliable. Before deploying critical services or client-server applications, infrastructure testing can measure throughput, capacity, reliability, and basic functionality of the network system.

Throughput, reliability, and functional testing can determine the stability of the existing infrastructure; validate the performance and stability of configurations, product releases, and technologies; and help isolate and resolve problems. Using these infrastructure testing procedures, specific tests can be developed that complement existing network management philosophy and capability.

For instance, one large bank buys only Cisco System routers. It does not do product evaluation tests, but it uses throughput and functional testing to help isolate problems. When monitoring tools detect that a router has an apparent problem, network support personnel immediately configure the router off-line and do an integrity check. The integrity check (regression test) verifies that a known sequence of tests work properly. If the router passes, it is put back on-line. If it fails, it is swapped with a replacement and set aside for future debugging. This shows how specific testing methodology can be incorporated into a network systems management process.

Another example is a major store chain that tests the network infrastructure early in the client-server development process to ensure that its performance and capacity will support the planned application.

The network infrastructure is composed of subsystems and internetwork configurations. Subsystems include routers, bridges, hubs, and switches. Internetworks are composed of multiple segments interconnected by subsystems. Subsystems can be treated as a common device type for the sake of discussion. In the following chapters, the term *router* applies collectively to routers, bridges, hubs, and switches. The primary difference in testing these subsystems is that the industry commonly measures throughput of routers and bridges in packets per second (PPS) or frames per second (FPS). Hubs and switches are more typically rated in megabytes per second (MBps) or kilobytes per second (KBps).

Subsystem and internetwork testing differ in two significant ways:

- **Scope:** Subsystem testing evaluates the unit under test to determine its behavior under different loads, port configurations, protocols, and features. Internetwork testing measures the network's behavior between two or more points across a complex configuration of multiple devices and interconnecting links. The intermediate links are not explicitly monitored or measured. Internetwork testing is not designed to evaluate specific characteristics of individual components or features.

- **Load Modeling:** The load model for subsystem testing is typically a packet stream. This approach accurately measures the effect on the device from small changes in traffic pattern and load. Throughput is measured in packets per second, and small variations in the load often create significant test differences. The internetwork load model is file I/O. Various file sizes are transferred between two end points (the requester and responder). Throughput is measured in KBps based on the amount of data transferred and the elapsed time.

Based on the test philosophy and methodology developed in Part I, Part II discusses testing subsystem and internetwork configurations of the network infrastructure for the following test objectives:

Reliability (Chapter 11)

Throughput (Chapter 12)

Feature/functionality (Chapter 13)

Regression (Chapter 14)

Acceptance (Chapter 15)

Product evaluation (Chapter 16)

Bottleneck identification and problem resolution (Chapter 17)

Reliability, throughput, and feature/functional testing are the core test objectives for the network infrastructure. Regression, acceptance, and product evaluation testing combine aspects of reliability, throughput, and functional testing to achieve their test objective. Bottleneck identification and problem resolution use basic testing principles to re-create and isolate problems. The following chapters describe test configurations, test execution, data collection, and data analysis for these seven test objectives.

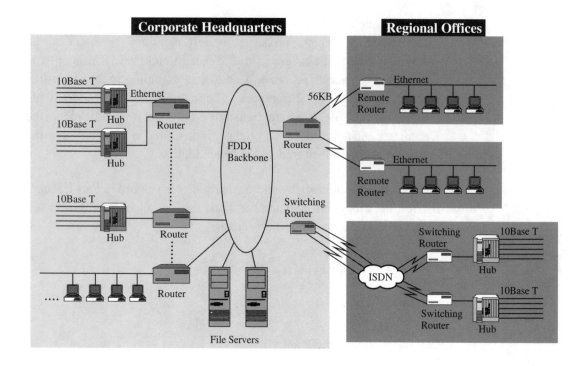

Figure 9.1   Large internetwork example.

Figure 9.1 represents a corporate headquarters and regional office internetwork configuration for a large company. For infrastructure testing, the internetwork test configuration, shown in Figure 9.2, is one example of how the production network can be modeled for testing. This model allows critical point-to-point paths to be tested. For subsystem testing, Figure 9.1 is divided into key subsystems, as shown in Figure 9.3.

This approach allows key subsystems to be tested and optimized individually, as well as to measure their interoperability with other subsystems in the internetwork. From a lab perspective, the same equipment is used for all the testing. For subsystem tests, it is configured, as shown in Figure 9.3. When an internetwork test is run, the devices are connected, as shown in Figure 9.2.

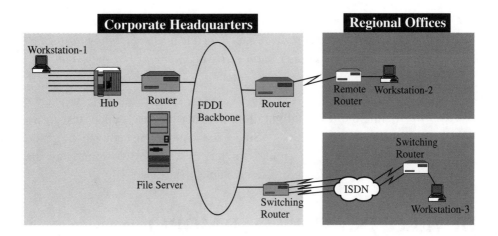

Figure 9.2 Internetwork test configuration for the production network in Figure 9.1.

Additional hardware on the subsystems will not impact internetwork level testing since the load model does not create traffic on the additional ports of the subsystem.

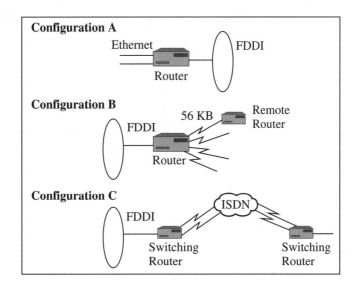

Figure 9.3 Subsystem test configurations for the production network in Figure 9.1.

Internetwork tests can also be conducted on the production network, where production loads provide excellent background loading for the test. Approaches are discussed in the test objective chapters for real-world testing.

Chapters 11 through 17 cover a specific test objective and outline how to define the test configuration, conduct the test, collect test measurements, and analyze the results. Since load modeling and load generation for the infrastructure are similar for all tests, these two topics are discussed in the remainder of Chapter 9 and Chapter 10, respectively.

DEVELOPING THE LOAD MODEL

There are two different load models required for infrastructure testing. Subsystem tests require a packet stream. Internetwork tests require a series of file I/O requests.

Several of the examples in Chapter 1 addressed the issue of developing load models for a network where the applications were not yet available or still in development. When a system is not available for baselining, testers must estimate the traffic patterns and load distributions. As the example companies found out, this is not easy, and upper management often gets nervous when they realize that there is not an exact capacity requirement on which to base comparisons and sizing. From my experience, the best way to approach this problem is the following:

1. Start with the best estimate of traffic patterns based on experience, gut feeling, or anything else available as input. Gather baseline information for existing networks and users that are comparable to the planned installation.

2. Bracket step 1 loads with at least two higher and one lower traffic pattern. By testing all five load points, you get factual information about system performance, degradation, and reliability as load changes. This provides both hard numbers and a perspective on the sensitivity of the network to load changes.

3. Estimate or predict network aging. Look at growth over one and three years. Use worse case scenarios to increase the loads in step 2 and rerun the tests. This will measure whether the network can sustain the growth and, if it can't, give some estimate of the cost to grow capacity.

4. As soon as portions of the network or applications are available, start baselining the system and compare the baseline numbers to the assumptions in steps 1 and 3. As a history of the baseline develops, compare this to the load models used and adjust them accordingly.

5. Continue testing and use the results to adjust the installed network, upgrades, and growth accordingly.

By the way, this is the approach being used by the financial services company in Example 1.3. The company is now part-way through its network implementation, which is going as planned, using the design and decisions based on test data and conclusions.

Subsystem Packet Stream Load Model

The load model is based on the production network baseline, or it uses "typical" network traffic patterns. The production system baseline is the preferred method, but requires more time and effort to develop. Both modeling approaches are discussed here.

Baselining the Production Network

Establishing a baseline for the production network is a process that requires an analyzer and several hours of work over a few weeks. This approach is more detailed than baseline methods discussed in books on network analyzers. Generally, baselining means collecting overall network utilization and error statistics, as shown in Figure 9.4, but this information does not provide sufficient detail for packet stream load modeling. The approach discussed next allows network traffic to be characterized in sufficient detail to ascertain traffic (packet) patterns that can be directly translated into a packet stream load model.

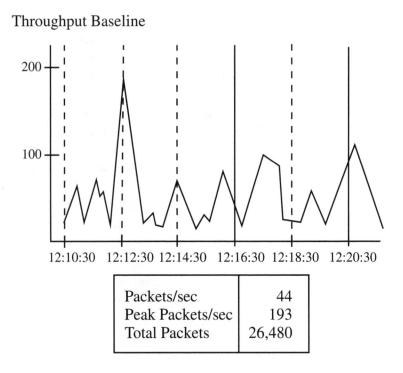

Throughput Baseline

Packets/sec	44
Peak Packets/sec	193
Total Packets	26,480

Figure 9.4A   Throughput statistics typically collected by a network analyzer for baselining.

Subsystem testing characterizes two load models: worse case and typical case. The models represent:

- **Worse case** = smaller packet sizes + peak load + many protocols + bidirectional traffic.

- **Typical case** = mixed packet sizes + average load + predominate protocols + bidirectional traffic.

To baseline the production network, measure the network segments connected to the subsystem(s) to be tested. The baseline for the corporate network shown in Figure 9.1 is developed by measuring traffic patterns through

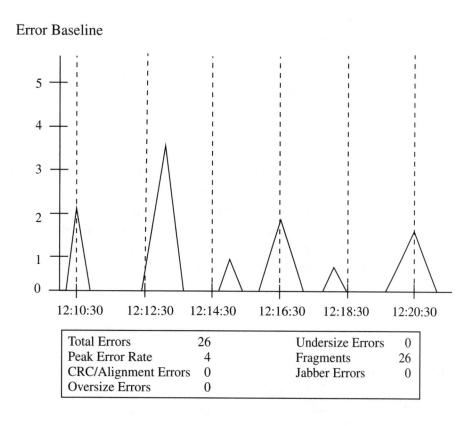

Figure 9.4B Error statistics typically collected by a network analyzer.

selected subsystems that will be tested, examples of which are depicted in Figure 9.3. The baseline does not attempt to replicate the entire network traffic pattern, but rather traffic flow through critical components that interconnect primary network topologies. Traffic measurements are collected for each of the segments attached to the subsystem to be tested.

Measurements on the segments should be taken at least three times a day:

- early morning for login, application downloads, and mail responses

- before lunch for end-of-morning work

- prior to quitting time for end-of-day load

These hours often represent the heaviest network use. If experience shows that your network's heaviest loads are during different periods, monitor the network during those times, and repeat the process for several days. If the network is used for end-of-month processing, take measurements during the month close.

The first step in baselining the network is to diagram the configuration(s) that will be monitored, including the network address of each port or segment on the subsystem. Segment addresses are required to set filters for packet capture during the baselining process. Figure 9.5 is an example subsystem configuration with address designations. Figure 9.6 shows the baselining steps for each of the three connected network segments.

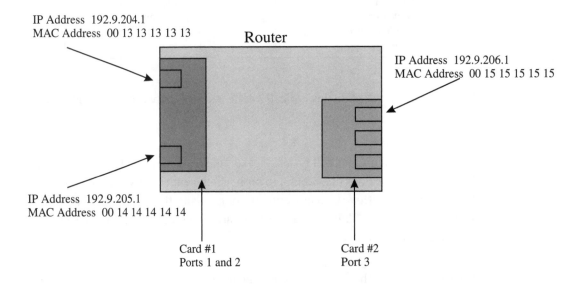

IP Address 192.9.204.1
MAC Address 00 13 13 13 13 13

Router

IP Address 192.9.206.1
MAC Address 00 15 15 15 15 15

IP Address 192.9.205.1
MAC Address 00 14 14 14 14 14

Card #1
Ports 1 and 2

Card #2
Port 3

Figure 9.5   Example subsystem diagram for baseline monitoring, including network and port addresses.

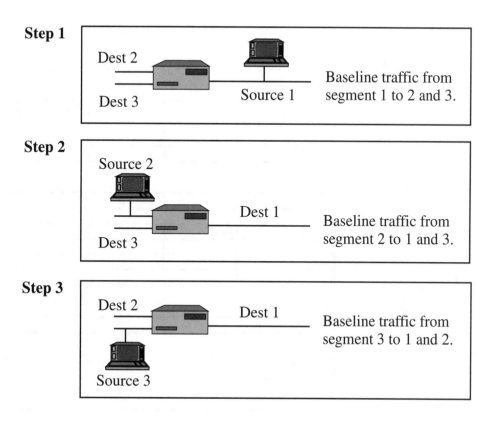

Figure 9.6 Baselining steps for the subsystem diagram in Figure 9.5.

Take each measurement for at least two minutes and repeat three times. Record the average of the three readings in the spreadsheet shown in Figure 9.7. Figure 9.7 records the following information for the production system baseline:

cell A = baselined segment address (required)

cell B = date and time of data capture (required)

cell C = destination segment address (required)

cell D = average PPS (required)

Baselined Segment   **(A)**   Date/Time   **(B)**

Destination Segment ID   **(C)**

Avg PPS		**(D)**	Max PPS		**(E)**
Protocol Detail					
Protocol ID	Total Pkts	Small	Medium	Large	
(G)	**(H)**	**(F)**			

Destination Segment ID   **(C)**

Avg PPS		Max PPS		
Protocol Detail				
Protocol ID	Total Pkts	Small	Medium	Large

Destination Segment ID   **(C)**

Avg PPS		Max PPS		
Protocol Detail				
Protocol ID	Total Pkts	Small	Medium	Large

Figure 9.7   Network baseline measurement spreadsheet.

cell E = maximum PPS (required)

cell F = packet size distribution (optional). Group the packet sizes into small (under 128 bytes), medium (128 to 1000 bytes), and large (greater than 1000 bytes). If cell G is not used, cell F is used for the distribution across all protocols.

cell G = active protocols (optional). One row for each protocol forwarded from the baselined segment to the destination segment. If tracking by protocol, cell F, packet size, is recorded for each protocol.

cell H = total packets per protocol (use only if recording cell G). Used to determine the percentage of each protocol from the source network to the destination network.

Cells C through H are recorded for each destination segment. Baselining for each protocol provides a more representative load model, but it requires more time. If the test objective is to measure how protocol mix impacts the subsystem, the load model must model the protocol percentages accurately.

Depending on the analyzer used, the exact process of capturing packet traffic will vary. For baselining by protocol mix, the process is:

1. Select the first segment for baselining.

2. Set prefilters for the protocol to be baselined and the packet destination segment address so that the analyzer will capture only packets of the prescribed protocol and destination address. For example, using Novell's LANalyzer, prefilter for the required packet addresses using the Edit Simple Filter menu.

3. Select the analyzer option that allows total packets, average PPS, maximum PPS, and packet size distribution to be captured for two minutes. Repeat three times and average the results. For LANalyzer, use the Run Global screen after setting the appropriate prefilters in step 2.

4. Repeat steps 2 and 3 for each protocol and each destination segment.

5. Move to the next segment to be baselined and repeat steps 2 through 4.

To baseline without protocol mix:

1. Select the first segment for baselining.

2. Set a prefilter for the packet destination address.

3. Select the analyzer option that allows average PPS, maximum PPS, and packet size distribution to be captured for two minutes. For example, with LANalyzer, use the Run Global screen.

4. Repeat steps 2 and 3 for each destination segment.

5. Move to the next segment to be baselined and repeat steps 2 through 4.

The baselining effort produces a series of spreadsheets. As shown, Figure 9.8 is the spreadsheet for segment 1. (NOTE: Similar spreadsheets would be created for segments 2 and 3.) The spreadsheet does not include protocol detail or segmentation in the baseline measurements. The number of spreadsheets created equals the number of times per day the baseline is conducted, times the number of segments baselined. In Figure 9.8, the spreadsheet represents one baseline time (4:00 P.M.) and three segments connected to the device shown in Figure 9.5. Order the spreadsheets by time and source segment. To determine the typical case and worst case loads, analyze the highlighted cells (average and maximum PPS) for each run. Comparing the highlighted cells, the worse case and typical case loads can be identified in a matrix, as shown in Figure 9.9. Since

Baselined Segment   1   Date/Time   6/20, 4:00PM

Destination Segment ID   2

Avg PPS		800	Max PPS	1400	
Protocol Detail					
Protocol ID	Total Pkts	Small	Medium	Large	

Destination Network ID   3

Avg PPS		450	Max PPS	600	
Protocol Detail					
Protocol ID	Total Pkts	Small	Medium	Large	

Figure 9.8   Partial network baseline matrix for the steps illustrated in Figure 9.6.

Worse Case Load

Segment				
	To	1	2	3
From 1			2000	2500
2		1400		600
3		600	850	
Total PPS		2000	2850	3100

Typical Case Load

Segment				
	To	1	2	3
From 1			1000	1000
2		800		400
3		450	550	
Total PPS		1250	1550	1400

Figure 9.9   Typical and worse case load matrix based on Figure 9.8 baseline data (without protocol mix).

no protocol mix was measured, a single protocol is assumed. This is usually the predominate protocol on the network.

If the baselining was done by protocol and packet size, the spreadsheets in Figures 9.8 and 9.9 would include that detail. Figure 9.10 illustrates how the protocol mix data can be summarized. Each entry includes the protocol type, such as IP or IPX, the packet size, and the packet rate in PPS. The total PPS did not change between Figures 9.9 and 9.10, but in Figure 9.10, the rate is divided between protocol types and packet sizes as measured on the production network.

This baselining technique provides representative load and traffic patterns; however, the resulting load model will not be an exact duplication of the packet

Worse Case Load

Segment	To 1	To 2	To 3
From 1		IP/64/1500	IP/64/2000
		IP/512/200	IP/512/200
		IPX/64/300	IPX/64/300
From 2	IP/64/1000		IP/64/600
	IP/512/200		
	IPX/64/200		
From 3	IP/64/400	IP/64/850	
	IP/512/200		
Total PPS	2000	2850	3100

Typical Case Load

Segment	To 1	To 2	To 3
From 1		IP/64/950	IP/64/800
		IP/512/50	IP/512/50
		IPX/64/200	IPX/64/200
From 2	IP/64/650		IP/64/350
	IP/512/50		
	IPX/64/150		
From 3	IP/64/300	IP/64/350	
	IP/512/100		
Total PPS	1250	1550	1400

Figure 9.10   Typical and worse case load matrix by protocol and packet size.

flow across the production network. This is because the baseline measurements are:

- Taken only at fixed points throughout the day.

- Represent only peak and average values.

The baseline data provides only a guide for developing the load model, but experience shows that this approach will provide useful test results because the real-world load on the device is bracketed by this method. The testing procedures described in the following chapters provide an envelope of results that bound the actual reliability, throughput, and so on of the device under test. With today's testing tools, this is the level of accuracy that can be achieved. The more precise the baselining (number of times the system is monitored and the level of detail captured by protocol and packet size) the more accurate the load model and the test results.

In addition to the typical and worse case developed from the baseline, the load model should represent planned growth. The simplest method is to multiply the baseline values by a factor (typically 10 to 30 percent) to develop a growth model. Either the baseline model, growth model, or both can be used in testing. Using both models, test results may show:

- The unit under test passes under both models. This provides higher assurance that there is excess capacity for growth.

- The unit under test passes for the baseline model, but fails under the growth model. This indicates that the system may not have any excess capacity for growth. This sets a "red flag" warning of potential problems as system utilization grows.

- The unit under test fails under the baseline model. This indicates a strong possibility of existing problems that must be addressed before considering future growth.

"Typical" Network Traffic Patterns

Experience shows that most networks exhibit a large number of small and large packets and a much smaller percentage of medium-size packets. This is caused by the request-response protocol between the workstations and servers. Requests tend to be small packets, such as a file open or file read, and responses tend to be large packets of information. Medium-size packets result from the termination packet in a string of larger packets during a file transfer. A distribution of 45 percent small packets (64 bytes), 10 percent medium packets (512 bytes), and 45 percent large packets (largest allowable for the network) is therefore a reasonable traffic pattern.

Packet rates and destinations must still be determined. To do so, measure the network segments connected to the subsystem to be tested two or three times during the day. The recommended times are early morning, before lunch, and prior to quitting time. Repeat the process for several days. If the network is used for end-of-month processing, take measurements during month close.

The first step is to diagram the configuration that will be monitored, including the segment address of each port on the subsystem. This is required for packet address filtering during the measurement process. Depending on the analyzer used, the exact process of capturing this information will vary, but the basic process is:

1. Select the first segment for baselining.

2. Set prefilters for the packet destination address so that the analyzer will capture only packets with that address. For example, using Novell's LANalyzer, prefilter for required packet addresses using the Edit Simple Filter menu.

3. Select the analyzer option that captures average PPS and maximum PPS. Repeat three times and average the results. For LANalyzer, use the Run Global screen after setting the appropriate prefilters in step 2.

4. Repeat steps 2 and 3 for each destination segment.

5. Move to the next segment to be baselined and repeat steps 2 through 4.

Use the spreadsheets and analysis process described previously in Baselining the Production Network to determine the typical case and worst case loads.

Determining Load Generation Scripts and Load Distribution

To determine the packet sequence required to produce the packet traffic and load on each segment, use the baseline load matrix, shown in Figure 9.9 or 9.10. Create a worse case and typical case packet sequence for each segment's load generator.

The packet sequence must model the same relative distribution of protocols and packet sizes identified in the baseline.

Since the protocol and packet sizes were not baselined in Figure 9.9, the load model uses the measured PPS rates, primary network protocol and "typical" network traffic patterns just described. For the segment 1 load generator, the worse case load in Figure 9.9 is 2000 PPS, 1400 PPS to segment 2, and 600 PPS to segment 3. If the primary network protocol is IPX, Figure 9.11 illustrates the resulting load model of 10 packets. The packet stream is distributed in a ratio that ensures 70 percent are forwarded to segment 2, and 30 percent are forwarded to segment 3 during each cycle of the 10-packet sequence. The PPS rate on the load generator is set at 2000.

Using the "typical" network traffic pattern, sizes are distributed across 64-byte (small), 512-byte (medium), and 1024-byte (large) packets. The distribution to segment 3 has two small packets and one large packet. This errs on the side of conservatism (higher load) since the typical packet distribution ratio couldn't be fully modeled in a 10-packet sequence. The load model could be refined by increasing the number of packets to more accurately model the packet pattern. The trade-off is time and effort versus better load model accuracy.

IPX packet	64 bytes	destination segment 2
IPX packet	64 bytes	destination segment 2
IPX packet	64 bytes	destination segment 2
IPX packet	1024 bytes	destination segment 2
IPX packet	1024 bytes	destination segment 2
IPX packet	1024 bytes	destination segment 2
IPX packet	512 bytes	destination segment 2
IPX packet	64 bytes	destination segment 3
IPX packet	64 bytes	destination segment 3
IPX packet	1024 bytes	destination segment 3

Figure 9.11 Simple packet sequence of 10 packets representing Figure 9.9's load model.

A slightly more complex model that provides a better distribution from segment 1 to segment 3 is Figure 9.12. The model more accurately represents the "typical" traffic patterns for small, medium, and large packets, and contains 28 packet definitions.

The load generators on segments 2 and 3 would have similar load models for their test packet sequence.

IPX packet	64 bytes	destination segment 2
IPX packet	64 bytes	destination segment 2
IPX packet	64 bytes	destination segment 2
IPX packet	64 bytes	destination segment 2
IPX packet	64 bytes	destination segment 2
IPX packet	64 bytes	destination segment 2
IPX packet	64 bytes	destination segment 2
IPX packet	64 bytes	destination segment 2
IPX packet	64 bytes	destination segment 2
IPX packet	1024 bytes	destination segment 2
IPX packet	1024 bytes	destination segment 2
IPX packet	1024 bytes	destination segment 2
IPX packet	1024 bytes	destination segment 2
IPX packet	1024 bytes	destination segment 2
IPX packet	1024 bytes	destination segment 2
IPX packet	1024 bytes	destination segment 2
IPX packet	1024 bytes	destination segment 2
IPX packet	1024 bytes	destination segment 2
IPX packet	512 bytes	destination segment 2
IPX packet	512 bytes	destination segment 2
IPX packet	512 bytes	destination segment 2
IPX packet	64 bytes	destination segment 3
IPX packet	64 bytes	destination segment 3
IPX packet	64 bytes	destination segment 3
IPX packet	1024 bytes	destination segment 3
IPX packet	1024 bytes	destination segment 3
IPX packet	1024 bytes	destination segment 3
IPX packet	512 bytes	destination segment 3

Figure 9.12 More accurate packet sequence of 28 packets representing Figure 9.9's load model.

Use the same approach for the matrix in Figure 9.10 to create the load model. Since the packet sizes and quantity were baselined in this example, the packet sequence reflects the measured protocol and packet size distribution rather than a "typical" distribution. This is shown in Figure 9.13.

Load scripts to create these packet sequences are dependent on the load generator used. Chapter 10 discusses several load generators for subsystem testing and how to create load scripts for each.

Bursty Traffic Patterns

The typical case and worse case load models define a continuous load on the unit under test. Traffic on a network, however, is generally not continuous, but bursty. For reliability and functional testing, the load model can be extended to generate bursty loading by taking the baseline packet sequence and modifying the PPS rate, the packet distribution, or the number of generators on the source segment. For example, by expanding the packet sequence in Figure 9.11 to 37 packets, a distribution is created that loads segments 2 and 3 with a burst of traffic during each pass through the packet sequence. The new sequence is shown in Figure 9.14. This can be created by copying the packet sequence and modifying a few destination addresses, as shown by the bold lines in Figure 9.14.

IP packet	64 bytes	destination segment 2
IP packet	64 bytes	destination segment 2
IP packet	64 bytes	destination segment 2
IP packet	64 bytes	destination segment 2
IP packet	64 bytes	destination segment 2
IP packet	512 bytes	destination segment 2
IPX packet	64 bytes	destination segment 2
IP packet	64 bytes	destination segment 3
IP packet	64 bytes	destination segment 3
IP packet	512 bytes	destination segment 3

Figure 9.13 Packet sequence of baseline protocol mix representing Figure 9.10's load model.

IPX packet	64 bytes	destination segment 2
IPX packet	64 bytes	destination segment 2
IPX packet	64 bytes	destination segment 2
IPX packet	1024 bytes	destination segment 2
IPX packet	1024 bytes	destination segment 2
IPX packet	1024 bytes	destination segment 2
IPX packet	512 bytes	destination segment 2
IPX packet	64 bytes	destination segment 3
IPX packet	64 bytes	destination segment 3
IPX packet	1024 bytes	destination segment 3
IPX packet	64 bytes	destination segment 2
IPX packet	64 bytes	destination segment 2
IPX packet	64 bytes	destination segment 2
IPX packet	1024 bytes	destination segment 2
IPX packet	1024 bytes	destination segment 2
IPX packet	1024 bytes	destination segment 2
IPX packet	512 bytes	destination segment 2
IPX packet	64 bytes	destination segment 3
IPX packet	64 bytes	destination segment 3
IPX packet	1024 bytes	destination segment 3
IPX packet	1024 bytes	destination segment 2
IPX packet	1024 bytes	destination segment 2
IPX packet	1024 bytes	destination segment 2
IPX packet	512 bytes	destination segment 2
IPX packet	**64 bytes**	**destination segment 2**
IPX packet	**64 bytes**	**destination segment 2**
IPX packet	**1024 bytes**	**destination segment 2**
IPX packet	64 bytes	destination segment 2
IPX packet	64 bytes	destination segment 2
IPX packet	64 bytes	destination segment 2
IPX packet	**1024 bytes**	**destination segment 3**
IPX packet	**1024 bytes**	**destination segment 3**
IPX packet	**1024 bytes**	**destination segment 3**
IPX packet	**512 bytes**	**destination segment 3**
IPX packet	64 bytes	destination segment 3
IPX packet	64 bytes	destination segment 3
IPX packet	1024 bytes	destination segment 3

Figure 9.14   Packet sequence that generates bursty traffic.

While the average number of packets destined for each segment remains the same, the distribution places a burst of traffic first on segment 2 and then on segment 3 from the grouped distribution of highlighted packets.

Another alternative is to have two load generators on the source segment where each generates approximately one-half the packet load. The packet generation sequence from each load generator would be synchronized so that once during each pass they would generate a burst of traffic to each destination segment.

The ability to create a long packet sequence or to cycle the PPS rate during packet transmission is dependent on the capability of the load generator. A few load generators provide for bursty traffic, as discussed in Chapter 10.

Internetwork File I/O Load Model

Internetwork throughput results are influenced by four factors:

- file transfer size

- NOS and protocol flow control

- load on the responder, typically the file server

- ratio of bidirectional traffic

Load modeling develops various combinations of:

- unidirectional and bidirectional traffic

- file transfer sizes—small, medium, large, very large

    250 bytes (database record)

    2 Kbytes (mail message)

10-20 Kbytes (word document)

100 Kbytes (large document)

250 Kbytes (graphics file)

1000 Kbytes (large graphics file).

- request/response scenarios with small files in one direction (I/O requests) and large files in the other direction (file downloads)

- random, bursty traffic patterns and continuous uniform traffic patterns

The more accurately the preceding combinations reflect the production load, the more accurate will be the test results. To baseline data traffic between critical workstations and servers, use a network analyzer or an application load monitor, such as Intel's LANDesk or CoroNet's Management System (CMS). The simplest approach is to select several "typical" users and monitor the data traffic for those users several times a day over a few weeks. These users and their servers represent the end points of the data flow, or the requester and responder, respectively.

A network analyzer is good at monitoring PPS or kilobytes per second (KBps). Unfortunately, it is difficult to relate these low-level measurements to individual file I/O activity, unless you capture and decode packet traffic to interpret file activity. Figure 9.15 is an example of how detail packet decoding can provide individual file information.

Packet decoding is a very tedious and time-consuming activity. It is better to use an analyzer to determine traffic patterns for bursty versus continuous traffic and the percent of bidirectional traffic between the two end points of the internetwork. Do not use it to obtain individual file information.

For file I/O, use an application monitor to capture activity between the server and the typical user. This provides traffic rate, but not file size. The best

```
┌─────────────────────────────────────────────────┐
│            NetWare Core Protocol (NCP)           │
│                                                  │
│  NPC Reply:  Create File                         │
│  Reply Type:  0X333 (Reply)                      │
│  Sequence Number:  98                            │
│  Connection Number Low:  4                       │
│  Task Number:  2                                 │
│  Connection Number High:  0                      │
│  Completion Code:  0(Success)                    │
│  Connection Status:  0X00                        │
│  File Handle:  0XFF 0XFF 0X48 0X24 0X00 0X00     │
│  File Name:  Test1.DOC                           │
│  File Attributes:  0X00                          │
│  File Execute Type:  0X00                        │
│  File Length:  0                                 │
│  Creation Date:  Aug. 30, 1995                   │
│  Last Access Date:  Aug. 30, 1995                │
│  Last Update Date:  Aug. 30, 1995                │
│  Last Update Time:  4:44:44 PM                   │
└─────────────────────────────────────────────────┘
```

Figure 9.15   Packet decoding can provide specific details on file size and activity.

way to estimate file size is to look at the file types and sizes in the user's directory. These two pieces of information are used to model the file I/O.

To create the load model, use one of the previous suggestions to define the traffic from each requester. Load models will typically be simple combinations of file I/O, such as reading a 1-Kbyte file 100 times, and measuring the transfer time, or reading a 1-Kbyte file for X seconds and calculating the effective Kbytes per second throughput.

For the internetwork test configuration in Figure 9.2, a load model may look like the following:

- **Workstation 1:**   File activity to the server is word processing and spreadsheet retrieves and saves. The load model would read and write a combination of 2-Kbyte (memos), 25-Kbyte (documents), and 50-Kbyte (spreadsheet) files.

- **Workstation 2:** File activity to the server is retrieving purchase orders and packing slips. The load model would read 4-Kbyte files.

- **Workstation 3:** File activity is mail messages and attachments. Typical file size is 4-Kbyte mail messages and 100-Kbyte attachments in the ratio of nine to one, respectively. The load model would read 4-Kbyte files with 100-Kbyte files in the ratio of nine to one.

Load scripts to create the file I/O sequences are dependent on the load generator used. Chapter 10 discusses several load generators for internetwork testing and how to create load scripts for each.

TESTING TERMINOLOGY

Subsystem test measurements are defined by the following terminology:

- **Maximum sustained throughput per segment:** This is the rate at which all packets sent on the source segment are forwarded to the destination segment. There are no dropped packets in the test.

- **Aggregate sustained throughput for the device:** This is the rate at which all packets sent on all source segments are forwarded to all destination segments. There are no dropped packets in the test. If a total of 20,000 PPS are sent on the source segments, 20,000 PPS are measured across the destination segments. Sustained rate should be used as the maximum load rate for the device. This provides a margin of safety or additional capacity to handle severe load spikes.

- **Maximum throughput per segment:** This is the maximum packet-forwarding rate from the source to destination segment without regard to the number of dropped packets. As the input and dropped packet rate increase, throughput degradation will occur. The test measures the input load at which throughput degradation occurs. If 10,000 PPS are sent from one source to one destination segment, and 9,800 PPS are measured on the destination segment, 200 PPS were dropped. If 11,000 PPS are sent from one source to one destination segment, and 10,500 PPS are measured on the destination segment, 500 PPS were dropped. The effective throughput, however, is still higher than with the 10,000 PPS source rate. If 12,000 PPS are sent from one source to one destination segment, and 10,200 PPS are measured on the destination segment, then 1,800 PPS were dropped. The throughput for the second load is higher than for the first load even though packets were dropped. However, throughput for the third load is less than the second since sufficient packets were dropped to degrade throughput.

- **Aggregate throughput for the device:** This is the maximum packet-forwarding rate from all sources to all destinations without regard to the number of dropped packets. As the input and dropped packet rate increase, throughput degradation will occur. The test measures the input load at which throughput degradation occurs. The difference between the aggregate sustained throughput and the maximum throughput is the excess capacity of the subsystem to handle load peaks.

- **Fairness of throughput across segments:** This determines how fairly the subsystem handles throughput across all ports. This is an important test measurement when ports of different rates are configured in the same device, or the device has a maximum port configuration and heavy loads.

- **Variance across test configurations:** This measures how throughput changes as port configurations change on the device.

- **Variance across protocol configurations:** This determines how efficiently the device manages multiple protocols, or how optimized individual protocols are compared to one another.

- **Variance based on features:** This measures the degradation on throughput, or the impact on reliability caused by various subsystem features, such as filtering, encapsulation, encryption, and data compression.

- **Packet or frame errors:** This measures how many packets received by the device could not be forwarded because the packet was dropped or there was an error in the packet.

- **Accuracy of device statistics versus analyzer statistics:** This correlates the statistics gathered by the product-under-test to an independent counter, such as a network analyzer. It verifies that the device can accurately report statistics under heavy load conditions.

Internetwork testing and measurements are defined by the following terminology:

- **Maximum throughput across the internetwork:** This measures the point-to-point (requester to responder) throughput across the internetwork.

- **Variance across test configuration topologies:** This measures how throughput or reliability change as intermediate components are varied.

- **Variance across protocols or configuration options:** This determines how throughput changes because of protocol flow control, feature settings, or other options selected for internetwork nodes.

TEST CONFIGURATION PROBLEM RESOLUTION TIPS

When multiple runs generate test results that vary by more than 4 percent, the results are considered unreproducible. The first step is to determine whether problems in the test configuration are skewing the results. If a problem is found, it must be fixed and the tests rerun. In the absence of any problem, the conclusion is that the unit-under-test is causing the inconsistent results and the test measurements are valid.

To verify that the test configuration is working correctly:

- **Physical connections:** Confirm that all connections are tight and that all cabling is correct.

- **Addressing:** Check that the load scripts, routing tables, and so on of the configuration have the correct entries.

- **Intermittent errors:** Rerun the test and use an analyzer to monitor the test configuration for intermittent errors, excessive broadcast packets, or other problems that could affect test results.

- **Monitor accuracy:** Often monitors, such as analyzers or other statistics-gathering software, are not uniformly accurate through a range of loads. Many drop counts at higher loads. Independently verify that the monitors can record accurate statistics using a simple independent test configuration of the load generator and load monitor. Verify monitor accuracy at the maximum load rates for the test.

- **Synchronization of load generators and monitors:** Make sure that all monitors are started at the same time. Try starting the monitors in a different order to see if the test results change. Choose a specific process for synchronization and use it for each test case.

Infrastructure Testing Tools

CATEGORIES OF TESTING TOOLS

There are two categories of tools used for network infrastructure testing. The first generates packets, frames, or cells (ATM). These are used for testing subsystems, such as routers, bridges, hubs, and switches. These tools are network operating system-independent; in fact, a NOS is not required to be installed on the test configuration when using the tool. However, the tools often require specific network interface cards, and not all tools support all media. This tool category includes network analyzers, software utilities, and specialized hardware devices.

The second tool category generates file I/O requests to a file server for testing internetwork configurations. These tools require a NOS on the test configuration, but generally the tool is not NOS-dependent; rather, they are typically workstation-dependent, and different versions are required for DOS, Windows, OS/2, and UNIX operating systems. This tool category includes programs such as Novell's Perform3 and Ziff-Davis' NetBench and ServerBench. Most of these programs can be acquired free of charge from bulletin boards, or on diskettes or CD-ROM directly from the developer. Other options, such as in-house-developed batch files or Visual BASIC programs, provide flexible, low-cost load generators for internetwork testing.

PACKET GENERATORS

As discussed in Chapter 9, creating a packet stream (*load script*) for subsystem testing requires flexibility in defining:

- protocol types, such as IP, IPX, DECNet, and AppleTalk

- subnet and node source and destination addresses

- packet sizes

- packet data field contents

- packet sequence combinations, such as mixing IP and IPX packets of different sizes and addresses in one packet stream

Additionally, the load generator must provide the flexibility to generate packet rates from a few PPS to 70 percent or more of the network media's bandwidth.

To collect test data, a load monitor is required to record the rate, type, and contents of packets on the destination segments. Typically, the load monitor is a network analyzer. There are five methods for individual packet creation. Load script creation and packet generation are dependent on the type of load generator used. These topics are discussed in the following two sections.

Packet Creation

For subsystem testing, important packet attributes are:

- **Source and destination address:** Implements the required traffic pattern for the load model.

- **Length:** Allows maximum (creates the most stress on buffer management), minimum (creates maximum stress on the subsystem processor and backplane), and illegal (verifies error handling) packet sizes for the network type.

- **Data field contents:** Generally used to pad the packet to the required length, and often used to assist in monitoring forwarded traffic for functional testing and debugging.

- **Header checksum:** If appropriate.

- **Packet type:** Packet type is important for functional testing, if the test is to determine how the subsystem handles a specific packet type, such as an Ethernet SNAP packet or a Token Ring Source Routing Protocol (SRP) packet.

Five methods of packet creation are:

Start from scratch.

Use examples provided with the load generator.

Edit captured packets from the network.

Edit packets from previous tests.

Have the load generator create the packet based on input criteria.

Starting from scratch requires knowledge of individual protocol packet structure. Books are available that discuss protocol packet architecture and information on packet fields and contents. For most testing requirements, however, starting from scratch is not required.

Load generators, such as LANQuest's FrameThrower, Alantec's PowerBits, and some analyzers, include sample packet definitions that can be used as a starting point. A sample packet, such as an Ethernet_802.3 frame type, can be used for a variety of testing by changing the packet attributes delineated previously. If a sample packet is not available, captured packets from the production network can be edited.

According to the test methodology outlined in Chapter 6, following each project, all the individual packets and load scripts used for the project should be archived. This provides an excellent source of packet definitions for future projects.

Some load generators provide capabilities for creating complex packet sequences based on packet templates and runtime input specifications. This allows repetitive packet sequences to be quickly created and revised. The exact steps for combining the packets into a load script and generating the packets on the test configuration is dependent on the type of load generator used. The following section discusses three load generator alternatives.

Load Generator Alternatives

As just introduced, there are three alternatives for packet traffic load generators:

- network analyzers

- software utilities

- specialized hardware

Network Analyzers

The primary function of network analyzers is to capture and decode packets, but most network analyzers also have the capability to generate or transmit a packet or packet stream. But, because packet generation is *not* their primary function, network analyzers usually provide less sophisticated packet transmission than the other two alternatives. For example, Novell's LANalyzer provides several packet transmission options. With LANalyzer, packets can be created from scratch, or captured packets can be edited. It provides six transmit channels, which means that one to six packet types (with different addresses, sizes, and contents) can be transmitted in a "round-robin" fashion with a specified relative frequency of each packet type. With these features, LANalyzer could support the packet streams identified in Figures 9.11, 9.12, and 9.13, but not the longer sequence identified in Figure 9.14. Since the LANalyzer controls packet transmission rate through an interpacket gap setting, the tester has to experiment with the transmission settings to reach the required PPS rate for each test. For most test objectives, this could be done, but for throughput testing, as described in Chapter 12, this would be a time-consuming procedure.

Figure 10.1 shows how the load script for Figure 9.11's packet stream would look for the LANalyzer. For ease of use, a template, an example of which is shown in Figure 10.1A, is used to define destination address and packet length. A template defines each packet to be transmitted by name. Figure 10.1B shows how each packet is assigned to an individual transmission channel and how the relative frequency at which each packet is transmitted is defined.

The biggest drawbacks to using network analyzers for packet generation are their inability to generate high packet rates, lack of flexibility for load script definition, and cost. Wandel and Golterman's (W&G) DA30 overcomes the first two objections, but not the last one. Another concern with all packet generators is that their packet definitions are not portable from one device to another. If different analyzers are used in a test, different definitions of the same packet must be created.

Figure 10.2 gives the network analyzer requirement for the test configuration presented in Figure 9.5. Since most analyzers cannot generate load and measure packet traffic at the same time, at least one analyzer would be required on each source segment, and one additional analyzer is required to move between the destination segments for data collection, as shown by the dotted lines in Figure 10.2A. Although using only one load monitor reduces cost, it also lengthens testing time. The W&G DA30 can be configured to both send and monitor traffic, and is shown as alternative B in Figure 10.2.

When using all analyzers or a combination of analyzers and packet generators as described in the next section, the simplest way to synchronize the generators and monitors is to start the generators, wait a few seconds, then start the monitors for a 30-second measurement. If only one monitor is used, start the generators with the monitor attached to one destination segment. Wait a few seconds, then start the monitor for a 30-second measurement. Complete the

A) Packet Template: Define packet contents in the
Edit Packet menu using a template.

Checksum	FFFF
Length	34
Transport Ctl	0
Packet Type	17
Destination Network	19 29 20 61
Destination Node	00 15 15 15 15 15
Destination Socket	0451
Source Network	19 29 20 41
Source Node	00 13 13 13 13 13
Source Socket	0000

B) Load Script: Create a packet sequence using the Edit Transmit menu
defining various packet sizes and relative frequencies.

Channel	Packet
1	64 byte with destination segment 2
2	1024 byte with destination segment 2
3	512 byte with destination segment 2
4	64 byte with destination segment 3
5	1024 byte with destination segment 3
6	(not used)

Channel	Relative Frequency
1	3
2	3
3	1
4	2
5	1
6	(not used)

Figure 10.1   Packet template and load script for LANalyzer based on Figure
9.11 packet stream definition.

measurement on the first destination segment, then move the monitor to each
subsequent destination segment and take the measurement. Do not stop the
generators while moving the monitor. The W&G automatically synchronizes the
sending and monitoring for the segments to which it is attached.

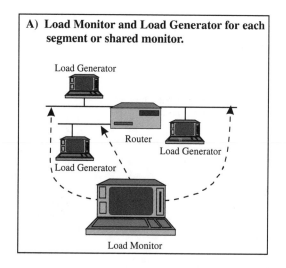

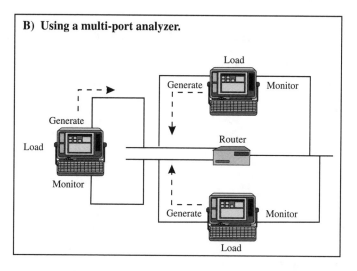

Figure 10.2   Using network analyzers as load generators and load monitors.

Most analyzers do not provide features for automatically varying the PPS rate during transmission. Bursty traffic can be created only through an expanded packet sequence, as discussed in Chapter 9, or the use of two analyzers per segment.

A) Packet Definition

File name = Eipx60.pkt

*IPX
This is a 60 byte IPX packet for use with the
FrameThrower packet generator program.

aa00 0400 0304   ; Dummy destination address. Modify here or
                                  ; use Destination address option.
0260 8c43 9593   ; Dummy source address. Will be filled in by
                                  ; Ethernet adapter.

0020 ffff 0020 00 11
0000 0120   ; Destination network number (in decimal).
aa00 0400 0104 4004   ; Destination node number and socket.
0000 0064   ; Source network number (in decimal).
0260 8c43 9593 4003   ; Source node number and socket.
013f
0000 0000 0000
0000 0000 0000 0000

Note: Adapter appends 4 byte CRC to above packet to create 64 byte transmitted packet.

B) Packet List

File name = Fig_9-11.pkl

ipx64_1
ipx64_1
ipx64_1
ipxT24_1
ipxT24_1
ipxT24_1
ipxT24_1
ipx64_2
ipx64_2
ipxT24_2

Note: T24 is a code for a 1024 byte packet. _X
in the file name designates the destination
segment address coded in the packet.

C) Load Script

EN;	Protocol
;	Destination
;	Packet Length
;	Text
Fig_9-11.pkl;	File #1
;	
;	
;	
100;	Transmission Rate
100;	Default Transmission Range
300;	Base Address
3;	Interrupt Request
AUI;	Connector

Figure 10.3   Packet definition, packet list, and load script for FrameThrower based on Figure 9.11 packet stream definition.

Software Utilities for Packet Generation

There are several software utilities that provide packet generation. One of the most flexible and easy to use is LANQuest's FrameThrower.

FrameThrower allows the tester to specify up to 1,000 individual packets in a "packet list." The packet list, plus information such as network type and target PPS transmission rate, are combined into a load script. Within the packet list, every packet can have different packet attributes, such as protocol type, length, address, and data field content. Versions of FrameThrower are available for Ethernet, Token Ring, FDDI, and ATM. FrameThrower also includes an extensive list of sample packets.

The primary drawback to FrameThrower is that packet definition and load script creation is a manual process in all but the ATM version. Figure 10.3 shows what a load script (FrameThrower calls this a packet list) and the individual packet definitions (FrameThrower calls these packets) look like for the load model defined in Figure 9.11. These are ASCII files that are edited using an internal text editor. To use captured packets off the production network, they must be typed into the FrameThrower format. However, FrameThrower provides an extensive sample library of packets that can be easily edited for required packet attributes.

FrameThrower also provides good packet generation price/performance, relative to most network analyzers. Figure 10.4 illustrates how the test configuration in Figure 10.2 would change if FrameThrowers were used as packet generators. Use the method described in the previous section to synchronize the generators and monitors.

For bursty traffic, FrameThrower supports expanded packet sequences. It also allows multiple load scripts to be combined in a BATCH file where each script is unique. By varying the scripts and script contents, complex bursty traffic can be created from a single FrameThrower node. FrameThrower/ATM has four transmission modes: timed, burst, continuous, and mixed.

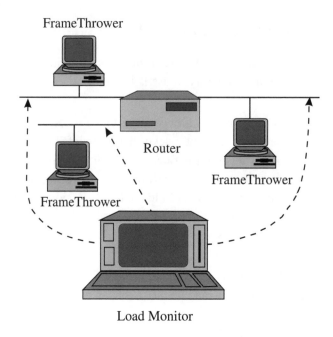

Figure 10.4   FrameThrower-based test configuration.

Specialized Hardware

There are several hardware devices that provide simple packet generation, such as pings or preformatted packets, but only Alantec's PowerBits provides the flexibility required for subsystem testing. Alantec is a router and hub manufacturer that has created a special version of its hardware for packet generation. The product provides both packet generation and monitoring for multiple segments concurrently. Load scripts can be prepared that provide automated packet creation and generation across a range of packet attributes. On the monitoring side, the product will automatically count the number of received packets. An example load script is shown in Figure 10.5 for the packet stream defined in Figure 9.11; a packet is defined as shown in Figure 10.5A. Packet groups define packet combinations of length and relative frequency, as shown in Figure 10.5B. A session, given in Figure 10.5C, defines which ports are used for sending and receiving the packet stream.

A) **Packet**

EPI	0	00 15 15 15 15 15	# Destination MAC Addr
EPI	6	00 13 13 13 13 13	# Source MAC S Addr
EPI	12	81 37	# Type ⟶ (8137 for IPX)
	14	00 00	# Checksum computed by PowerBits
	16	00 2E	# Length (00 2E=46 bytes)
	18	00	# Transport Ctrl
	19	17	# Packet Type ⟶ (17=NCP Packet)
	20	19 29 20 61	# Destination Network
	24	00 15 15 15 15 15	# Destination MAC Addr
	30	04 51	# Destination Socket ⟶ (0451=NCP)
	32	19 29 20 41	# Source Network
	36	00 13 13 13 13 13	# Source MAC Addr
	42	00 00	# Source Socket

B) **Packet Group**

C) **Session:** Send port, Receive port, List of packet groups.

```
ag 1  64:3  1024:3  512:1        as 1   1   2   1 2
ag 2  64:2  1024:1               es 1       3
```

Figure 10.5 Load script for PowerBits based on Figure 9.11 packet stream definition.

With PowerBits, the need for an analyzer is eliminated in the test configuration, as shown in Figure 10.6. PowerBits provides more automation than FrameThrower, but supports only Ethernet and FDDI media. PowerBits includes predefined tests, such as burst and sustained throughput. PowerBits also automatically synchronizes the transmission and monitoring of the traffic for up to six Ethernets and two FDDI DOS connections.

Selecting Your Load Generator

Network analyzers are usually the first packet generator most testers use. However, for a serious tester and a network test lab, the other alternatives provide more flexibility and performance at a lower price.

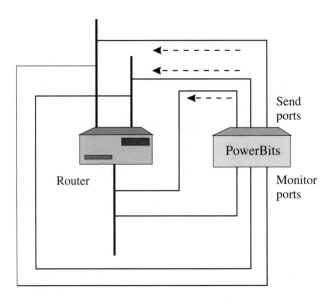

Figure 10.6   PowerBits-based test configuration.

The best way to select load generators is to identify the type and configuration of sub-system testing, and the complexity of the load model. Then evaluate in-house network analyzers to determine if they can meet the needs before looking at new products. For ease-of-use and load script consistency, it is best to select one load generator, however, today's reality is that no single load generator provides a broad solution set. More than one type will be needed to satisfy broad test objectives.

Part IV includes a list of products available in the above three categories of load generators.

FILE I/O GENERATION

As discussed in Chapter 9, file I/O for internetwork testing requires unidirectional and bidirectional data flow for various file sizes and traffic patterns (bursty versus continuous transmission) between a requester and responder.

File activity can be created by a broad range of software utilities and programs. For internetwork testing, the test designer needs flexibility to specify file size, frequency, and repetition of data transfer to model application file transfer across the internetwork. A software utility that emulates file I/O is preferred over the actual application.

There are four categories of software that are easy to use and very inexpensive for internetwork testing. These are:

- DOS batch files

- Novell's Perform3

- File I/O emulator, such as Ziff-Davis' Server Benchmarks

- In-house developed program in C or BASIC

The following sections discuss how these are used to create internetwork load scripts.

DOS Batch File

A batch file can be equivalent to a simple software program that includes program language features, such as flow control, variables, error codes, remarks, linking, and branching. It can be used to create broad and complex traffic patterns between a requester (workstation) and responder (file server).

Batch files can include most commands executable from the DOS prompt. For load scripts, the commands most often used are:

- **COPY** Creates file I/O read and write activity between the requester and responder.

- **DIR** Creates file read activity against the responder.

LD_GEN.BAT

```
@echo off
set copycmd=/y
Echo Start Test_%1>>Audit
For %%A IN (1 2 3) DO Call I_O %%A
Erase trash
Erase temp_1
Erase temp_2
Erase temp_3
Echo Completed Test_%1>>Audit
```

TIME_MRK.BAT

```
@Echo off
If NOT EXIST Rtn GOTO Miss
Echo %1>>Audit
Time<Rtn | FIND "Current">>Audit
GOTO End
:MISS
Cannot find RTN file
:End
```

I_O.BAT

```
Call time_mrk Start_%1
Echo off
FOR %%B IN (1 2 3 4 5 6 7 8 9 10) DO Copy File_%1.txt temp_%1>>Trash
Call Time_Mrk Done_%1
```

Audit Log

```
Start Test_a
Start_1
Current time is 4:36:31.67p
Done_1
Current time is 4:36:33.21p
Start_2
Current time is 4:36:33.53p
Done_2
Current time is 4:36:35.02p
Start_3
Current time is 4:36:35.35p
Done_3
Current time is 4:36:36.89p
Completed Test_a
Start Test_b
Start_1
Current time is 4:36:44.19p
Done_1
Current time is 4:36:45.62p
Start_2
Current time is 4:36:45.95p
Done 2
Current time is 4:36:47.32p
Start_3
Current time is 4:36:47.60p
Done_3
Current time is 4:36:49.02p
Completed Test_b
```

Figure 10.7 Batch file load script for Figure 9.16, workstation 1; includes three linked batch files and example audit file of test results.

- **CALL** Allows batch flies to be chained to create complex load scripts from simple individual files.

- **FOR** Creates loops of activity for file I/O.

- **DOS commands:** Commands for accessing drives, directories, and applications can be used to redirect file I/O and change data paths.

- **Date and Time:** File operations are date and time stamped so that throughput rates can be calculated. These stamps can be labeled and redirected to a printer or file during the test.

Figure 10.7 is a simple batch file load script for workstation 1 in Figure 9.16. There are actually three batch files in the script:

- LD_GEN.BAT controls the number of copy iterations. It calls a second batch file, I_O.BAT.

- I_O.BAT performs the file copies. I_O.BAT calls a third batch file, TIME_MRK.BAT.

- TIME_MRK.BAT creates time stamps that measure the file copy duration and redirect the time to an audit file for data reduction and analysis.

The audit file, as shown in Figure 10.7, contains a start and completion time for each file copy. Based on file size and transfer time, an effective throughput can be calculated. Remember, each file COPY actually moves twice the amount of data across the network because the file is transferred to (read) and from (written) the workstation for each copy request. Another approach is to record only a global start and completion time for all the file copies. This would provide an average throughput for the total bytes transmitted. To write or read files, the workstation hard disk could be used as the starting or ending point of the copy, respectively.

To use this batch file, three files must be created in a directory on the responder (file server). For this example, the files would be 2, 25, and 50 kilobytes in size. The batch files could be expanded to initially create the files, or to record and log the file sizes used in the I/O. The audit file data reduction could be done by hand for a small test series, or a BASIC or C program could be written to scan the audit file, extract test data, and calculate throughput.

Novell's Perform3

Perform3 is a widely used software utility that reads cached data from a file server and calculates effective throughput. File sizes from 64 bytes to 65,000 KBytes and read times from 12 to 65,000 seconds can be used in the test. Perform3 creates the required file in the server's cache and performs sequential block reads of the file for the specified duration. At the end of the test, it calculates effective throughput (KBps) based on the total KBytes read during the elapsed time. As input parameters, a start, stop, and step size for the file can be specified. Perform3 will automatically increment the file size and calculate the throughput for each file size read. Perform3 does not perform file writes.

This utility can be controlled in a batch file or combined with other commands, such as COPY, to create both reads and writes. For the load model in Figure 9.16, Perform3 is not a good file emulation tool since it only does cached I/O, and the three-workstation load model does not include files that would typically be cached. Perform3 would work better for database I/O emulation where the data is often cached and may actually be read as small records of hundreds rather than thousands of bytes.

Ziff-Davis' (ZD) Server Benchmarks

Since the internetwork test model is primarily workstation to file server I/O, these utilities can be used to emulate appropriate file activity. ZD developed these tests to measure server and client-server performance, but they can be also used to create network activity to measure the internetwork. Measuring response time between the requester and responder effectively measures the throughput and reliability of the internetwork links.

ZD's Server Benchmarks include two test suites. NetBench emulates typical file I/O between a workstation and server. ServerBench emulates I/O in a client-server environment where transactions rather than complete files are transferred between the workstation and server.

NetBench provides the following individual tests:

- disk mix: random read, random write, random read/write

- sequential read

- sequential write

- NIC test

ServerBench contains numerous individual tests that create transactions that are sent to the server. A client never sends a file to the server; it always sends a transaction. The individual tests include disk tests, a processor test, and network tests. ServerBench packages the transactions in a test mix and places the test mix in a test suite. A test suite can contain more than one mix.

ServerBench reports its results in terms of TPS, or transactions per second. ServerBench only measures completed transactions. It calculates a transaction as the amount of time it takes for a client to issue a request and get a response back from the server.

ServerBench provides the following tests:

- **One processor test:** This test would not be used for internetwork testing.

A) QBASIC Program: LDGEN.BAS

```
CLS
DIM ARRAY(100) AS STRING
DIM IFILES(3) AS STRING
DIM LENGTH(3) AS INTEGER
OPEN "C:\TEMP\AUDIT_LG" FOR OUTPUT AS #10
INPUT "Enter Test Id:";ID$
INPUT "ENTER TEST FILE ID1"; IFILES(1)
INPUT "ENTER LENGTH OF RECORD TO READ";LENGTH(1)
INPUT "ENTER TEST FILE ID2"; IFILES(2)
INPUT "ENTER LENGTH OF RECORD TO READ";LENGTH(2)
INPUT "ENTER TEST FILE ID3"; IFILES(3)
INPUT "ENTER LENGTH OF RECORD TO READ";LENGTH(3)
WRITE #10, IFILES(1), IFILES(2), IFILES(3)
WRITE #10 LENGTH(1), LENGTH(2), LENGTH(3)
WRITE #10, "TEST ID=", ID$
a%=1
DO
  B%=a%+3
  C%=1
  WRITE #10, "START", a%, TIME$
  DO
    OPEN IFILES(a%) FOR INPUT AS #1
    OPEN "C:\TEMP\TEMP" FOR OUTPUT AS #2
    DO
      L%=LENGTH(a%)
      ARRAY$=INPUT$(L%,#1)
      WRITE #2, ARRAY$
    LOOP UNTIL EOF(1)
    CLOSE #1
    CLOSE #2
    C%-C%+1
  LOOP UNTIL C%=11
  WRITE #10, "COMPLETE", a%, TIME$
  a%=a%+1
LOOP UNTIL a%=4
CLOSE
PRINT "TEST COMPLETE", ID$
END
```

B) Screen Input:

```
ENTER TEST FILE  ID1
C:\TEMP\F1
ENTER LENGTH OF RECORD TO READ
10
ENTER TEST FILE  ID1
C:\TEMP\F2
ENTER LENGTH OF RECORD TO READ
40
ENTER TEST FILE  ID1
C:\TEMP\F3
ENTER LENGTH OF RECORD TO READ
1
```

C) Audit Log

```
"C:\TEMP\F1","C:\TEMP\F2","C:\TEMP\F3"
10,40,1
"TEST ID=","1"
"START",1,"15:29:05"
"COMPLETE",1,"15:29:06"
"START",2,"15:29:06"
"COMPLETE",2,"15:29:06"
"START",3,"15:29:06"
"COMPLETE",3,"15:29:06"
```

Figure 10.8   QBASIC program load script for Figure 9.16, workstation 1; includes the program, input parameters, and audit file of test results.

- **Five disk tests:** These tests can be used to create various traffic patterns between the client and server. The disk tests are sequential read and write, random read and write, and append.

- **Two network tests:** These generate the highest load, and stress the internetwork more than the disk tests.

NetBench could be used to model the loads for Figure 9.16 and for application testing. ServerBench would be more appropriate for a client-server environment, as discussed in Part III, Application and Presentation Layer Testing.

C or BASIC Programs

Another cost-effective alternative is to develop small programs in-house to generate file I/O. A C or BASIC program to create the file I/O discussed in the previous batch file example would not be much longer than the batch file, and would provide greater flexibility for varying block I/O sizes and traffic patterns, including bursty traffic, across the internetwork.

Figure 10.8A illustrates a simple BASIC program that generates file I/O similar to the previous batch file. The BASIC program is called LDGEN.BAS. It sequentially reads three files of varying block sizes until the end of file (EOF) is reached. Figure 10.8B shows the input to the program, which includes the input file name and the block size to read from the file. Figure 10.8C illustrates the audit file that records the start and stop times for the file I/O. In this example, the amount of data read was too small, typically 80 bytes, to generate usable test data. The start and stop times of some of the reads are within the same second, or the limit of accuracy of the time stamps.

Infrastructure: Throughput Testing

TEST MATRIX

Throughput and reliability are the predominate test objectives for the infrastructure. Throughput testing of the network infrastructure is conducted for subsystems, such as a router, and for internetwork configurations. Test Case 1 discusses subsystem throughput testing using emulated configurations and loads. Test Case 2 discusses internetwork throughput testing using emulated loads and emulated and real-world configurations.

TEST CASE 1: SUBSYSTEM THROUGHPUT TESTING

Subsystem throughput testing measures how the device performs under various port and feature configurations. It does not measure the impact on the device by other nodes on the network or internetwork.

Test Measurements

Throughput test measurements can be used to determine the following information about the device under test:

- maximum sustained throughput per segment

- aggregate sustained throughput for the device

- maximum throughput per segment

- maximum aggregate throughput for the device

- fairness of throughput across segments

- variances across test configurations

- variances across protocol configurations

- variances based on features

- packet or frame errors

- accuracy of device statistics versus analyzer statistics

Test Configurations

All test configurations are emulated. The configurations must represent the most critical or typical production network components. To determine which configurations to test, consider:

- Nodes that support a mix of media, such as an Ethernet segment and an ATM or FDDI connection, or a slow-speed WAN link. Testing experience has shown that buffering transmissions across such configurations often severely impacts throughput.

- Nodes that support more than two protocols. Since each protocol option is implemented in a different software module, one protocol will often perform better than another. When multiple protocols are supported, the subsystem's overall performance is often impacted.

- Nodes that have a maximum number of segments, such as a fully configured switch or hub. The backplane or switching fabric and buffering can impact throughput and fairness algorithms across the segments.

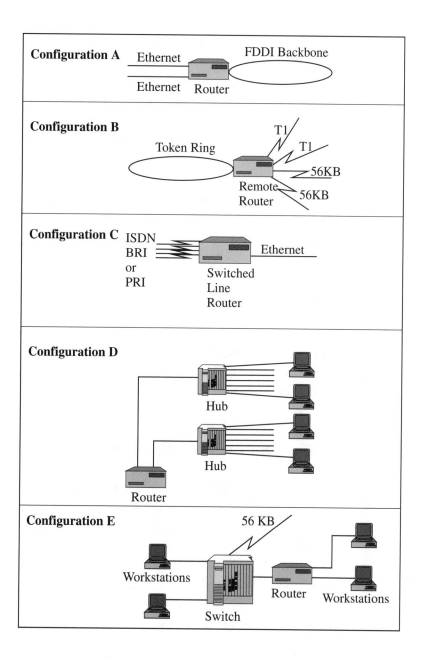

Figure 11.1 Examples of throughput test configurations for routers, hubs, and switches.

One or two segments can get in "resonance" and become favored ports on the device.

Figure 11.1 shows typical subsystem configurations that are tested for a facility's backbone interconnection, remote office access, and switched network configuration. Use these as a guide, but define specific test configurations that emulate your unique network topology.

Before starting the test project be sure to start a test journal, document the test configuration hardware and software, and create data reduction spreadsheets as described in Chapter 6.

Load Model

Refer to the section in Chapter 9 entitled Developing the Load to create the test scripts for this test. Depending on the type of load generator (Refer to Chapter 10 for details on several possible alternatives), develop the load generator scripts for the typical case and worst case load models.

Test Execution and Data Collection

Run the typical case load first, then repeat the steps for the worse case load. Record all test data in the spreadsheet shown in Figure 11.2. The spreadsheet measurements are in packets per second (PPS). Throughput in kilobytes per second (KBps) or kilobits per second (Kbps) is easier for some people to understand and is typically how switches and hubs are measured. To translate PPS into KBps or Kbps, use the following formulas:

KBps = PPS * packet size in bytes

Kbps = PPS * packet size in bytes * 8 (for 8 bits per byte)

Thus, 512-byte packets transmitted at 1,000 PPS generate 4,096,000 bits, 4,096 Kbps, or 512 KBps load.

Cell definitions in the Figure 11.2 spreadsheet are:

cell A = total packets per second (PPS) transmitted on the source segment as defined by the load model. The packet destinations will be one or more of the destination segments, depending on the destination address in each of the packets.

cell B = expected PPS capture rate on the destination segment based on the load model. If all packets are received, then the unit under test forwarded all transmitted packets from the source segment to the targeted destination segment.

cell C = actual PPS measured on the destination segment. This represents what the unit under test forwarded from the source to the destination segment.

cell D = loss is the number of packets per second not forwarded by the unit under test from a source to a destination segment. $D = B - C$. Cell D is zero if all packets are successfully forwarded.

cell E = sum of the measured PPS on each destination segment from the specified source segment. $E = SUM(Cs)$. If the unit under test is forwarding all the packets that it is receiving from the source segment, cell E will equal cell A (within a margin of error of 4 percent).

cell F = loss through the device under test for the specified source segment. $F = A - E$.

cell G = percent PPS loss. $G = F/A$.

cell H = aggregate PPS transmitted from all the source segments to the unit under test based on the load model. $H = SUM(As)$. This represents the total load on the unit under test.

Run ID

Run 1

Segment	Generated PPS	Segment	Expected PPS	Actual PPS	Loss	Segment	Expected PPS	Actual PPS	Loss	Throughput PPS	Total Loss	% PPS Loss
	Source		Destination							Summary		
1	(A)	2	(B)	(C)	(D)	3				(E)	(F)	(G)
2		1				3						
3		1				2						
Aggregate Input	(H)											
Aggregate Output			(I)	(J)	(K)					(L)	(M)	(N)

Run 2

Segment	PPS	Segment	Expected PPS	Actual PPS	Loss	Segment	Expected PPS	Actual PPS	Loss	Throughput PPS	PPS Loss	%PPS Loss
	Source		Destination							Summary		
1	(A)	2	(B)	(C)	(D)	3				(E)	(F)	(G)
2		1				3						
3		1				2						
Aggregate Input	(H)											
Aggregate Output			(I)	(J)	(K)					(L)	(M)	(N)

Run 3

Segment	PPS	Segment	Expected PPS	Actual PPS	Loss	Segment	Expected PPS	Actual PPS	Loss	Throughput PPS	PPS Loss	%PPS Loss
	Source		Destination							Summary		
1	(A)	2	(B)	(C)	(D)	3				(E)	(F)	(G)
2		1				3						
3		1				2						
Aggregate Input	(H)											
Aggregate Output			(I)	(J)	(K)					(L)	(M)	(N)

Figure 11.2   Data reduction spreadsheet for subsystem throughput testing.

cell I = aggregate expected PPS capture rate on the destination segment from load transmitted on all the source segments based on the load model. I = SUM(Bs).

cell J = aggregate actual PPS measured on a destination segment from load transmitted on all the source segments. J = SUM(Cs). This represents what the unit under test forwarded from all source segments to a specific destination segment.

Run ID
Run 1

	Source		Destination								Summary		
Segment	Generated PPS	Segment	Expected PPS	Actual PPS	Loss	Segment	Expected PPS	Actual PPS	Loss		Throughput PPS	PPS Loss	% PPS Loss
1-IP	(A)	2	(B)	(C)	(D)	3					(E)	(F)	(G)
1-IPX													
1-DecNet													
2-IP		1				3							
2-IPX													
2-DecNet													
3-IP		1				2							
3-IPX													
3-Decnet													
Aggregate Input	(H)												
Aggregate Output			(I)	(J)	(K)						(L)	(M)	(N)

Figure 11.3 Spreadsheet for measuring throughput contribution by protocol, packet size, or type.

cell K = loss per destination segment is the number of packets per second not forwarded by the unit under test from all source segments to a specific destination segment. K = I - J.

cell L = aggregate sum of the measured PPS across all destination segments. L = SUM(Js). If the unit under test is forwarding all the packets that it is receiving from the source segments, cell L will equal cell H (within a margin of error of 4 percent).

cell M = aggregate loss through the device under test. This is the difference between the sum of all packets transmitted and the sum of all packets measured across the destination segments. M = H - L.

cell N = percent PPS aggregate loss. N = M/H.

Since most tests include bidirectional traffic, each segment is both a source and destination segment in the spreadsheet. The spreadsheet can be refined to show the contribution of packets by each protocol or packet size by expanding the rows to include data for each protocol type or packet size in the test. Figure 11.3 illustrates how this would look for up to three protocols or packet sizes.

Run ID 1

Source		Destination								Summary		
Segment	Generated PPS	Segment	Expected PPS	Actual PPS	Loss	Segment	Expected PPS	Actual PPS	Loss	Throughput PPS	Total Loss	% PPS Loss
X	5000	Y	2000			Z	3000			0		0
Y	6000	X	3150			Z	2850			0		0
Z	2000	X	750			Y	1225			0		0
Aggregate Input	13000											
Aggregate Output			5900				7075					0

Run ID 2

Source		Destination								Summary		
Segment	Generated PPS	Segment	Expected PPS	Actual PPS	Loss	Segment	Expected PPS	Actual PPS	Loss	Throughput PPS	Total Loss	% PPS Loss
X	5000	Y	2000			Z	3000			0		0
Y	6000	X	3150			Z	2850			0		0
Z	2000	X	750			Y	1225			0		0
Aggregate Input	13000											
Aggregate Output			5900				7075					0

Run ID 3

Source		Destination								Summary		
Segment	Generated PPS	Segment	Expected PPS	Actual PPS	Loss	Segment	Expected PPS	Actual PPS	Loss	Throughput PPS	Total Loss	% PPS Loss
X	5000	Y	2000			Z	3000			0		0
Y	6000	X	3150			Z	2850			0		0
Z	2000	X	750			Y	1225			0		0
Aggregate Input	13000											
Aggregate Output			5900				7075					0

Figure 11.4   Data reduction spreadsheet prior to first test run.

The test sequence is:

1. Start the load generators. Verify that the test configuration is working properly, that the load generators can attain the target source PPS rates, and that packets are being routed to their correct segments using the test monitors. Chapter 10 describes how to synchronize the generators and monitors.

2. Set up a spreadsheet for the first test load and fill in the source and expected PPS rates in the spreadsheet, as shown in Figure 11.4.

3. Shut down and restart the load generators using the typical case load. Run the test for 30 seconds and record for each segment the total packets

or PPS sent and received. If total packets are recorded, divide the number by 30 to get PPS. After each test, enter the results into the data reduction spreadsheet. Enter the measured rates for destination segments in C cells. Repeat the test three times to ensure that the results are reproducible. Based on the source and destination measured rates, the spreadsheet calculates other cell values. After the third run, compare the PPS numbers in the M cells. If the values differ by more than 4 percent across the three runs, the test configuration is not generating reproducible results. Determine why before proceeding with additional tests. See Test Configuration Problem Resolution Tips at the end of Chapter 9.

4. Analyze the test measurements.

- **No dropped packets:** If there are no dropped packets (N is less than 4 percent, typically the margin of error allowed between test runs), increase the source packet rate by 5 percent on each load generator, duplicate the spreadsheets, enter the new expected PPS, and repeat steps 2 through 4 until dropped packets occur on the segments. *The highest rate prior to measuring dropped packets determines the sustained throughput rate for the device within 5 percent of the actual number.* For a finer measurement, start at the sustained throughput rate and repeat this process increasing the load by 2 percent until dropped packets occur. The highest rate prior to the test measuring dropped packets determines the new sustained throughput rate for the device.

- **Dropped packets:** If there are dropped packets (N is greater than 4 percent across the three runs, or the results are mixed and average greater than 4 percent), decrease the packet rate by 5 percent, duplicate the spreadsheets, enter the new expected PPS, and repeat steps 2 through 4 until dropped packets do not occur on the segments. *The first test run in which no dropped packets are measured determines the sustained throughput rate for the device.* For a finer measurement, start at the sustained throughput rate and repeat this process increasing the load by 2 percent until dropped packets occur. The highest rate prior to the test measuring dropped packets determines the new sustained throughput rate for the device.

5. Shut down and restart all the load generators using the worse case packet rate or the sustained throughput rate, whichever is higher, from step 4. Run the test for 30 seconds and record for each segment the total packets received. Repeat the test three times to ensure that the results are reproducible.

6. Analyze test measurements. If the test does not fail, increase the packet rate by 5 percent and repeat step 5 until the test fails. The highest rate prior to the test failing determines the maximum throughput rate for the device. To get a finer measurement, start at the maximum throughput rate and repeat this process increasing the load by 2 percent until the test fails. The highest rate prior to the test failing determines the new maximum throughput rate for the device.

A test failure has occurred when one or more of the following conditions occur:

•   **Aggregate throughput decreases:** The aggregate throughput decreases from the previous test run. A decrease in the aggregate throughput signifies that the device under test is experiencing congestion severe enough to create a performance bottleneck. Note: Initially, the aggregate throughput may continue to increase even as dropped packets increase. At some point, the volume of dropped packets will cause a decrease in the aggregate throughput.

•   **Throughput fairness problem:** Throughput on one or more segments decreases by greater than 20 percent from the previous test run.

•   **Subsystem failure:** The device under test fails to forward packets to all the segments or crashes during the test.

Some load generators, specifically PowerBits and the W&G DA30, automate several of the steps just outlined. The process remains the same, but

Run ID

Source		Destination								Summary		
Segment	PPS	Segment	Expected PPS	Actual PPS	Loss	Segment	Expected PPS	Actual PPS	Loss	Throughput PPS	Total Loss	% PPS Loss
X	5000	Y	2000	2000	0	Z	3000	3000	0	5000	0	0.000
Y	6000	X	3150	3100	50	Z	2850	2800	50	5900	100	0.017
Z	2000	X	750	750	0	Y	1225	1225	0	1975	25	0.013
Aggregate Input	13000											
Aggregate Output				5900	5850	50		7075	7025	50	12875	125	0.010

Figure 11.5   Example of sustained throughput.

some of the monitoring and load incrementing and decrementing is done by the load generator, which accelerates the test process.

Data Interpretation

As each test case is run, enter results in the data reduction spreadsheet, which calculates throughput per segment, aggregate throughput, and packet loss. This information is required to determine the next test case input packet rate as described previously under Test Execution and Data collection steps. The spreadsheet data can be used to quickly determine various test results, as illustrated in the following figures.

Figure 11.5 shows a test where aggregate input and output are within 1 percent (note the highlighted cells). The unit under test was able to sustain

Run ID

Source		Destination								Summary		
Segment	PPS	Segment	Expected PPS	Actual PPS	Loss	Segment	Expected PPS	Actual PPS	Loss	Throughput PPS	Total Loss	% PPS Loss
X	6538	Y	2615	2583	32	Z	3923	3920	3	6503	35	0.005
Y	7846	X	4119	4100	19	Z	3727	3725	2	7825	21	0.003
Z	2616	X	981	979	2	Y	1635	1632	3	2611	5	0.002
Aggregate Input	17000											
Aggregate Output				7715	7662	53		9285	9277	8	16939	61	0.004

Figure 11.6   Example of maximum sustained throughput.

Run ID

Source		Destination								Summary		
Segment	PPS	Segment	Expected PPS	Actual PPS	Loss	Segment	Expected PPS	Actual PPS	Loss	Throughput PPS	Total Loss	% PPS Loss
X	7623	Y	3049	3000	49	Z	4574	4570	4	7570	53	0.007
Y	9148	X	4803	4755	48	Z	4345	3500	845	8255	893	0.100
Z	3029	X	1136	1120	16	Y	1893	1800	93	2920	109	0.036
Aggregate Input	19800											
Aggregate Output			8988	8875	113		10812	9870	942	18745	1055	0.053

Figure 11.7   Example of maximum throughput.

forwarding of all received packets. However, this does not represent the maximum sustained throughput capacity of the unit.

Figure 11.6 shows that the maximum sustained throughput is reached at 17,500 PPS for the device. Testing at higher source rates showed that the unit was not able to sustain forwarding all packets. Figure 11.7 shows a higher maximum throughput, though a much higher number of packets are dropped (note the highlighted cells). Since most protocols automatically retransmit dropped packets, data integrity is maintained. This type of performance is typical of most routers.

If the number of dropped packets becomes too large, throughput degradation occurs, as shown in Figure 11.8. Although the input rate is higher in Figure 11.8 than in Figure 11.7, the throughput in Figure 11.8 is lower (note the highlighted cells), which indicates that performance is degrading under the heavier load. This can become a rapidly accelerating downward spiral of

Run ID

Source		Destination								Summary		
Segment	PPS	Segment	Expected PPS	Actual PPS	Loss	Segment	Expected PPS	Actual PPS	Loss	Throughput PPS	Total Loss	% PPS Loss
X	8004	Y	3201	2950	251	Z	4803	4500	303	7450	554	0.070
Y	9605	X	5043	4145	898	Z	4562	4101	461	8246	1359	0.141
Z	3180	X	1193	800	393	Y	1988	1805	183	2605	575	0.181
Aggregate Input	20789											
Aggregate Output			9437	7895	1542		11353	10406	947	18301	2488	0.120

Figure 11.8   Example of degraded throughput because of excessive dropped packets.

Run ID

	Source			Destination							Summary		
	Segment	PPS	Segment	Expected PPS	Actual PPS	Loss	Segment	Expected PPS	Actual PPS	Loss		Throughput PPS	Total Loss	% PPS Loss
	X	7623	Y	3049	3000	49	Z	4574	4570	4		7570	53	0.007
	Y	9148	X	4803	4755	48	Z	4345	3500	845		8255	893	0.100
	Z	3029	X	1136	1120	16	Y	1893	1800	93		2920	109	0.036
Aggregate Input		19800												
Aggregate Output				8988	8875	113		10812	9870	942		18745	1055	0.053

Figure 11.9 Example of a problem in the fairness algorithm across multiple segments.

performance degradation as more retransmissions cause higher load and, subsequently, more dropped packets.

Figure 11.9 is an example of an easily misleading test result. The maximum throughput increased from the previous test in Figure 11.7. However, one destination segment, Y, is not being handled fairly by the device (note the highlighted cell), and it exhibits a significant performance degradation, over 280 percent, from the previous test. Therefore, test failure condition number two

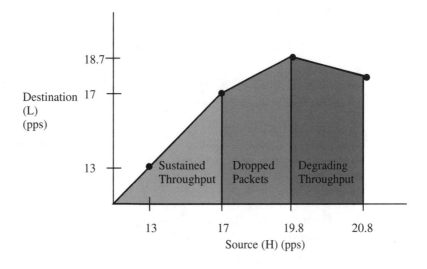

Figure 11.10 Aggregate throughput characterization of the device under test.

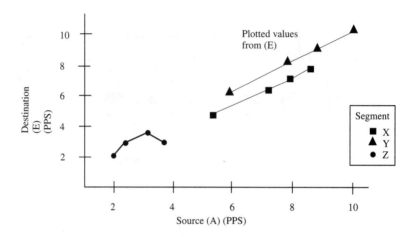

Figure 11.11   Throughput characterization of individual segment traffic.

applies, and this cannot be considered a successful test. The results should not be used to determine maximum throughput. The results in Figure 11.9 may be the effect of a:

- bad configuration

- problem in the segment fairness algorithm of the device under test

- problem with a specific protocol or protocol combination

The data collection and reduction spreadsheets provide too much detail for presenting test results. Graphs can be used to communicate the same information in a more easily understood form. Using the previous examples, the following figures illustrate two test conclusions presented in graphical format.

Figure 11.10 shows the aggregate sustained throughput, aggregate maximum throughput, and throughput degradation as source loads increase. This data is from cells H and L in Figures 11.5, 11.6, 11.7, and 11.8. These results summarize performance of the unit and provide an aggregate throughput threshold for monitoring the device on the production network.

Figure 11.11 provides similar information to Figure 11.10, but on a segment-by-segment basis. This is important when traffic on one segment is expected to increase at a higher rate than on the other segments. It is also a visual representation of the relative performance and degradation across segments. Look at the slope of each curve as performance begins to degrade to determine which degrades more quickly. This data is from cells A and E in Figures 11.5, 11.6, 11.7, and 11.8.

The data collection and reduction spreadsheets can be expanded to record source and destination data by protocol, packet type, or packet size to do more detailed analysis as required for a particular project. The same basic test process, data collection, and interpretation principles apply.

Testing Feature Impact

Test scenarios that measure the impact on throughput when additional features or other loads are activated include:

- Testing with address or packet type filtering enabled.

- Testing with data compression, encryption, or protocol encapsulation enabled.

- Testing with additional scripts that represent route table updates.

This testing is important when comparing competitive products, planning for network segmentation or firewalls, determining the effect of a specific feature on the devices' throughput capacity, and collecting nodal data for simulation studies.

Feature testing requires a baseline test and a feature test. Follow the preceding procedures to test the device without the feature enabled. Next, enable, the feature and retest the device; for example, to measure the impact on protocol encapsulation, run two test series, one series with protocol encapsulation enabled and another with it disabled. Compare the throughput results to determine the change in performance caused by protocol encapsulation.

Analyze the test runs for differences in segment and aggregate throughput and fairness across the segments. Also monitor the tests to verify that the filtering, encryption, encapsulation, and other features are working correctly. Usually, failures occur because of a clog (no packets are forwarded) or a rip (incorrect packets are forwarded) in the feature under test. Failures often appear at medium to high loads and become worse as the load increases.

TEST CASE 2: INTERNETWORK THROUGHPUT TESTING

Internetwork throughput testing measures throughput across multiple devices and connecting links. This is important when the devices have very different performance capability, or when throughput is determined by the devices' ability to expand bandwidth on demand, such as for switched line routers or communication gateways. Internetwork testing does not attempt to measure the same level of isolation as subsystem testing (PPS by source, destination, packet size, and protocol). Its objective is to measure point-to-point throughput in kilobytes per second (KBps).

Test Measurements

Throughput test measurements can be used to determine the following information about the device under test:

- maximum throughput across the internetwork based on the load model

- variance across test configurations

- variance across protocols or configuration options

Test Configurations

All test loads are emulated. Test configurations can be emulated, or real-world configurations can be used for some testing. A few workstations and a server can be added to the production network for the test. Using the production network as background load, the test can be conducted on a real-world configuration. When running the test, increase the load incrementally by adding additional requesters. Always analyze the previous test impact (degradation) on the production network before increasing load. Stop the test before the production

Configuration A

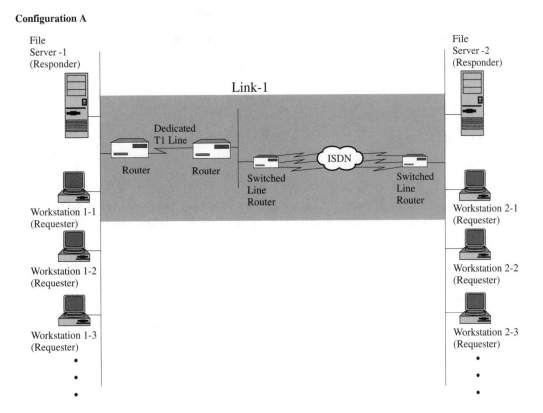

Figure 11.12A   Example of internetwork throughput test.

Configuration B

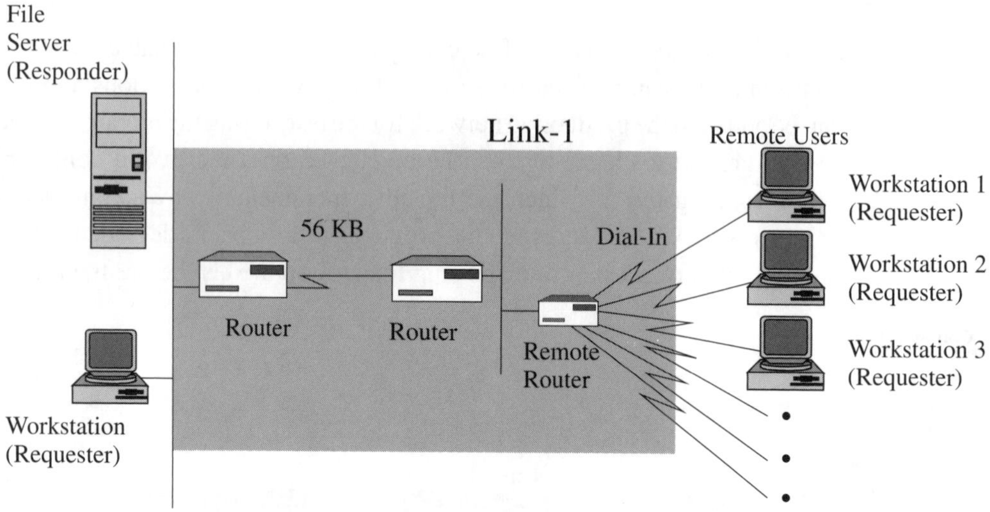

Figure 11.12*B*   Example of internetwork throughput test.

network degradation becomes intolerable, as discussed shortly.   This test provides both throughput results for the new load and a measure of the production network degradation that will be caused by the new loads.

The test configurations must represent the most critical or typical production network configurations.   To determine which configurations to test, consider:

- Paths that have highly disparate segments, such as an Ethernet segment and an ATM or FDDI connection or a slow-speed WAN link.   Testing experience has shown that throughput across such paths is highly dependent on protocols and traffic pattern.

- Paths where bandwidth on demand determines effective throughput capacity. The algorithms for acquiring and relinquishing bandwidth will be key to the effective throughput rate across the internetwork.

- Paths or responders that are under constant, heavy load.

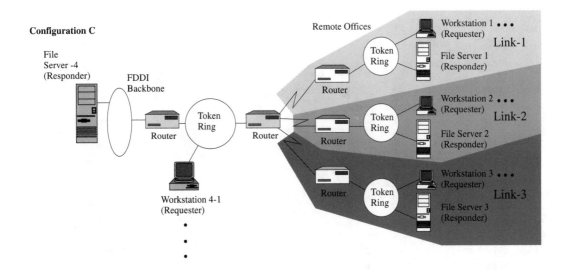

Figure 11.12C Example of internetwork throughput test.

Internetwork testing measures point-to-point throughput. It does not attempt to isolate individual performance of connecting nodes. Figures 11.12A, B, and C show typical configurations that could be tested for a switched network, remote access server at a regional office, and regional office connections to corporate headquarters. This testing uses multiple load generators (workstation requesters) and responders (file servers) to create bidirectional traffic.

Internetwork testing can become very complex by introducing too many requesters and responders on intermediate segments, as shown in Figure 11.13. Such configurations make it difficult to coordinate the data collection across all segments and to interpret the cause of performance changes.

Rather than complicating the test configuration, as in Figure 11.13, it is recommended that subsystem tests and small internetwork configurations be used to isolate and analyze individual segment and nodal throughput, as shown in Figure 11.14. During the internetwork test, individual segments can be monitored

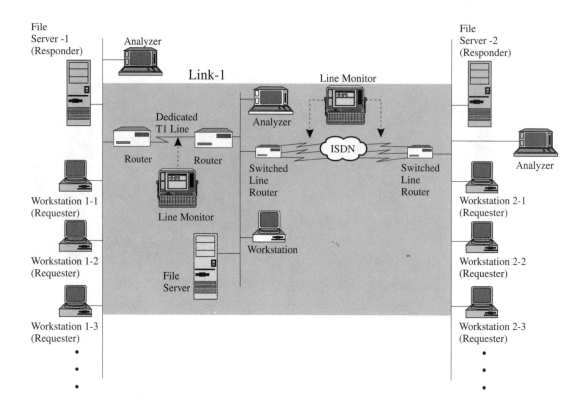

Figure 11.13 Internetwork throughput test configurations with intermediate segment requesters and responders are to complex to analyze.

and trace data used to create a load model for the subsystem test configurations shown in Figure 11.14. This approach allows the individual subsystems to be more easily analyzed without the effect of other internetwork components.

Before starting the test project, start a test journal, document the test configuration hardware and software, and create data reduction spreadsheets as described in Chapter 6.

Configuration A

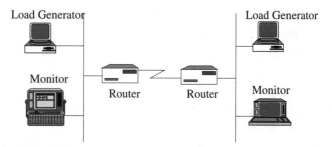

Configuration B

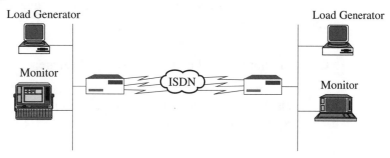

Figure 11.14   Preferred method of isolating individual internetwork segment and node throughput.

Load Model

The load model for internetwork testing is very different from the one used for subsystem testing. The primary differences are:

- Traffic patterns are collected at the test end points rather than for individual segments.

- The load generation uses file I/O rather than packet streams.

Refer to the section Internetwork File I/O Model in Chapter 9 to create the test scripts for this test. Depending on the type of load generator (refer to Chapter 10 for details on several possible alternatives), develop the load generator scripts for the load model.

Test Execution and Data Collection

Use the sample data collection and reduction spreadsheet shown in Figure 11.15. The spreadsheet is formatted for one link, one workstation (requester) on each segment, and one file server (responder) on each segment from Figure 11.12 test configuration A.

Cell definitions in the Figure 11.15 spreadsheet are:

cell A = total bytes to be transferred across the internetwork from the requester to the responder.

Run ID

		Requester					Test Results		
	ID	Load Script	Kbytes Transferred	Responder ID	Link ID		Transfer Time (sec)	Throughput KBps	Aggregate KBps
Run 1			(A)				(B)	(C)	
									(D)
Run 2									
Run 3									

Figure 11.15 Data collection and reduction spreadsheets for internetwork throughput testing across one link.

Run ID

Run 1

	Requester					Test Results		
	ID	Load Script	Kbytes Transferred	Responder ID	Link ID	Transfer Time (sec)	Throughput KBps	Aggregate KBps
Link 1	Stn-1			FS-4	Link1			
	Stn-4			FS-1	Link1			
Link 2	Stn-2			FS-4	Link2			
	Stn-4			FS-2	Link2			
Link 3	Stn-3			FS-4	Link3			
	Stn-4			FS-3	Link3			
Aggregate								
Internet TP								

Run 2

	Requester					Test Results		
	ID	Load Script	Kbytes Transferred	Responder ID	Link ID	Transfer Time (sec)	Throughput KBps	Aggregate KBps
Link 1	Stn-1			FS-4	Link1			
	Stn-4			FS-1	Link1			
Link 2	Stn-2			FS-4	Link2			
	Stn-4			FS-2	Link2			
Link 3	Stn-3			FS-4	Link3			
	Stn-4			FS-3	Link3			
Aggregate								
Internet TP								

Run 3

	Requester					Test Results		
	ID	Load Script	Kbytes Transferred	Responder ID	Link ID	Transfer Time (sec)	Throughput KBps	Aggregate KBps
Link 1	Stn-1			FS-4	Link1			
	Stn-4			FS-1	Link1			
Link 2	Stn-2			FS-4	Link2			
	Stn-4			FS-2	Link2			
Link 3	Stn-3			FS-4	Link3			
	Stn-4			FS-3	Link3			
Aggregate								
Internet TP								

Figure 11.16 Data collection and reduction spreadsheet for internetwork throughput testing across multiple links.

cell B = time for the transfer in seconds.

cell C = calculated throughput in KBps between one requester and responder. C = A/B.

cell D = aggregate throughput across the link. D = SUM(Cs).

A complete test series would consist of multiple runs where the number of requesters is increased to generate a load versus throughput curve. A spreadsheet for runs of 2, 4, and 8 requesters can be easily formatted by increasing the number of rows in Figure 11.15, so that there is one row per run for each requester and responder session. If the test configuration has more links or requesters, expand the number of row groups in the spreadsheet. Figure 11.16 illustrates how the spreadsheet would expand for configuration C, in Figure 11.12.

The test sequence is:

1. Start the load generators. Verify that the test configuration is working properly, that the load generators can access the file server, and that files are being read from the correct servers. Chapter 10 describes how to synchronize the load generators.

Run ID

	Requester					Test Results		
	ID	Load Script	Kbytes Transferred	Responder ID	Link ID	Transfer Time (sec)	Throughput KBps	Aggregate KBps
Run 1	Stn-1	L01PGE.SCR	100000	FS-2	T1-ISDN	0	0	
	Stn-2	L02PGE.SCR	120000	FS-1	T1-ISDN	0	0	
								0
Run 2	Stn-1	L01PGE.SCR	100000	FS-2	T1-ISDN	0	0	
	Stn-2	L02PGE.SCR	120000	FS-1	T1-ISDN	0	0	
								0
Run 3	Stn-1	L01PGE.SCR	100000	FS-2	T1-ISDN	0	0	
	Stn-2	L02PGE.SCR	120000	FS-1	T1-ISDN	0	0	
								0

Figure 11.17   Data reduction spreadsheet prior to first test run for Figure 11.12 configuration A.

Run ID

	Requestor					Test Results		
ID	Load Script	Kbytes Transferred	Responder ID	Link ID	Transfer Time (sec)	Throughput KBps	Aggregate KBps	
Run 1	Stn-1	L01PGE.SCR	10000	FS-2	T1-ISDN	174	57.471	
	Stn-2	L02PGE.SCR	12000	FS-1	T1-ISDN	210	57.143	
								114.614
Run 2	Stn-1	L01PGE.SCR	10000	FS-2	T1-ISDN	176	56.818	
	Stn-2	L02PGE.SCR	12000	FS-1	T1-ISDN	206	58.252	
								115.071
Run 3	Stn-1	L01PGE.SCR	10000	FS-2	T1-ISDN	174.5	57.307	
	Stn-2	L02PGE.SCR	12000	FS-1	T1-ISDN	208.4	57.582	
								114.889

Figure 11.18 Comparing runs to determine reproducibility of test results.

2. Set up a spreadsheet for the first test series and fill in the Run ID, Test Script ID, Load Script ID per Requester, Link IDs, and bytes transferred, as shown in Figure 11.17.

3. Shut down and restart the load generators for the first test load. Run the test and record the time it takes to transfer the files across the internetwork for each requester. Enter the time for the data transfer into cell B in the data reduction spreadsheet. Based on the KBps transferred and the transfer time, the spreadsheet calculates throughput from point to point and aggregate throughput per link, as shown in Figure 11.18. Figure 11.18 shows the calculated values for three runs of a single requester at each end point. After the third run, compare the throughput (cell D) for the three runs.

4. In this test, the margin of error was .003 percent. If the values differ by more than 4 percent across the three runs, the test configuration is not generating reproducible results, which means there is a problem in the configuration, such as a bad connection, or that the internetwork configuration does not provide consistent times from run to run. Determine the cause before proceeding with additional tests. See Test Configuration Problem Resolution Tips at the end of Chapter 9.

5. Increase the number of requesters and repeat step 3. Graph or visually compare the load versus throughput to determine maximum throughput, as discussed in the Data Interpretation section.

6. Repeat steps 3 and 4 for additional test loads.

There are no commercially available integrated tools to assist in internetwork throughput testing. If this testing is done infrequently, the manual process works well. However, for those who plan on doing extensive testing, many of the test procedures, data capture, and data reduction discussed herein can be automated through batch files, simple programs, and spreadsheet macros developed in-house.

Data Interpretation

As each test case is run, results should be entered into the data reduction spreadsheet. The spreadsheet calculates throughput from point to point and aggregate throughput per link. Data interpretation charts the results as the number of requesters is increased, and compares results from run to run as the load conditions are changed.

To reiterate what was discussed in Chapter 9, throughput results will be influenced by four factors:

- File size used for the transfer.

- NOS and protocol.

- Load on the responder, typically the file server.

- Ratio of bidirectional traffic. Results will be affected by the fact that the traffic is evenly distributed as compared to a unidirectional flow.

Analysis is typically done for the following test combinations:

- unidirectional traffic versus bidirectional traffic

- various file sizes—small, medium, large, very large

- small files in one direction (I/O requests) and large files in the other (file downloads)

- random, bursty traffic patterns versus continuous uniform traffic patterns

The closer the model reflects the production loads, the more relevant the test results. The following figures illustrate how these comparisons may look graphically.

Figure 11.19 illustrates how throughput is influenced by the number of

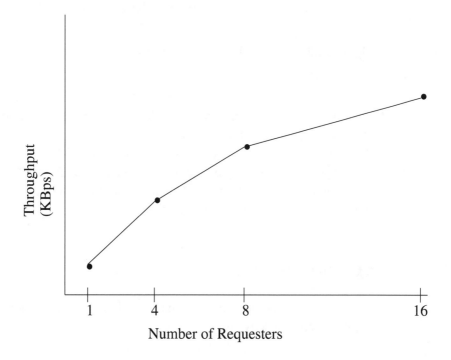

Figure 11.19 Throughput based on load (number of requesters).

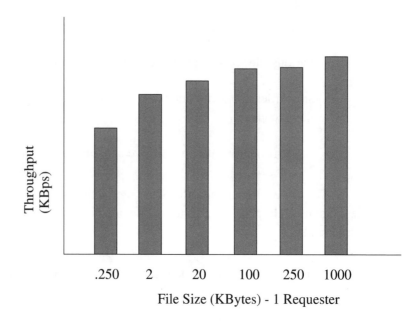

Figure 11.20   Throughput influenced by file size.

requesters. A decreasing slope to the curve indicates that throughput per requester decreases as more requesters are added. Figure 11.20 illustrates how throughput is influenced by file size. Larger file I/O often results in higher throughput. Figure 11.21 shows the possible effect on performance of unidirectional versus bidirectional traffic flow. Unidirectional flow represents best case, while bidirectional represents real-world activity.

Testing Other Impacts

Test scenarios that measure the impact on throughput when additional features or other loads are active may include:

- Testing with data compression, encryption, or protocol encapsulation enabled across one or more segments in the point-to-point link.

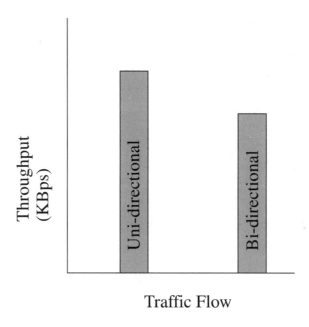

Figure 11.21   Throughput influenced by traffic flow.

- Testing with scripts that add more loads to one or more of the internetwork components.

- Testing with different line speeds or multiple paths.

- Tests that add local traffic to the responder (file server).

This testing requires a baseline test and an impact test. First test the internetwork throughput without the change. Next retest with the change implemented. For example, to measure the impact on throughput when additional load is applied to the file server, run tests with and without the additional file server load. Compare the throughput results to determine the change in performance caused by the additional file server load.

Infrastructure: Reliability Testing

TEST MATRIX

Reliability testing forces the unit under test or the internetwork to handle in a compressed time period the activity it would normally experience over weeks, months, or years on a production network. The testing uses accelerated loading techniques to apply and maintain high load on the unit under test for prolonged periods of time (24 to 72 hours or more).

Reliability testing attempts to accelerate failure of the subsystem or internetwork caused by:

- **Cumulative errors:** These are the result of repeating an operation multiple times in a fashion that results in an error. A simple example would be a port requesting I/O buffers, but not always releasing the buffers back to the buffer pool when they are no longer needed. If this happened over a period of time, the subsystem would run out of available buffers for other ports.

- **Timing errors:** These errors are caused by two time-dependent operations that occur out of sequence or without the proper delay. Typically, the problem is manifested when the system becomes very busy and one operation is delayed or impacted relative to another. Example 6.1 in Chapter 6 is an excellent illustration of a timing problem.

- **Statistical errors:** In developing and testing a complex software system, it is virtually impossible to test and verify every possible path through the code. However, statistically, over time, every path will be traversed, either because of an error condition or a seldom-invoked sequence of events. Reliability testing increases the probability that a statistical error will occur.

Reliability testing of the network infrastructure can be conducted for a subsystem, such as a router, and an internetwork configuration using an emulated configuration and load. Test Case 1 discusses subsystem reliability testing. Test Case 2 discusses internetwork reliability testing.

TEST CASE 1: SUBSYSTEM RELIABILITY TESTING

Subsystem reliability testing measures how well the device maintains operation under various loads, port, and feature configurations. For a subsystem that can be configured with many different interface boards and software options, the reliability of the subsystem may vary significantly across different test configurations. It does not measure the impact on the device by other nodes on the network or internetwork.

Test Measurements

Reliability testing provides two key measurements:

- **Operational reliability:** Subsystem-sustained operation under sustained load.

- **Stressed reliability:** Subsystem-sustained operation under peak load.

The first measurement determines how reliable the subsystem is under a sustainable load where virtually all received packets are correctly forwarded to the destination segment(s). The second measurement determines how stable the subsystem is under peak loads. Figure 12.1 illustrates the differences between these two measurements. Operational reliability requires the system to be stable for a long time at medium to heavy loads. Under stressed reliability, subsystems almost always fail; it is the mode of failure and test duration that are important.

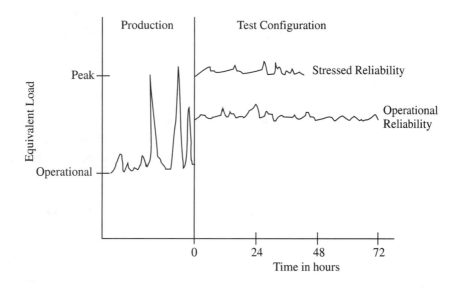

Figure 12.1 Operational versus stressed reliability.

Typical test results show:

- The subsystem cannot maintain the sustained load for long periods.

- The subsystem can maintain sustained loads, but fails under peak loads.

- The subsystem can maintain both sustained and peak loads.

- The subsystem encounters noncritical or recoverable errors under one or both loads.

Test Configurations

All test configurations are emulated. The test configurations must represent the most critical or typical production network configurations. In determining which configurations to test, consider:

- Nodes that support different media, such as an Ethernet segment, an ATM or FDDI connection, or a slow-speed WAN link. Testing experience has shown that load-induced reliability problems are common across such configurations.

- Nodes that have more than two protocols. Since each protocol is implemented in a different software module, one protocol may be less reliable than another, or multiple protocols may interact differently with the core operating software.

- Nodes that have a maximum number of segments, such as a fully configured switch or hub. Excessive load on the backplane or switching fabric can result in reliability issues.

The same configurations are used for throughput and reliability testing, therefore, refer to Figure 11.1 for typical subsystem configurations that can be tested for a facility's backbone interconnection, remote office access, and switched network configuration. Study these examples, then create specific test configurations that emulate your unique network topology.

It is best to have a load generator and load monitor on each segment, but a reliability test can be conducted similar to a throughput test by periodically moving the monitor from one segment to another and using the statistics-gathering capabilities of the subsystem to supplement the monitor. The Test Execution and Data Collection section discusses both approaches.

Before starting the test project, be sure to start a test journal, document the test configuration hardware and software, and create data reduction spreadsheets, as described in Chapter 6.

Load Model

The reliability test load model can be developed from either the production network baseline, as discussed in Chapter 9, or from Chapter 11 throughput test results.

Production Network Baseline Load Model

Using the production baseline load model, reliability testing measures the reliability of the subsystem under test relative to the current production system loading. It tells how the subsystem will work, if there are no changes in the network traffic or load. If throughput testing hasn't been conducted on the subsystem, this is the best load model to use. For example, if the production system baseline shows that the subsystem is forwarding an average aggregate 10,000 PPS, then this load would be used in the reliability test to determine the subsystem stability under sustained loading. For the maximum load, the baseline peak aggregate load would be used. Refer to the section in Chapter 9 on subsystem packet stream load modeling to create the test scripts for this test.

Depending on the type of load generator (refer to Chapter 10 for details on several possible alternatives), develop the load generator scripts for the sustained and peak load models.

Throughput Test Results Load Model

This approach measures the reliability of the subsystem under test relative to the sustained and maximum throughput of the subsystem based on throughput test results. It is a more conservative measurement than using the production network baseline load model, and automatically factors in network traffic growth.

For example, if the production system baseline shows that the subsystem is forwarding an average aggregate 10,000 PPS and throughput test results show that the subsystem aggregate sustained throughput is 14,400 PPS, the reliability test would use the higher PPS loading to determine the subsystem stability under sustained loading. For the maximum load, the maximum aggregate rate from the throughput test would be used. This approach places more load on the subsystem and, therefore, measures the subsystem's ability to reliably handle loads beyond the existing production network traffic.

As throughput tests measure subsystem capacity, this test effectively measures subsystem "stress capacity," as diagrammed in Figure 12.2. Operational and peak loads are from the production system baseline. Sustained

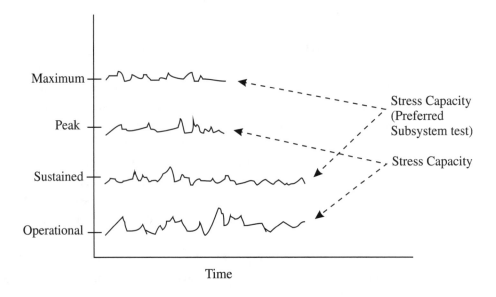

Figure 12.2   Measuring subsystem reliably, "stress capacity."

and maximum are from throughput tests. The difference between the reliability curves in Figure 12.2 indicate the capacity of the subsystem to reliably handle additional load.

This is the preferred method of reliability testing. If the subsystem fails this test, it can be re-tested using the production baseline loading to determine if the subsystem can handle existing network traffic. This testing provides a margin of comfort that the production baseline modeling does not. Another advantage of using this load model is that the load scripts can be reused from throughput testing.

Load Modeling Bursty Traffic

During a reliability test, the loading should not be constant, but bursty, as is typical of most network data transmission. This can be done using two techniques:

- Create a load script that varies the number of packets forwarded from the source to the destination segment, as discussed in Chapter 9.

- Vary the PPS rate or number of load generators concurrently running. This depends on the capabilities of the load generator(s) used and is discussed in Chapter 10.

Make sure that when using bursty traffic, the average PPS rate measured over a minute increment is equal to the load model average and peak PPS rates for operational and stressed reliability, respectively.

Test Execution and Data Collection

Depending on the load model chosen, run the average or sustained load first (lowest load), then repeat the steps for the peak or maximum loading (highest load). Record all test data in the spreadsheet shown in Figure 12.3. Reliability testing includes three key measurements:

test duration

throughput

detected errors

Cell definitions in the Figure 12.3 spreadsheet are:

cell A = run ID.

cell B = time and date when measurements are recorded.

cell C = segment ID. There should be one column for each segment connected to the unit under test. If only one segment is monitored at a time, enter the collected data into the appropriate segment column and leave the other columns blank.

Run ID	(A)
Time/Date	(B)
Segment	(C)
Load Script	(D)
Avg PPS Gen	(E)
Avg PPS Measured	(F)
Peak PPS	(G)
Total Throughput	(H)
Errors	
Critical	(I)
Noncritical	(J)

Figure 12.3   Data reduction spreadsheet for subsystem reliability testing.

cell D = load script ID.

cell E = PPS generation rate.

cell F = average PPS measured.

cell G = peak PPS measured.

cell H = total PPS measured.

cell I = critical errors. This can be expanded with additional rows of error types that are expected to occur or treated as a summary value as shown in the spreadsheet. Record the number of critical errors here and enter details for each in the problem log. For different media types, there will be different error types to record.

cell J = noncritical errors. This can be expanded with additional rows of key error types that are expected to occur or treated as a summary value. Record the number of noncritical errors here and enter details for each in the problem log. Typically, the number of dropped packets and so on for each segment or port are recorded.

Problem reports and the test journal should be used to describe error conditions in detail and to record resolutions, as appropriate. The test sequence is:

1. Start the load generators. Verify that the test configuration is working properly, that the load generators can attain the target source PPS rates, and that packets are being routed to their correct segments using the test monitors. Chapter 10 describes how to synchronize the generators and monitors.

2. Set up a spreadsheet for the first test load and fill in the Run ID, start date and time, segment IDs, and PPS rates in the spreadsheet, as shown in Figure 12.4.

Run ID	1		
Time/Date	12/1-9:00 am		
Segment	1	2	3
Load Script	L01PGE	L02PGE	L02PGE
Avg PPS Gen	5,000	7,200	8,250
Avg PPS Measured			
Peak PPS			
Total Throughput			
Errors			
Critical			
Noncritical			

Figure 12.4   Data reduction spreadsheet prior to first run.

3. Shut down and restart the load generators using the lowest load. Run the test for 72 hours.

4. Every 12 hours, record the following data:

    -   date and time of measurement

    -   total packets received by the monitors

Run ID	1		
Time/Date	12/1-9:00 am		
Segment	1	2	3
Load Script	L01PGE	L02PGE	L02PGE
Avg PPS Gen	5,000	7,200	8,250
Avg PPS Measured	4,878	7,250	8,277
Peak PPS	5,020	8,500	9,230
Total Throughput	100,592 MBps	150,793 MBps	259,005 MBps
Errors			
Critical	0	0	0
Noncritical	2	3	7

Time/Date	12/1-9:00 pm		
Segment	1	2	3
Load Script	L01PGE	L02PGE	L02PGE
Avg PPS Gen	5,000	7,200	8,250
Avg PPS Measured	4,900	7,133	8,270
Peak PPS	5,050	7,899	9,145
Total Throughput	101,002 MBps	150,633 MBps	260,301 MBps
Errors			
Critical	0	2	0
Noncritical	2	5	10

Figure 12.5   Data reduction spreadsheet with two 12-hour measurements completed.

- total errors and error types recorded by the monitors

- total packets forwarded by the subsystem, if available

- total errors and error types recorded by the subsystem, if available

5. If the test configuration is using only one monitor, move the monitor to a new segment for the next 12-hour period. Figure 12.5 shows a partially completed spreadsheet for two 12-hour periods. Note that the critical error rate on segment 2 is increasing slowly. This should be monitored as a possible point of failure later in the test.

6. Analyze the test results to determine whether there is significant throughput degradation for the subsystem or for individual segments, or an increase in the error rate since the last measurement. Look for significant differences between the monitor's statistics and the statistics provided by the subsystem.

7. If the subsystem completes the 72-hour test at the lower load, shut down and restart all load generators using the higher packet rate. Run the test for 24 hours and repeat the previous recording procedure and monitor relocation, if applicable, every six to eight hours.

Data Interpretation

A test failure has occurred when one or more of the following conditions takes place:

- An error stops the subsystem from forwarding or transmitting packets.

- A hardware component on the device fails.

- An unrecoverable error stops the subsystem from forwarding or transmitting data on one or more segments.

- An error occurs that causes one or more system features to become inoperable, such as filtering, data encapsulation, or network management capabilities.

The last three failure conditions have a degree of latitude in their interpretation. If an error occurs that causes a fault that can be corrected *without* restarting the subsystem, the failed component may be reset or replaced and the test continued. If the subsystem allows hot-swapping of interface boards, a failed board can be replaced without interrupting the operation of the remainder of the subsystem. This type of reliability testing is valuable because it mimics real-world operation. A good rule of thumb is: "Three strikes and it's out!" Even if the third problem is recoverable, the number and frequency of problems indicates an unstable environment and the subsystem should not pass the reliability test.

How firm are the load and time duration guidelines for a reliability test? Experience has shown that if a subsystem survives the preceding tests, there is a high probability that it will not fail on the production network. But, what if the subsystem runs the stressed reliability test for 18 or 20 hours before a failure occurs? The first step is to rerun the test to determine whether there is a consistent failure mode or time period. If the subsystem fails consistently, or in a majority of the tests, then the reliability test has failed. If the subsystem does not fail a second time, or a second failure is different than the first failure, interpreting the test results must be based on the criticality of the failure. For instance, in separate tests, one segment on the subsystem (not necessarily the same in each test) shuts down after 20 hours. It can be re-started without interfering with the other subsystem operations. Based on the test parameters, the test has failed, but the reality is that the subsystem will probably provide acceptable uptime for the production network. If similar failures occur in 8 or 10 hours, instead of 20 hours, the test failure would be viewed more severely, and the test would be considered a failure.

Reliability test results often have a large gray area of interpretation. The best advice is to start with the guidelines just given, and temper the data interpretation based on experience with specific products and vendors.

Testing Feature Impact

Test scenarios that measure the impact on reliability when additional features or other loads are activated may include:

- Testing with address or packet type filtering enabled.

- Testing with data compression, encryption, or protocol encapsulation enabled.

Such testing is important when comparing competitive products, planning for network segmentation or firewalls, and determining the effect of a specific feature on the devices' reliability.

Feature testing requires a baseline test and a feature test. First test the device without the feature enabled. Enable the feature and follow the procedures and steps outlined to retest the device. For example, to measure the impact on protocol encapsulation, run two test series, one series with protocol encapsulation enabled and another with it disabled. Then compare the reliability results to determine any change in reliability or performance caused by the protocol encapsulation.

Monitor the tests to confirm that the filtering, encryption, encapsulation, and other features are working correctly. Usually, failures occur because of a clog (no packets are forwarded) or a rip (incorrect packets are forwarded or counted). This will not stop the subsystem from operating. However, the forwarding or trapping of incorrect packets does cause the subsystem to fail the reliability test.

TEST CASE 2: INTERNETWORK RELIABILITY TESTING

Internetwork reliability testing measures reliability across multiple devices and connecting links. Since every network is virtually a unique combination of heterogeneous, multivendor devices, this is a particularly important test. Vendors spend a large amount of money and time testing their products, but they cannot verify more than a small number of combinations of their products' interoperability with other products. An internetwork test can measure your individual network's reliability.

Internetwork testing does not attempt to measure the same level of isolation as subsystem testing. Its objective is to measure point-to-point reliability and interoperability.

Test Measurements

Test results provide the following information:

- Reliability of the internetwork path between two points.

- Reliability of the internetwork when multiple paths are traversed concurrently.

Test Configurations

While most test configurations are emulated, a point-to-point test can be conducted on the production network for operational reliability. Stressed reliability should be conducted only on emulated test configurations, because of the high potential for causing a network failure.

The test configurations must represent the most critical or typical production network configurations. In determining which configurations to test, consider:

- Paths that have bursty, high peak loads. Experience has shown that components servicing this type of demand may have unstable operation during periods when the duration of the peak load is long or when "ramping up" to service a quickly increasing load.

- Paths that have high continuous loads.

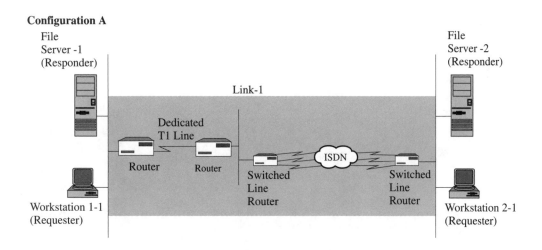

Figure 12.6A Example of internetwork reliability test configuration A.

- Paths where bandwidth on demand determines effective capacity. The time it takes for acquiring bandwidth may cause clogs in other portions of the system that result in unstable operation.

Internetwork testing measures path reliability. It does not attempt to isolate the reliability of individual connections or nodes. Figure 12.6 shows typical configurations that could be tested for a switched network, remote access server at a regional office, and regional office connection to corporate headquarters. This testing usually uses one or more load generators (requesters) and one responder (file server) at each point to create bidirectional traffic, as shown in Figure 12.6, configurations A and C. Another configuration may have many load generators and only one responder, as in Figure 12.6, configuration B. The exact configuration depends on the loads that must be created to adequately stress the path. This is discussed in the following section, Load Model.

Before initiating the test project, start a test journal, document the test configuration hardware and software, and create data reduction spreadsheets, as described in Chapter 6.

Configuration B

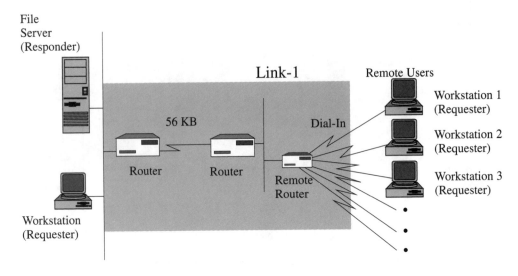

Figure 12.6*B*   Example of internetwork reliability test configuration B.

Load Model

The load model for internetwork reliability testing must:

- Create high bandwidth demands on the interconnecting links.

- Create high CPU demands on the responder and intermediate nodes.

- Create bursty traffic.

Referring to Figure 12.6, configuration A:

- All interconnecting links should be loaded to 50 percent and 70 percent of bandwidth for operational and stressed reliability testing, respectively.

- Responder and interconnecting node CPU utilization should be at 60 and 90 percent of capacity for operational and stressed reliability testing, respectively.

The target load on the interconnecting links and the target load on the responders can be reached by increasing the number of requesters on the end segments, as shown in Figure 12.7. Some additional requesters create internetwork load, while others perform local file I/O against the responder (file server). Run preliminary tests and adjust the number of requesters until the desired loads are achieved.

If the intermediate nodes (routers, switches, and so on) typically have more connections than emulated in the test configuration, increase their CPU utilization to represent the load that the other segments would create. This is considered background load. The simplest method of increasing CPU load on the intermediate nodes is to use packet generators on the intermediate segments with

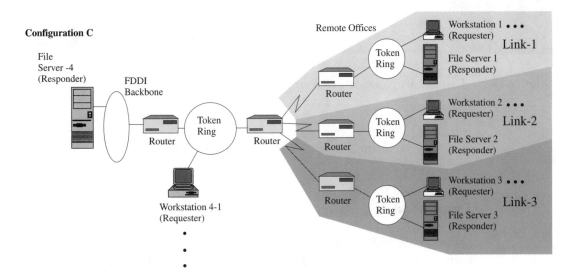

Figure 12.6C Example of internetwork reliability test configuration C.

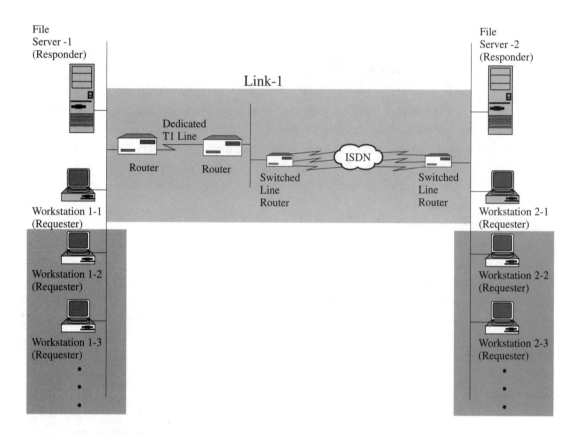

Figure 12.7   Using more requesters to increase load.

load scripts that simply create forwarded traffic through the node, as shown in Figure 12.8.

Load Modeling Bursty Traffic

During a reliability test, the loading should not be constant, but bursty, as is typical of most network data transmission. This can be done using two techniques:

- Create a load script that varies the file I/O rate, as discussed in Chapter 9.

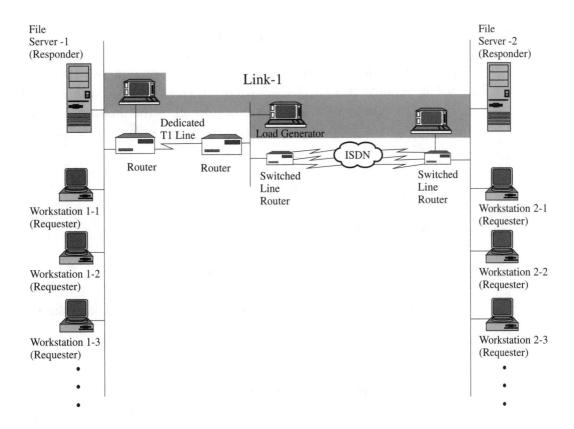

Figure 12.8   Using load generators to increase intermediate node utilization.

- Vary the PPS rate or number of load generators concurrently running. This depends on the capabilities of the load generator(s) used, as discussed in Chapter 10. Many routers do not provide CPU statistics, so it is difficult to determine the actual CPU utilization for the unit. In place of CPU utilization, use the load generators to create bursty loads equal to peak loads measured on the production network.

Make sure that when using bursty data, the average load measured over a minute increment meets the required percent of link and CPU utilization for the test.

Test Execution and Data Collection

For this task, use the data collection and reduction spreadsheet shown in Figure 12.9. The example spreadsheet assumes that there is only one link in the test and that there is bidirectional traffic with multiple workstations (requesters) and a single file server (responder) at each end point, from Figure 12.6 test configuration A.

Cell definitions in the Figure 12.9 spreadsheet are:

cell A = test ID.

cell B = time and date when measurements are recorded.

cell C = link ID.   There should be one column per link in the test configuration.

Run ID	(A)
Time/Date	(B)
Link ID	(C)
Test Script	(D)
CPU (File Server - 1)	(E)
CPU (File Server -2)	
Link 1 (Throughput)	
CPU (Routers)	
Errors	
Critical	(F)
Noncritical	(G)

Figure 12.9   Data collection and reduction spreadsheet for internetwork reliability testing.

cell D = test Script ID.

cell E = CPU and throughput utilization of the servers, routers, and links.

cell F = critical errors. This can be expanded with additional rows of key errors that are expected to occur or treated as a summary value. Record the number of critical errors here and enter details for each in the problem log.

cell G = noncritical errors. This can be expanded with additional rows or treated as a summary value. Record the number of noncritical errors here and enter details for each in the problem log.

The test sequence is:

1. Start the load generators. Verify that the test configuration is working properly, that the load generators can access the file server, that files are being read from the correct servers, that packets are being forwarded by the intermediate nodes, and that the link and CPU utilization are at the correct levels. For reliability testing, load generator and monitor synchronization is not required, as long as they are started within a minute of each other.

Run ID	1
Time/Date	12/1-9:00 am
Link ID	1
Test Script	T01PGE
Total Throughput	
Errors	
Critical	
Noncritical	

Figure 12.10 Data reduction spreadsheet prior to first test run.

2. Set up a spreadsheet for the first test load and fill in the Run ID, start date and time, Test Script ID(s), Link ID, and link and CPU utilization targets in the spreadsheet, as shown in Figure 12.10.

3. Shut down and restart the load generators using the lowest load. Run the test for 72 hours.

4. Every 12 hours, record the following data:

   - date and time of the test measurement

   - CPU utilization

   - link throughput

   - total errors and error types recorded by the monitors and intermediate nodes, as appropriate

5. If the test configuration is using only one monitor, move the monitor to a new segment for the next 12-hour period. Figure 12.11 shows a partially completed spreadsheet after two 12-hour periods.

6. Analyze the test results to determine whether there is significant throughput degradation for the internetwork or for individual segments

Run ID	1
Time/Date	12/1-9:00 am
Link ID	1
Test Script	T01PGE
Total Throughput	100,592 MBps
Errors	
Critical	0
Noncritical	2

Time/Date	12/1-9:00 pm
Link ID	1
Test Script	T01PGE
Total Throughput	101,002 MBps
Errors	
Critical	0
Noncritical	2

Figure 12.11   Data reduction spreadsheet for two 12-hour measurements.

or an increase in the error rate since the last measurement. Look for significant differences between the monitor's statistics and the statistics provided by intermediate nodes.

7. If the internetwork completes the 72-hour test at the lower load, shut down and restart all the load generators using the higher load. Run the test for 24 hours and repeat the previous recording procedure and monitor relocation, if applicable, every six to eight hours.

Data Interpretation

As each test case is run, the results should be entered into the data reduction spreadsheet. A test failure has occurred when one or more of the following conditions take place:

- An error stops data flow across the internetwork.

- A hardware component on a device in the internetwork path fails.

- An unrecoverable error stops an intermediate node from forwarding or transmitting data on one or more segments.

- An error occurs that causes one or more system features to become inoperable, such as network management capabilities, on one of the intermediate nodes.

- One of the responders (file servers) fails.

- One of the requesters (workstations) fails.

The second through fifth failure conditions have a degree of latitude in their interpretation. The tester can be strict or lenient in determining the criteria for stopping or continuing the test. The failure of one requester is rarely sufficient grounds for failing the test.

If an error occurs that causes a fault that can be corrected while the remainder of the internetwork continues to function correctly, then the test can continue. The capability can be reset or replaced. If intermediate components allow hot-swapping of interface boards, a failed board can be replaced without interrupting the operation of the remainder of the subsystem. If a file server fails and is rebooted, the test can continue. This type of reliability testing is valuable because it mimics real-world operation. A good rule of thumb is: "Three strikes and it's out!" Even if the third problem is recoverable, the number and frequency of problems indicates an unstable environment, and the internetwork does not pass the reliability test.

The loading and time duration for an internetwork reliability test has the same degree of flexibility as discussed previously for the subsystem test. Reliability test results often have a large gray area of interpretation. Start with the guidelines given, and temper the data interpretation based on experience with specific products and vendors.

Testing Other Impacts

Test scenarios that measure the impact on reliability when additional features or other loads are active may include:

- Testing with data compression, encryption, or protocol encapsulation enabled across one or more segments in the point-to-point link.

- Testing with scripts that add more loads to one or more of the internetwork components or responders.

- Testing with different line speeds or multiple paths.

Such testing allows the effect on reliability to be measured when changes are made to the internetwork. It requires a baseline test and an impact test as discussed under subsystem testing.

Infrastructure: Functionality Testing

TEST MATRIX

While feature/functional testing is associated with applications, functional infrastructure testing is useful across a wide range of objectives. Functional testing of the network infrastructure can be conducted for a subsystem, such as a router, using an emulated test configuration and load. Functional testing is seldom done on an internetwork configuration. Using internetworked test configurations, it is done for network-wide applications, such as a name service or Lotus Notes. This testing is at the application/presentation layers and is discussed in Part III.

SUBSYSYEM FUNCTIONAL TESTING

Functional testing verifies hardware and software features and capabilities of the subsystem. For example, if a specific feature, such as data encapsulation, is critical to the network, functional testing can ensure that it works properly across a range of protocols and load scenarios.

Functional testing is also used to determine support costs for a family of subsystems. Testing for ease of use, configuration, management, and support can help determine the life cycle cost for installing, configuring, and maintaining the subsystem. Routers are historically high-support systems, particularly for installation and configuration. Installing routers in remote offices is often a great expense for a network management group. When vendors introduced remote routers that didn't require significant on-site support, life cycle costs for these products was much lower than for previous models. Router, switch, and hub products vary significantly in their user interfaces, and these differences can equate directly to higher support costs.

Functional testing can verify how a subsystem handles error conditions, such as illegal packets, broadcast storms, and so forth, and how well the unit recovers after the error condition is removed. The robustness of the product contributes directly to lower support costs. In addition, functional testing can be as diverse as the range of product features, and its results can be used for a variety of benefits, from verifying feature operations to estimating support costs. One company used functional testing to evaluate the increase in effective throughput across wide area communication lines using data compression, only to discover that the compression algorithm generally did not provide more than 20 percent improvement. At high loads, throughput actually decreased. Based on test results, another company found that installation time and cost varied significantly across different products. The results played an important role in selecting one product over another, and saved the company an estimated $250,000 in installation and support costs.

Test Measurements

The subsystem can be tested for hardware and software functionality. Although any function of the subsystem can be tested, the following outlines the most commonly tested features. Figures 13.1 and 13.2 illustrate hardware and software areas for functional testing.

Hardware Testing

Hardware testing is used to verify that features, such as hot-swapping of interface boards, switch-over of redundant power supplies, and maximum port configurations function properly, as shown in Figure 13.1. The test objective is to ensure that the system continues to function properly either during or after the hardware change has been made.

Software Testing

Software testing falls into three categories, as shown in Figure 13.2:

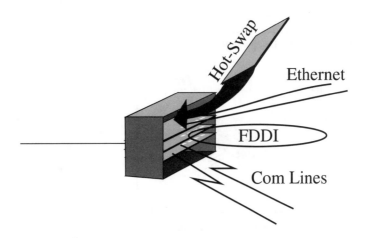

Figure 13.1   Typical areas of subsystem hardware functional testing.

- **Configuration and management feature testing:** This testing is performed to verify that new configuration options and remote management
  capability work as documented. It can also measure how long specific
  management tasks take and estimate the life cycle cost for product
  support. For a single unit, this is not important, but if a company is
  installing units at hundreds of locations, the cumulative cost of support
  is a significant factor. Understanding how product features or requirements affect life cycle cost is an important measurement.

- **Network management software testing:** This testing is performed to
  verify that network management agents work with a particular network
  management station. It is also used to check that subsystem agents
  accurately capture throughput statistics and errors at high loads.

- **Feature testing:** This testing ensures that a specific feature, such as data
  encapsulation, data compression, or filtering works under various subsystem configurations and loads. It can also verify the level of error-han-
  dling by the subsystem.

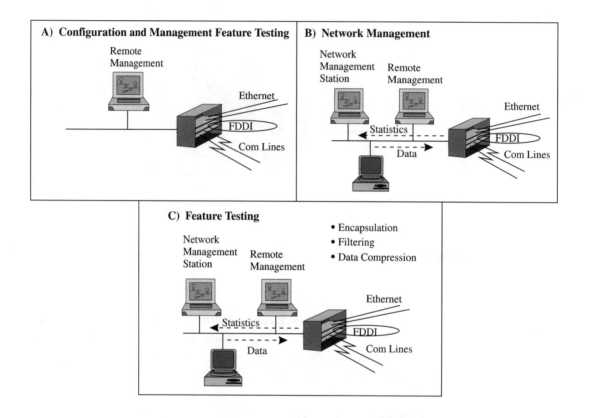

Figure 13.2   Typical areas of subsystem software functional testing.

The following sections discuss how to perform functional testing for the hardware and three software areas listed here.

Test Configurations

All test configurations are emulated, and must represent a typical production network configuration. In determining which configuration(s) to test, consider:

- In which configuration(s) will a feature be used.

- What the predominate subsystem configuration is on the production network.

Typically, functional testing a single, common configuration will provide representative results, unless test results are load-dependent, in which case, several configurations may be necessary to confirm how results vary across different configurations and loads.

Before initiating the test project, start a test journal and document the test configuration hardware and software.

Load Model

The load model and test scripts for functional testing can be leveraged or modified from the other test objectives. Details on creating these are discussed in Chapters 9, 10, 11, and 12.

Hardware testing rarely requires tailored test scripts. The test script is primarily used to create load on the unit under test to:

- Verify that a maximum subsystem configuration can forward data across all ports concurrently.

- Verify that a hardware change, such as hot-swapping an interface board, does not disrupt subsystem operation on other ports, and that the replaced ports come back on-line gracefully.

- Measure what an induced error, such as cutting off the primary power supply (on a redundant power supply subsystem), does to the subsystem.

Test scripts from throughput or reliability testing can be used for hardware functional testing with minor or no modification. Since the testing is not protocol-, packet size-, data content-, or load-dependent, the only changes needed in test scripts are destination and source addresses for the specific test configuration.

The three categories of software functional testing usually require test script tailoring. Often, throughput or reliability scripts can be used, as these contain representative production network packet sequences. The test script changes are different for each of the three test objectives:

- **Configuration and management software:** Testing configuration software requires the tester to manually input and verify the changes to the subsystem. Test scripts are used to verify that the subsystem functions properly after the configuration changes are made. Use regression, throughput, or reliability test scripts and modify them to exercise the new configuration. For example, to verify the maximum configuration of 10 ports for the subsystem, copy an existing test script and change the appropriate destination and source addresses as a fast and simple way to create new test scripts for the functional test.

    Ease of use, management, configuration, and support testing are primarily manual tasks that do not require automated test scripts. They do require a list of the specific tasks that are to be measured. Examples may include: out-of-the-box hardware set-up time, configuration time for one or two different port configurations, and time for routing table modification.

- **Network management software:** Network management feature testing requires both manual testing of the user interface and management functions and test script loading to verify that the subsystem collects accurate throughput and error statistics under high load. For example, running the test script that creates maximum throughput for the subsystem is an easy way to determine whether the subsystem can accurately capture throughput statistics under very heavy load.

- **Features:** Testing specific features, such as data encapsulation, data compression, filtering, and so on requires test scripts that exercise the functions to be tested. For encapsulation, compression, and features that work across any packet size and contents, test scripts from other tests can generally be used. For tests that require specific packet content, such as address filtering, packet sequences can be edited to include the required address ranges. Start with throughput test scripts and use both sustained and maximum rate tests to verify that the feature works properly for different load points.

Test Execution and Data Collection

Before starting a functional test, identify the measurement technique and expected test result. The following are examples of measurement techniques.

Hardware Testing

Use load monitors on the destination segments to ensure that all traffic is correctly forwarded. If the hardware change is a hot-swap of a faulty interface board, verify that packet flow during the hot-swap is not affected on the other segments, and that packet flow on the affected segment(s) returns to normal after the replacement.

Run the test for a sufficient amount of time to make and verify the hardware change, and to confirm that the subsystem has returned to normal operation. Usually a 2- to 10-minute test is sufficient. Hardware tests do not have to be repeated to verify reproducibility, since hardware functionality is very repetitive. If it works once, it works every time unless there is a faulty board, which brings up an interesting example. A hot-swap test was run in which the replacement board was also faulty (not planned). The faulty board generated symptoms that were originally assumed to be a problem caused by the swapping process. If such problems arise, first rerun the test using another piece of hardware. For hardware testing, always have at least two, or preferably three, samples of the item to be tested.

Configuration Changes

Check the new configuration file to verify that the change was implemented. Next, run a test script to ensure that the system still works properly. Finally, use load monitors to verify that all traffic is properly routed from source to destination segments. For example, if the configuration change increased the number of ports and protocols, the test script can verify these changes by ensuring that the subsystem forwards packets across all ports and protocols. Once the functionality of the change is verified, other tests for throughput and reliability are run.

Run the functional test for two minutes. Generally, these tests do not have to be repeated to verify reproducibility.

Ease of Use

This measures the time and effort required to install, maintain, and support the unit under test. The steps, execution time, and level of automation can be tested and measured. The basic measurement is the time it takes to complete a series of tasks. Recording the number of steps and level of automation also provides an indication of how error-prone the operations may be. More steps and less automation indicate a higher probability of errors. Several studies have found that the single highest cause of system problems is system administration errors.

Another important step is measuring the vendor's customer support response time, helpfulness, and ability to solve problems. For this, use actual problems encountered in the testing or create problem scenarios. Contact customer support and measure its ability to solve the reported problem. This will indicate what can be expected of the staff when the products are installed and in use.

In general, the process for ease-of-use testing entails:

1. Defining a list of tasks to be tested.

2. Having one person execute the procedure and another record the time and steps to accomplish the task.

3. Rerunning the test with one or two additional people. As a person becomes more familiar and comfortable with a system, his or her speed will improve.

4. Repeating the first three steps for other system features to be tested.

Network Management Statistics

The accuracy of statistics provided by the subsystem's agent to the network management station can be measured by comparing them to an independent load monitor, such as a network analyzer.

- Run test scripts that create high sustained throughput. Throughput test scripts are the best and easiest to use, since their PPS rates are already calibrated from the throughput tests.

- Run test scripts that induce dropped packets and other errors. Use the maximum throughput test script to measure dropped packets. Use a modified sustained throughput test script to verify other types of error recording by introducing faulty packets to the packet stream. Edit the script to include bad header checksums, truncated and over-length packets, corrupted fields, and bad addresses.

Problems usually occur at higher loads when the subsystem statistics collection cannot keep pace with the packet flow.

Specific Feature Tests

Set the load monitor options to capture packets that verify the operation of the feature. For example, if a filtering test is constructed to filter based on packet type or address, set the monitor on the destination segment to capture only packets containing the address or type. If the monitor does not capture any packets during the test, the subsystem has correctly filtered the packets. Inversely, to measure if the subsystem is filtering valid packets, set the load generator to transmit a specific number and verify that all packets were forwarded.

For data encapsulation tests, use the monitor to verify that the transmitted packets are properly encapsulated. This will require decoding random packets from the forwarded packets to verify all field contents. For data compression, create a packet sequence that has a well-defined data field. Use the monitor to measure effective throughput, and check that the data field is decompressed correctly on the destination segment. The expected throughput should be calculated prior to the test and verified by the monitor.

Running Functional Tests

For hardware, configuration changes, and ease-of-use testing, the general test process is outlined under the item. For network management statistics and specific feature tests, the test process is more structured and includes the following steps:

1. Start the load generators and use a monitor to verify that the packet sequences contain the required packets to exercise the feature under test.

2. Stop the load generators. Restart the load generators. Start the monitors with the appropriate setting to capture the required test traffic.

3. Capture traffic for 30 seconds.

4. Analyze the traffic to ensure that the feature is working properly.

5. Stop the load generators. Restart the load generators with the second test script to verify that the feature is *not* affecting other traffic flow, as discussed. Start the monitors with the appropriate setting to capture test traffic that should not be affected by the feature.

6. Capture traffic for 30 seconds.

7. Analyze the traffic to confirm that the feature is working properly and not impacting other traffic.

8. Run each test three times and verify that the results are reproducible. Record the results in the test journal.

Data Interpretation

First verify that the test results illustrate the expected operation of the subsystem feature, and that the results are reproducible as discussed under Test Execution.

Generally, as network managers and support personnel become familiar with a product, time to perform tasks decreases. Experience has shown that the minimum test time for any task will become the average time for that task in the production network. Therefore, when estimating operational task effort, use the best test time. For a conservative time estimate, average the time across the testers.

To calculate estimated life cycle support costs, estimate the number of units that will be installed, the number of times the units will be reconfigured, and multiply the cost of that time by the test measurement times. For example, if 600 units are to be installed, the life cycle costs may be calculated as:

- Installation cost = 600 units x 1 hour per install x $35/hour = $21,000

- Configuration cost = 600 units x 3 hours per configuration x $ 35/hour = $63,000

- Reconfiguration cost = 600 units x 1.5 re-configurations per product life cycle x 4.5 hours per reconfiguration x $35/hour = $141,750

- Total estimated life cycle cost = $225,750

These are only estimated costs, but they are valid comparisons to consider when selecting a product. If the process time for two products differs by 20 to 40 percent, the life cycle costs can be significantly different. Support savings may actually pay for several production units. Many vendors position products based on ease of use. Companies who have done ease-of-use testing are often surprised by the vast differences between products. As feature content, performance, and reliability of products become less variable, issues such as ease of use and support become significant differentiators. This is a good test to determine whether the product meets vendor claims.

Analyzing Unexpected Results

The difficult part of functional testing is analyzing why results are not as expected. The following provides tips and steps on how to analyze unexpected test results.

Hardware

If the hardware change causes the subsystem not to perform as expected, take the following steps to isolate the problem:

1. Rerun the test to determine whether the failure is reproducible.

2. Rerun the test with a different hardware component.

3. Verify that the test configuration is properly cabled.

4. Verify that the hardware change followed the procedures outlined in the manual.

5. If the test introduces a fault, such as disconnecting a power supply, reevaluate the method used and try another approach to create the fault, if available.

6. Rerun the test and verify that the load generators and monitors work correctly without the hardware disruption.

7. Rerun the test with a replacement subsystem.

8. If the previous steps do not isolate or identify a problem, then the test process should be considered to be working properly and the fault lies in the subsystem or component under test.

Configuration Changes

1. Verify the configuration file or reenter the change through the configuration menu. Rerun the test.

2. Rerun the test with another test script to determine whether the subsystem works under different load conditions.

3. Change back to the original configuration and run the first test script to determine whether the subsystem works under the original configuration.

4. Replace the hardware and rerun the test.

5. If the previous steps do not isolate or identify a problem, then the test process should be considered to be working properly and the fault lies in the subsystem under test.

Network management statistics

1. Verify that the monitor is capable of capturing the statistics required under the load applied. Many network analyzers lose accuracy at high loads. Run a test with the load generator and analyzer on the same segment. Send a known stream of packets at a known rate (high) to the load monitor and confirm that it captures the data, including errors, accurately.

2. Verify that the monitor and subsystem are configured to capture and display the same statistics.

3. Verify that the monitor and subsystem variables are set to zero before the test.

4. Verify that the monitor and subsystem are capturing data over the same time period, usually 30 seconds.

5. Verify the monitor and subsystem operation by sending a small, well-defined packet sequence and by checking that correct data is recorded. Then increase loading until discrepancies occur. Determine whether the differences between the subsystem and monitor values are load dependent. This should indicate which one is not accurately capturing the statistics.

6. If these steps do not isolate why the systems are recording different statistics, then the test conclusion is that the subsystem statistics are not accurate.

Specific feature tests

1. Verify that the load monitor is configured to collect the correct packets.

2. Verify the subsystem configuration and feature options.

3. Verify that the load generator is working correctly by connecting it directly to the load monitor and validating the generated packet sequence.

4. If the previous steps do not isolate or identify a problem, then the test process should be considered to be working properly and the fault lies in the subsystem under test.

Infrastructure: Regression Testing

TEST MATRIX

Regression testing is not one test, but a series of tests that measure critical aspects of the subsystem and internetwork. For example, if a specific feature, such as data encapsulation, is critical to the network, regression testing ensures that it functions properly in each new release. Regression testing is a combination of other test objectives. *A regression test plan identifies which basic test objectives should be run against each new product release.*

Regression testing of the network infrastructure can be conducted for a subsystem, such as a router, and an internetwork configuration using an emulated test configuration and load. Test Case 1 describes subsystem regression testing. Test Case 2 explains internetwork regression testing.

TEST CASE 1: SUBSYSTEM REGRESSION TESTING

Regression testing verifies that a hardware or software upgrade to the subsystem does not impact its performance, reliability, or functionality. It does not measure the impact on the device by other nodes on the network or internetwork. Regression testing does not measure new features or capabilities; such tests fall under feature/functional testing, as discussed in Chapter 13.

Test Measurements

Regression test measurements depend on which capabilities are defined as critical to the production network and which corresponding tests are included in the regression test plan. As a minimum, throughput (Chapter 11) and reliability (Chapter 12) should be verified for each upgrade. Functional testing (Chapter 13) can also be performed to verify that current release features work properly in the upgrade.

The key to regression testing is establishing pass/fail criteria as discussed in the upcoming Data Interpretation section.

Test Configurations

All test configurations are emulated, and must represent the most critical and typical production network configurations. In determining which configurations to test, consider:

- Which is the predominate subsystem configuration on the production network.

- Which is the most complex hardware and software configuration on the production network.

- Which configurations have been tested for throughput, reliability, and functionality.

- Which configurations and vendor products have caused past problems during upgrades.

Typically, regression test between one and three different configurations based on the preceding selection criteria. If a configuration has not been previously tested, you should first run tests against the current version before testing the upgrade. Without a baseline against which to compare the upgrade, it cannot be determined if the subsystem has improved or regressed.

After determining which test objectives will be included in the regression test plan, refer to the appropriate chapter (11 through 13) for examples of typical subsystem test configurations. Before beginning the test project, start a test journal, document the test configuration hardware and software, and create data reduction spreadsheets. Also establish pass/fail criteria for each test as discussed in the Data Interpretation section.

Load Model

The load model and test scripts for regression testing are leveraged from the other test objectives. Details on creating these are discussed in Chapters 9, 10, and in the appropriate test objective chapters. It is very important to confirm that the load model used is the exact one used in the previous test against which the regression test results will be compared. If you have followed the test methodology outlined in Chapter 6 for documenting and archiving test project information, it will be easy to leverage load scripts from previous tests.

Test Execution and Data Collection

For each test objectives included in the regression test plan, follow the instructions contained in that test objective's chapter for test execution and data collection. Use the following data interpretation procedures rather than the procedures included in the test objective chapter.

The order of conducting regression tests is important because some results will influence subsequent tests, as discussed in Data Interpretation. The preferred order of testing is reliability, functional, and throughput. A first-pass reliability test is performed to verify that the upgrade is sufficiently stable to conduct the other tests. This can save time and effort.

Data Interpretation

Let's consider throughput, reliability, and functional testing as components of the regression test plan, and identify issues in establishing pass/fail criteria for each test.

Functional

Of the three tests discussed, regressive functional testing is the easiest to conduct and the easiest to interpret. Regression testing a feature is simpler than testing the feature originally, as covered in Chapter 13. In a regression test, the configuration and load model are defined by the original test. If a good test journal and test script archive have been maintained, reproducing the test on the upgrade is straightforward.

Interpreting the test results is also straightforward. The intent of regression testing is to ascertain that the product works as used in the production system. The upgrade should work like the existing product, therefore the test results should be the same as in the previous functional test. Regression testing does not attempt to address new features or capabilities.

As discussed in Chapter 13, the key to functional testing is to measure the before and after state of the subsystem and packet traffic to verify that the function worked correctly. For example, in a filtering test, verify that the input contains packets to be filtered and that the output does not include any packets that should not have been forwarded. For system configuration management, a functional test of a remote management capability includes reviewing a printout of the configuration file before and after making the configuration change. Be sure that the subsystem still works correctly after the re-configuration; often, you may be surprised by the results.

Throughput

Baseline throughput measurements, as discussed in Chapter 9, provide the production system average (X) and peak (Y) load in PPS. Previous tests on the current subsystem measured sustained aggregate throughput (A) and maximum aggregate throughput (B), where A=X and B>Y. Based on these equations, what are acceptable throughput measurements for the upgrade under test?

The upgrade must have a sustained aggregate throughput equal to or greater than X to provide the same performance as the current version. For maximum aggregate throughput, however, the pass/fail criteria is not as straightforward.

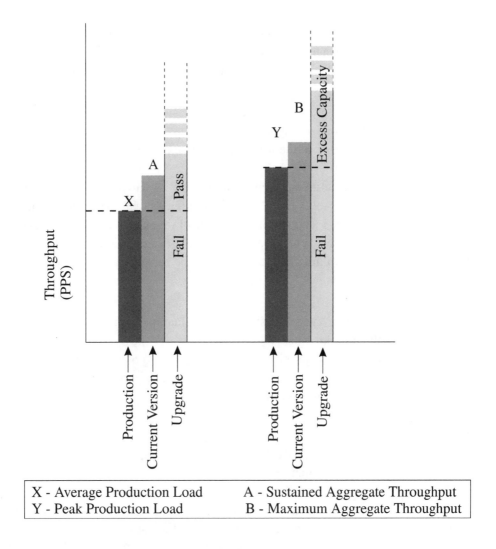

Figure 14.1 Differences between sustained and maximum aggregate throughput indicate subsystem growth capacity.

Under ideal circumstances, the upgrade measurements should be equal to or greater than B. However, since B is greater than the production system requirement (Y), the upgrade may be acceptable if its performance is between Y and B. A reduction in the maximum aggregate throughput should not impact performance of the production network, but it does indicate that the upgrade provides less growth capacity than the current version, as indicated in Figure 14.1. This could become important if production load increases after the upgrade is deployed.

The subsystem upgrade may be tested under several test configurations, and it is likely that throughput measurements could meet or exceed the current values on all but one of the test configurations. Since router, bridge, switch, and hub throughput are typically configuration-, protocol-, and feature-sensitive, such mixed results are often encountered. It is hard to predict in advance how to handle these test results. It is basically a judgment call that must consider the number of impacted locations and the extent of the risk. If the throughput measurements are only a few percent lower than the current version, the risk and degradation is probably minimal and may actually be related to the margin of test error more than to any real change in the product.

Often, the greatest risk in evaluating such results is the potential of a problem lurking just below the surface. The test results may be an indication of a more serious problem that wasn't fully exposed based on the load model and test configuration. The best approach is to verify results with the vendor and expand the number of test cases.

1. Report the test results and concern to the vendors. Invite them to the lab to verify the test results. Ask them if they have additional test results from their testing.

2. Rerun the tests, making one permutation to the hardware configuration and then one permutation to the software configuration. If there is a serious underlying problem, this approach will often expose other symptoms.

Reliability

Based on throughput test results, the upgraded subsystem has a sustained aggregate throughput (C) and maximum aggregate throughput (D), where $A>C=X$ and $B>D>Y$. Based on these equations and the reliability of the current revision, what is an acceptable expectation of reliability for the upgrade under test?

There are two criteria against which to measure reliability:

- Based on the sustained aggregate throughput (C) or the production system average load (X), the upgrade should run for 72 or more hours without a failure.

- Based on the maximum aggregate throughput (D) or the production system peak load (Y), the upgrade should run for 24 hours without a failure.

How rigid are the loading and time duration for a reliability test? Experience has shown that if a subsystem survives the previous tests, there is a high probability that it will not fail in the production network. However, these times are not "set in stone." Refer to the data interpretation guidelines outlined in Chapter 12 for more information.

Reliability test results often have a large gray area of interpretation. Start with these guidelines, and temper the data interpretation based on experience with specific products and vendors.

Regression Test Conclusions

A graduate professor in aeronautics at the University of Maryland gives only two grades to his students—pass or fail. He believes that the answer is either right or wrong. In designing aircraft and space vehicles, "almost right" doesn't count.

As discussed, interpreting regression test results isn't always that clearcut. Reliability and throughput results are often open to interpretation. There is, however, a clear point at which the test results indicate a failing grade. Experience indicates this point is reached when conclusions on two or more of the test cases must be made based on "judgment calls." Then it's possible to conclude that the upgrade has several problems relative to the current release, and to effect deployment is only asking for trouble on the production network.

TEST CASE 2: INTERNETWORK REGRESSION TESTING

Internetwork regression testing measures the effect on the internetwork based on the upgrade of one or more components. In a subsystem test, you can control the test scope by changing only one component at a time in order to determine its effect on the subsystem. In internetwork testing, the interaction of the subsystems and components is multidimensional, and it is often very hard to pinpoint why a failure or degradation occurs. Comparing internetwork regression test results to current version test data measures changes at the macro level, but does not isolate the exact cause of the difference. If adding an upgrade to the internetwork test configuration causes a failure, it cannot be deduced with certainty whether the upgrade failed or the upgrade stressed another borderline component that failed.

For example, in Figure 14.2, the switched routers were upgraded with additional ISDN PRI (Primary Rate Interface) lines and internetwork throughput improved. Reliability tests, however, failed within 10 hours because the sessions between the file server and workstations were dropped. The questions to be answered are: Where is the failure occurring? Is there a problem with the server under higher loads? Is there a problem with the routers handling additional lines? Is there some other problem not directly related to the additional lines? This scenario makes debugging difficult because the real cause is often masked by other symptoms. In this actual test case, the problem was in the router's data compression algorithm. As load increased, optimization techniques in the data compression algorithm that predict repetitive sequences had errors, which caused session responses to decrease to a point where they timed out and were dropped by the server. The problem was not directly caused by the additional lines, but resulted from the higher loads they caused.

As stated at the beginning of this chapter, regression testing is a series of tests that measure critical aspects of the internetwork test configuration. For example, if end-to-end throughput of X Kbytes is required, then the regression test should verify that the throughput level is attainable and reliable under various traffic patterns. Internetwork regression test plans usually include throughput and reliability testing. The test plan identifies which of these tests should be run against each new upgrade on the internetwork.

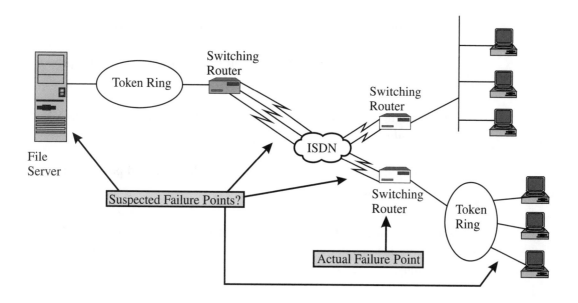

Figure 14.2   Isolating a problem in internetwork tests is often difficult; the problem frequently is not where it is expected to be!

Test Measurements

Test measurements will depend on which capabilities are defined as critical to the production network and which corresponding tests are included in the regression test plan. Typically, throughput (Chapter 11) and reliability (Chapter 12) are verified for upgrades to the internetwork. The key to successful regression testing is establishing pass/fail criteria for the testing, as discussed in the Data Interpretation section.

Test Configurations

All test configurations are emulated, and must represent the most critical or typical production network configurations. Typically, an internetwork test configuration should include:

- The predominate configurations on the production network.

- The most complex hardware and software configurations on the production network.

- Configurations that have been previously tested for throughput and reliability.

- Configurations and vendor products that have caused problems during past upgrades.

Once the test objectives for the regression test plan have been defined, refer to the appropriate chapter (11 and 12) for examples of typical subsystem test configurations.

Before starting the test project, start a test journal, document the test configuration hardware and software, and create data reduction spreadsheets. Also establish pass/fail criteria for each test, as discussed in the Data Interpretation section.

Load Model

The load model and test scripts for regression testing are leveraged from the other test objectives. Details on creating these are discussed in Chapters 9 through 12. It is very important to ensure that the load model used is the exact one used in the previous test against which the regression test results will be compared.

Test Execution and Data Collection

For each of the test objectives included in the regression test plan, follow the instructions contained in that test objective's chapter for test execution and data collection. Use the following data interpretation procedures rather than the procedures included in the test objective chapter.

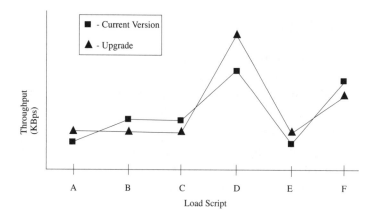

Figure 14.3 Internetwork test results for various load scripts.

Data Interpretation

Consider the two test objectives identified previously.

Throughput

Regression tests compare throughput from run to run as load conditions change, as well as compare upgrade to current version results. These comparisons provide two important data points:

- How the system performs across the tested load conditions.

- Whether the system's relative throughput has changed compared to the current version.

Figure 14.3 shows how an upgrade did not significantly change throughput, except for Load Script C. If Load Script C represents large file transfers, this indicates that the upgrade has improved the handling of large packets across the internetwork. These exact results were measured several years ago when NOSs incorporated features supporting layer Token Ring packets.

Reliability

Whether testing a new internetwork test configuration or performing a regression test for an upgrade, the most effective method of measuring internetwork reliability is to load the system and critical components to a prescribed level and run the test configuration for 24 to 72 hours, as discussed in Chapter 13. Follow the procedures described in Chapter 13 and compare the test results, including errors and failures, to current version data, if available. Good test documentation and detailed error tracking are extremely important in regression testing, as the following example illustrates.

A reliability test configuration is upgraded with new NOS software and a 72-hour test fails after 70 hours with "Not ready reading drive D:" error messages on several workstations. The natural conclusion is that the new software is causing the problem. However, a search of well-maintained test journals and problem resolution logs uncovers that the same problem occurred with an earlier version of an adapter driver and Windows 3.1. All the failed workstations are Windows 3.1, which are checked and found to have the faulty driver installed. The driver is upgraded to the latest version and the test is rerun successfully. Without good test documentation, the test group would have had to isolate the same problem over again.

Similar to subsystem reliability testing, test conclusions are not always straightforward and require judgment on the severity of the problem and the risk of it occurring on the production network. Refer to Chapter 13 for helpful hints on interpreting test results.

Regression Test Conclusions

As already discussed for subsystem testing, interpreting regression test results isn't always clearcut. When tests require judgment calls, the conservative approach is to fail the regression test, and either not deploy the upgrade or conduct further tests to clarify the issues.

Infrastructure: Acceptance Testing

TEST MATRIX

Acceptance testing of the network infrastructure is conducted for an internetwork configuration using a real-world test configuration and emulated load. Acceptance testing is not conducted on a subsystem because the subsystem is not a final target configuration. See Chapter 5, Acceptance Testing, for more information on test configuration criteria.

Like regression testing, acceptance testing does not have a single objective, but a combination of one or more test objectives. For the infrastructure, these test objectives are specifically throughput (Chapter 11) and reliability (Chapter 12).

INTERNETWORK ACCEPTANCE TESTING

Internetwork acceptance testing should be performed on the complete and final network just prior to deployment. It measures the network's or internetwork's ability to meet specific acceptance criteria, usually performance and reliability. One or two test cases covering performance and one case covering reliability is a good mix. Functional testing in an acceptance test is usually conducted at the application/presentation layers. This is discussed in Part III, Chapter 27. Figure 15.1 illustrates a new regional office network after it has been installed but is not yet productional.

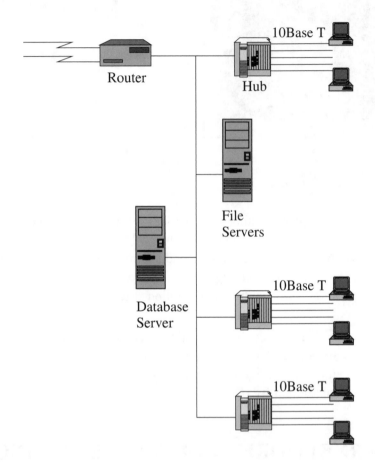

Figure 15.1   A network ready for final acceptance testing.

Test Measurements

The objective of these tests is not to isolate specific errors, but to verify that under the defined load conditions the network performs as expected.

The key to successful acceptance testing is defining meaningful test cases and establishing pass/fail criteria for the testing, as discussed in Chapter 5 and in the following Data Interpretation section.

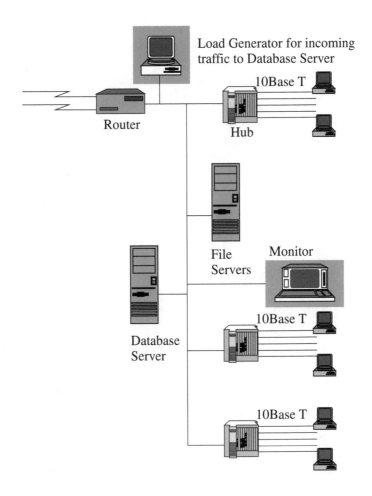

Figure 15.2 Adding load generators and monitors to the preproduction network for *throughput* testing.

Test Configurations

The test configuration is the production network with additional components for load generation and monitoring. Figures 15.2 and 15.3 illustrate how the preproduction network shown in Figure 15.1 would be supplemented for acceptance testing.

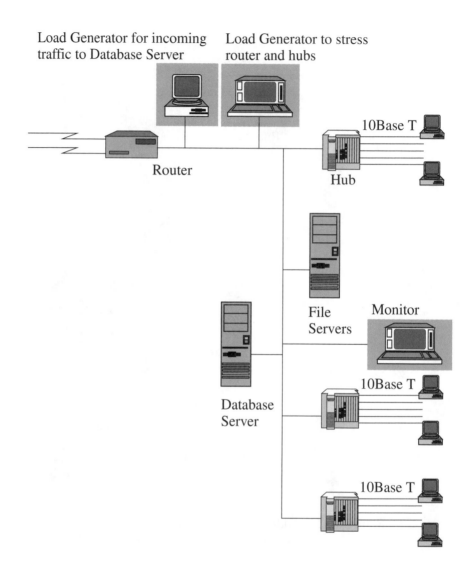

Figure 15.3   Adding load monitors and load generators to the preproduction
network for *reliability* testing.

Before starting the test project, begin a test journal, document the test
configuration hardware and software, and establish pass/fail criteria for each test,
as discussed in the Data Interpretation section.

Load Model

Unlike application/presentation layer acceptance test scripts that are created during the development cycle, infrastructure acceptance test scripts are usually developed just prior to testing. Once developed, these same scripts can also be used for regression testing product upgrades. Details on creating these are discussed in Chapters 9 and 10. Remember to adhere to the rules discussed in Chapter 5, and repeated briefly here, when developing the load model:

1. Base the criteria on business or technical requirements.

2. Be selective in defining the criteria.

3. State the criteria in measurable terms.

For throughput testing, the test scripts should measure at least two or more paths concurrently. Figures 15.4 shows the loading required to test the example network illustrated in Figure 15.3.

For the infrastructure, this testing measures that a specified (based on the load model) KBps rate can be achieved and sustained through the internetwork, and that there are no critical errors encountered during the test. The paths selected for the testing are the most critical paths. In Figure 15.4, the acceptance test verifies that the regional office file server can sustain the required throughput for the local users, and that the database server can sustain throughput from the local office and the home office. In Figure 15.4, only five load paths are shown by the numbers, because only a few workstations are used to generate equivalent user loading for the test. There are other throughput tests that could be run, but this was defined as the most critical for the operational status of the network.

For reliability testing, the test scripts should measure all links and nodes concurrently. Figure 15.5 illustrates one possible reliability test load model. Each workstation attached to a hub creates load to verify the reliability of its individual path. In Figure 15.5, this equates to many loads as shown by the numbers. The only equivalent user load is the incoming home office database

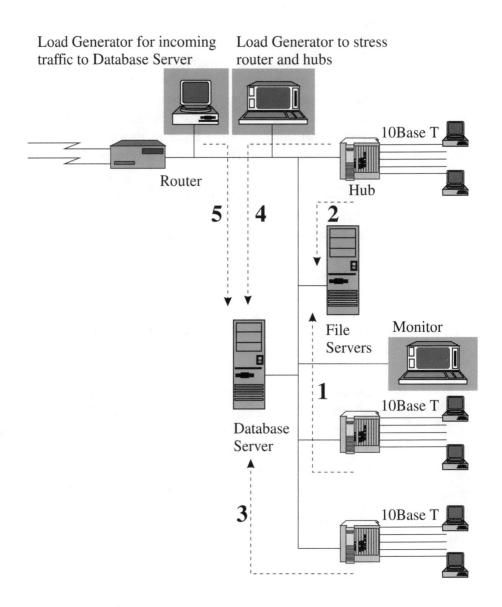

Figure 15.4   Concurrent throughput testing across multiple paths.

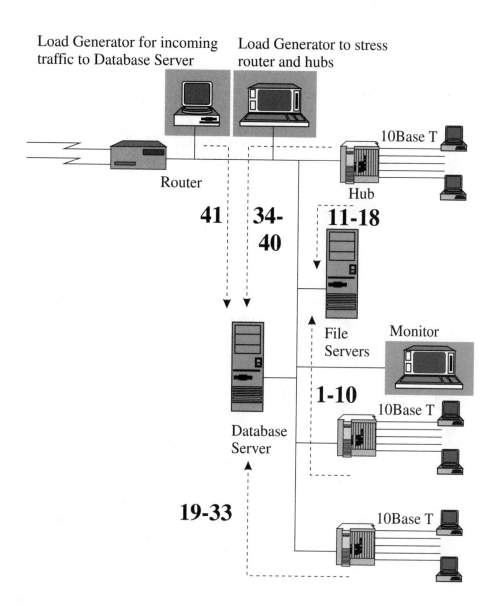

Figure 15.5 Reliability testing requires that all links and nodes be exercised concurrently.

traffic emulation, number 41. For reliability tests, each node should be verified as shown by load paths 1 through 40.

Test Execution and Data Collection

For each of the test objectives included in the acceptance test plan, follow the instructions detailed in this section.

Throughput

The test sequence is:

1. Start the load generators. Verify that the test configuration is working properly, that the load generators can access the file server, that files are being read from the correct servers, and that the load is as specified in the acceptance test plan.

2. Set up a spreadsheet for the first test load and fill in the run ID, test script, load script IDs, and bytes to be transferred. The data collection spreadsheet is discussed in Chapter 11, Figure 11.15.

3. Shut down and restart the load generators for the first test load. Make sure to synchronize the load generators, as discussed in Chapter 10. Run the test and record the time it takes to transfer the files across the internetwork for each load generator. Enter the time for the data transfer into cell B in the data reduction spreadsheet. Based on the KBps transferred and the transfer time, the spreadsheet calculates aggregate throughput across the link.

4. Repeat steps 2 and 3 for the remaining test loads.

Reliability

This test is usually run over a weekend for 48 or more hours. The objective is to determine that the network transport mechanism is stable. The test sequence is:

1. Start the load generators. Verify that the test configuration is working properly, that the load generators can access the file server, that files are being read from the correct servers, that packets are being forwarded by the intermediate nodes, and that the link and CPU utilization are at the correct levels. Chapter 10 describes how to synchronize the load generators.

2. Set up a spreadsheet for the first test load and fill in the run ID, start date and time, test script ID(s), link ID(s), and link and CPU utilization targets in the spreadsheet. Spreadsheet details are discussed in Chapter 12, Figure 12.9.

3. Every 12 hours, record the following data:

   • date and time of the measurement

   • link and CPU utilization

   • total errors and error types recorded by the monitors and intermediate nodes, as appropriate

4. At the end of the test period, usually 48 to 72 hours, record the final test data and shut down the load generators and monitors.

Data Interpretation

Throughput

If the internetwork throughput measurements are within 4 percent of the target, then the system passes the acceptance test. If the throughput is below the target rate:

1. Verify that the network cannot sustain more throughput by adding one more requester. This is important across wide area communication links because some protocol implementations, specifically TCP/IP, throttle data flow based on response time from the server. Test results

may prove that there is unused server and link bandwidth available for additional workstations.

2. If throughput increases, this shows that there is unused bandwidth. If throughput remains below target, the network has not passed the acceptance test.

3. If throughput increases by adding another requester, add more requesters until throughput is maximized. This indicates that the original load model was incorrect, throughput is traffic pattern-dependent, or the reason may be as discussed in item 1. This must be investigated and resolved, but not as part of the acceptance test. The test fails.

In Chapter 5, the section If the Acceptance Test Fails provides further actions that should be taken if the test fails.

Reliability

If the test runs without critical errors, the system passes the acceptance test. If the test completes the time duration, and noncritical errors are recorded, the system passes. The cause of the noncritical errors should be investigated and resolved before the system is deployed into production.

If critical errors are encountered, or portions of the network fail, the test fails. Read the Chapter 5 section, If the Acceptance Test Fails, for further actions that should be taken.

Infrastructure: Product Evaluation

TEST MATRIX

Product evaluation testing of the network infrastructure can be conducted for subsystems, such as routers, and a technology, such as ATM or FDDI, using an emulated test configuration and load. Product evaluation testing is not done on an internetwork configuration because there are too many variables in such a configuration to achieve a valid comparison.

Since many companies have selected their router, hub, or switch vendor, classical product comparisons are often not done. The question often asked, then, is not which product to choose, but which technology to choose, and how to compare different technologies. Therefore, product evaluation testing has expanded in scope to include technology evaluation.

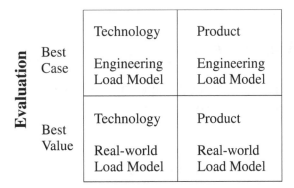

Figure 16.1 Product evaluation alternatives and objectives.

In addition to comparing products or technologies using best case engineering loads and measurements, experienced testers make comparisons using real-world loads. Real-world loads indicate how the product will perform in a specific network environment, and the difference between engineering results and real-world results indicate the excess capacity available in the unit under test. Figure 16.1 shows the expanded dimensions of product evaluation.

SUBSYSTEM EVALUATION TESTING

Evaluation testing compares like features or capabilities of a subsystem or technology. Products or technologies are compared across performance, reliability, feature set, ease of installation, configuration, use, and management.

Creating a product evaluation test is basically creating a regression test. In a product evaluation test, two or more different products are compared; in a regression test, an upgrade is compared to an earlier version. Many times, the criteria used in selecting a product is also valid for ensuring that product upgrades work correctly. This is an excellent way of leveraging the testing done in the planning and design phase. The initial product evaluation test suites can be refined in the deployment stage for acceptance testing, and used in the evolution phase for regression testing.

Test Measurements

Consult the specifics outlined in the throughput, reliability, and functional testing chapters for the type of measurements for each test objective.

Test Configurations

All test configurations are emulated. The test configuration does not have to represent a typical production network configuration for product comparison.

Any valid, unbiased configuration should provide an accurate relative ranking of the tested products. However, the more closely the test configuration and load model represent the real world, the more accurately the test results will predict the operation on your network.

There are two procedures when installing and configuring the test network that should be strictly adhered to:

1. *Ensure that the latest versions of all the test components are included in the configuration.* If a prerelease version from one vendor is used, solicit from other vendors comparable levels of hardware and software. Make the test as fair and consistent as possible to achieve best results. Be cautious in testing prereleases, since release dates often slip, and making a decision on pre-release results could delay the project. Also, prerelease products often "change" by the time they reach production, therefore prerelease product results may differ from released product test results.

2. *Be consistent in comparing "out-of-the-box" or "tuned" versions of the products. This can make a significant difference in test results and can create an apples-to-oranges comparison. If the products are tuned, confirm that all configuration settings are documented in the test journal.*

For product evaluation, all elements in the test configuration are held constant except the product under test. This is very important to ensure that results are truly comparing apples to apples. For subsystems, this is straightforward, since one subsystem is swapped with another in the test configuration, as shown in Figure 16.2.

For technology evaluation, the objective is to compare the technologies; therefore, often several elements of the test configuration must be changed. The important thing is not to modify the source and destination configurations. Figure 16.3 illustrates the test configuration for comparing T1 dedicated lines to switched ISDN lines. In this configuration, both the communication lines and the boxes (routers) may need to be changed. The traffic load and end point configurations remain the same across the tests.

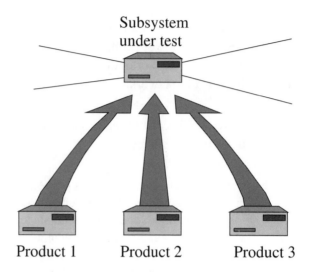

Figure 16.2   Subsystem testing keeps all test configuration attributes constant except the subsystem under test.

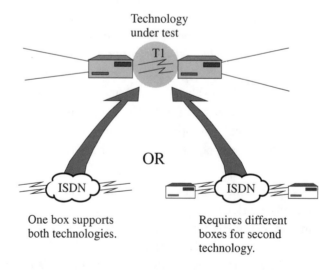

Figure 16.3   Technology testing may require that several test configuration components be swapped between tests, depending on product features.

Before beginning the test project, start a test journal and document the test configuration hardware and software. Be very specific about any configuration settings.

Load Model

The load model and test scripts for product evaluation testing can be constructed to measure best case engineering results or real-world differences in the subsystems or technologies under test. Each approach provides a unique and important measurement, and it is important that the tester understand how these tests differ.

Engineering measurements are best case differences between the products or technologies, and hence, often do not illustrate the difference that will be seen in the production environment. Real-world measurements can be better related to expected differences on a production network, but do not provide insight into product capacity for growth. If time allows, run tests with both loads. Generally, testers only have time to do one test series and choose best case comparisons. Most publications and independent test reports also provide best case comparisons. Based on the measured results, the upcoming Data Interpretation section discusses how to evaluate price and performance numbers relative to production system needs.

Refer to Chapters 9 through 13 for information on how to create load models for the respective tests. For real-world throughput and reliability loading, follow the guidelines in Chapter 9 for baselining the production network and creating the load model. For engineering loads, follow the procedures in Chapter 11 for maximum aggregate throughput, and Chapter 12 for stressed reliability.

Test Execution and Data Collection

For each of the test objectives included in the product evaluation test plan, follow the instructions contained in that test objective's chapter for test execution, data collection, and data interpretation.

The order of conducting tests is not important in product evaluation testing, because, typically, this is not a one-pass sequence, but an iterative process. As tests generate new information, often previous tests are rerun to confirm earlier data, or rerun with slight differences to evaluate another facet of the product. In addition, vendors often provide new product releases or prereleases during evaluation against which various tests must be rerun. Be sure to maintain a good test journal and problem log to avoid confusion during the project.

Data Interpretation

The following discussion, covering Figures 16.4 through 16.6, illustrates how basic test data can be coupled with other information to create different comparisons or "cuts" across the products under test. Figure 16.4 shows that price and performance measurements of the products can be misleading if there is not a baseline against which to compare them. That baseline is the average and peak production network requirements.

In Figure 16.4, chart A has no baseline for comparison, therefore, product M with the best price/performance ratio is top ranked. Chart B illustrates the average and peak loads for the production network. With this baseline, product O is the best alternative, even though its price/performance ratio is slightly lower. Based on the production network requirements, products N, O, and P are overkill. Chart C shows another production network baseline that changes the product selection criteria. There, only product N can meet the peak system throughput demand.

Test measurements plus pricing provide a quantitative method of accurately comparing current product value and anticipated product return over its life cycle. Figure 16.5 shows how price/performance can be mapped to anticipated network growth to establish current and future product return. The conclusions drawn from Figure 16.4, chart B, change when anticipated network growth is overlaid on the chart, as shown in Figure 16.5. Based on forecasted growth, the life cycle for all the products, except N, is less than 18 months. Therefore, to support anticipated growth, product N is the better long-term alternative.

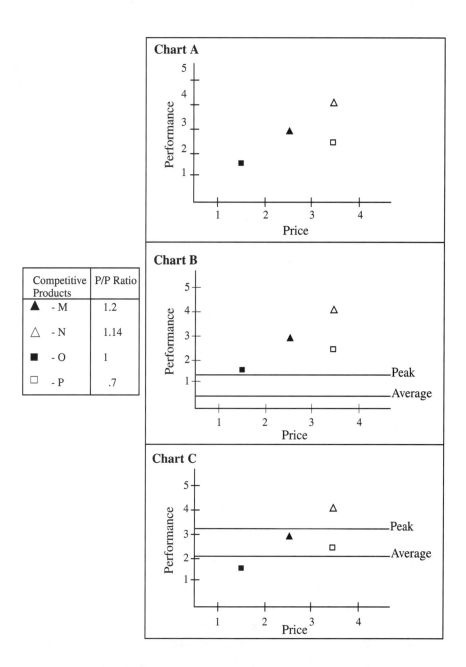

Figure 16.4 Production network baseline requirements are a critical element in product evaluation.

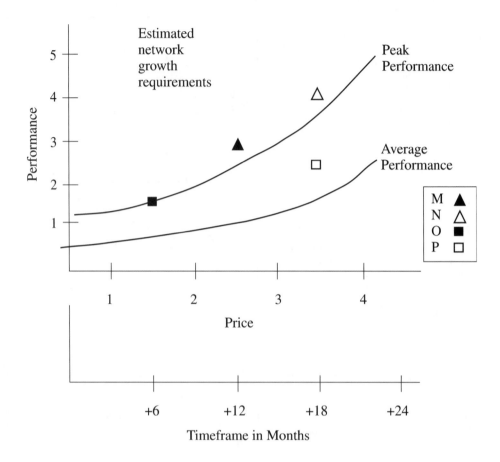

Figure 16.5 Anticipated production network growth is also critical to product evaluation conclusions.

Figure 16.6 illustrates a similar comparison for manageability, using the procedures outlined in Chapter 13, Functional Testing, for estimating product support costs. The total estimated expenditures for the products over 24 months illustrate that products N and P maintain their same relative cost structure, while the cost for product O increases significantly and is roughly equivalent to product M. Using these lifetime costs, the price/performance ratio of the products changes significantly from Figure 16.4.

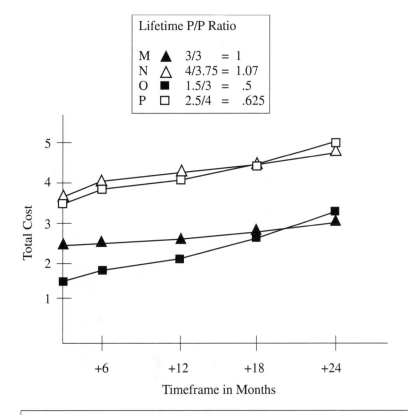

Figure 16.6   Anticipated management costs illustrate that the lowest-price product may not result in the lowest lifetime costs.

Evaluation testing with real-world loads provides product comparison information relevant to the production network. The differences between the engineering and real-world results can be used to gauge performance and reliability growth capacity for the products, as shown in Figure 16.7. Products M, N, and P provide a reasonable level of excess capacity, while product O measures both lower performance and capacity. All the products show good

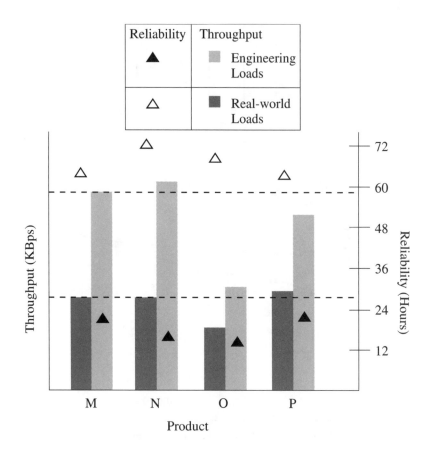

Figure 16.7 Taking both engineering and real-world load measurements allows growth capacity and reliability to be compared.

operational (real-world load) reliability (over 65 hours), but both N and O show lower stability under engineering loads.

Infrastructure: Problem Resolution

INTRODUCTION

Identification and resolution of network infrastructure problems can be improved using testing techniques. *Debugging, as it is commonly called, is much less procedural than the other test objectives, and the following are guidelines and suggestions that are successfully employed by some companies today.*

Most debugging is done using network analyzers. This approach works well if the condition that causes the fault can be trapped and decoded using the analyzer. This is often the hardest part of the debugging process. Using testing techniques in conjunction with a network analyzer can improve the process by:

- Verifying that a suspected component or node can or cannot perform basic required functions. This can be done by running known test cases against the component and determining whether its behavior has changed from previous tests. This may either confirm what is working, thereby eliminating certain areas to investigate, or point to the cause of the problem.

- Reproducing the problem off-line so that it can be isolated, debugged, and corrected.

A large U.S. bank uses testing to perform integrity checks on production network routers that are suspected of problems. If a problem is identified, or the test results vary from previous tests, the router is swapped out of the production network and set aside for further debugging. This allows the bank to quickly

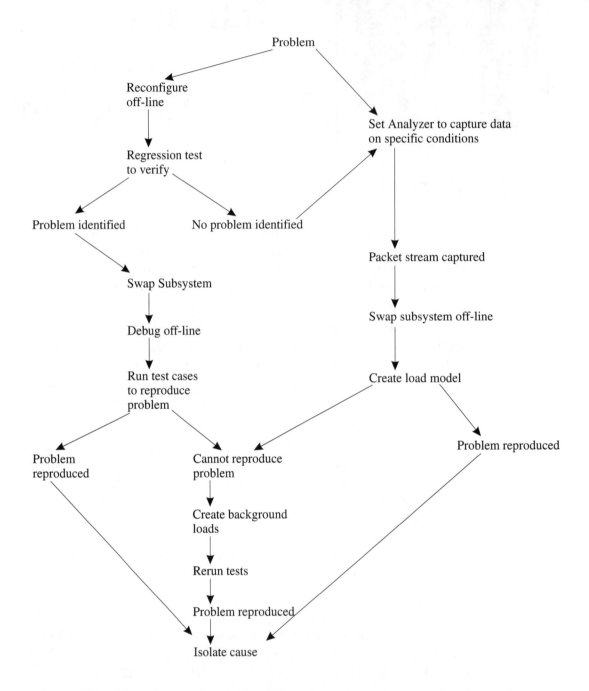

Figure 17.1   Flow diagram for problem debugging using analyzers and testing tools.

ascertain if a subsystem's characteristics have changed and take appropriate action. It does not solve the subsystem problem immediately, but it does allow the production network's operation to continue with minimal disruption.

A major securities firm runs daily tests across its network to verify that the system has not changed over the last 24 hours. These tests are run during off-hours. Any day-to-day change measured by the testing is immediately investigated. The firm's objective is to avoid problems by detecting symptoms early and addressing them before a problem arises.

Today's testing tools, particularly for the infrastructure, are not well-suited for problem debugging or execution on the production network. These tools can, however, assist in problem debugging on emulated test configurations by following the flow diagram shown in Figure 17.1.

Debugging is simply the application of existing test scripts from reliability, throughput, and functional testing for the reproduction and isolation of problems.

DEBUG TESTING

In throughput, reliability, and functional testing, the test measurements are designed to collect data on how well the unit under test is running. When these same tests are used in debugging, the measurement emphasis switches focus. In debugging, the objective is to create and trap problems or symptoms that point to an underlying problem.

For example, if a router is running multiple protocols, throughput testing is designed to measure the sustained and maximum throughput of the router. If the suspected problem is that, under peak loads the router drops excessive packets, the throughput test can be used to measure under what test conditions dropped packets occur. One test case on a well-known router showed that when the router was running IPX, IP, DECNet, and AppleTalk protocols, a peak in IPX traffic on any segment caused a significant increase in dropped DECNet packets on all segments. While this didn't solve the problem, it led to further testing that showed other protocol combinations caused similar problems, one of which was the configuration of the suspect router.

Similarly, reliability testing can be used to accelerate the time domain, and attempt to re-create a problem. For debugging, the time the test runs is not nearly as important as failures or problems trapped along the way. These are often reproductions of the problems encountered on the suspect unit. If problems on the network often occur during month-end closing, when activity is high, accelerated tests can be run to emulate the higher loads with the intent of re-creating the problems in a short time frame. If a problem can be reproduced on a repetitive basis, it is much easier to isolate the cause.

Functional testing can be used to confirm that the product works properly, thereby eliminating possible areas for debugging. The functional tests can also be modified to create forced error conditions that are suspected of causing a problem. This can help determine if the unit under test correctly handles a particular error condition.

Test Configurations

All test configurations are emulated and should represent as closely as possible the production network configuration on which the problem exists.

Load Model

The load model and test scripts for debugging can be modeled from the conditions on the production system when the problem occurred, or they can be the basic scripts used for other test objectives. The former modeling is the best, but often it is hard to accurately trap and re-create the conditions just prior to a failure or problem. A network analyzer is an excellent tool for recording conditions, if specific criteria can be defined to trigger data capture by the analyzer. Most analyzers require that an operator be at the analyzer to start the recording when the problem is detected. This is both time-consuming and boring, but it is how companies debug their networks.

Often, a perceived problem on one segment is caused by conditions in the subsystem due to load or problems on other attached segments. Therefore, it may be required to capture data from multiple segments to re-create the background traffic that actual caused the problem. This can be very difficult and time-consuming, which is one reason that it is often easier, more timely, and as effective to use or modify existing test scripts to reproduce problems.

Test Execution and Data Collection

Referring to the flow diagram in Figure 17.1, the following provides additional detail on the steps and test execution for problem debugging:

1. For a suspected or detected problem, a network analyzer can be used to trap the specific conditions prior to the problem; or the unit can be tested off-line to verify its integrity. Existing regression test script(s) can be used for the integrity testing.

2. If a problem or irregularity is identified through the testing, the unit can be swapped out and debugged later.

3. If no problem is detected in item 2, an analyzer can be used to attempt to trap the error conditions.

4. If production network conditions are not recorded, existing test scripts can be used to attempt to reproduce and isolate the problem. If a trace has been successfully captured, test scripts can be modified or designed to re-create the conditions prior to the problem.

5. If testing cannot reproduce the problem, it may indicate that other factors, such as background traffic on that segment or load on the subsystem from other segments, contribute to the cause of the problem. This would require expanding the test configuration to more accurately model the production system.

6. Once the problem can be reproduced on a repetitive basis, cause isolation and resolution can be achieved.

Part

III

Testing Application Layers

PART III INTRODUCTION

A horse, a horse, my kingdom for a horse !

King Richard III in Shakespeare's play by the same name lead by example. Without his leadership and inspiration, the kingdom infrastructure of knights, armies, and castles had little function or direction. Similarly, without direction from applications, the network infrastructure has little function. A network, like a country, cannot exist without a solid infrastructure; but to be useful it needs direction. In a country, this is called leadership; on a network, these are called applications and services.

Striking a balance between what is desired and what is achievable are the keys to success for a network and a kingdom. King Richard's actions often put England in peril. Network managers are more fortunate: proactive testing can help them balance growth and risk, and reduce perils on the production network.

The most reliable network, possibly in the whole world, has been running for over seven years without a single failure. When the network administrator was asked how this had been accomplished, his answer was simple. He took a conservative approach to growth, which reduced risk and problems. None of the components has been changed or upgraded since they were installed, thereby eliminating problems caused by change. The network has one file server, one workstation, and one application, thereby keeping network load to a minimum. Based on the single workstation configuration, only one user can access the network at a time, thus eliminating multiuser problems. This is certainly a unique network with very little growth or risk. In fact, many people wouldn't even call this a network.

Let's say that the Widgets Company business is booming and the company has plans for adding two more workstations, an upgrade to the NOS, and a new application for account receivables. The new application will integrate with the current application that tracks widget inventory. What are the chances for a smooth upgrade? Is there something easy and inexpensive that it could or should do to reduce risk? Even for such a small network, the answer is *yes*.

The network manager could take the two new workstations and configure a small network (not surprisingly, two nodes, just like their current network), install the existing NOS and application, and perform a practice upgrade to determine problems and issues before upgrading the production network. The staff could also perform functional and response time tests on the new application. With this information in hand, there is a higher probability of a smooth upgrade with minimal risk. In fact, using this approach, the network manager may have been convinced years ago to grow the network faster.

This fictitious example illustrates that even the simplest network can benefit from proactive testing that minimizes the risk and fear brought about through change. In reality, this wouldn't be done because of time and cost, but maybe it should be.

Example 18.1 Even small networks benefit from testing.

My wife recently got a statement from our health insurance company that had a medical charge reconciliation on it for which we had never been billed by the doctor. Naturally, she called the doctor to investigate. She found that the office network of three workstations and one server had just been upgraded with new hardware and software. In the upgrade process, the patient database somehow got a mixture of new and old patient information. The database had our correct name, phone number, and social security number, but the wrong address. Bills that were automatically generated by the application were being sent to the wrong address. This is a good case in point where there was probably little or no implementation or acceptance testing. The nontechnical doctor's office just assumed that everything would work. Unfortunately, my wife wasn't the only patient that had a billing problem and the staff found out the hard way that they shouldn't assume; they should have verified that things worked. The only way to do that is to test the application.❏

As networks grow, the same arguments (no time, money, or resources) are often used for not doing testing. This is how many companies and network managers get into trouble. The old adage that "it is easier to do it twice than to do it right the first time" is the way many networks are managed. The network is implemented. When it doesn't work, it is debugged and reengineered. As networks grow, the upper layers begin to dominate the quality, reliability, and performance of the system. These must be tested, just like the infrastructure, to proactively attack a primary cause of network problems.

*Part III discusses network application/presentation layer testing, which addresses the upper layers of the network. These layers are composed of applications, database software, GUI interfaces, and desktop presentation software, which collectively provide the user's interface to the network. From a testing perspective, these layers are all considered to be "network applications" and are called the **application layers**. Experience has shown that it is best to test these layers together because of their inter-dependence.*

*There is also enabling software and hardware, the NOS, file servers, and workstations, which run below the applications and above the network infrastructure. Combined, they are called the **network platform**, and are tested as a single subsystem.* Network applications are dependent on the network platform used; for example, different applications are required on a Sun NFS network than on a Novell NetWare system.

Figure 18.1 illustrates application layer and network platform testing focus. Application layer testing measures applications, GUI interfaces, and database software as the user sees and perceives them. Network platform testing measures the NOS distributed across the file server(s) and workstation(s) and the hardware it runs on. For application and network platform testing, the infrastructure of the network is treated as much as possible as a "black box."

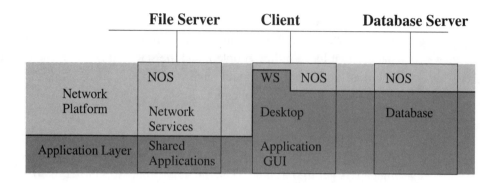

Figure 18.1   Difference between application layer and network platform focus.

For the application/presentation layers, the key test objectives are response time, reliability, throughput, and capacity. These overlap the primary test objectives for the network infrastructure, reliability and throughput, and add two objectives that are weighted heavily toward client-server applications.

Part II discussed how proactive testing is used to provide a reliable, high-performance network infrastructure capable of supporting client-server applications and company-wide services, such as electronic mail and Lotus Notes. Part III shows how proactive testing also improves the reliability, responsiveness, and usability of network applications, user interfaces and services—the leading causes of both user satisfaction and dissatisfaction. Figure 18.2 depicts the area of coverage of subsystem, internetwork, network platform, and application layer testing presented in Parts II and III.

Two types of load modeling are required. File I/O load scripts, similar to those used in internetwork testing, are used for network platform testing. For application layer and some network platform testing, load scripts composed of application commands and mouse point-and-click movements are required to emulate user interaction with the application and presentation (desktop) layers. For database testing, the application front end is circumvented. Similar to testing a router with packet streams in Part II, transaction streams are preferred because they provide finer control of load and traffic patterns against the database server.

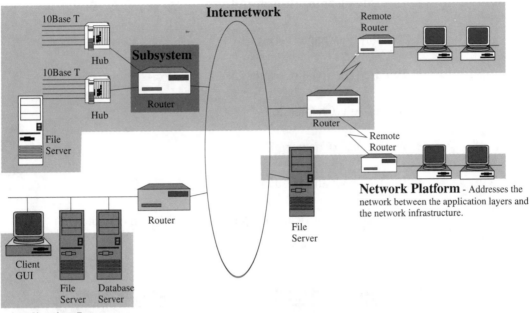

Figure 18.2 Coverage of subsystem, internetwork, network platform, and application layer testing.

> *For application testing, the load generator is the actual application GUI; for database testing, it is a transaction generator; for network platform testing, the load generator is often a batch file or program that emulates file I/O.*

Based on the test philosophy and methodology developed in Part I, Part III discusses testing applications and network platform configurations for the following test objectives:

- Response time (Chapter 20)

- Throughput (Chapter 21)

- Configuration sizing (Chapter 22)

- Capacity planning (Chapter 23)

- Reliability (Chapter 24)

- Feature/functional (Chapter 25)

- Regression (Chapter 26)

- Acceptance (Chapter 27)

- Product evaluation (Chapter 28)

- Bottleneck identification and problem resolution (Chapter 29)

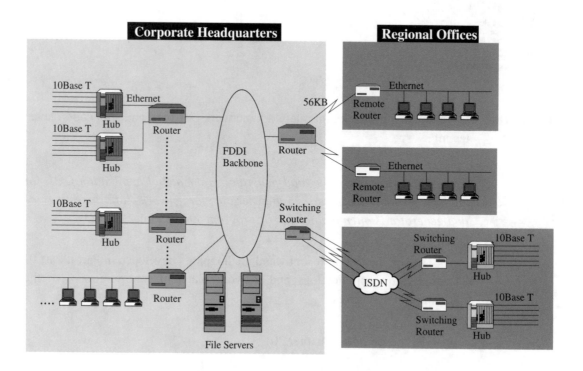

Figure 18.3   Large internetwork example.

Response time, throughput, configuration sizing, and capacity planning tests are the core test objectives for network application/presentation layer testing. Regression, acceptance, and product evaluation testing combine aspects of response time, throughput, capacity planning, and reliability testing to achieve test plan objectives. Bottleneck identification and problem resolution use basic testing principles to re-create and isolate problems. The chapters in Part III describe test configurations, test execution, data collection, and data analysis for applications and network platform testing for the above 10 test objectives.

Figure 18.3 illustrates a corporate headquarters and regional office internetwork configuration for a large company. For discussion purposes, this is the same example network used in Part II, Figure 9.1. As a refresher, for infrastructure testing, the internetwork test configuration used is shown in Figure 18.4. This model allows critical point-to-point paths through the internetwork to be tested. For subsystem testing in Part II, Figure 18.3 was divided into key subsystems, as shown in Figure 18.5.

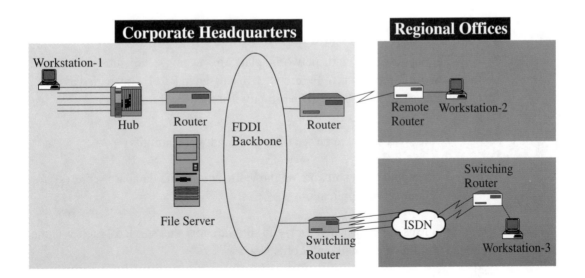

Figure 18.4   Internetwork test configuration for the production network in Figure 18.3.

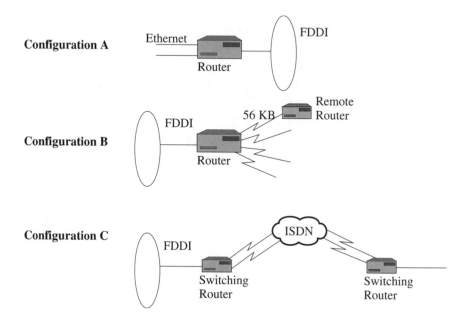

Figure 18.5   Subsystem test configurations for the production network in Figure 18.3.

For application and network platform testing, the subsystems and internetwork components of Figure 18.3, discussed in Part II, are treated as much as possible as a "black box." The primary test focus is the end points:

- the NOS software on the file server and workstation(s)

- the application software on the workstations and database server(s), for client-server applications

- the user interface and back-end software for other services, such as name or directory, mail, and Lotus Notes

- the server and workstation hardware

A) Application test configurations

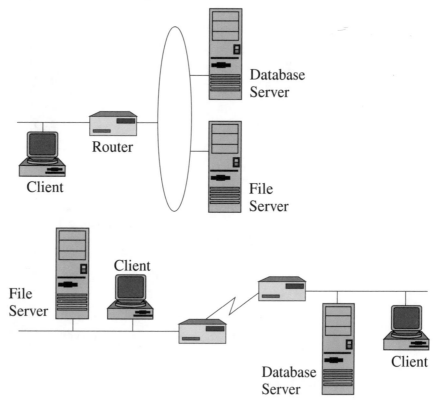

Figure 18.6A Test configuration examples for application layer testing.

Figures 18.6A is a test configuration example for application layer testing based on the corporate network shown in Figure 18.3. Application and network platform test configurations must allow access to the file and database servers to be measured both locally and remotely as they will be used across the network. Modeling all possible media and path combinations is not required as long as the highest and lowest performance media are covered in the tests.

B) Network platform test configurations

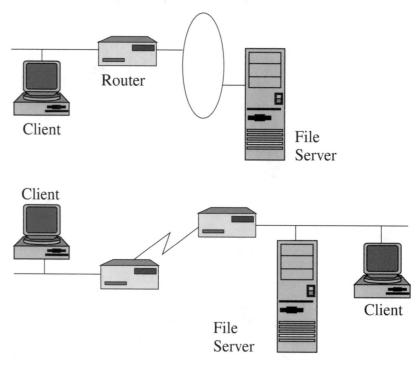

Figure 18.6B   Test configuration examples for network platform testing.

Figure 18.6B is used for network platform testing, and is like Figure 18.6A, but without the database servers. *From the preceding figures and discussion, it may already be apparent that infrastructure and application/presentation layer testing is not quite as simple as the previous partitioning implies.* Network baseline measurements in PPS are the direct result of application requests for file opens, record reads and writes, and other file server or database server requests. Application response times are dependent on both server response and internetwork path throughput between the server and workstation. You may be wondering, then, why Parts II and III partitioned the network into different testing layers.

The interaction between the many components that make up a network is very complex, in fact too complex to accurately model and analyze in a single configuration. Testing and measuring a complex network may provide lots of data, but the contribution of individual network parts cannot be isolated from the whole. *The Art of Testing Network Systems* presents a test philosophy that identifies network layer testing that facilitates isolating, testing, and analyzing key network parts separately. It does not, however, mean these network parts can be analyzed independently. In fact, the opposite is true. Test data from a Part II infrastructure test is often critical to modeling and analyzing a Part III application test, and vice versa. Testing is usually an iterative process in which results from one test influence or define parameters for subsequent tests.

The following examples illustrate how the measurements and processes discussed under various test objectives in Parts II and III are interrelated and used in analyzing the network from top to bottom.

Example 18.2 Isolating a throughput bottleneck.

A new client-server application, which is scheduled to support several hundred

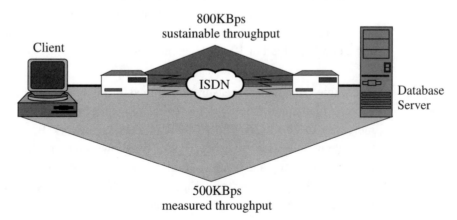

Figure 18.7   Comparing network sustainable throughput and client-server application throughput across the internetwork.

Network A: 100 Equivalent Users   **Network B: 200 Equivalent Users**

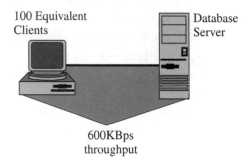

100 Equivalent   Database
Clients   Server

600KBps
throughput

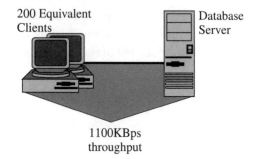

200 Equivalent   Database
Clients   Server

1100KBps
throughput

Figure 18.8   Client-server application throughput without internetwork paths.

users, is to be added to an existing internetwork. Internetwork throughput testing measures sustainable rates of 800KBps. When the client-server application is tested across the internetwork with an emulated load of 100 equivalent users (Figure 18.7), the measured throughput is only 500KBps, 50 percent below the expected requirement of 750KBps for the 100 users.

Since the internetwork can support a load greater than what was measured, the immediate assumption is that the database server is the bottleneck. A second test is run on a single segment network, shown in Figure 18.8, network A, using the same emulated load of 100 equivalent users.

The single segment test measures combined throughput of over 600KBps, which is better than the internetwork test results, but still below the target. The load is increased to 200 users, shown in Figure 18.8, network B, and the measured throughput increases to 1100KBps. This shows that the database server has additional capacity and is not the bottleneck. Repeating the 200-user load on the internetwork measures throughput of 794KBps. This approximates the maximum sustained rate for the internetwork.

These test results have not identified the bottleneck, but they have eliminated the internetwork and database server as the source, and point to the workstation software. Another test is run that eliminates the GUI front end. Transactions are sent to the database server from a C program. This test measures maximum server throughput of 1400KBps.

In this example, the test organization first tested the internetwork to determine whether it could sustain the estimated application throughput and determined that it could. It next tested the new application across the internetwork and discovered a bottleneck. Since the internetwork was not the bottleneck, the next step was to determine whether the database server could sustain adequate throughput. When it was found that the server had excess throughput capacity, the application GUI interface was suspected and then shown to be the bottleneck. An effort is next required to isolate the GUI bottleneck. There are numerous application QA test utilities, including Mercury System's WinRunner and Microsoft Test, that can be used to diagnose the GUI front end. A combination of test results from internetwork and application layer testing provided results that pinpointed the application bottleneck.❏

Example 18.3 Determining production system capacity for new applications.

A new client-server application is tested on a single segment network. Response time is measured at 2.5 seconds average per client for up to 50 clients, which is the design target. Using a network analyzer, the total kilobytes and average KBps are recorded during the test.

The test group does not have the equipment available to set up an internetwork configuration for performance testing. It does, however, have a spare server and workstations that can be added to the production system. Using the measured KBps from the client-server test as the throughput requirement, a test is configured to measure the excess capacity on the company internetwork between the points at which the client-server workstations and database server will be located, as shown in Figure 18.9. The test is run at various times per day for one week. The test is only one minute long, thereby minimizing production network impact.

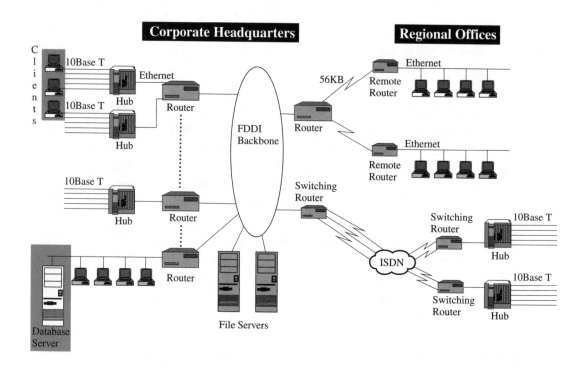

Figure 18.9   Measuring network infrastructure capacity based on client-server application load requirements.

The average and standard deviation of KBps for the test is calculated; it is below the required rate. Based on the results, the company internetwork cannot provide adequate KBps support. Therefore, the target response time of 2.5 seconds for the new application cannot be achieved across the internetwork.❑

This example used a combination of application testing during development and real-world internetwork throughput testing to determine that insufficient capacity exists in the network infrastructure before deploying the new application. Further internetwork testing is required to isolate the bottleneck and expand capacity of the production network.

Example 18.4 Acceptance test.

A new regional office network for 100 users is installed, as diagrammed in Figure 18.10. Prior to bringing the network on-line, an acceptance test is conducted to ensure that the network is reliable. The test is run for 48 hours over a weekend. Figure 18.10 illustrates how internetwork, regional office network platform and distributed client-server application tests are run simultaneously as part of the acceptance test.

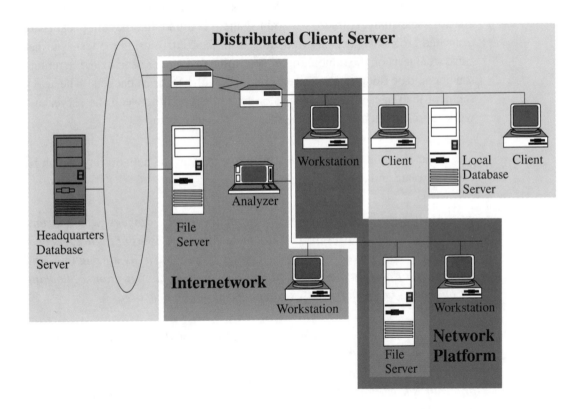

Figure 18.10 New network acceptance testing.

Although the servers and workstations do not crash, by the end of 24 hours, the servers have dropped several user sessions, and the analyzer has recorded a high number of errors on the file server's segment. Almost all the error statistics are runt packets, but no actual packets were captured. The errors are initially ignored, based on the assumption that the file server became overloaded and dropped sessions. A network platform test is conducted to measure the reliability of the file server with a very large emulated user load. The server runs for 24 hours without a single dropped session.

Since the file server test shows that it is stable, the test is rerun with the analyzer set to capture runt packets. The test fails after 26 hours when the file server crashes. The analyzer trace is examined and it is found that the runt packets are truncated broadcast packets originating from the router during the test. Further subsystem tests on the remote router determine that, under peak load, the remote router could be flooding the server's segment with broadcast packets. The heavy segment load caused the transmission to be disrupted between the server and workstations, which caused the server to time-out sessions.❏

This example shows how test results from various network layers can be used to isolate and debug a network problem.

As illustrated in these examples, proactive testing provides two important data points: First, test results can eliminate suspected areas of failure; second, test results can provide known reference points, such as throughput and reliability, for correlating results across different test configurations. Looking for anomalies between test cases can help isolate problem areas.

Testing is rarely a single step. Loads generated or measured in one test are often used as input for a subsequent test. One set of test results often lead to additional testing in order to fully analyze the network. Many times, the test procedures from Parts II and III must be used in combination to achieve project objectives.

Figure 18.11 shows the interrelationship between the four distinct tests covered in Parts II and III. Use this as a guide when formulating overall test plans

Measurement	Throughput	Reliability	Response Time	Capacity
Subsystem	Per node	Per node	Indirect contribution	Max-Min Throughput
Internetwork	Point-to-point across interconnecting path	Interoperability	Indirect contribution	Max-Min Throughput
Network Platform	End point capacity	Interoperability	Indirect contribution	NOS and File Server
Application Layer	Server software and hardware	Software	System-level measurement	Application and database

Figure 18.11 Relationship between subsystem, internetwork, network platform, and application/presentation layer tests.

for verifying, debugging, or planning network throughput, reliability, and capacity.

Chapters 18 through 29 cover specific test objectives and outline how to define the test configuration, conduct the test, collect test measurements, and analyze results. Since load modeling and load generation are similar for all the tests, these two topics are discussed in the remainder of Chapters 18 and 19, respectively.

DEVELOPING THE LOAD MODEL

There are three basic load model formats required for application/presentation layer testing:

- Application tests require a command or mouse point-and-click sequence as input to the application program or GUI.

- Database server tests require transaction streams.

- Network platform tests require a series of file I/O requests.

As discussed in the Chapter 1 examples and Chapter 9, Developing the Load Model, often the test project must develop a load model before the actual loading is known or even before the applications are developed. The outline in Chapter 9 for estimating, aging, and baselining for load model development applies equally for applications as for the network infrastructure. The outline is repeated below for ease of reference:

1. Start with the best estimate of traffic patterns based on experience, gut feel, or anything else available as input. Gather baseline information for existing networks and users, if available.

2. Bracket step 1 loads with at least two higher and one lower traffic pattern. By testing all five load points, you get factual information about system performance, degradation, and reliability as load changes. This provides both hard numbers and a perspective on the sensitivity of the network to load changes.

3. Estimate or predict network aging. Look at growth over one and three years. Use worse case scenarios to increase the loads in step 2 and rerun the tests. This will measure whether the network can sustain the growth, and, if it can't, give some estimate of the cost to grow capacity.

4. As soon as portions of the network and applications are installed, start baselining the system and compare the baseline numbers to the assumptions in steps 1 and 3. As a history of the baseline develops, compare this to the load models used and adjust them accordingly.

5. Continue testing and use the results to adjust the installed network, upgrades, and growth accordingly.

Application Load Modeling: Command Sequences and Transaction Streams

Load models for application testing typically take one of six forms:

- **Network centric:** These load scripts are focused on generating maximum network activity based on the GUI front end or a program-generated transaction stream. These scripts attempt to stress the file server and database server with a minimum amount of workstations. A transaction generator eliminates GUI front-end overhead and allows a higher rate of transaction flow with less test hardware. It also helps to isolate bottlenecks between the GUI and back-end server. Network centric scripts are used for response time, reliability, throughput, configuration, capacity, and regression testing.

- **Real-world:** Real-world scripts try to mimic actual user interaction. They include a wide range of application commands, pauses for think time, verification of responses, and often, induced error conditions. These scripts are often used for regression testing or when a large network configuration is available for testing, such as Novell's Super Lab. To generate high-network load requires many more workstations than for the network centric scripts.

- **Key features:** These scripts are limited to 5 to 10 of the most widely used and important application features. They are often used for acceptance testing, as they generate high loads as well as verify critical application features.

- **Key functions:** These scripts are limited to load-sensitive operations associated with database servers and distributed network services, such as name directories, groupware, and mail. For database servers, these include background operations, such as transaction logging, transaction rollback, data synchronization, and backup.

- **Workstation/GUI centric:** As a previous example illustrates, the workstation GUI and desktop can have a significant impact on overall system and application performance. These scripts attempt to measure response delays either in the GUI software or in switching between desktop overlays, as is typical on a securities trading desk or customer support desk, where many integrated applications are needed by the user. These scripts generate network overhead based on downloading overlays, saving temporary files, and swap file activity between workstations, and file or database servers. Generally, these scripts are run in conjunction with other scripts, often a network centric script.

- **QA test script:** A good QA test verifies every application feature and command, similar to the way users actually access the application. These scripts are used for network feature testing involving a few workstations and are more complex than required for most network tests.

The key to creating scripts is to create a script library of individual modules that can be combined into more complex scripts and modified to create new scripts. For example, network centric, real-world, and key feature scripts may have 50 percent of the same commands. Adding pauses to a key feature script creates a real-world script. Cutting a QA script apart is a good start at network centric and key feature scripts. The point is, don't create one monolithic script; rather, create small, focused scripts that can be reused and modified over and over. Script preparation takes time, and this approach saves time and effort.

Defining Script Contents

For deployed systems, the best source of script input is from users and monitoring software. For new development, the best approach is to build scripts based on the requirements specification and modify them based on actually testing the software.

Real-world, key feature, key function, workstation/GUI centric, and QA script types are developed based on application commands or requests. Network centric and sometimes key function scripts, however, require transactions rather than commands. It is often hard to equate a specific application command or request with the appropriate transaction sequence. This is particularly true for "chatty" programs. As discussed in Example 1.1, a simple database request for record access generated 120 network transactions. Several companies doing client-server application testing have found that a new version of CoroNet's CMS product is very good for monitoring the application transaction flow.

The sequence of events for baselining the application and loading the database server is:

1. Identify a database request, such as a record access, sort, record update, and so on.

2. Run the request and monitor the application activity using CMS.

3. From CMS data, create the transaction sequence that corresponds to the request.

4. Use Mercury Interactive's LoadRunner to generate the transaction stream against the database server.

Application Load Scripts are as varied as the applications they test, therefore, script formats and contents cannot be specifically defined in this book. The following guidelines, however, will help in developing good scripts.

1. Network-oriented scripts are different from QA test scripts. Network scripts should not attempt to exercise every application feature. Usually, a few well-selected features that create network traffic make a better script than many different features. For example, a client-server application script would include accessing a random record, changing the record key, writing the record back as a new entry, and repeating the process 1,000 times. Commands, such as editing, sorting, and printing are often-used functions, but don't create significant workstation-to-server activity. These functions place load on the workstation or database server and are used for GUI/workstation and server CPU testing.

2. When measuring response time, always exclude startup and shutdown activities from the timed loop of commands. If included, these activities will skew test results. If startup and shutdown timing is important, measure them in a separate test.

3. Scripts that test the database server are more effective if they bypass the GUI and generate transaction streams against the server.

4. For response time tests, use keystrokes to invoke commands and do not verify the content of server response, as these typically reduce the load on the workstation and allow more transactions to be generated per workstation.

5. Verify mouse operations and server responses in QA feature-oriented test scripts, not in network test scripts.

6. For real-world and key feature scripts, use the interface most likely to be used by the users. In most GUI environments, this will be mouse point-and-click operations.

7. Reliability tests sometimes verify responses to ensure correct operation of the application, particularly when problems are suspected.

8. Make sure the script runs correctly on a single workstation, then try it on two or three workstations concurrently. This will identify any conflicts with multiple users accessing the same record before larger multiuser tests are run.

Load scripts are dependent on the load generator used. Chapter 19 discusses load generators for application testing, including an example load script.

Estimating Equivalent-User Loading

When developing an equivalent-user load, it is important to understand how many users each workstation or session emulates. The simplest method uses equivalent wall clock time to estimate the emulated number of users per workstation. In this method, a user goes through a predefined script at a rate that corresponds to actual user interaction with the system. One pass of the load script is run and timed. The ratio between the two times is used to determine the equivalent number of emulated users. For example, a user completes the script in 10 minutes. The automated test script takes one minute to complete the same operations. There is a 10 to 1 ratio of automated versus manual script execution. Each workstation represents 10 users. If the test network has 20 workstations, either 20 actual users can manually run the test, or 200 (20 x 10) equivalent users can run the test.

Equivalent user estimates should be developed for each script. If a script is very long or very repetitive, such as doing an operation 1,000 times, an estimate of equivalent loading can still be made by timing only one pass through the script and multiplying the time to estimate script duration. Generally, this will be sufficiently accurate for emulated load testing.

Verifying Application Response

This is particularly important for QA and feature/functional testing, but generally not for network testing. Response verification is sometimes used in regression, acceptance, and reliability tests, but is rarely needed in other tests.

When verifying responses, it is useful to measure the time from the request to the response. This provides a measure of turnaround time on the server. Tracking the time between acceptance of a response and the next request measures workstation GUI performance, as shown in Figure 18.12.

Bursty Traffic Patterns

All network data traffic is bursty. Therefore, similar to infrastructure reliability testing, application/presentation layer reliability testing benefits from bursty traffic patterns against the unit under test. Since each workstation in the test is generating as many transactions as possible, and each session between the workstation and server is asynchronous in nature, the only method of creating

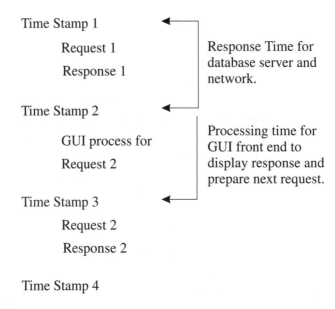

Figure 18.12   Example of setting time stamps to measure network and workstation GUI performance.

bursty traffic is to have additional workstations (that is equivalent users) log on and run test scripts on a random basis. Since there are no testing tools that provide this capability, either a manual process must be used, an in-house program must be written to wake up and shut down additional workstations, or, as is typically done, the test uses a uniform load, without bursty traffic.

File I/O Load Model

Network platform tests use file and record I/O scripts similar to those used for internetwork testing. When developing a load script that emulates an application, it is important to get the following combinations in the correct proportions:

1.   average and maximum file and record sizes read and written

2. percentage of reads versus writes

3. percentage of cached versus hard disk access

4. downloads of new application overlays from the application server to the workstation to satisfy user selections of menu items

Load modeling typically uses the following corresponding values for the preceding combinations when exact numbers are not present:

1. Estimated file size based on experience and application type. Typical file sizes used are: 2Kbytes (mail message), 10 to 20Kbytes (word document), 100Kbytes (large document), 250Kbytes (graphics file), 1000Kbytes (large graphics file).

2. Four reads to one write.

3. Data models use all cached data by preloading the file into cache before beginning the test, or they use all disk I/O by defining a small cache size or a large file to avoid any caching. Segmenting the I/O between cache and hard disk hits—as occurs in the real-world—is very difficult and therefore, rarely modeled. Running one test with all cached data and one with all hard disk-based data will provide upper and lower bounds on performance and capacity.

4. This is usually not modeled.

The more accurately the model reflects the production load, the more accurate will be the test results. Use a network analyzer or one of the newer application load monitors, such as Intel's LANDesk or CoroNet's Management System (CMS), to baseline data traffic between a single workstation and the server.

Have a user walk through the desired application series of commands at the workstation. Capture the wall clock time, file I/O activity (reads and writes), and

	Manual Test	**Load Script**
Duration	5 Min.	1.2 Min.
Bytes Read	10,000,000	17,000,000
Bytes Written	5,600,000	3,500,000
Time Ratios	4.166	(5/1.2)
Bytes Read Ratio	1.7	(17,000,000/10,000,000)
Bytes Written Ratio	1.6	(5,600,000/3,500,000)
Approx. Equivalent users	7	(Time Ratio*I/O Ratio=4.2*1.65)

Figure 18.13   Illustrates correlating manual loading to script loading.

network throughput. Then create a file I/O load script based on the captured data. Run the load script and compare network I/O to the manual session. Use the measurements to create an estimated equivalent user loading per workstation for the test script. Figure 18.13 illustrates this process.

Load scripts to create file and record I/O sequences are dependent on the load generator used. Chapter 19 discusses several load generators for network platform testing and how to create load scripts for each.

TEST CONFIGURATION PROBLEM RESOLUTION TIPS

When multiple runs generate test results that vary by more than 4 percent, the results are considered unreproducible. The first step is to determine whether problems in the test configuration are skewing the results. If a problem is found, it must be fixed and the tests rerun. In the absence of any problems, the conclusion is that the unit under test is causing the inconsistent results and the test results are valid.

To verify that the test configuration is working correctly, check:

- **Physical connections:** Confirm that all connections are tight and that all cabling is correct.

- **Timing:** Synchronize the clocks on all clients and workstations so they are set to the same time.

- **Synchronization of load generators:** Make sure that all load generators are started at the same time. Try starting the load generators in a different order to see if the test results change. Choose a specific process for synchronization and make sure it is used for each test case.

- **Intermittent errors:** Rerun the test, and use an analyzer to monitor the test configuration for intermittent errors, excessive broadcast packets, or other problems that could affect test results.

- **Load Scripts:** Verify that correct load scripts are used on all clients.

- **Configurations:** Verify parameter and INI file setting on all clients and servers.

Application Layer Testing Tools

CATEGORIES OF TESTING TOOLS

There are two categories of tools used for application/presentation layer testing. The first testing tool category generates load based on application commands and mouse point-and-click sequences. These utilities are called by many names in the industry, such as GUI automated development tools, automated software quality (ASQ) products, and client-server testing tools, as referred to in this book. They are used for testing applications and graphical desktops or presentation managers, such as MS Windows, Macintosh, OSF/Motif, and OS/2 Presentation Manager. The tools are workstation- and network operating system-dependent, as are the applications and GUIs they test. Client-server testing tools with the proper test scripts and test configuration can be used to test the application GUI, the workstation presentation layer (desktop), and the database server. Tools in this category include Mercury Interactive's WinRunner, Microsoft Test by Microsoft, AutoTester by AutoTester, Inc., and QA Partner by Seque Software, Inc. Refer to Part IV for additional product information.

The second tool category generates file I/O requests to the file server. These are used for testing the network platform in much the same way as they are used for testing the internetwork infrastructure in Part II. The test tools are similar, but the testing focuses on a higher layer of the network, and includes the file server, workstations, and NOS. These tools require a NOS on the test configuration, but generally the tool is not NOS-dependent. The tools are typically workstation-dependent and different versions of the tools are required for DOS, Windows, OS/2, and UNIX operating systems. This tool category includes programs such as Novell's Perform3 and Ziff-Davis' ServerBench. Most of these programs can be acquired free of charge from bulletin boards, on diskettes, or on CD-ROM directly from the developer. Other options, such as in-house-developed batch files or Visual BASIC programs, provide flexible, low-cost load generators for network platform testing.

CLIENT-SERVER TESTING TOOLS

Most client-server testing tools allow the test script to be developed either programmatically or through recording keyboard and mouse events. The two approaches provide flexibility for creating test scripts based on requirements or functional specifications before the actual application is completed, and recording user sessions with the application once it is functional.

Script Structure

For a network test, a good test script should include three sections:

1. startup

2. test execution

3. shutdown

Startup

The startup phase coordinates the loading of applications or load generators on each workstation in the test, linking to required files, linking to an audit log or file for recording test results; it also provides a method of coordinating the start of each test execution on the workstations. Depending on the client-server testing tool used, these steps may be manual or automated. A manual sequence of events would be:

1. Log on each workstation and link to directories on the file server.

2. Load and start the test script.

3. The first command in the test script loads, starts the load generator, and opens an audit file for logging purposes. The test script then pauses.

4. When all workstations have loaded and started their respective load generators, the tester starts the test on each workstation by depressing a key. There is a small delay between the first and last workstation starting, but experience has shown that if this is only a few seconds in a three-minute test, overall results are not affected.

If the load generator is fully automated, the test script would perform all the same steps, but would not require manual intervention.

Test Execution

This phase performs the commands, timing, response verification, and other steps included in the test script. It can also perform logging of time stamps as long as there is not significant overhead associated with that process. One way to verify the impact from logging is to run this portion of the script first with logging on, then turned off. Compare the difference in execution time, then calculate the percent increase in execution time due to logging. If the percentage is greater than 2 or 3 percent, logging is impacting execution time.

Usually the test execution is controlled either by a loop count or a timer in the test script. For response time and reliability testing, this portion of the script is run multiple times. For response time testing, usually 20 repetitions or five minutes are sufficient to get a representative average response time. For reliability testing, the script may run from 12 to 72 hours. For other test objectives, usually one pass is sufficient.

For most testing, a time stamp at the beginning and end of the loops is sufficient. The total elapsed time can be used, or it can be divided by the number of repetitions to get a per-pass time. For purely comparative purposes, the former is sufficient.

Shutdown

The final steps in the script clean up the test environment. These chores include logging time stamps, exiting the application, unlinking, and logging out, as appropriate for the test. It is important that individual workstations do not start these steps until all workstations have completed the test. Otherwise, the "last" workstations' times may be skewed because of these new loads on the network.

The following example illustrates how a typical interactive recording session proceeds and the corresponding programmatic script it creates.

Example 19.1 Creating an application load script.

Most client-server testing tools provide record and playback features that allow a test script to be developed by recording the keystrokes and mouse point-and-click interaction of the user. Also, most tools use a programming language to define the script, which allows a recorded script to be modified or a new script to be created without using the recording. This latter feature is useful for script development in parallel with application development. Test scripts can be ready when the application menus are finished, to facilitate their testing. From a network testing perspective, this isn't as important as the ability the programming language provides for modifying existing scripts without having to re-create them through the recording mode.

The following example uses Mercury Interactive's WinRunner product for illustration. This product works with Microsoft Windows for scripting GUI application interfaces. Steps for creating the test script using the recording process are:

1. Start WinRunner and select the **Record** feature.

2. Switch to the client-server application window, called Name Database in this example.

3. Define the startup state for the test. For this test, open an existing file by selecting **Open** on the Names Database **File** menu. When the **Open** menu appears, type the file name, Mail_Lst, and select **OK**.

4. The data entry window appears. Type in the following information for a new entry, and the menu will look like Figure 19.1:

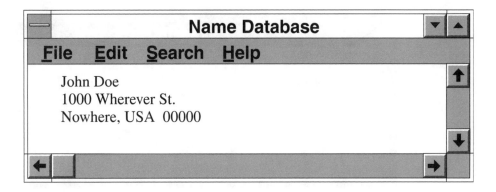

Figure 19.1   New database entry.

John Doe

1000 Wherever Street

Nowhere, USA

5. Search for other surnames of Doe by selecting **Find** from the menu in
    Figure 19.1 and typing in Doe in the **Find What** edit field, Figure 19.2.

6. Press the **Find Next** button. A window will appear listing the
    information on Mary Doe, as shown in Figure 19.3. Press the **Cancel**
    button in the **Name Record** window.

7. To conclude the test, return the Name Database application back to its
    original state. Select **New** on the Name Database File menu. When the
    dialog box appears asking if you wish to save the new entry, press Yes.

8. Switch back to the WinRunner menu and select **Stop**. The resultant test
    script is shown in Figure 19.4. The test commands are easy to read and
    they illustrate essentially each step that was performed through the
    Name Database menu interface.❑

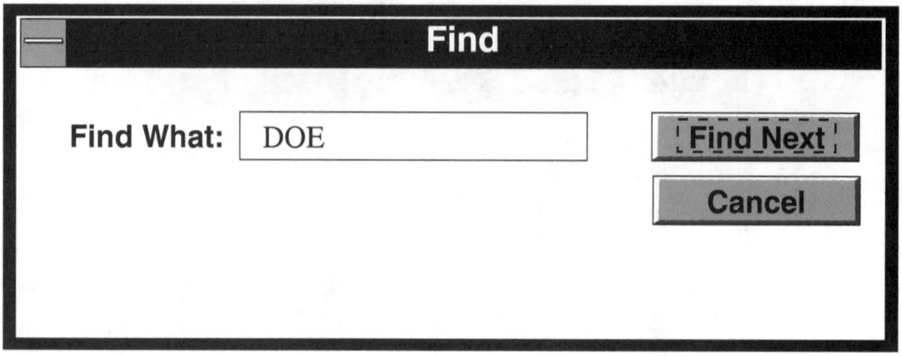

Figure 19.2   Search for matching record, keyword DOE.

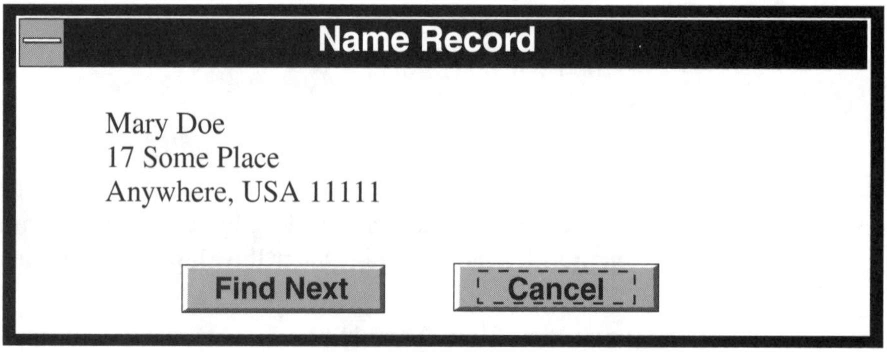

Figure 19.3   Displays first record found, keyword DOE.

Selecting Your Load Generator

There are many aspects to selecting a client-server test tool as a network load generator. Most of these tools have roots in GUI and application QA testing on a single platform. Many have since expanded capabilities that enable them to be run across a network. In running a load generator on the network, consider your individual needs for:

```
                    set_window ("Name Database");
                    menu_select_item ("File;Open");
                    win_activate ("Open");
                    type ("Mail_Lst");
                    button_press ("OK");
                    edit_set_insert_position ("edit",0,0);
                    type ("John Doe");
                    edit_set_insert_position ("edit",10,0);
                    type ("1000 Wherever St.");
                    edit_set_insert_position ("edit",20,0);
                    type ("Nowhere, USA 00000");
                    menu_select_item ("Search; Find");
                    win_activate ("Find");
                    type ("Doe");
                    button_press ("Find Next");
                    button_press ("Cancel");
                    set_window ("Name Database");
                    menu_select_item ("File;New");
                    set_window ("Name Database");
                    button_press ("Yes");
```

Figure 19.4 Test script generated through menu input.

centralized control

cross-platform support

multiuser emulation

test script management

Centralized Control

Centralized control provides better test management through automation of test synchronization, data collection, and monitoring of the workstations running test scripts. The control mechanism between the workstations and the management station should not prohibit the workstations from being placed on other segments and across internetwork links. This flexibility is important for test configurations where users are on different segments from the database or file server. The central station should be able to monitor, start, stop, and interrupt testing. If a test is interrupted, the management station should be able to resynchronize and restart the test without manual intervention.

Cross Platform Support

Many networks support a broad range of workstation hardware, while others have standardized on Microsoft Windows. Some test tools provide a broad range of workstation support, while others go one step farther and provide portability of a single test script across different GUIs. The largest support is for Microsoft Windows, with many products supporting OS/2 and X Windows.

Multiuser Emulation

Since client-server applications may have hundreds to thousands of planned users, the test tool should be able to control at least 50 separate workstations or equivalent sessions. If each workstation or session represents up to 10 actual users, this provides the equivalent of at least 500 users.

Test Script Management

As discussed in Chapter 6, storing, referencing, and accessing test scripts and test results for future use can leverage the test effort considerably. Many client-server test tools are beginning to provide features for test management.

The question is not which testing tool or scripting language is superior, but which tool does the job. Many of the test tools available will support application layer load scripts and cover all the test objectives discussed in the following chapters. If a company is already using a test tool in client-server application development, that tool is the best choice for network testing because it allows the development and test groups to share test scripts. Application layer testing cannot be accomplished without a scripting tool, and this testing may be the most overlooked opportunity for network improvement of all proactive test objectives. Any serious network test organization needs a client-server testing tool.

FILE I/O AND TRANSACTION GENERATION

File I/O test scripts for network platform testing are very similar to the test scripts discussed in Chapter 10 for internetwork testing. The primary difference between the test scripts is the load orientation. For internetwork testing, the load is designed to stress the internetwork links and paths. For network platform testing, the load is designed to stress specific aspects of the file server or workstation, such as cached I/O versus hard disk I/O, or multiple network ports versus single port access.

Network platform file activity can be created with the same software utilities and programs used for internetwork test script development. These include:

DOS batch files

Novell's Perform3

file I/O emulators, such as Ziff-Davis' Server Benchmarks

in-house-developed C or BASIC programs

Tailoring Test Scripts for Network Platform File I/O Testing

Chapter 10's File I/O Generation section explains how these tools can be used to create internetwork test scripts. Because the same approach is used for network platform testing, refer to Chapter 10 for details and examples on basic test script development before reading the following section.

This section details the requirements of network platform testing not pertinent to internetwork testing, and how the test tool scripts can be expanded to encompass these needs.

A) LD_GEN.BAT

```
@echo off
set copycmd=/y
Echo Start Test_%1 >> Audit
For %%A IN (1 2 3) DO Call I_O %%A
Erase trash
Erase temp_1
Erase temp_2
Erase temp_3
Echo Completed Test_%1 >> Audit
```

B) I_O.BAT

```
Call time_mrk Start_%1
Echo off
FOR %%B IN (1 2 3 4 5 6 7 8 9 10) DO Copy File_%1.txt temp_%1 >> Trash
Call Time_Mrk Done_%1
```

C) TIME_MRK.BAT

```
@Echo off
If NOT EXIT Rtn GOTO Miss
Echo %1>> Audit
Time <Rtn | FIND "Current" >> Audit
GOTO End
:MISS
Cannot find RTN file
:End
```

Figure 19.5   Batch file load script; includes three linked batch files.

Figure 19.5, copied from Figure 10.7 (page 228), is a simple batch file load script for workstation 1 in Figure 9.16. There are actually three batch files in the script:

LD_GEN.BAT controls the number of copy iterations. It calls a second batch file, I_O.BAT.

I_O.BAT performs the file copies. I_O.BAT calls a third batch file, TIME_MRK.BAT.

TIME_MRK.BAT creates time stamps that measure the file copy duration and redirect the time to an audit file for data reduction and analysis.

This load script is designed to create basic file I/O activity across the internetwork without regard to whether the I/O is from cached or disk-based data. The test files are read and written to the same temporary directory. Functionally, this means that the file is first transferred (read) from the server hard disk to workstation memory, then retransferred (written) from workstation memory to the server's hard disk. For larger files, this process will be repeated several times until the entire file is transferred. For generating internetwork traffic, this is a good mechanism, but for a network platform test this may not be appropriate.

If the test objective is to measure maximum file server throughput for cached file reads, the preceding will not provide accurate data. For this objective, either the batch file can be modified as explained next, or another test utility, Novell's Perform3, can be used to read cached data.

Modified Batch File

The batch file has to be modified to:

1. Force the data file to be cached before the reads are initiated.

2. Read, but not write data.

This can be done by ensuring that the server cache is sufficient to hold the entire file and by prereading the file into the server cache. On the workstations, the file can be "copied" to a RAM disk (Drive E:), rather than the workstation hard disk. Since the RAM disk is essentially a memory-to-memory transfer, the time for this will be orders of magnitude faster than the network I/O and can be ignored in the final transfer time calculations. Figure 19.6 shows the required batch file changes. Similar changes would be required for the BASIC program illustrated in Chapter 10, Figure 10.8.

A) Modified LD_GEN.BAT

```
@echo off
set copycmd=/y
Copy File_1.txt d:temp_1>>Trash
Copy File_2.txt d:temp_2>>Trash
Copy File_3.txt d:temp_3>>Trash
Echo Start Test_%1 >> Audit
For %%A IN (1 2 3) DO Call I_O %%A
Erase Trash
Erase Temp_1
Erase Temp_2
Erase Temp_3
Echo Completed Test_%1 >> Audit
```

B) Modified I_O.BAT

```
Call time_mrk Start_%1
Echo off
FOR %%B IN (1 2 3 4 5 6 7 8 9 10) DO Copy File_%1.txt D:temp_%1 >> Trash
Call Time_Mrk Done_%1
```

C) TIME_MRK.BAT

```
@Echo off
If NOT EXIT Rtn GOTO Miss
Echo %1 >> Audit
Time < Rtn | FIND "Current" >> Audit
GOTO End
:MISS
Cannot find RTN file
:End
```

Figure 19.6 Changes to Figure 19.5 batch file to precache files and write to RAM disk.

Novell's Perform3

Perform3 is a widely-used software utility that reads cached data from a file server and calculates effective throughput. Input variables allow file sizes from 64 bytes to 65,000 Kbytes and read times from 12 to 65,000 seconds. Perform3 creates the required file on the server and performs sequential block reads of the file for the specified duration. At the end of the test, it calculates effective throughput

(KBps) based on the total kilobytes read during the elapsed time. Input parameters for file start, stop, and step size can be specified. Perform3 will automatically increment the file size and calculate the throughput for each file size read. It does not perform file writes, and therefore is the perfect test tool for calculating maximum file server throughput for cached reads, actually better than the modified batch file.

C or BASIC Programs for Transaction I/O

C or BASIC programs can be developed to emulate file I/O to the file server. Such programs are very useful when planning and evaluating the network platform's capacity to support as yet undeveloped client-server applications. Even without the client-server application, test data can be generated during the planning and design stage using C and BASIC programs.

One company spent over a year developing a client-server application with a GUI front end, only to find that, in initial tests, the underlying network environment could not support the response time targets for the application. If a transaction generator had been developed first, this testing could have been accomplished without expenditure of a year's development time.

Transaction generators are also valuable tools for testing the back end of a client-server system, as noted in Example 18.1. This tool allows the front-end GUI to be eliminated from the equation, and can be useful in configuration sizing, bottleneck identification, throughput, and reliability testing.

Ziff-Davis' (ZD) ServerBench for Transaction I/O

ServerBench contains numerous individual tests that create transactions that ServerBench sends to the server. (A client never sends a file to the server; it always sends a transaction.) The individual tests include disk tests, a processor test, and network tests. ServerBench packages the transactions in a test mix and places the test mix in a test suite. A test suite can contain more than one mix.

ServerBench reports its results in terms of TPS, or transactions per second; it only measures completed transactions. It calculates a transaction as the amount of time it takes for a client to issue a request and get a response back from the server.

ServerBench provides the following tests:

- **One processor test:** This test would not generally be used for network testing.

- **Five disk tests:** These tests can be used to create various traffic patterns between the client and server. The disk tests are sequential read and write, random read and write, and an append test.

- **Two network tests:** These generate the highest load, and can be used to stress the internetwork more than the disk tests.

ServerBench is a good emulation tool that can be used to pretest the network platform throughput and capacity in preparation for developing and deploying a client-server application. It may be too limiting in many situations for specifying a transaction stream for specific client-server applications, but since it is free, it is definitely worth checking out.

Application: Response Time Testing

TEST MATRIX

Response time testing is the predominate test objective for network applications. This test, more than any other, reflects how the user will perceive the network. Response time testing is primarily conducted for application layer test configurations. Test Case 1 discusses application response time testing using emulated configurations and loads. Test Case 2 discusses response time testing using emulated loads and real-world configurations. This same methodology can also be applied to:

- **Network platform response for command sequences, such as logon:** The response of the network for logon may be particularly important if many users concurrently log on early in the morning. A load script, essentially the logon commands, can be run to determine how long it takes for 100 equivalent users to concurrently log on to the network. Generally, the primary objective of this testing is not to measure response time, but rather to optimize the logon process, which is highly server- and NOS-dependent. This testing, therefore, is covered in Chapter 22, Configuration Sizing.

- **Desktop presentation manager performance:** Often, a user environment is composed of many interrelated applications, such as found on securities trading, customer support, and telesales desktops. The desktop is driven by the interactive and arbitrary nature of the customer's requests; therefore, the time to switch between windows and applications directly affects the ability of the user to service the customer. Load scripts that emulate this random behavior can be developed similar to application load scripts to measure system response time for loading new windows, applications, and overlays. This testing is not load sensitive, because it is based on workstation, not server performance. The primary objective of this testing is not to measure response time, but rather to optimize the presentation manager and workstation platform. This testing, therefore, is covered in Chapter 22, Configuration Sizing.

Using the test methodology discussed in this chapter and in Chapter 21:

- Chapter 22 discusses techniques for optimizing configurations for improved response time and throughput.

- Chapter 23 describes how to determine excess capacity.

- Chapter 29 discusses how to identify bottlenecks.

TEST CASE 1: EMULATED TEST CONFIGURATION

As a systems-level test, application response time tests use a load script of application commands to measure how the combined application GUI front-end, back-end database (for a client-server application), file server, network platform, and network infrastructure perform under various user loads. As a transaction-based test, it measures all aspects of the system except the GUI. The GUI front end is replaced by a program that sends transactions to the database server. This allows the server and network response time to be decoupled from the GUI response time for purposes of identifying bottlenecks in the GUI and server.

Test Measurements

Response time measurements are usually shown as a load versus response time curve. The load is represented as equivalent users, and the response time is shown in seconds or minutes. Response time is taken as the average across all the workstations or sessions in the test. A different chart or line graph can be used to represent different load scripts, as illustrated in Figure 20.1. These load scripts represent basic functions, such as queries, record updates, and database sorts.

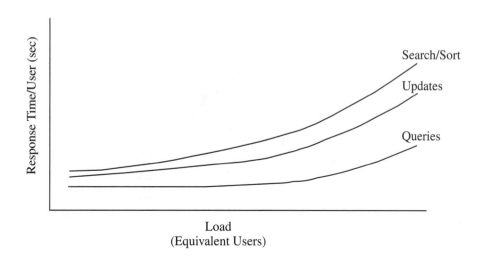

Figure 20.1   Load versus response time curve for different load scripts.

Test Configurations

Test configurations are emulated, and are single segments with the file server, database server, applications server (if required), and workstations. If the application users are distributed across different segments from the database server or file server, and the interconnecting paths include slow speed links that could affect performance, these are included in the test configuration to measure their impact on response time. Figure 20.2 illustrates test configuration options. Note the network analyzer on the test configuration. If errors are detected during the test, they will have to be investigated. If a problem is found, the tests must be rerun to get relevant response time measurements. Use these configurations as a guide, but define specific test configurations that emulate your unique network topology.

Running the test with a number of users who represent the planned user community measures response time for the anticipated production load. If the number of users is increased until response time degrades, the test also provides a measure of system capacity to support more users. Once the equivalent user

Configuration A

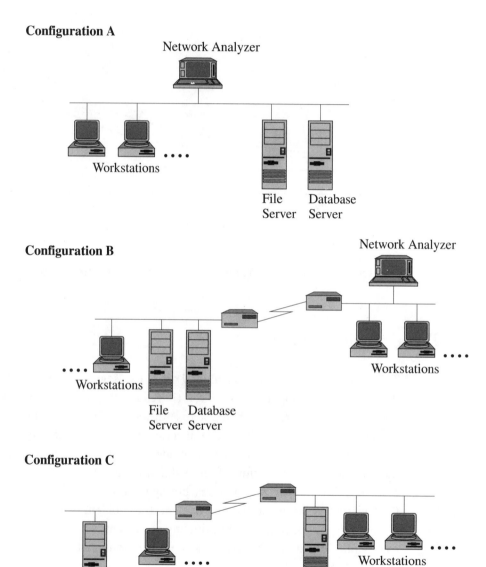

Figure 20.2   Example test configurations for application response time tests.

loading is estimated as described in Chapter 18, Estimating Equivalent User Loading, configure workstations to conduct one of the following test scenarios:

- Create a load curve of increasing equivalent user load until response time degrades. The loading would increase in increments, such as 1,10, 20, 30, 60, 120, and so on, or 1, 50, 100, 200 depending on the estimated capacity of the system.

- Create a load curve that brackets the expected number of production users. If the system is expected to support 200 users, the load increments would look like 150, 200, 225, 250, 300, and so on.

Before starting the test project, begin a test journal, document the test configuration hardware and software, and create data reduction spreadsheets, as described in Chapter 6.

The test configuration requires that the application and database software under test be installed on the database server, application server, or file server as it will be deployed on the production network. If the application user interface will be used on the workstations as the load generator, then it must be installed as planned for the production network. If a transaction generator program is run on the workstations as the load generator, it must be installed so that it will not be intrusive to the testing. The transaction program can be stored in a shared directory on the file server and downloaded to the workstations during the startup phase of the load script.

For GUI/front-end testing, load model 3, only a single workstation is run against the server. The focus is to measure front end, GUI, and workstation response and bottlenecks. The server must provide excess capacity for the workstation to ensure that any delays are at the workstation.

Load Model

Refer to the section in Chapter 18 on Developing the Load Model to create the test scripts. Load models can include:

- **Load Model 1:** Network centric load model to measure the response time of the server and network to peak load with minimal test hardware. Either an application command load script or transaction load script can be used. Be careful to minimize GUI front-end overhead in the application script in order to generate maximum transaction rates.

- **Load Model 2:** Key feature load model to measure the response of the application's critical features. If the correct set of functions are chosen, this test measures responsiveness under typical user loads.

- **Load Model 3:** Workstation/GUI centric load model to measure the response of the application to presentation and context-switching operations. For instance, if large quantities of data must be displayed, windows must be redrawn when certain functions are selected, or overlays must be downloaded from the server when a feature is selected. The time to complete these operations may be perceived as slow application responsiveness by the user.

In a response time test, all workstations typically run the same "homogeneous" load script. As equivalent homogeneous users are added, this allows a load versus response time curve to be generated based on the average response for the users.

If the application is such that a "heterogeneous" mix of users is more typical and the mix can be accurately defined, a test can be run in which different load scripts are used across the workstations. For example, one group of customer service representatives may primarily interact with customers and do database queries and updates, while another group of users in accounting mainly generates billings from the database.

The heterogeneous load scripts are constructed so that they each run for the same duration. Response time is based on test duration time divided by the number of test iterations completed. For example, one load script performs record access based on a random key, and another script performs sequential record access and report generation. The number of loops or iterations each script performs in a given time will change as load increases, based on the design and

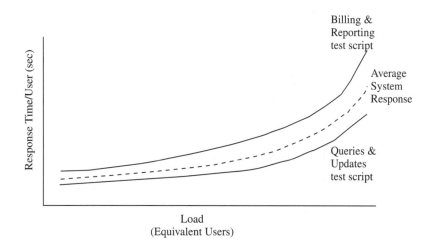

Figure 20.3   Load versus response time chart for averaged and individual test script.

capability of the application and server. Heterogeneous load scripts provide important real-world data for performance and capacity planning. Figure 20.3 shows how charts would look for a heterogeneous load versus response time curve for averaged and individual script response times.

Depending on the type of client-server testing tool you use, develop the load generator scripts using the recording or programming mode of that tool. Some client-server testing tools provide a transaction generator that captures and replays transactions independent of the application front end (workstation software). If this is not available, a C program will have to be written to generate transactions.

Test Execution and Data Collection

Most client-server testing tools provide automated data collection and reduction facilities. All data reduction should include an average per run, an average across multiple runs (the recommendation is three runs), and standard deviation across

Run ID (A)

	Station ID	Test Script ID	Run 1 Response Time	Run 2 Response Time	Run 3 Response Time
	(B)	(C)	(D)		
Average for Run			(E)		
Average Across Runs			(F)		
Standard Deviation			(G)		

Figure 20.4   Data reduction spreadsheet for application response time testing.

runs (to insure reproducible results). If the testing tool does not provide data reduction, the spreadsheet given in Figure 20.4 can be used as a guide in developing data reduction. This spreadsheet can also be used to compare results across different load scripts, as shown in Figure 20.3.

Cell definitions in the Figure 20.4 spreadsheet are:

cell A = Run ID

cell B = Workstation ID

cell C = Test Script ID

cell D = response time is minutes or seconds

cell E = average response time for the run

cell F = average response time for two or three runs

cell G = standard deviation for two or three runs

The test sequence is:

1. Start the client-server testing tool. Verify that the test configuration is working properly and that all workstations can access the server. Run a practice test with several workstations.

2. If required, set up a spreadsheet for the load increments and fill in the Run ID and Load Script ID(s).

3. Shut down and restart the client-server testing tool for the first load point of X equivalent users. Run the test three times. After each test, enter the results into the data reduction spreadsheet or log the results through the mechanism provided by the testing tool. After the third run, compare the average response time for the three runs and calculate the standard deviation. If the values differ by more than 4 percent across the three runs, the margin of error is too high, and the test is not generating reproducible results. The reason for this must be determined before proceeding with additional tests. See Test Configuration Problem Resolution Tips at the end of Chapter 18.

4. Analyze the results:

   - **Minimal or no degradation:** If there is little or no degradation in response time across three consecutive load points, continue increasing the load incrementally. For example, if the test is using 20 user increments, increment to 40 or 80 users until degradation is measured.

   - **Significant degradation:** If there is significant degradation between the last and the current load point, halve the load until the "knee" of the curve is reached. Figure 20.5 illustrates how this is done with two examples. In the first example, degradation increases sharply between 180 and 190 equivalent users. In example 2, degradation increases sharply after 160 equivalent users. If the degradation occurs before the target load is reached, stop the test; sufficient data has been collected to conclude that the system is not capable of supporting the target load and response time.

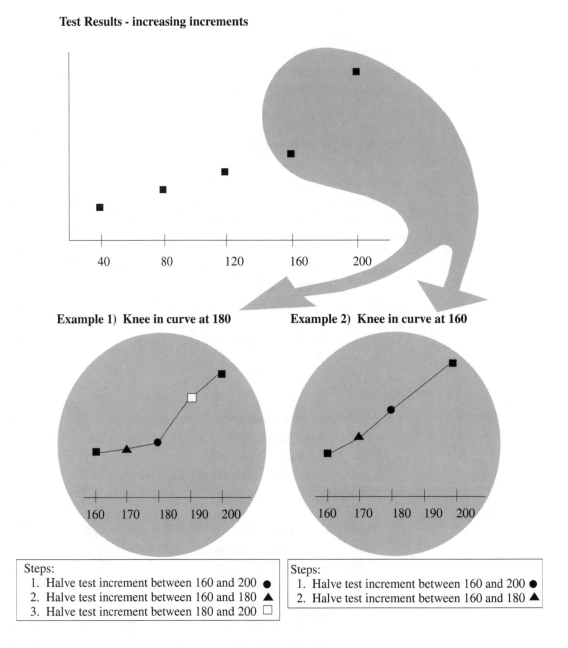

Figure 20.5 Determining the "knee" in the load versus response time curve.

5. Repeat steps 3 and 4 for each load point.

6. Repeat steps 1 through 5 for each test script.

Data Interpretation

As each test case is run, the results should be entered into the data reduction spreadsheet. The spreadsheet calculates average response time and standard deviation between test runs, information required to determine the next test load as described under Test Execution.

Response time is probably the single most important measurement of user satisfaction, followed closely by reliability. Technically, we all know that different operations will have different response times, but, often, users have an expectation of X second response time and do not take into account the operation being performed. If standard operations, such as a database query, record update, record sort, report formatting, and so on, are tested, test results can be used to set user expectations on system performance. Recommended rule of thumb is to always set expectations at twice the measured time.

Response time is a high-level measurement of the application and network system's ability to satisfy user demand. Depending on the load model used, it can isolate aspects of performance to the GUI front end or the server back end, but it cannot pinpoint which component is causing a bottleneck. Response time load scripts are often used as a measurement standard for configuration sizing, capacity planning, and acceptance testing, as described in Chapters 22, 23, and 27, respectively.

TEST CASE 2: REAL-WORLD TEST CONFIGURATION

Response time is a system-level measurement that is highly dependent on network activity. The results from Test Case 1 are very useful for measuring and tuning the application during development, but they tend to be best case and may not represent what users will actually experience on the production network.

To achieve better real-world measurements:

1. Add network platform, internetwork and subsystem loads to the application test configuration to emulate the production network load caused by other network activity.

2. Run response time tests on the production network, using the same load scripts as in the emulated test configuration of Test Case 1.

Application testing on the production network is not as risky as it may appear, once the application is stable and Test Case 1 results are available to guide the incremental loading. Do not do real-world testing until the application has been measured in an emulated test configuration.

Real-world testing is very similar to emulated testing with the addition of:

1. Establishing a control group on the production network in order to measure degradation of the production network due to increased load from the new application.

2. Establishing load increments based on the network activity measured in Test Case 1.

Test Measurements

Response time measurements are shown in a load versus response time chart. The load is represented as equivalent users, and the response time is shown in seconds or minutes. The response time is taken as the average across all the workstations or sessions in the test. A second graph is used to represent the change in production system throughput for the control group, as illustrated in Figure 20.6. Typically, as the application test load is increased, production throughput degrades. The test tries to anticipate the knee in the production network curve without creating severe degradation.

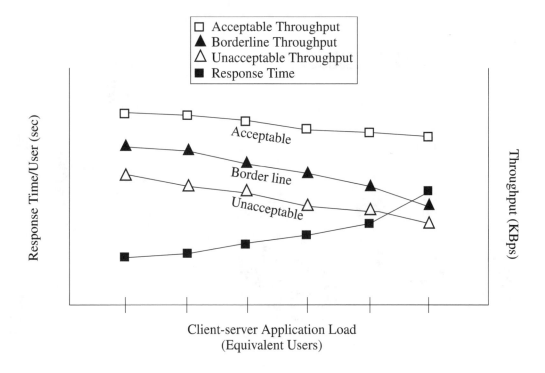

Figure 20.6 Load versus response time chart for the application and production network control group.

Test Configurations

The test configuration is the production network with the new servers and workstations located as they will be deployed across the network. Two or three key production network operations are treated as a control group to determine degradation caused by the new application load. Figure 20.7 shows how this may look for the corporate network discussed in Chapter 18, Figure 18.3.

Before initiating the test project, start a test journal, document the test configuration hardware and software, and create data reduction spreadsheets as described in Chapter 6.

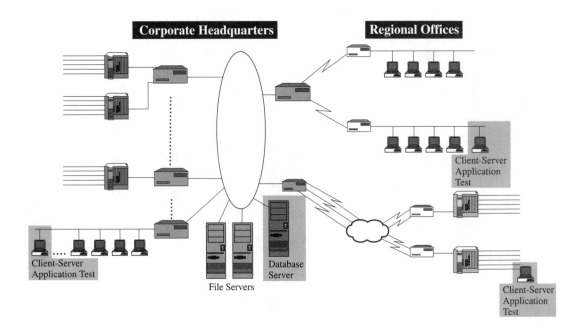

Figure 20.7   Corporate network client-server upgrades for real-world application response time testing.

Load Model

The load model for real-world application testing is the same one used in Test Case 1 for the new application. Make sure that the script runs between one and two minutes. A short script that causes some degradation is tolerable, but longer scripts may create unacceptable impact to the production network. Additionally, a load monitor, such as an analyzer, or control group load scripts are required to measure the degradation on the production system due to the application load.

A control group load model that works well is network platform file I/O. Create a control group load script using Perform3, which reads small block sizes,

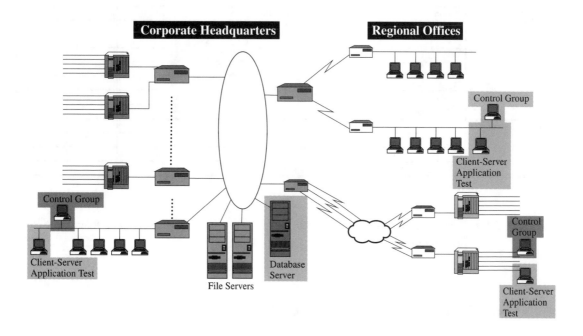

Figure 20.8 Adding control group load scripts for real-world application response time testing.

and run it on two or three workstations on the production network both with and without the new application load. As the new application load is increased, use the Perform3 throughput results to determine degradation on the production network.

Be sure to define the control group load model so that all key paths are measured. Figure 20.8 shows how the load scripts would be distributed to measure both file server and link degradation on the production network from Figure 20.7. Control test stations are added to test local and remote file server access. This placement allows all critical links that may be impacted by the new application, FDDI backbone/local router, ISDN/router, and 56KB lines/router, to be measured.

Run ID (A)				Date/Time	(B)		
Application	Station ID	Test Script ID	Baseline	Load 1	Load 2	Load 3
	(G)	(H)		(I)		
	Avg. Response Time for Run			(J)		
	Emulated Response Time			(K)		
	% Degradation			(L)		
Control Group	(C)	(D)	(E)	(M)		
	Average Throughput		(F)	(N)		
	% Degradation from Baseline			(O)		

Figure 20.9   Data reduction spreadsheet for real-world application response time and production network control group testing.

Test Execution and Data Collection

Many client-server testing tools provide automated data collection and reduction facilities. All data reduction should include an average per run, an average across three runs, and the standard deviation across runs (to insure reproducible results). For this test, the data reduction must include both the client-server testing tool results and Perform3 throughput results. Figure 20.9 shows how these results should be recorded.

Cell definitions in the Figure 20.9 spreadsheet are:

cell A = Run ID

cell B = date and time of test measurements on production network

cell C = Workstation ID of control group workstations

cell D = Test Script ID for control group workstations. Different stations can run different test scripts

cell E = throughput measurements for control group baseline test

cell F = average throughput for the baseline test

cell G = Workstation ID of client-server application workstations in test

cell H = Test Script ID for client-server application workstations. In this example, all stations run the same script, but different stations can run different test scripts

cell I = response time measurements for the client-server workstations

cell J = average response time for the load point

cell K = response time measurement for emulated loading

cell L = percent response time degradation between emulated and real-world test data

cell M = throughput measurements for the control group workstations

cell N = average throughput for the load point tests

cell O = percent throughput degradation between baseline and load point test data

The test sequence is:

1. Start the control group (Perform3) load scripts. Verify that the test configuration is working properly and that all workstations can access the server. Run a practice test with several workstations.

2. Start the client-server testing tool. Verify that the test configuration is working properly and that all workstations can access the server. Run a practice test with several workstations.

3. Set up a spreadsheet for the load increments and fill in the Run ID and Load Script ID(s). From the emulated test results, Test Case 1, choose three load increments to test. Enter the Test Case 1 load points and emulated test results into the spreadsheet. Either choose three points bracketing the expected number of production users or the three points that bracket the knee in the curve. This will ensure that the overall test time on the production network is kept to a minimum, and will provide sufficient data to create a load versus response time curve for both the application and production network.

4. Run Perform3 without the client-server load and enter results into the spreadsheet. Run the client-server testing tool and Perform3 for the first load point of X equivalent users. Enter the results into the data reduction spreadsheet and compare the average response time for the application and the production network, as shown in Figure 20.10. Always analyze the previous test impact (degradation) on the production network before increasing the load. If production network degradation is unacceptable or it decreased significantly (20 percent or more) between test points, stop the test.

5. Repeat step 4 for the second load point. Calculate the percent production network degradation and application response time change between the successive runs.

Run ID	C-5 Payroll			Date/Time		12/13/95	
Application	Station ID	Test Script ID	Baseline	Load 1	Load 2	Load 3
	Stat-1	T0104PR		45	46.9	
	Stat-2	T0104PR		45.5	47.3	
	Stat-3	T0104PR		44	47.5	
	Stat-4	T0104PR		43.5	46.4	
	Avg. Response Time for Run			44.5	47	
	Emulated Response Time			40	42	
	% Degradation			11.3	11.9	
Control Group	Stat-5	T0202FC	500	500	498	
	Stat-6	T0302FC	525	522	518	
	Average Throughput		512.5	511	508	
	% Degradation from Baseline			0.3	0.9	

Figure 20.10   Spreadsheet entries for the control group baseline and two load points.

Run ID	C-5 Payroll		Date/Time	12/13/95		
Application	Station ID	Test Script ID	Baseline	Load 1	Load 2	Load 3
	Stat-1	T0104PR		45	46.9	48.2
	Stat-2	T0104PR		45.5	47.3	48.5
	Stat-3	T0104PR		44	47.5	47.9
	Stat-4	T0104PR		43.5	46.4	48.3
	Avg. Response Time for Run			44.5	47	48.2
	Emulated Response Time			40	42	43
	% Degradation			11.3	11.9	10.7
Control Group	Stat-5	T0202FC	500	500	498	480
	Stat-6	T0302FC	525	522	518	502
	Average Throughput		512.5	511	508	491
	% Degradation from Baseline			0.3	0.9	4

Figure 20.11   Spreadsheet entries for three load points.

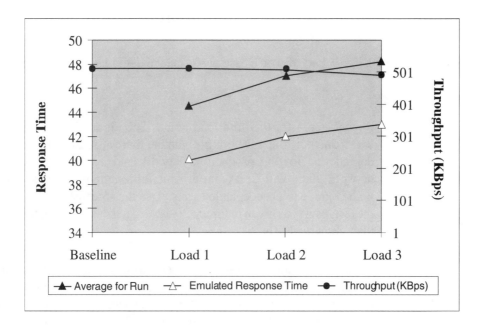

Figure 20.12   Chart of Figure 20.11 test results.

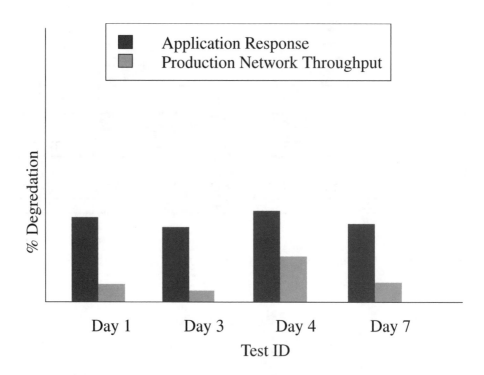

Figure 20.13   Chart of worse case performance degradation across four days.

6. Repeat step 5 for the third load point. See Figure 20.11 for example data from three runs. Determine whether there is a pattern to the percent degradation for the production network and application. For each network, there will be a point at which throughput, response time, or both degrade to unacceptable levels. Use the spreadsheet data to chart the test results, as given in Figure 20.12. Visual data is easier to interpret than numerical lists.

7. Repeat steps 1 through 6 at other times during the day, week, and month to determine an average for the application response across different production system loads. Look for periods when production system or application degradation is severe. Figure 20.13 charts the worst case load results at four different test times. These are shown as a percent degradation from Test Case 1 results and throughput measurements

without application load, respectively. If the worse case degradation is unacceptable, then system enhancements must be made to improve response time and throughput to acceptable levels before deploying the new application.

8. Repeat steps 1 through 7 for other test scripts.

Data Interpretation

The test data in Figure 20.12 shows that production network throughput does not degrade for the first two load points. It degrades only marginally for load point number three. Client-server application response, however, is about 11 percent lower than measured in the emulated test. This illustrates a problem in the emulated test configuration and loading. Emulated results are providing consistent, but not accurate production network response numbers.

Reality is that an 11 percent difference indicates that the test setup and load model are pretty good; you shouldn't expect to be much more accurate. This is why testers never rely on a single load point, but always bracket the expected loading to understand how the system reacts with the estimated loading and higher load levels.

These results provide a high level of confidence that the new client-server application will not significantly degrade the production network, and that response time targets for the application can be met. This is only one point in time, however. As per step 7, these measurements must be taken at different times to confirm that overall network performance and response time are consistent and acceptable.

Application: Throughput Testing

TEST MATRIX

Throughput testing is used to measure network servers, both file and database, and workstation-to-server connections. It is also conducted for client-server database servers and network platform test configurations. Test Case 1 describes client-server testing using emulated configurations and loads. Test Case 2 explains network platform testing using emulated configurations and loads. This chapter discusses how to create load scripts and measure throughput of the file or database server's network interface, CPU, and hard disk.

Using the testing methodology discussed in this chapter and Chapter 20:

- Chapter 22 discusses techniques for optimizing configurations for improved response time and throughput.

- Chapter 23 describes how to determine excess capacity.

- Chapter 29 discusses how to identify bottlenecks.

TEST CASE 1: CLIENT-SERVER THROUGHPUT TESTING

For a client-server application, transaction-based throughput testing is similar to PPS router throughput testing. Both objectives attempt to measure the sustainable rate of transactions per second. In router testing, the rate of transactions (packets) is the governing factor: a large number of small packets puts maximum stress on the router. For a database server, the transaction stream is not quite that simple. There are four potential bottlenecks to consider:

- **The network interface:** A large number of transaction requests will stress the server's network interface. This is essentially like sending a large number of small packets to the server. A single network interface is bound by the number of packets it can receive per second.

- **The server's hard disk:** Transaction requests cause data transmission to the client. If the data is not cache-resident, the server must read it from the hard disk. The hard disk's speed, fragmentation, and interface will determine how quickly the data can be transferred.

- **The server's CPU:** Transaction requests cause the database server to perform tasks. A transaction request for a record entry causes cache or hard disk I/O. A transaction request to sort the database and calculate record averages, for example, causes significant hard disk I/O as well as CPU load. Each transaction type places different loads on the server's CPU and hard disk.

- **The network transport:** A single transaction can result in a large response, which must be broken down into packets to be sent to the workstation. A single network interface is bound by the number of packets it can handle per second and the required time to reset between send and receive mode. Total data transfer is bounded by the network transport and the slowest link in the path between the workstation and server.

Test Measurements

Throughput measurements for a client-server database typically measure transactions per second, TPS. It is also valuable to measure equivalent KBps, particularly when transactions result in large responses. KBps measurements can be recorded on a network analyzer, and comparing these measurements can determine if the network adapter or transport is constraining throughput. Figure 21.1 illustrates how TPS and KBps can vary across transaction type.

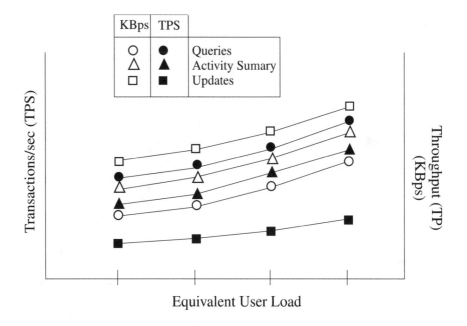

Figure 21.1   Variations in TPS and KBps based on transaction mix.

Test Configurations

All test configurations are emulated. The same configuration should be used for response time, throughput, configuration sizing, and capacity planning tests.

As originally presented in Chapter 20, test configurations are often a single segment network with the file server, database server, applications server (if required), and workstations. If the application users are distributed across different segments from the database server or file server, and the interconnecting paths include slow speed links that could affect performance, these are included in the test configuration to measure their impact on throughput. Figure 21.2 illustrates several test configuration options. Note the network analyzer on the test configuration to measure KBps and network error. If errors are detected

Configuration A

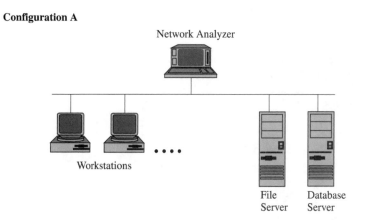

Configuration B

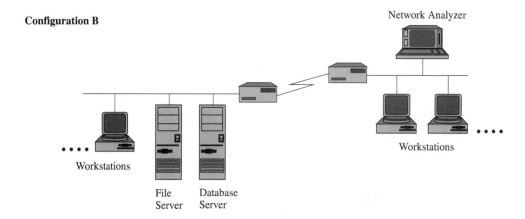

Configuration C

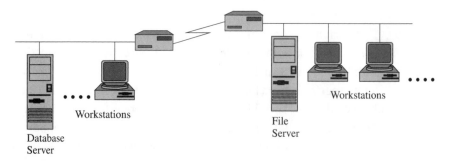

Figure 21.2 Example test configurations for application throughput tests.

during the test, they have to be investigated. If a problem is found, the tests must be rerun to get relevant response time measurements. Use these configurations as a guide, but be sure to define specific test configurations that emulate your unique network topology.

Before starting the test project, begin a test journal, document the test configuration hardware and software, and create data reduction spreadsheets as described in Chapter 6.

The test configuration requires that the database software under test be installed on the database server, application server, or file server as it will be deployed on the production network. The application user interface will not be used on the workstations. The load generator is a transaction generator program. To be nonintrusive to the testing, the transaction program can be stored in a shared directory on the file server and downloaded to the workstations during the startup phase of the load script.

Load Model

Refer to the section in Chapter 18, Developing the Load Model, to create the test scripts for this test. Load models can be created to measure system-level transaction throughput or any one of the four potential bottlenecks identified previously:

- **Load Model 4:** Network centric load model to measure throughput of the server and network to peak transaction load. Transactions, such as database queries, are small and require minimal server processing and response. All transactions should be handled from cached data. This can be done by reading the same record over and over across all workstations in the test. This allows maximum transaction load to be achieved with minimal hardware.

- **Load Model 5:** Modified network centric load scripts from the network interface tests are used to determine how quickly requests are processed from the server cache. Cache size and transaction type are configured to ensure that all requests are satisfied from cached data. Usually, a broader range of representative transaction types are used than in Load Model 4. Monitor the number of cache hits and "dirty" cache buffers during the test.

- **Load Model 6:** Server CPU test where transactions require server processing. The test must monitor server CPU utilization and TPS. The objective is to achieve 100 percent CPU utilization and measure resultant TPS.

- **Load Model 7:** Network centric load scripts, Load Model 5, are reused to measure hard disk throughput. By eliminating server caching, all requests must be processed off the hard disk; therefore, the hard disk will become the bottleneck.

- **Load Model 8:** Network transport capacity and efficiency can be measured using transactions that generate large data volume responses. The test must monitor network bandwidth utilization, network interface utilization, and TPS. The objective is to achieve 100 percent bandwidth utilization.

In a throughput test, all workstations run the same "homogeneous" load script. As equivalent homogeneous users are added, a load versus throughput curve can be generated based on the average KBps and TPS.

Similar to response time testing, a representative load curve can be generated for "heterogeneous" transaction mixes, if equivalent heterogeneous users are added in the same percentage, but this is not recommended. Throughput testing tries to isolate results to specific components, and heterogeneous scripts make isolation more uncertain and data interpretation more difficult. It is hard to capture conclusive results in such tests.

Some client-server testing tools provide a transaction generator that captures and replays transactions independent of the application front end (workstation software). If this is not available, a C program has to be written to generate transactions.

Run ID (A)

			Run 1		Run 2		Run 3	
Station ID	Test Script ID		TPS	KBps	TPS	KBps	TPS	KBps
(B)	(C)		(D)	(E)				
Average for Run			(F)	(G)				
Average Across Runs					(H)	(J)		
Standard Deviation					(I)	(K)		

Figure 21.3   Data reduction spreadsheet for client-server application throughput testing.

Test Execution and Data Collection

Figure 21.3's data reduction spreadsheet can be used to record throughput in TPS and KBps.

Cell definitions in the spreadsheet are:

cell A = Run ID

cell B = Workstation ID

cell C = Test Script ID

cell D = measured transactions per second

cell E = measured kilobytes per second

cell F = average transactions per second for the run

cell G = average kilobytes per second for the run

cell H = average transactions per second across two or more runs

cell I = standard deviation of average transactions per second for two or three runs

cell J = average kilobytes per second across two or more runs

cell K = standard deviation of average kilobytes per second for two or three runs

In addition to TPS, KBps must be recorded. If KBps is not available from the transaction load generator, use the network analyzer to monitor the network and record KBps.

The same basic test sequence is used for all load models, with slight variations in the data measurements and data interpretation. The following steps outline the test sequence with load model dependent instructions, as required:

1. Start the load generator and network analyzer. Verify that the test configuration is working properly and that all workstations can access the server. Run a practice test with several workstations.

2. Set up a spreadsheet for the load increments and fill in the Run ID and Load Script ID(s).

3. Shut down and restart the load generators for the first load point of X equivalent users. Run the test three times. After each test, enter the results into the data reduction spreadsheet or log the results through the mechanism provided by the testing tool. After the third run, compare the average throughput for the three runs and calculate the standard deviation. If the values differ by more than 4 percent across the three runs, the test configuration is not generating reproducible results. You must determine why before proceeding with additional tests. See Test Configuration Problem Resolution Tips at the end of Chapter 18.

4. Analyze the results:

- **Minimal or no degradation**: If there is little or no degradation in TPS and KBps as the load increases, continue increasing the load incrementally. For example, if the test is using 20 user increments, increment to 40 or 80 users until degradation is measured.

  For Load Model 6, determine whether CPU utilization has reached 100 percent. If it has, measure throughput at one more load point. This will determine if TPS and KBps degrade or level off once CPU capacity is reached. If CPU utilization is below 100 percent, continue increasing the load as described.

  For Load Model 8, determine whether the capacity of the slowest link has reached 100 percent. If it has, measure throughput at one more load point. This will determine if TPS and KBps degrade or level off once bandwidth of the link is reached. If bandwidth utilization is below 100 percent, continue increasing the load as described.

- **Significant degradation**: If there is significant degradation between the last and the current load point, reduce the transaction load until the "knee" of the curve is reached. Figure 21.4 illustrates how this would look. If the degradation occurs before the target load is reached, stop the test. Sufficient data has been collected to conclude that the system is not capable of supporting the target TPS. When measuring TPS and KBps, the knee occurs when the throughput drops off suddenly. When measuring response time, the knee occurs when the response time increases suddenly.

5. Repeat steps 3 and 4 for each load point.

6. Repeat steps 1 through 5 for each test script.

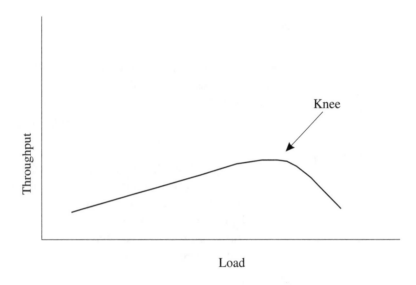

Figure 21.4   Determining the knee in the load versus TPS curve.

Data Interpretation

After each test case is run, the results should be entered into the data reduction spreadsheet. The spreadsheet calculates average TPS, KBps, and standard deviation between test runs. This information is required to determine the next test load, as described under Test Execution.

Figure 21.5 illustrates how test data from different load models provides information on database server throughput:

- **Load Model 4—network interface:** Figure 21.5 shows the peak sustainable transaction rate of the database server configuration. This is an indication of how fast the server can turn around a transaction. It measures the internal queuing, buffering, processing, and cache access of the database software. It does not measure peak server throughput in KBps, since the overhead of the database software typically reduces effective server throughput. Peak server throughput is measured using Test Case 2, which will provide the upper bound or curve in Figure 21.5.

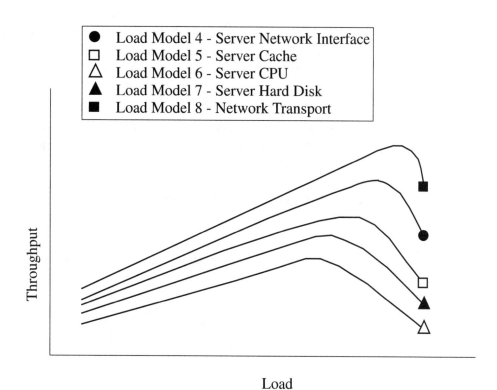

Figure 21.5   Analyzing throughput test data.

- **Load Model 5—server cache:** The second test measures the same data as the first test, when a broader mix of representative transactions are serviced from cache. Both TPS and KBps are typically lower than in Load Model 1 tests, and the knee of the curve will be experienced at a lower load. Load Model 1 tests represent engineering maximums. This test is more representative of what users would experience when most requests (80 percent) can be serviced from cache.

- **Load Model 6—server CPU:** The third test measures TPS and KBps for CPU-intensive operations, such as numerical calculations. The TPS and KBps will not be as high as Load Models 1 and 2 tests. The objective of the test is to determine maximum TPS at 100 percent CPU utilization.

- **Load Model 7—server hard disk:** This test measures the same data as the second test, when the majority of the transactions are serviced from the hard disk rather than cache. Both TPS and KBps will be lower than in Test 2. The difference in results between Tests 2 and 4 indicate the contribution to throughput from cache memory I/O. If the results are about equal, it indicates that there is a bottleneck in the server, which affects both cache and hard disk I/O. This could be the adapter, protocol, CPU, or software.

- **Load Model 8—network transport:** This test measures the throughput of the slowest network link.

These tests provide an indication of the contribution of each part of the database and network system.

If there is a significant throughput difference between Load Models 4 and 5, a problem exists in the database software when handling a mix of transaction types and sizes.

If throughput results from Load Model 4 and 7 are very close, then the server's adapter may be constraining throughput, and a higher-speed adapter should be used. If Load Model 4 results are significantly higher than 7, server throughput can be improved by upgrading the hard disk for faster data access.

If Load Model 6 throughput is close to that of Load Model 4, the server's adapter may be constraining throughput. If Load Model 6 throughput is much less than that of Load Model 4, throughput can be improved by upgrading the server CPU.

If Load Model 8 throughput is significantly below the other throughput measurements, this indicates that the network path has a slow link that is constraining throughput.

Once these tests have been run individually, a combined load model using Load Models 5, 6, and 7 can provide a representative measure of the TPS and

KBps that the production system will provide. Create the load model using a percentage mix of cache hits versus hard disk I/O, and I/O versus CPU-bound transactions. Since these mixes are difficult to estimate, use the following recommended process:

1. Construct a load model, Load Model M, with 4 to 1 read versus write transactions with an estimated 50 percent cache hit and 75 percent I/O requests versus 25 percent CPU transactions. Run three load points that bracket the knee of Load Model 7 tests.

2. Change the load model to a different estimate of I/O distribution, such as 3 to 1 read versus write and 30 percent cache hits.

3. Rerun the test.

4. Change Load Model M to a different percentage of I/O versus CPU transactions, such as 60/40.

5. Rerun the test.

Since every application and system is different, there is no way to predict how the load changes will effect TPS and KBps. However, this will provide three data points that create a performance curve and should illustrate a trend. As the system is deployed and the utilization rates are measured, these test results will indicate probable performance changes depending on the actual mix of user transactions.

TEST CASE 2: NETWORK PLATFORM TESTING

Network platform and client-server application throughput testing measure similar attributes for the file server and database server, respectively. Workstation throughput can also be measured to determine effective data transfer between the workstation and file server. Workstation throughput is important to ensure that it can support client-server application and other file I/O demands.

While client-server application testing uses a transaction load, network platform testing uses file I/O loads to represent typical reads and writes from productivity applications, such as spreadsheets, word processors, and drawing utilities.

Test Measurements

Throughput measurements for a network platform typically are presented in KBps. KBps measurements can be recorded on a network analyzer or calculated by the load generator. The analyzer can also monitor for network errors during the test. Anytime a performance test is conducted, the system should be monitored for errors, as errors can significantly impact measured performance and skew the results.

Test Configurations

All test configurations are emulated. The same configuration should be used for response time, throughput, configuration sizing, and capacity planning tests. As originally presented in Chapter 20, the test configurations are often a single segment with a file server and workstations. This can be the same hardware as used for client-server testing. If the application users will usually be on different segments from the database server or file server, and the interconnecting paths include slow speed links that could affect performance, these are included in the test configuration to measure their impact on throughput. Figure 21.6 illustrates several test configurations options.

When testing workstation side throughput, run only one workstation against the server. This will guarantee that the throughput bottleneck is within the workstation and not the server, since the server should have excess capacity supporting only one workstation.

Use these configurations as a guide, but be sure to define specific test configurations that emulate your unique network topology.

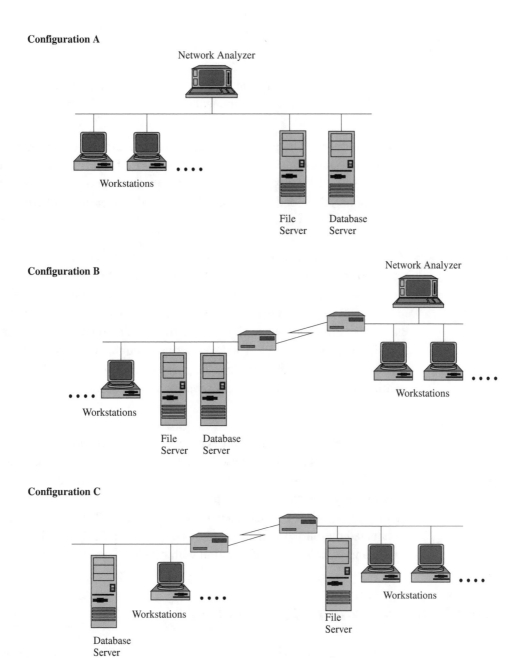

Figure 21.6   Example test configurations for network platform tests.

Load Model

The load model for network platform testing is file I/O, with slight changes in the test script depending on which component of the file server is to be measured:

- **Load Model 9:** The test script measures maximum server throughput by reading data exclusively from server cache. Perform3 is the preferred test utility. The measured KBps represents both server and network throughput. This load model can also be used to measure workstation throughput.

- **Load Model 10:** The test script measures maximum hard disk through-put. Perform3 reads only cached data; therefore, batch files or program load generators must be developed for this test. By eliminating server caching, all requests must be processed off the hard disk; therefore, the hard disk is the bottleneck. By reading the same amount and format of data in Load Models 9 and 10, the effective throughput improvement of cached versus hard disk I/O can be measured. By both reading and writing data, the load model better represents real-world server loading and throughput.

- **Load Model 11:** Since most file servers tend to be I/O, rather than CPU bound, more attention is focused on the other test objectives, as they return higher dividends. This test is not discussed. To measure maxi-mum throughput based on 100 percent CPU utilization often requires multiple network segments and high complex loads. This testing can be conducted by following the procedures described under Load Models 9 or 10, and using a test configuration with multiple server segments.

Test Execution and Data Collection

Perform3 provides automated data collection and reduction for each workstation in the test. For other load generators, automated data reduction will have to be developed, or data will have to be manually recorded and reduced. All data reduction should include an average per run, an average across three runs, and

Run ID (A)

	Station ID	Test Script ID	Run 1 KBps	Run 2 KBps	Run 3 KBps
	(B)	(C)	(D)		
Average for Run			(E)		
Average Across Runs				(F)	
Standard Deviation				(G)	

Figure 21.7   Data reduction spreadsheet for network platform throughput testing.

the standard deviation across runs (to insure reproducible results). Figure 21.7 shows a spreadsheet for data reduction. When using Perform3, only the run averages have to be entered in the spreadsheet. For other load generators, the spreadsheet provides a collection and reduction method for each workstation in the test.

Cell definitions in the Figure 21.7 spreadsheet are:

    cell A = Run ID

    cell B = Workstation ID

    cell C = Test Script ID

    cell D = measured kilobytes per second

    cell E = average kilobytes per second for the run

    cell F = average kilobytes per second across two or more runs

    cell G = standard deviation of average kilobytes per second for two or three runs

Run ID 2 Stations

Station ID	Test Script ID	Run 1 KBps	Run 2 KBps	Run 3 KBps
Stat-1	Perf3/512			
Stat-2	Perf3/512			
Average for Run		501.5	501.5	501.75
Average Across Runs			501.5	501.6
Standard Deviation			0	0

Figure 21.8   Spreadsheet entries for one load point (Run ID) test repeated three times.

Run ID 2 Stations

Station ID	Test Script ID	Run 1 KBps	Run 2 KBps	Run 3 KBps
Stat-1	Perf3/512			
Stat-2	Perf3/512			
Average for Run		501.5	501.5	501.75
Average Across Runs			501.5	501.6
Standard Deviation			0	0

Run ID 3 Stations

Station ID	Test Script ID	Run 1 KBps	Run 2 KBps	Run 3 KBps
Stat-1	Perf3/512			
Stat-2	Perf3/512			
Stat-3	Perf3/512			
Average for Run		707	707.3	707.4
Average Across Runs			707.2	707.2
Standard Deviation			0	0

Run ID 4 Stations

Station ID	Test Script ID	Run 1 KBps	Run 2 KBps	Run 3 KBps
Stat-1	Perf3/512			
Stat-2	Perf3/512			
Stat-3	Perf3/512			
Stat-4	Perf3/512			
Average for Run		695	694.9	695.1
Average Across Runs			695	695
Standard Deviation			0	0

Figure 21.9   Spreadsheet entries for three runs at different load points of two, three, and four workstations.

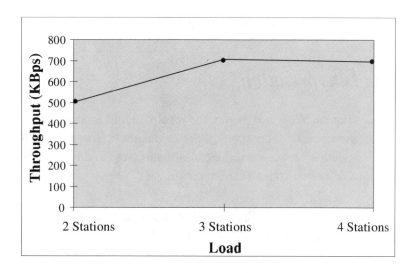

Figure 21.10   Chart of Figure 21.9 test results.

The test sequence for Load Models 9 and 10 is:

1. Start the load generators. Verify that the test configuration is working properly and that all workstations can access the file server. Run a practice test with several workstations.

2. Set up a spreadsheet for the load increments and fill in the Run ID and Load Script ID(s).

3. Run the test at the first load point three times, Figure 21.8. Enter the results into the data reduction spreadsheet and compare the total and average KBps throughput across the three runs. Record the CPU utilization of the server in the test journal.

4. Repeat step 3 for additional load points, Figure 21.9. For each network there will be a point at which throughput will degrade to an unacceptable level. You need to determine this point for your network. Use the spreadsheet data to chart the test results, as diagrammed in Figure 21.10. Visual data is easier to interpret than numerical data.

5. Repeat steps 1 through 4 for other test scripts.

Data Interpretation

After each test case is run, the results should be entered into the data reduction spreadsheet. The spreadsheet calculates average TPS, KBps, and standard deviation between test runs, information required to determine the next test load as described under Test Execution.

Figure 21.11 illustrates how test data from different load models provides information on file server throughput:

- **Load Model 9:** The first test results in Figure 21.11 determine peak data throughput in KBps. This is an indication of how fast the server, adapter, and network can handle file reads. It measures the internal queuing, buffering, processing, and cache access. Since the server software

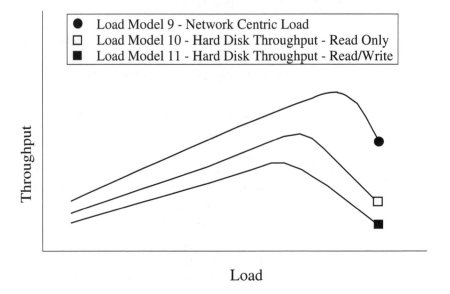

Figure 21.11   Analyzing throughput test data.

(NOS) is not CPU-intensive in this test, measured server CPU utilization indicates how much CPU is used by the server adapter's software driver to maintain the throughput rate. For instance, if the adapter driver is using 50 percent of the CPU, this may indicate that adding another adapter to the server will decrease throughput per segment. If, in the production network, servers support other tasks that require the CPU, then the measured throughput may also degrade or the services may degrade because of CPU contention.

- **Load Model 10:** The second curve in Figure 21.11 measures the same data as the first test, when the majority of the transactions are serviced from the hard disk rather than cache. This compares hard disk to cache access at a system level.

The third curve in Figure 21.11 shows throughput for reads and writes for a normally-configured server with reasonable cache. This curve best represents real-world throughput capacity of the server.

If throughput results from Load Models 9 and 10 are very close, then the server's adapter may be constraining throughput and a higher-speed adapter should be used. If Load Model 9 results are significantly higher than those of 10, server throughput can be improved by upgrading the hard disk (faster access) and CPU.

Application: Configuration Sizing

TEST MATRIX

Configuration sizing attempts to optimize network system performance. It addresses each component in the network path: the client-server application, the presentation manager, the workstation, workstation-to-server connection, the file server, the database server, and the database software. Configuration sizing is used to:

- Measure how key configuration settings affect system performance and confirm that all settings are optimally configured.

- Determine the settings to achieve a required response time, TPS, or KBps.

Configuration sizing uses the test procedures and measurements discussed in Chapters 20 and 21 to measure the performance difference when parameters and components are changed in the test configuration. Configuration sizing is an iterative process that is both labor- and time-intensive.

Example 22.1 Configuration sizing a NOS.

At the initial release of 3Com's 3+Open, which was based on Microsoft's LAN Manager, I managed a project to evaluate the effect of various configuration parameters and options on server performance. It took two months of testing to analyze about 80 parameter permutations. At the completion of the testing, the conclusion was that only a few parameters significantly affected server throughput, while the majority of the parameters had little effect (in the range of 2 to 4 percent). What was learned from that project was a method for minimizing the iterative process of the testing. If we had employed the process initially, the testing could have been completed in three to four weeks.❏

Some changes that improve performance may not be practical to implement. If testing identifies that 32MB of RAM per workstation improves performance by 5 percent, but there are 500 workstations, the cost to upgrade all workstations, approximately $500,000, may be prohibitive. If testing shows that a higher-performance adapter in the server improves performance, but requires significant CPU cycles, the cost of the adapters is small, but the cost of additional servers may be high. In configuration sizing, conclusions must be balanced to determine which changes can be financially and technically implemented on a large production network.

This chapter outlines a procedure that addresses major configuration aspects of the network system that affect performance and throughput, while minimizing the iterative process. This reduces the time and effort of configuration sizing.

Test Measurements

The most important aspect of configuration sizing is defining the set of parameters and components that will be evaluated in the test. Figure 22.1 provides a recommended list of test configuration options that should be evaluated for client-server application network components. Figure 22.2 is a comparable list for database servers. Figure 22.3 is the list for sizing the network platform. Use these lists as a guideline and supplement or delete items based on experience and test results. In configuration sizing, the 80-20 rule applies. Changes in a few parameters and components provide the majority of improvement, as discussed in the previous example. Subsequent changes may provide additional improvement, but often it is very difficult to evaluate these more subtle changes, and generally the return does not justify the effort.

	Configuration Parameter	Load Model	Recommended Evaluation
Client-server Application GUI/WS	Memory Size/Allocation	2/3	* See NOTE
	Video RAM Data Cache	2/3	* 1 vs 2MB * Total cache and block/page size. For random I/O, minimize network I/O; for sequential I/O, maximize cached data.
	RAM Disk Swap file location and size	2/3	* For swap and temp files. * RAM disk, local hard disk, or network drive.
	Processor Foreground/background allocation	2/3	* See NOTE
			(*NOTE: Refer to Microsoft Windows and DOS 6.2 User Guide for configuration options to evaluate.)
	Application temp file location	2/3/9	RAM drive, local or remote hard disk.
	Hard disk speed	2/3	Only important if used for file access by application. Use root or subdirectory off root.
	Hard disk structure	2/3	Only important if used for file access by application. Use root or subdirectory off root.
	CPU speed	2/3	Test X MHz and 2X MHz to determine performance difference.
	Network adapter	4/9	Lower cost vs higher performance. Throughput should be 20% greater than application throughput requirements.

Figure 22.1 Recommended list of configuration parameters and components to evaluate for client-server applications.

	Configuration Parameter	Load Model	Recommended Evaluation
Database	Cache size and utilization	4/5	Increase until diminishing returns.
	Cache block/page size	5	Equal to largest record.
	I/O Buffers	4/5	Increase until diminishing returns.
	Processes	6	Double default to determine effect on throughput.
	CPU	4/6	Faster is better. Want 80% utilization for production system.
	Hard Disk Access	2/7	Faster is better. Less than 5 times slower than cache access.
	Data Compression	2/7	Measure CPU overhead vs. performance.
	Adapter	4	High throughput, low CPU use.
	Number of network adapters	4/6	1 vs. 2
	Other NOS/network features, e.g. streaming	4	Evaluate throughput enhancement.

Figure 22.2   Recommended list of configuration parameters and components to evaluate for database servers.

	Configuration Parameter	Load Model	Recommended Evaluation
Network Platform	Cache size and utilization	9/10	Increase until diminishing returns.
	Cache block/page size		Equal to largest record.
	I/O Buffers	9/10	Increase until diminishing returns.
	Processes		Double default to determine effect on throughput.
	CPU		Faster is better. Want 80% utilization for production system.
	Hard Disk Access	10	Faster is better. Less than 5 times slower than cache access.
	Data Compression	9/10	Measure CPU overhead vs. performance.
	Adapter	9	High throughput, low CPU use.
	Number of network adapters	9	1 vs. 2
	Other NOS/network features, e.g. streaming	9	Evaluate throughput enhancement.

Figure 22.3   Parameters and components to consider when sizing the network platform.

Based on the load model tests presented in Chapters 20 and 21:

- Client-server application response time is used to determine the effective performance difference between various parameter settings for the application GUI, presentation manager, workstation operating system, and database server. Column 3 in Figure 22.1 illustrates how various load models are used to size client-server application network components.

- Often, the effect of the workstation hardware, OS software, and GUI on client-server performance is underestimated. For example, workstation throughput testing has uncovered a broad range of bottlenecks, including:

    The adapter/driver combination limited throughput to 500KBps when the server could sustain significantly more.

    The workstation cache was too small, which effectively required the cache to be rewritten for each read request, because most, but not all, of the required data was available in the cache. This eliminated any benefit of workstation caching.

    The workstation buffering was such that it required two writes for each record requested.

    Swapping to the local hard disk was actually slower than to the file server hard disk.

- Database server throughput measurements in TPS and KBps are used to determine the effective performance difference between various server and workstation configurations for the NOS, workstation and server network interfaces, and database server software. Column 3 in Figure 22.2 illustrates how various load models are used to size the database server and network.

- File server throughput in KBps is used to determine the effective performance difference between various configurations for the NOS and workstation and server network interfaces. Column 3 in Figure 22.3 illustrates how various load models are used to size the network platform (NOS, workstation, and file server).

Test Configurations

All test configurations are emulated. The same configuration should be used for response time, throughput, configuration sizing, and capacity planning tests. As originally presented in Chapter 20, the test configuration is a single segment with the file server, database server, applications server (if required), and workstations. If the application users will usually be on different segments from the database server or file server, and the interconnecting paths include slow speed links that could affect performance, these should be included in the test configuration to measure their impact on response time. Figure 22.4 illustrates several test configurations options. Note the network analyzer on the test configuration: If errors are detected during the test, they will have to be investigated; if a problem is found, the tests must be rerun to get relevant response time measurements.

The test configuration requires that the application and database software under test be installed on the database server, application server, or file server as it will be deployed on the production network. The workstations should represent a mix of the workstations that will be used on the production network; therefore, several workstation configurations may have to be tested for configuration sizing. Use these configurations as a guide, but, as always, define specific test configurations that emulate your unique network topology.

Before starting the test project, begin a test journal, document the test configuration hardware and software, and create data reduction spreadsheets as described in Chapter 6.

Load Model

Use the homogeneous load scripts described in Chapters 20 and 21 to test the various aspects of the servers, workstations, and applications as outlined in

Configuration A

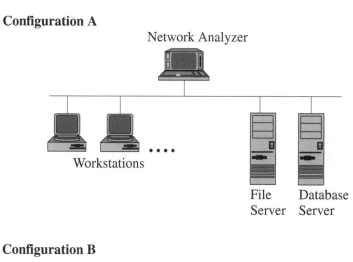

Configuration B

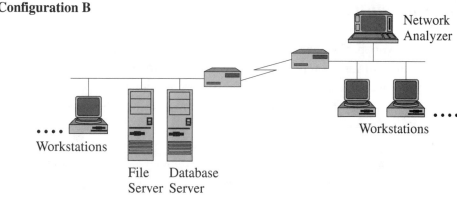

Configuration C

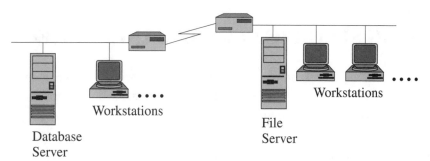

Figure 22.4   Example test configurations for configuration sizing.

Figures 22.1, 22.2, and 22.3. Estimate the number of users for the initial production load and the growth over the first year. Use these two user load points to define equivalent user loading. For example, the initial load may be 100 users, with 20 percent growth forecasted over the next 12 months. The load points are 100 and 120 equivalent users.

"Heterogeneous" transaction mixes can be used as test cases, but for tuning, these provide a complex load that does not facilitate test data analysis. However, it is a good practice to run a test before and after configuration sizing to determine performance improvement.

Test Execution and Data Collection

Network performance is the result of the interaction of many individual software and hardware components. Generally, improving each network component improves overall network performance, but not to the same degree. Some changes make significant improvements, while others provide very little improvement.

As noted earlier, configuration sizing can be used to meet specific performance targets or to optimize the system configuration. The former test objective is narrower in scope than the latter, and the testing process is different for the two objectives.

MEETING SPECIFIC PERFORMANCE OBJECTIVES

The test process for this objective analyzes various parameter and configuration changes that should improve performance until the target performance is reached, at which time testing is completed.

From experience, the recommended order of tuning is to evaluate parameters and settings that affect the following areas in the order listed:

1. server I/O

2. server processes

3. network I/O

4. workstation I/O

5. workstation processes

With this in mind, the test sequence is:

1. Define the starting test configuration and configuration settings. Use either out-of-the-box settings, or tune the system based on vendor recommendations or experience.

2. From response time and throughput testing, run the following load models to baseline the test configuration for client-server applications:

   Load Model 2: Measure overall system response time.

   Load Model 3: Measure GUI response time.

   Load Model 4: Measure server and network throughput.

   Load Model 5: Measure server transaction throughput.

   Load Model 6: Measure server CPU throughput.

   Load Model 7: Measure server hard disk throughput.

   For a file server or network platform, run the following load models:

   Load Model 9: Measure server and network throughput.

   Load Model 10: Measure hard disk throughput.

3. Use the suggested spreadsheet formats from Chapters 20 and 21 to record the raw test measurements. Record the average measurements and the parameter settings in a consolidated spreadsheet, such as shown in Figure 22.5. Determine whether the test results meet the target requirements for response time and throughput. If they do, stop the test; the configuration meets requirements. Otherwise, proceed to step 4.

4. Based on Figure 22.2 for a database server or Figure 22.3 for the network platform, increase one of the recommended configuration items by 50 to 100 percent and rerun the appropriate tests of step 2.

5. Record test data in the spreadsheet and calculate the percent change in performance. Determine whether the test results meet the target requirements for response time and throughput. If they do, stop the test; the configuration meets requirements. Otherwise, proceed to step 6.

6. If the change improves performance, double the change and rerun the tests. Continue this process until there is no improvement or the change exceeds the bounds of financial or technical enhancement options. If the change does not improve performance, reset the configuration.

7. Repeat steps 2 through 6 until the target requirements are met or all configuration changes have been evaluated. If the target requirements have not been met, proceed with step 8 for tuning the workstation.

Target Response Time   _____
Target Throughput   _____

Run ID	Parameter	Setting	Response Time	Throughput

Figure 22.5   Data reduction spreadsheet for configuration sizing.

8. Based on Figure 22.1 for a client-server application, increase one of the configuration items by 50 to 100 percent and rerun the appropriate tests of step 2 for client-server applications.

9. Record the data in the spreadsheet and calculate the percent change in performance. Determine whether the test results meet the target requirements for response time and throughput. If they do, stop the test; the configuration meets requirements. Otherwise, proceed to step 10.

10. If the change improves performance, double the change and rerun the tests. Continue this process until there is no improvement or the change exceeds the bounds of financial or technical enhancement options. If the change does not improve performance, reset the configuration.

11. Repeat steps 8 to 10 until the target requirements are met or all configuration changes have been evaluated. If, after evaluating all configuration changes, the target requirements have not been met, the current network system as defined and implemented cannot support the performance requirements.

OPTIMIZING THE SYSTEM

The test process for this objective first determines the contribution from each element, and then combines those changes that provide the most individual improvement. The test objective is to achieve the best possible configuration.

From experience, the recommended order of tuning is to evaluate parameters and settings that affect the following areas in the order listed:

1. server I/O

2. server processes

3. network I/O

4. workstation I/O

Target Response Time _____
Target Throughput   _____

Run ID	Parameter	Setting	Response Time	Throughput

Figure 22.6   Performance comparisons across test configuration.

5. workstation processes

The test sequence is:

1. Define the starting test configuration. Use either out-of-the-box settings or tune the system based on vendor recommendations or experience.

2. From response time and throughput testing, run the following load models to baseline the test configuration for client-server applications:

   Load Model 1: Measure overall system response time.

   Load Model 3: Measure GUI response time.

   Load Model 4: Measure server and network throughput.

   Load Model 5: Measure server transaction throughput.

   Load Model 6: Measure server CPU throughput.

   Load Model 7: Measure server hard disk throughput.

   For a file server or network platform, run the following load models:

Load Model 9: Measure server network throughput.

Load Model 10: Measure hard disk throughput.

3. Record the reduced test data in a spreadsheet, such as in Figure 22.6.

4. Make the first test configuration change based on the key configuration parameters shown in Figures 22.1, 22.2, and 22.3.

    For client-server applications, test the database server first. Make a change from Figure 22.2.

    For file servers, make one NOS or file server change from Figure 22.3.

5. Rerun the appropriate TPS and throughput tests from step 2. Record all test data in the spreadsheet.

6. If the change improves performance, double the change and rerun the test. Continue this process until there is no improvement or the change exceeds the bounds of financial or technical enhancement options.

7. Reset the parameter changed in step 4 and change another parameter. Rerun the tests of step 2. Record all test data in the spreadsheet.

8. If the change improves performance, double the change and rerun the test. Continue this process until there is no improvement or the change exceeds the bounds of financial or technical enhancement options.

9. Repeat steps 4 through 8 until all the basic parameter changes have been made.

10. For a client-server application, repeat the previous process for the application GUI using Figure 22.1 as a guideline.

11. Analyze the single change results from the previous tests. Determine which changes had the greatest impact on performance.

12. Select the top two to four changes from step 11. Make the test configuration changes and rerun the tests. Use the spreadsheet from Figure 22.6 to record all parameter changes and the measured response time and throughput measurements.

13. Compare the results from steps 11 and 12. If the combined changes improved performance by more than 5 percent over the best case single change, use the combined change values. Otherwise, use the single change that generated the best performance improvement at the lowest cost.

The outline given here provides a methodical process for evaluating a broad combination of changes. This effort may appear to be very time-consuming, but most tests are very short, and data interpretation is straightforward. Often, reconfiguration takes up the majority of project time. The number of test cases can be tempered by experience and results of previous runs.

Application: Capacity Planning

TEST MATRIX

Either a system that has been optimally configured through configuration sizing or any existing configuration can be measured for excess capacity, which is the number of users who can be supported beyond the planned or estimated production load without degrading performance to an unacceptable level. Capacity planning measures system capacity and component or key resource capacity, such as server I/O, server CPU, and network bandwidth.

As a systems-level test, capacity testing uses a load script of application commands to measure how the combined application GUI front-end, back-end database (for a client-server application), file server, network platform, and network infrastructure perform. Starting with an equivalent user load that represents the planned or estimated production load, the user load is increased until response degradation occurs. The difference between the starting and ending equivalent user load represents the excess capacity of the system. Test Case 1 discusses system-level testing.

As a key component test, capacity testing measures the relative capacity of a component as compared to the overall system. For example, if, in the system-level test, user response degrades at 500 users with X KBps throughput, component capacity testing can determine which component is limiting system throughput. It can also measure the excess capacity of the nonbottleneck components. Test Case 2 discusses component-level testing.

TEST CASE 1: SYSTEM-LEVEL CAPACITY TESTING

This test uses a test script of application commands, Load Model 2, Chapter 20, to measure the response time of the system for increasing load.

Test Measurements

Response time measurements are usually shown as a load versus response time curve. The load is represented as equivalent users, and response time is shown in seconds or minutes. The response time is taken as the average across all the workstations or sessions in the test.

Test Configurations

All test configurations are emulated. The test configuration should be used in configuration sizing or in an existing configuration for which excess capacity needs to be measured. A network analyzer should be used to measure KBps and record errors during the test.

Running the test with an equivalent user load equal to the production load measures baseline performance. As the number of users is increased until response time degrades, the test provides a measure of the system's capacity to support more users.

Before initiating the test project, start a test journal, document the test configuration hardware and software, and create data reduction spreadsheets as described in Chapter 6.

Load Model

To accurately measure the excess capacity in a production environment, Load Model 2 should be used. It includes a set of typical user commands covering the system's key functionality.

In a capacity test, all workstations typically run the same load script. As equivalent users are added, a load versus response time curve can be generated based on the average response for the users.

If the application is such that a "heterogeneous" mix of users is more typical and the mix can be accurately defined, it can work well for capacity planning. Load increments can include any mix of new users, and the results will be relevant comparable to the baseline. For example, if one group of customer service representatives mainly interact with customers and do database queries and updates, and another group of users in accounting mainly generate billings based on database order entries, load points could include the following increments, and all results could be compared to the baseline to determine excess capacity for the specific mix:

- **Baseline:** 50 customer service representatives, 5 accounting users

- **Load Point 1:** 75 customer service representatives, 8 accounting users

- **Load Point 2:** 60 customer service representatives, 5 accounting users

- **Load Point 3:** 70 customer service representatives, 5 accounting users

- **Load Point 4:** 100 customer service representatives, 8 accounting users

Test Execution and Data Collection

Most client-server testing tools provide automated data collection and reduction facilities. All data reduction should include an average per run, an average across three runs, and the standard deviation across runs (to ensure reproducible results). If the testing tool does not provide data reduction, the spreadsheet provided in Figure 23.1 can be used as a guide in developing your own data reduction.

Cell definitions in the Figure 23.1 spreadsheet are:

cell A = Run ID

Run ID (A)

	Station ID	Test Script ID	Run 1		Run 2		Run 3	
			Response Time	Throughput	Response Time	Throughput	Response Time	Throughput
	(B)	(C)	(D)	(H)				
Average for Run			(E)	(I)				
Average Across Runs			(F)	(J)				
Standard Deviation			(G)	(G)				

Figure 23.1   Data reduction spreadsheet for application response time testing.

cell B = Workstation ID

cell C = Test Script ID

cell D = response time is minutes or seconds

cell E = average response time for the run

cell F = average response time for two or three runs

cell G = standard deviation for two or three runs

cell H = throughput in KBps

cell I = average throughput for the run

cell J = average throughput for two or three runs

The test sequence is:

1. Start the client-server testing tool. Verify that the test configuration is working properly and that all workstations can access the server. Run a practice test with several workstations.

2. If required, set up a spreadsheet for the load increments and fill in the Run ID and Load Script ID(s).

3. Shut down and restart the client-server testing tool for the first load point of X equivalent users. This is the planned or estimated production load. After each test, enter the results into the data reduction spreadsheet or log the results through the mechanism provided by the testing tool. Measure both response time and KBps at the server. After the third run, compare the average response time for the three runs and calculate the standard deviation. If the values differ by more than 4 percent across the three runs, the test configuration is not generating reproducible results. You must determine why before proceeding with additional tests. See Test Configuration Problem Resolution Tips at the end of Chapter 18.

4. Analyze the results.

   - **Minimal or no degradation**: If there is little or no degradation in response time as the load increases, continue to do so in increments equal to 20 percent of the production load.

   - **Significant degradation**: If there is significant degradation between the last and the current load point, halve the load until the knee of the curve is reached. This is the same procedure that was used in Chapter 20, Figure 20.5.

5. Repeat steps 3 and 4 until degradation occurs.

Data Interpretation

As each test case is run, the results should be entered into the data reduction spreadsheet. The spreadsheet calculates average response time and standard deviation between test runs. This information is required to determine the next test load as described under Test Execution.

Since the load model only approximates the distribution of transactions on the production network (best estimate), the capacity measurements are not exact. However, the test results will provide a level of risk measurement:

- If excess capacity is under 25 percent, the system may already be in trouble or will be shortly after it is deployed. Changes in the system should be considered to increase excess capacity to the next level.

- If excess capacity is between 25 and 60 percent, there is a reasonable performance cushion. As system use grows, it should be monitored and the production network traffic patterns baselined in order to create a better load model. The tests should be rerun with the improved load model.

- Over 60 percent excess capacity implies that the system is overly designed or implemented, and probably it can be cost reduced if some components are downsized. Downsizing can be analyzed using configuration sizing in reverse.

The knee of the response time curve also determines the effective KBps of the system. This data is used in Test Case 2 to determine the capacity of individual components relative to the system.

TEST CASE 2: COMPONENT CAPACITY TESTING

Once the excess capacity of the system has been determined, individual components can also be measured using response time and KBps measurements from the system tests.

Test Measurements

Measurements are KBps that are compared to Test Case 1 throughput to determine the relationship between system and component capacity.

Test Configurations

The test configuration must be identical to that used in Test Case 1 to achieve meaningful and comparative results. Before starting the test project, begin a test journal, document the test configuration hardware and software, and create data reduction spreadsheets as described in Chapter 6.

Load Model

Use the load model(s) from Test Case 1 that are pertinent to the component under test. The five component-level tests most often run are:

- server throughput capacity using Load Model 5

- server CPU capacity using Load Model 6

- server hard disk capacity using Load Model 7

- network bandwidth using Load Model 8

- GUI/front-end response using Load Model 3

Test Execution and Data Collection

Many client-server testing tools provide automated data collection and reduction facilities. All data reduction should include an average per run, an average across three runs, and the standard deviation across runs (to ensure reproducible results). For this test, the data reduction must include TPS, KBps, CPU utilization for Load Model 6, and network utilization for Load Model 8.

The test sequence is:

1. Start the client-server testing tool. Verify that the test configuration is working properly and that all workstations can access the server. Run a practice test with several workstations.

2. From Test Case 1, determine the KBps throughput required and the TPS necessary to achieve the throughput for the load model to be run. If Load Model 7 is used, determine how many TPS are required to generate equivalent throughput to Test Case 1 results.

3. Set up a spreadsheet for the load increments and fill in the Run ID and Load Script ID(s). Fill in the TPS and KBps from step 2. Increase the TPS by 20 percent and measure KBps.

4. Analyze the results.

    •   **Minimal or no degradation:** If there is little or no degradation in response time as the load increases, continue to do so in increments equal to 20 percent of the production load.

    •   **Significant degradation:** If there is significant degradation between the last and the current load point, halve the load until the knee of the curve is reached. This is the same procedure that was used in Chapter 20, Figure 20.5.

5. Repeat steps 3 and 4 until degradation occurs.

6. Repeat steps 2 to 4 for other load models.

Data Interpretation

As each test case is run, the results should be entered into the data reduction spreadsheet. The spreadsheet calculates average response time and standard deviation between test runs. This information is required to determine the next test load as described under Test Execution.

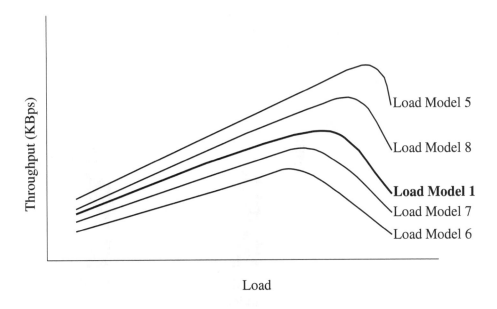

Figure 23.2   A system degrades differently under different load models.

Based on Test Case 1 and 2 test results, a load versus throughput (KBps) curve can be created that illustrates how the system and each component degrades under load and where the knee of the curve is for each test as diagrammed in Figure 23.2. Any Test Case 2 results that fall on or near the Test Case 1 throughput should be suspected as bottlenecks.

GUI/front-end testing, comparing Test Case 1 and 2 results, illustrates how graphic-intensive and application-swapping operations affect performance, as shown in Figure 23.3. Test Case 1 measured average response time for key functions and transactions of the system, which probably includes some of GUI and swapping load, but also includes other features and transactions. The Test Case 2 results show that response time changes as GUI and swapping overhead increase. If these response times are significantly different, the results indicate front-end bottlenecks that will impact system performance on a slow workstation. Further tests to isolate separate menu operations and transactions, can identify

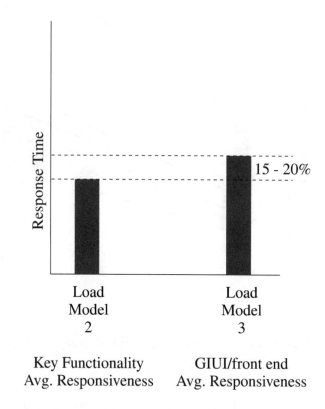

Figure 23.3   GUI overhead often significantly impacts user response time.

those activities that are the slowest and point to where optimization effort should be spent.

Application: Reliability Testing

TEST MATRIX

Application/presentation layer reliability testing is similar to network infrastructure reliability testing. Both tests use accelerated loading to create in a matter of hours loads that the system would normally experience over weeks and months of normal use.

Reliability testing attempts to accelerate failure of the application, presentation layer, workstation OS, NOS, and network platform caused by:

- **Cumulative errors:** These are the result of repeating an operation multiple times in a fashion that results in an error. A simple example would be dirty cache buffers. If the algorithm for dirty cache buffer writes does not update pointers correctly, eventually the cache could become populated with free, but unavailable buffers, possibly resulting in degraded performance and eventually a system crash.

- **Timing errors:** These errors are caused by two time-dependent operations that occur out of sequence or without the proper delay. Typically, the problem is manifested when the system becomes very busy and one operation is delayed or impacted relative to another. Heavy multiuser record access and updates that result in incorrect information reported to a user would be an example of one possible timing error.

- **Statistical errors:** In developing and testing a complex software system, it is virtually impossible to test and verify every possible path through the code. However, statistically, over time, every path will be traversed, either because of an error condition or a seldom-invoked sequence of events. Reliability testing increases the probability that a statistical error will occur.

Reliability testing is conducted for the application/network system or for a file or database server.

TEST CASE 1: SERVER RELIABILITY TESTING

The server is the single most critical point of failure. For a typical network, the file server and application server comprise the hub of the system; for a client-server application, it is the database server. If the server isn't reliable, there is no value in testing other network components, therefore, server testing is first on the agenda.

Test Measurements

The most important measurement is to determine whether the server survives the test. Average throughput, test duration, and network errors are recorded at intervals during the test.

Test Configurations

All test configurations are emulated and very simple. Since maximum server loading is required, the test configuration should include a very high-speed network between the workstations and server, such as will be used in the production environment. Each workstation generates as much activity as possible against the server. Figure 24.1 shows simple test configurations that can be used for file server, database server, and workstation tests.

Before starting the test project, begin a test journal, document the test configuration hardware and software, and create data reduction spreadsheets as described in Chapter 6.

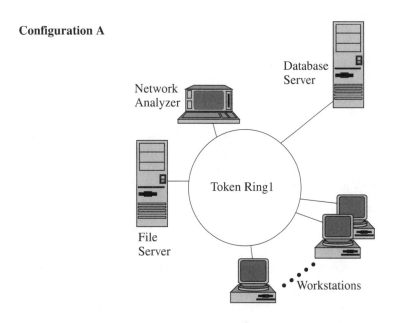

Figure 24.1 Simple server reliability test configurations for maximum server loading.

Load Model

The following sections discuss several types of load models.

Server Tests

The maximum load possible is generated against the server, so the load model must eliminate overhead from all components that could degrade server load. Therefore, the recommended scripts for database servers are Load Models 5, 6, 7, and 8, Chapter 21. For file servers or other servers, use Load Models 9 and 10, Chapter 21.

These load models are designed to run for a few iterations or a short time, therefore test scripts have to be modified to run for the required test duration. Consequently, either set a time parameter or have the scripts run for a large number of iterations. The number of required test iterations can be estimated by running a short test of X iterations and timing the wall clock duration for the test. Divide the wall clock time into the required test duration to get a multiplier for the number of iterations. For example, if it takes five minutes to run 10 iterations and the test duration is 24 hours, divide 24 hours (1,440 minutes) by 5. The multiplier is 288. Multiply 288 by 10, which equals 2,880. This is the number of iterations required for the 24-hour test.

The transaction or file I/O load should be sufficient to create:

- Throughput (KBps) demand on the server equal to the 70 to 90 percent of the maximum sustainable throughput of the media, or

- 95 to 100 percent CPU utilization, whichever occurs first.

Based on the target loads, this is a stressed reliability test.

Workstation Tests

Using Load Models 2 and 3, Chapter 20, workstation reliability tests can also be run. These tests are important if several different workstation models and

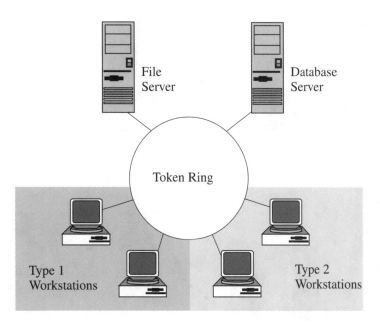

Figure 24.2 Workstation reliability testing.

configurations are used for the client-server application. Using the same rationale, this also applies to throughput testing. Always run workstation pairs, as shown in Figure 24.2, during reliability testing, and run different test scripts on the workstations. This is the first step toward isolating problems as hardware or software failures.

Load Modeling Bursty Traffic

As with infrastructure reliability testing, the preferred loading is bursty traffic, which better emulates data transmissions. This is partially achieved by using different load models, as illustrated in Figure 24.3. Without enforced synchronization, the test scripts generate a natural variation of load during the long test duration. Additional bursty traffic can be achieved by running more application load generators. A packet load generator, sending short bursts of directed packets to the server, can also be used to create more perceived transactions on the server and increase media utilization. While these packets are

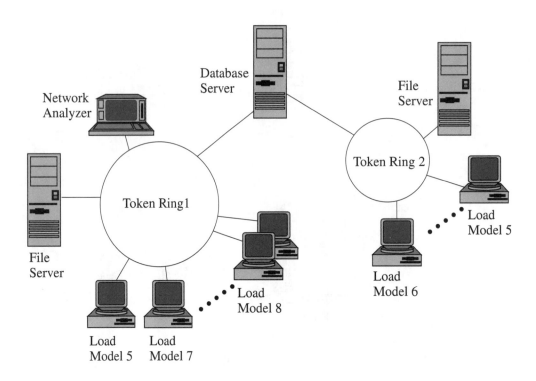

Figure 24.3 Using different load models creates bursty traffic through the varying transaction mix.

discarded at a very low level in the server protocol stack, the fact that they must be handled affects server CPU usage and network throughput.

Test Execution and Data Collection

Most products that provide client-server transaction load generation provide end-of-test throughput results, but don't necessarily provide intermediate results. Since a reliability test is effectively a very long test, it may not be possible to collect throughput data from the load generators during the run. If the test tool cannot provide intermediate results, use the average throughput reading on the network analyzer to determine whether system performance degrades during the test duration. If the tool is an in-house-developed transaction generator, add a

Run ID	(A)
Time/Date	(B)
Server ID	(C)
Test Script	(D)
No. of Workstations	(E)
CPU Utilization	(F)
Throughput	(G)
Errors	
Critical	(H)
Noncritical	(I)

Figure 24.4   Data reduction spreadsheet for server reliability testing.

feature that allows intermediate results on demand to be output. This small overhead in a multihour reliability test will not affect overall results.

Cell definitions in the Figure 24.4 spreadsheet are:

cell A = Test ID.

cell B = time and date when measurements are recorded.

cell C = Server ID.

cell D = Test Script ID.

cell E = number of load generators.

cell F = CPU utilization of the server.

cell G = throughput.

cell H = critical errors. This can be expanded with additional rows of key errors that are expected to occur, or treated as a summary value. Record the number of critical errors here and enter details for each in the problem log.

cell I = noncritical errors. This can be expanded with additional rows, or treated as a summary value. Record the number of noncritical errors here and enter details for each in the problem log.

The test sequence is:

1. Start the load generators. Verify that the test configuration is working properly and that all workstations can access the server. Run a practice test with several workstations.

2. Set up a spreadsheet and fill in the Run ID and Test Script ID.

3. Run the test scripts and increase the load until the required KBps throughput and CPU utilization are achieved. Record the configuration details, including the number of workstations and the load script run on each workstation, in the test journal.

4. Shut down and restart the load generators with the configuration recorded in step 3.

5. Run the test for 24 hours.

6. Every six hours, record the following data, as shown in Figure 24.5:

    -   date and time of test measurement

    -   average KBps throughput and CPU utilization of the server

    -   errors recorded by the network analyzer

7. Analyze the test results to determine whether there is significant throughput degradation for the system or an increase in the error rate

Run ID	1
Time/Date	12/13/95 16:00
Server ID	FS-1
Test Script	T0107FS
No. of Workstations	7
CPU Utilization	89
Throughput	600KBps
Errors	
Critical	0
Noncritical	2

Run ID	2
Time/Date	12/13/95 22:00
Server ID	FS-1
Test Script	T0107FS
No. of Workstations	7
CPU Utilization	91
Throughput	612KBps
Errors	
Critical	0
Noncritical	0

Figure 24.5   Data reduction spreadsheet with the first two six-hour measurements completed.

since the last measurement. Ensure that the CPU utilization and throughput is being maintained in the proper range for the test.

8. Stop the test after 24 hours or when a failure occurs as outlined in the following section.

Data Interpretation

At each six-hour recording milestone, the results should be entered into the data reduction spreadsheet.

A test failure has occurred when one or more of the following conditions manifests:

1. Response time or throughput degrades significantly, greater than 20 percent.

2. An error causes the server to fail.

3. An error causes the link(s) between the server and workstation(s) to be dropped.

If other failures occur, such as a crashed workstation, this does not represent a test failure since the major test objective is to verify server reliability. However, if workstation failures cause the test load to fall below the target rate, the test has to be rerun to get relevant results. It is worthwhile investigating such failures before rerunning the test, and if they persist, the problem must be fixed.

TEST CASE 2: SYSTEM-LEVEL RELIABILITY TESTING

System-level reliability testing does not attempt to measure or isolate specific components or errors. Its objective is to measure reliability and interoperability as the user perceives the system. Any failures that prevent the user or application from interfacing with the GUI or server or impact data retrieval are considered errors.

Establishing Baseline Reliability

Application/presentation layer reliability testing should be conducted on a network that is known to be stable and reliable. This testing is actually a two-step process. First, a combined network platform and internetwork reliability test is run to ensure that the network system and components are reliable. Load Model 9 is used, as illustrated, to test local and remote links and server access. Second, the applications are added to the network, and application/presentation layer reliability tests are run against both the local and remote servers using a load model mix that is representative of estimated production system loads. Figures 24.6 and 24.7 illustrate these two steps.

If application/presentation layer reliability testing is conducted on a network that has *not* been tested for reliability, subsequent problems and errors will be much harder to isolate and resolve.

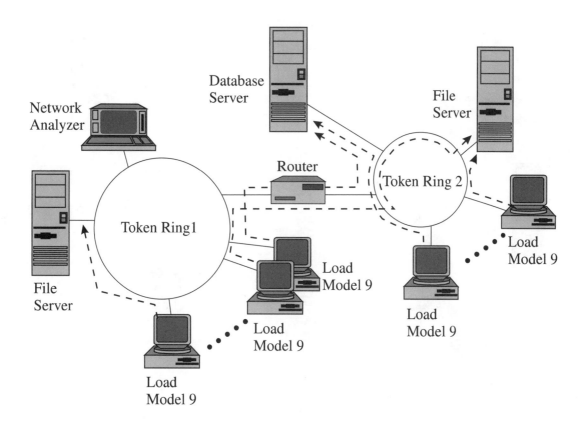

Figure 24.6 First step, network infrastructure reliability testing.

Use test results from application response time and throughput testing to define the load model for the internetwork testing as outlined in Chapter 12, Internetwork Reliability Testing. If test data is not available:

- Throughput (KBps) demand on the server should be equal to 70 to 90 percent of the maximum sustainable throughput of the media, or

- 95 to 100 percent CPU utilization should be achieved, whichever occurs first.

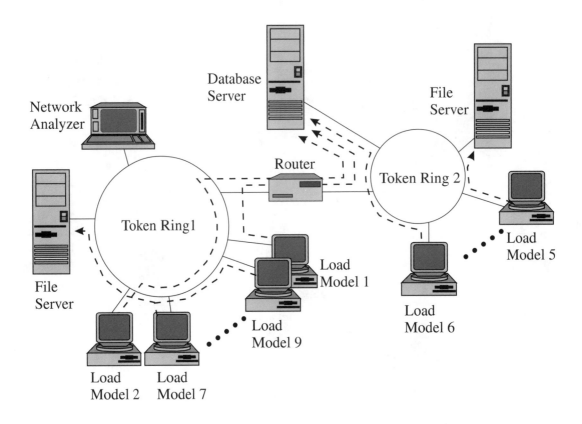

Figure 24.7 Second step, application presentation layer reliability testing on a known baseline from Figure 24.6.

Use the same test configuration as in Chapter 20, Response Time Testing on Emulated Configurations. Run the test for the duration planned for the application reliability testing, either 24 or 72 hours.

Test Measurements

The most important measurement is that which determines whether the system survives the test. Average response time, throughput, test duration, and network errors are recorded at intervals during the test.

Test Configurations

All test configurations are emulated. Use the same configuration as in the previous section, Establishing Baseline Reliability, example Figure 24.6. This configuration has a tested level of baseline reliability for subsequent system-level testing of the client-server application.

Before beginning the test project, start a test journal, document the test configuration hardware and software, and create data reduction spreadsheets as described in Chapter 6.

Load Model

The recommended scripts are Load Model 2 (Chapter 20) and Load Models 6, 7, and 9 (Chapter 21). These scripts exercise basic system functionality and major components.

These load models are designed to run for a few iterations, therefore the test scripts have to be modified to run for the required test duration. To do so, either set a time parameter or have the scripts run for a large number of iterations. The number of required test iterations can be estimated by calculating the time for X iterations and dividing the time into the required test duration to get a multiplier for the number of iterations. For example, if it takes five minutes to run 10 iterations and the test duration is 24 hours, divide 24 hours (1,440 minutes) by 5. The multiplier is 288. Multiply 288 by 10, which equals 2,880. This is the number of iterations required for the 24-hour test.

The equivalent user load should be sufficient to create:

- Throughput (KBps) demand on the file and database server equal to the 70 to 90 percent of the maximum sustainable throughput used in the baseline testing

- 60 to 90 percent CPU utilization on the file and database server

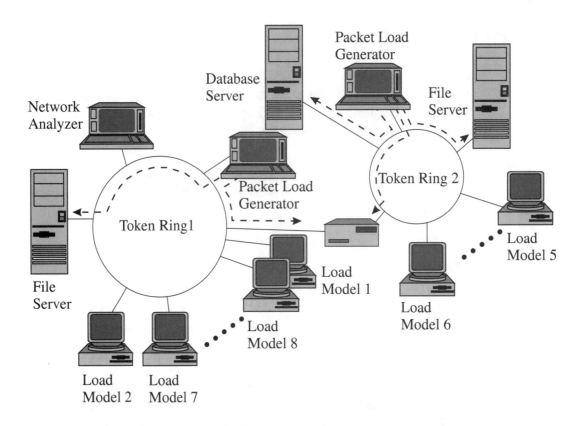

Figure 24.8   Using packet load generators to increase server and link loads.

The lower percentage is used for operational reliability testing, and the higher percentage is used for stressed reliability testing.

Load Modeling Bursty Traffic

As with other reliability testing, the preferred loading is bursty traffic, which better emulates data transmissions. This is partially achieved by using the four different load models. Running the test scripts on different workstations with no enforced synchronization causes a natural variation of load during the long test. Additional bursty traffic can be achieved by running other application load generators, which cause more load on the server or connecting links. A packet load generator, sending short bursts of packets to servers and routers, can be used to create more perceived transactions on the server, as shown in Figure 24.8. While these packets are thrown away at a very low level in the server protocol stack, this loading will affect server CPU and network throughput.

Test Execution and Data Collection

Most client-server testing tools provide automated data collection and reduction facilities. Test results are usually presented at the end of the test run, as most products do not provide intermediate results. Since a reliability test is effectively a very long test, it may not be possible to collect response time data during the run. If the test tool cannot provide intermediate results, use the average throughput reading on the network analyzer to determine whether system performance degrades during the test duration.

Cell definitions in the Figure 24.9 spreadsheet are:

cell A = Test ID.

cell B = time and date when measurements are recorded.

cell C = Server ID.

cell D = Test Script ID.

cell E = number of load generators.

cell F = CPU utilization of the server.

cell G = throughput.

cell H = average response time, if available.

cell I = critical errors. This can be expanded with additional rows of key errors that are expected to occur, or treated as a summary value. Record the number of critical errors here and enter details for each in the problem log.

cell J = noncritical errors. This can be expanded with additional rows, or treated as a summary value. Record the number of noncritical errors here and enter details for each in the problem log.

The test sequence is:

1. Start the client-server testing tool. Verify that the test configuration is working properly and that all workstations can access the server. Run a practice test with several workstations.

2. Set up a spreadsheet, Figure 24.9, and fill in the Run ID and Load Script ID.

3. Run the test scripts and increase the equivalent user loading until the required KBps throughput and CPU utilization are achieved for operational reliability testing. Record the number of equivalent users

Run ID	(A)
Time/Date	(B)
Server ID	(C)
Test Script	(D)
No. of Workstations	(E)
CPU Utilization	(F)
Throughput	(G)
Average Response Time	(H)
Errors	
Critical	(I)
Noncritical	(J)

Figure 24.9   Data reduction spreadsheet for system-level application reliability testing (similar to Figure 12.9).

in the spreadsheet. Record the configuration, including the number of workstations and the test script run on each workstation.

4. Shut down and restart the client-server testing tool with the equivalent user loading from step 3. Run the test for 72 hours.

5. Every 12 hours, record the following data, as shown in Figure 24.10:

   - date and time of test measurement

   - average response time, if available

   - average KBps throughput across the links

   - average CPU utilization of the servers

   - errors recorded by the network analyzer

6. Analyze the test results to determine whether there is significant response time or throughput degradation for the system or an increase in the error rate since the last measurement. Ensure that the CPU utilization and throughput is being maintained in the proper range for the test.

7. If the system completes the 72-hour test at the operational load, repeat steps 2 through 6 using stressed loading. Run the test for 24 hours and repeat the preceding recording procedure every six to eight hours.

Data Interpretation

At each recording milestone, the results should be entered into the data reduction spreadsheet.

A test failure has occurred when one or more of the following conditions manifests:

Run ID	1
Time/Date	12/13/95 9:00
Server ID	FS-1
Test Script	T0207FS
No. of Workstations	7
CPU Utilization	89
Throughput	600KBps
Average Response Time	4 min. 8 sec.
Errors	
Critical	2
Noncritical	0

Run ID	2
Time/Date	12/13/95 21:00
Server ID	FS-1
Test Script	T0207FS
No. of Workstations	7
CPU Utilization	91
Throughput	612KBps
Average Response Time	4 min. 3 sec.
Errors	
Critical	0
Noncritical	0

Figure 24.10   Data reduction spreadsheet with the first two 12-hour measurements completed.

1. Response time or throughput degrades significantly, greater than 20 percent.

2. An error causes the database, file, or application server to fail.

3. An error causes the workstation(s) to fail.

4. An error causes the link(s) between the server and workstation(s) to be dropped.

5. A device, such as a router, in the internetwork path fails.

6. Other nodes or components, such as a print or fax server, on the test configuration fail.

Either significant degradation or a failed server flukes the reliability test. Failure conditions 3 through 6 have a degree of latitude in their interpretation. The tester can be strict or lenient in determining the criteria for stopping or continuing the test. The failure of one workstation is rarely sufficient grounds for failing the test. Often, a workstation failure is isolated to a hardware or software problem in that particular system, which is why at least two of each workstation should be used. Dropped links need to be investigated because they often indicate simple time-out conditions that can be easily fixed. This may, however, indicate a system overload where the server is too busy to respond to requests on a timely basis, which may require configuration sizing or application and database server changes.

Failure conditions 5 and 6 indicate that the infrastructure reliability testing did not adequately model the application load, therefore, the baseline reliability loading should be reviewed and modified to better emulate the application load.

Application: Functionality Testing

TEST MATRIX

Most client-server applications, productivity software, and NOSs are tested for features and functionality during development on the developer's workbench and during quality testing in a network configuration. Feature testing initially includes one user and expands to several users on a small network as the software becomes stable. Feature testing focuses on verifying that the GUI interface, commands, and transactions work properly under the various contexts by which they can be invoked. There are many good application QA testing tools that help in providing comprehensive coverage of the GUI front end and application features.

There exists a level of network-oriented feature/functional testing beyond the feature and functional tests just mentioned. This testing measures multiuser network activities and system features that may be sensitive to high network or application loads. Figure 25.1 illustrates the three levels of feature and functional testing.

Comparing these three levels of testing to a school for elegant French cuisine may help to clarify their differences. At the cooking school, students are first taught the basics of food groups, spices, and so on. The student chefs then learn to prepare individual entrees, appetizers, and desserts. They progress to cooking a complete seven-course meal. The food is excellent, and they pass their first-level test as chefs. But, being a good chef and managing a restaurant's kitchen are separate tasks that require different talents and capabilities. Managing a kitchen requires doing many tasks concurrently, and some of these tasks are random in selection and quantity, depending on the crowd and customer menu selections. Other tasks are basic and repetitive, such as making sure sufficient

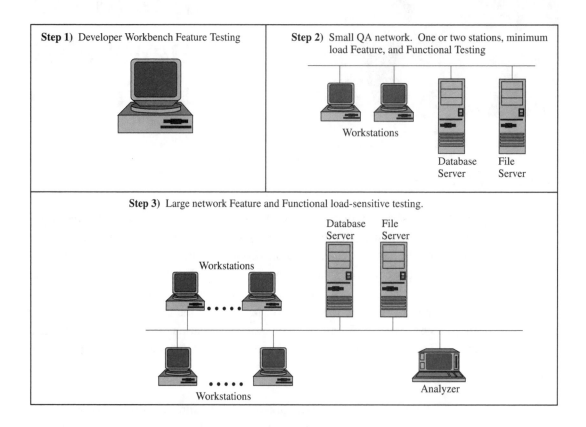

Figure 25.1   Three levels of feature and functional testing.

supplies are in place and dishes are cleaned for reuse. Naturally, not all chefs make good kitchen managers. Similarly, a client-server application that works well with a small "crowd," may not work as well when more users arrive. Like the chef who performs well in specific areas, such as desserts or entrees, but who cannot manage multiple disparate tasks, some parts of the client-server application may degrade as more load and varying requests are placed on it.

The objective of QA testing is predominately focused on verifying that the GUI and application features work properly, similar to being able to prepare a seven-course meal without dropping food on the floor. The objective of network-oriented functional testing is like verifying that a great chef can also handle a busy kitchen. It confirms that neither crowds nor background tasks degrade the client-server application's ability to service the users or handle routine operations on the server.

Since feature testing is unique for each application, exact test objectives and transaction scripts cannot be enumerated here. Consequently, the following test procedures provide guidelines that are appropriate for network-oriented functional test projects that have one or more of the following attributes:

- multiuser, concurrent record access

- time-sensitive tasks

- background, "cycle-stealing" operations

Functional testing for client-server applications is discussed under Test Case 1. Test Case 2 describes testing multiple servers where distributed data must be synchronized across the servers.

TEST CASE 1: CLIENT-SERVER FUNCTIONAL TESTING

Features of the application and network system that may be affected by network load, traffic patterns, or data volume are included in client-server functional testing. The testing process loads the server with background transactions, and specific test scripts are required to exercise the functions under test.

Test Measurements

The objective of the test is to verify that operation of the feature under test completed successfully. Before starting the test there must be a defined manner for accomplishing test verification. When a single user performs an operation, it is easy to determine that it completed successfully by manually verifying the change to the database or other end-of-transaction status. In a network test, however, data volume and timing issues often make verification more difficult and may require automated data reduction and analysis.

For some tests, response verification features in client-server testing tools help in determining that the application recognized and responded to a specific request or command. But, a correct response on the screen does not ensure that the actual record was updated, an in-process transaction was successfully rolled back, or that a backup of the database captured every changed record. Often, the only way to verify the test results is to manually or programmatically scan or interrogate the database or other data storage to confirm that the change took place.

In addition to checking that a specific function happened, it is also pertinent to validate that other functions, specifically the transactions used to create load on the server, also functioned properly. For example, to confirm that a heavily loaded server can correctly roll back an in-progress transaction, the tester must verify both the transaction was properly rolled back and that other similar transactions against the same record were correctly processed. This requires test scripts to test both functions.

Test Configurations

All test configurations are emulated. For client-server testing, heavy server loading is required. The test configuration should include a very high-speed network media between the workstations and server, such as will be used in the production environment as shown in Figure 25.2, and a sufficient number of workstations (equivalent users) to create a heavy load on the server. Keep the configuration as simple as possible to reduce the interpretation of a large amount of test data.

Before beginning the test project, start a test journal and document the test configuration hardware and software as described in Chapter 6.

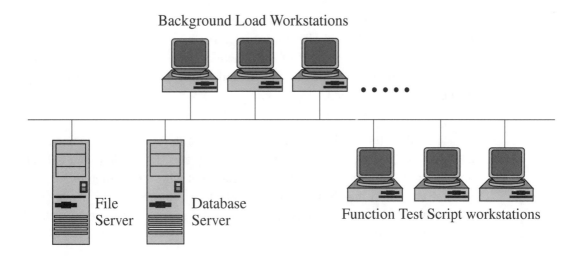

Figure 25.2   Client-server functional test configuration.

Load Model

For client-server functional testing, the test is conducted with a heavy load against the server. The recommended scripts for database server functional testing are Load Models 5, 6, 7, and 8, from Chapter 21. Test scripts that exercises the feature-under-test and its converse operation are needed. For instance, three workstations might run a script that attempts to access, update, and roll back similar transactions against the same record. This could be representative of an on-line airline reservation database when three sales representatives all request reservations for the same flight and then all cancel the reservations concurrently. Another test script would concurrently apply a converse or completed transaction to the record that would not be rolled back. This network testing guarantees that the application maintains database integrity under heavy load. It can only be accomplished through network functional testing.

The functional test scripts typically run for one iteration, and it may be easier or required to start all test scripts concurrently through the client-server testing tool. In this case, the functional test scripts must run long enough to ensure that the server is heavily loaded when the actual test occurs. This can be accomplished by having a delay in the start of the functional test script, or by performing "dummy" commands for the first few seconds while the background test scripts create a heavy server load.

To reduce testing time, many functional tests scripts can be combined into a single run. This works well and saves time if the tests are independent of one another, and a failure in one test doesn't impact another. It is often impossible to know absolutely that the tests and the evaluation of the test results will be fully independent. Nevertheless, this is a widely used approach that works well 90 percent of the time.

Test Execution and Data Collection

The test sequence is:

1. Start the load generators. Verify that the test configuration is working properly and that all workstations can access the server. Run a practice test with several workstations.

2. Start the background load test scripts and increase the load until a heavy KBps throughput and CPU utilization are achieved. Record in the test journal the number of workstations, equivalent users, and the test script run on each workstation.

3. Start the functional test scripts. Monitor the test to determine that all transactions have completed, or that there has been a failure that prevented the transactions from completing.

4. Verify manually or through an automated process the status of the operations tested.

Data Interpretation

Verify that the function-under-test and its converse operation both completed successfully. Analyze the test results to determine whether there was any throughput degradation, dropped sessions, or other problems while the test scripts were running. The test passes when all functions complete successfully and the system does not degrade while performing the operations.

TEST CASE 2: DATA SYNCHRONIZATION TESTING

When network systems include multiple servers that share common data (such as groupware, name service, mail applications, and distributed databases), automated and reliable data distribution or updates are critical to application data integrity and system operation.

One large utilities company has an ongoing concern that all its name servers, which number in the hundreds, are properly updated with moves and changes in a timely manner. Another worldwide communications corporation has multiple service centers that operate off a service ticket database that must share information across all the centers.

To determine whether the synchronization of the multiple servers can be interrupted by server load and network activity, a functional test must be conducted that measures data synchronization under heavy background load.

Test Measurements

A distributed name service is designed to synchronize entries twice a day. It is relatively easy to enter a block of new entries in each distributed server, but it is more difficult to verify that all the entries are properly posted to other distributed name servers. Figure 25.3 illustrates how a relatively simple test configuration

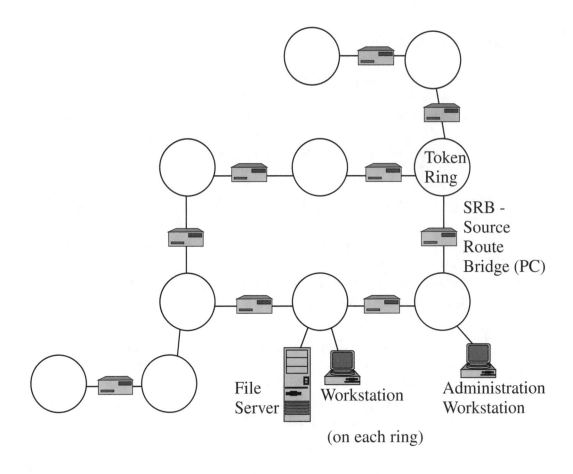

Figure 25.3   Simple test configuration for complex distributed data synchronization.

can emulate a complex distributed name server configuration. The configuration creates 10 network segments using only 31 nodes (2 PCs per segment plus routers).

Additionally, although it is planned that all synchronization will occur at off-hours, it is prudent to understand how synchronization is impacted when the name servers are under moderate to heavy load, versus no load. Figure 25.4 illustrates how the expanded loading would look. One PC is added per segment to create name service queries. Since name service access is not generally a

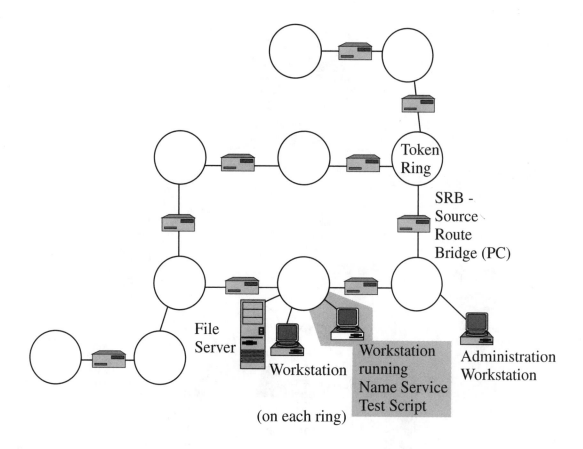

Figure 25.4   Complex distributed data synchronization under heavy network activity.

high-load environment, the single PC can create the equivalent loading of hundreds to thousands of users. This test can help plan for problem avoidance as the user base grows.

Test Configurations

For more real-world data synchronization or distribution tests, an internetwork test configuration, as diagrammed in Figure 25.5, should include small network

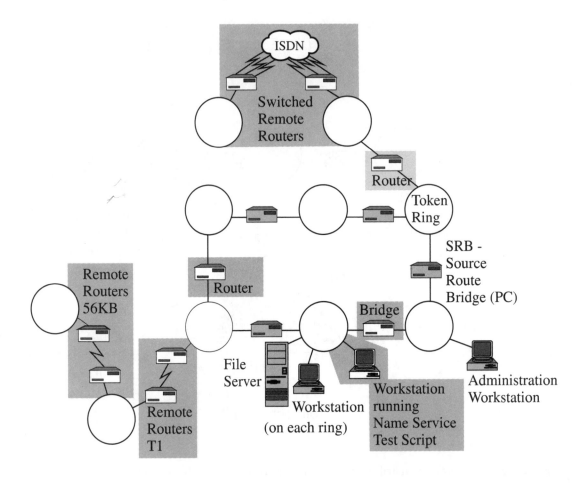

Figure 25.5   Test configuration for data synchronization or distribution.

segments with a server and a workstation to generate load, the server under test if different from the file server, and a variety of interconnecting links representative of the production system.

Before starting the test project, begin a test journal and document the test configuration hardware and software as described in Chapter 6.

Load Model

Entries can be entered manually or through an automated test script into the distributed servers. Since testing may be repeated many times during a test project or in future regression testing, a test script may take more time to develop initially, but can save substantial time in future tests. Also, a test script that rolls back all entries or reloads each server to reset the servers for subsequent tests is a real timesaver. It will speed up test time and reduce potential test errors caused by the large volumes of data being manipulated.

Almost any throughput load model can be used for file server loading. For the test, three or four separate load models are required:

- Test scripts to update the name services on each segment, with entries that must be synchronized.

- Test scripts to create name server load.

- Test scripts to create segment and internetwork background load.

- A test script to reset the name servers to their initial state for rerunning the tests. This is a required step, but can be done manually. Experience suggests that this step will be done many times, and an automated approach saves time and is less error-prone. If the starting state of the name servers is not consistent, the test may "fail" even through the servers are working properly.

Test Execution and Data Collection

The test sequence is:

1. Start the servers and verify that the test configuration is working properly and that all servers are communicating with one another, as appropriate.

2. Enter the server updates, but do not allow the servers to start synchronizing them until step 4.

3. Start the background load and server test scripts. Increase the load until a heavy KBps throughput and CPU utilization are achieved on the servers. Record in the test journal the load and the test script run on each workstation.

4. Allow the servers to start synchronization.

5. Monitor the individual segments for throughput and errors.

6. Monitor the servers to determine that all servers have completed the synchronization, or that there has been a failure that prevented the synchronization.

7. Check the servers manually or through an automated process to determine that all the servers were correctly updated.

Data Interpretation

Verify that the synchronization process completed successfully. Analyze the test results to determine whether there was any throughput degradation, dropped sessions, or other problems while the synchronization was in progress. The test passes when all functions complete successfully and the system does not degrade significantly while performing the operations.

Application: Regression Testing

TEST MATRIX

Regression testing is not one test, but a series of tests that measure critical aspects of the application, presentation layer, database server, or network platform under test. For each new release of software and server or workstation hardware, regression testing ensures that the upgrade will function properly prior to deployment on the production network. A regression test plan identifies which basic test objectives should be run against each new product release.

Regression testing can be conducted for the client-server system, including the application software, workstation, GUI front end, and database server. It can also be run for the network platform, including the NOS, file server, and workstation. Test Case 1 discusses client-server application regression testing. Test Case 2 details network platform regression testing.

More than one company have deployed new software or hardware only to experience a failure in the field. The cost of deploying and fixing or removing the offending hardware or software costs substantially more in both effort and loss of user satisfaction than a regression test project. This is true for both in-house-developed software and purchased products. Although a product has been QA tested by its developer, it cannot have been tested on a configuration that included your unique network configuration. Therefore, a regression test may uncover problems specific to your configuration or traffic patterns.

One large international company found that it had continued problems running multiple revisions of a product, and because its network contained over 10,000 nodes, it was impossible to upgrade all nodes simultaneously. In fact, as you can guess, it was even hard to keep track of the product versions on all nodes.

By regression testing a new release with two back releases, it found that it was possible to determine problem areas and either find workarounds or warn users of problems before they uncovered them.

TEST CASE 1: CLIENT-SERVER REGRESSION TESTING

Client-server application regression testing can verify that a hardware or software upgrade does not impact performance, reliability, or functionality of the production system. It indirectly measures impact on the upgrade by other nodes on the network or internetwork based on the test configuration. Regression testing does not, however, measure new features or capabilities. Such tests fall under feature and functional testing, as discussed in Chapter 25.

For a client-server application, regression testing is used to verify upgrades to all system components, as illustrated in Figure 26.1.

Test Measurements

Regression test measurements depend on which capabilities are defined as critical to the production network and which corresponding tests are included in the regression test plan. As a minimum, response time (Chapter 20), throughput

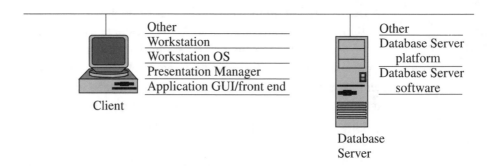

Figure 26.1   Regression testing components of a client-server application.

(Chapter 21), and reliability (Chapter 24) should be verified for a new release of software and selected hardware upgrades. Functional testing, Chapter 25, should be performed to verify critical functions for each new release of software.

Use test data from the preceding individual test objectives or a past regression test project as the baseline for the current regression test. If no current data exists, first run tests against the current application and database versions before testing the upgrade. Without a baseline against which to compare the upgrade, it cannot be determined whether the client-server application system has improved or regressed.

The key to successful regression testing is establishing pass/fail criteria as discussed in the upcoming Data Interpretation section.

Test Configurations

All test configurations are emulated. If all workstations and servers on the production system will be upgraded concurrently, use the same test configuration as for response time and throughput testing, shown in Figure 26.2.

If the upgrades will be deployed across workstations and servers over several weeks to months, start with the test configuration used for response time and throughput testing, then add additional hardware and software to allow cross-platform testing between the current revision and the upgrade, as shown in Figure 26.3.

Cross-platform testing confirms that workstations and servers with the current release can interoperate with workstations and servers with the upgrade without lose of functionality, reliability, or performance.

Before starting the test project, begin a test journal, document the test configuration hardware and software, and create data reduction spreadsheets as described in Chapter 6. Also establish pass/fail criteria for each test, as discussed below under Data Interpretation.

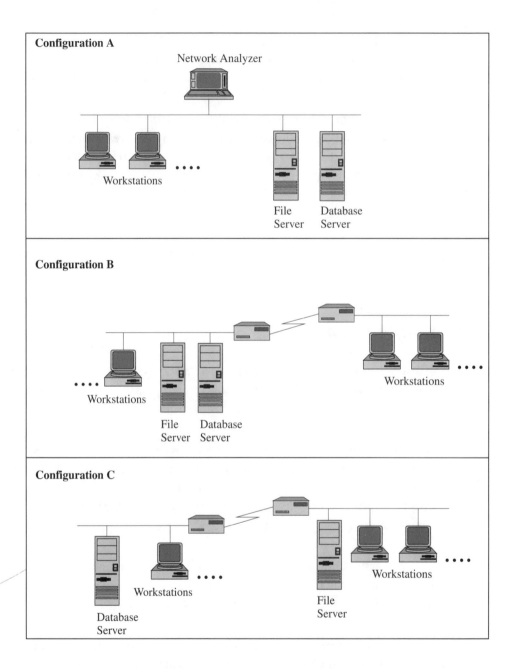

Figure 26.2   Regression test configuration for concurrent upgrade of all nodes.

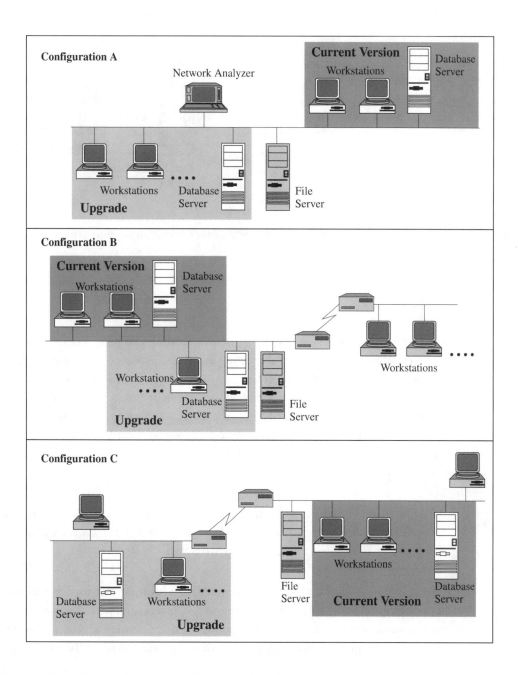

Figure 26.3 Regression test configuration for phased upgrades (cross-platform testing).

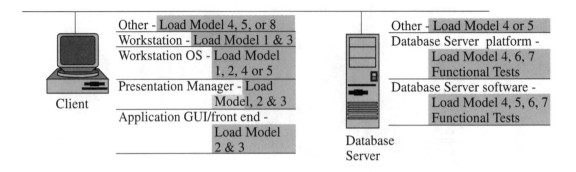

Figure 26.4   Load models typically used in client-server application regression testing.

Load Model

The load model and test scripts for regression testing can be leveraged from the other test objectives. Details on creating these are discussed in Chapters 18, 19, and in the appropriate test objective chapters. Figure 26.4 shows which load model(s) to use for the various components that can be tested. For example, Load Models 4, 5, 6, and 7 can be used for database software to measure maximum throughput, cached I/O, CPU-intensive operations, and hard disk I/O. Note that for new server hardware, Load Model 5 *isn't* used because its focus is cache I/O. Cache efficiency is more software than hardware influenced.

Functional test results are server-, not workstation- dependent, therefore, network functional testing is not used to regression test workstation changes. Feature tests should be run against new workstation software.

It is *very important* that the load model used is the exact load model used in the previous test against which the regression test results will be compared. If the test methodology outlined in Chapter 6 for documenting and archiving test project information has been followed, it should be easy to reuse the load scripts from the previous tests.

Additionally, the load model should be supplemented with selected functional test scripts that were run on the current release but are not in the existing regression test suite. As the release numbers increase, so does the scope of the regression test:

- Regression test, v 3.0 = regression test, v 2.0 + selected functional tests for v 2.0

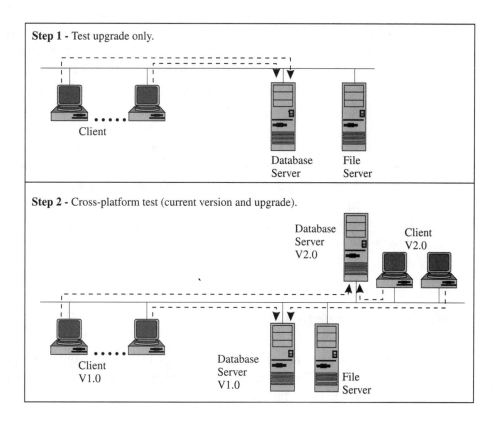

Figure 26.5 Regression testing for upgrade verification and cross-platform interoperability.

Test Execution and Data Collection

For each of the test objectives included in the regression test plan, follow the instructions contained in that test objective's chapter for test execution and data collection.

For upgrade-only tests, shown in Figure 26.2, run one pass of each test case against the configuration with the upgraded software or hardware. For cross-platform tests, shown in Figure 26.3, run one pass of each test case against the upgraded software or hardware. This provides a measurement of how the upgrade compares to the current version. Next, run the same test with cross-platform access, to measure performance differences and interoperability between the current version and the upgrade. Figure 26.5 shows this two-step process.

Use the following data interpretation procedures rather than the procedures included in the test objective chapters. The order in which you conduct regression tests is important because some test results will influence subsequent tests, as discussed under Data Interpretation. The preferred order is reliability, functional, response time, and throughput. Reliability testing is done before functional testing to verify that the upgrade is sufficiently stable to conduct the other tests. If the upgrade isn't reliable, this approach saves time and effort.

Data Interpretation

Let's consider a regression test plan that includes reliability, response time, throughput, and functional testing as components of the plan, and identify issues in establishing pass/fail criteria for each test.

Reliability

Chapter 24 discusses reliability testing for the application system and for an individual file or database server. For regression testing, the system approach is recommended because it measures the system as the user sees it, and provides the highest return for the shortest time and least amount of effort. If server problems are indicated, a second test can be run to isolate the server.

A test failure has occurred when one or more of the following conditions manifests:

1. Response time or throughput degrades significantly, greater than 20 percent.

2. An error causes the database, file, or application server to fail.

3. An error causes the workstation(s) to fail.

4. An error causes the link(s) between the server and workstation(s) to be dropped.

Either significant degradation or a failed server flunks the reliability test. Note though that failure conditions 3 and 4 have a degree of latitude in their interpretation. The tester can be strict or lenient in determining the criteria for stopping or continuing the test. If the upgrade was to the server, failure of one workstation is rarely sufficient grounds for failing the test. But, if the upgrade was to the workstation, a single workstation failure is cause for failing the test.

In evaluating test duration, the first consideration is to determine whether the upgrade ran as long as the current system. Assume, for instance, that the current system failed the 72-hour test. It ran for 58 hours, but was still deployed. If this is causing no problems in the production network, then the upgrade pass/fail criteria should be based on a 58-hour test. If, on the other hand, reliability has been a problem, or the upgrade specifically includes improved reliability features, a 58-hour pass/fail criteria is not sufficient. Seventy-two hours should be the target.

Functional

Regressive functional tests for network infrastructure components are often the easiest to perform. Regressive functional testing for applications and presentation managers, however, is often viewed as a lower-confidence test because comprehensive coverage is difficult to achieve. For in-house-developed applications and software, functional testing is conducted as part of the formal QA process. With purchased products, there is often no initial functional testing, though such testing is a valuable step in the evaluation and deployment phases of the product's life cycle. Once a product is deployed on the production network, future releases should be verified through regression testing.

Regression testing a feature is simpler than testing the feature originally, because the configuration and load model are defined by the original test. If a good test journal and test script archive have been maintained, reproducing the test on the upgrade should be straightforward. Interpreting the test results is also straightforward. The intent of regression testing is to ascertain that the product works as used in the production system. Because the upgrade should work like the existing product, the test results should be the same as the previous functional test.

The basic test process just described is a required, but not sufficient, measurement of system functionality. The difficulty in regressive functional testing is that, often, one operation creates a state or condition that affects the next operation. As new product features are added, the specific feature being tested can often be arrived at or accessed through a variety of paths, particularly in a sophisticated GUI front end. But, while the regression test may verify that existing paths work correctly, it may overlook new paths created by new or upgraded features.

Comprehensive functional testing may require that new test cases be added based on analysis of how changes expand paths through the application system. As a simple illustration, a well-known presentation manager provides several modes for exiting and returning to the desktop. A new feature let the user exit through one mode and return using one of several different commands. The feature was checked during QA testing, but regression testing did not include the new feature in combination with existing features. Fortunately, during a response time test, a tester used the new feature, followed by an older exit command and found a bug. The problem was fixed before release, but this illustrates how complex and difficult GUI regression testing can be.

Interoperability testing confirms that the same command executed against the current version and upgrade produces the same results. This is easiest to do when only four workstations and two servers are used. This limits the analysis effort, and experience has shown that the results provide a high-confidence level.

Rerunning existing test scripts for feature and functional regression will verify most changes. Just be aware that comprehensive testing is very difficult to achieve and requires constant tuning and extension of the test scripts.

Response Time

Response time, as mentioned previously, is probably the single best measure of how the user perceives the application system. In a regression test, Load Models 1, 2, and 3 from Chapter 20, can be used, depending on what the upgrade changed, as depicted in Figure 26.4. Load Model 1 measures peak server performance, Load Model 2 measures system responsiveness, and Load Model 3 measures any changes in the GUI. If any of these response time measurements degrade, the upgrade may be perceived by the users as a step backward. It is not advisable to deploy an upgrade that increases user response time, unless you are lonely and want to hear from a lot of people.

Load Model 1 response time measurements are the only ones that may not impact users if it increases. If the response times for Load Models 2 and 3 do not increase for the upgrade, the user will not perceive any immediate change, even if Load Model 1's times increase. This is because Load Model 1 measures peak load response, and unless the system is running at peak loads, excess capacity can decrease without impacting the users. However, if Load Model 1's times increase, it indicates a decrease in system capacity, as illustrated in Figure 26.6.

In evaluating response time test results for cross-platform access, the following guidelines should be used:

1. If there are no performance-specific enhancements included in the upgrade, comparable response times should be measured for cross-platform access.

Current User Base

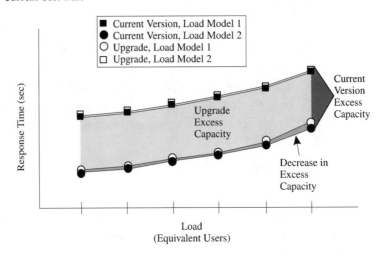

Projected User Growth

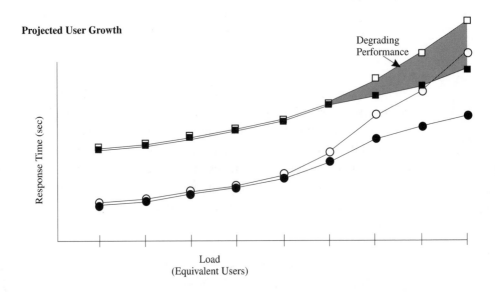

Figure 26.6   Response time as a measure of server capacity using Load Model 1.

2. If there are no performance-specific enhancements included in the upgrade, but comparable response times are not measured:

   - It will usually be acceptable to have a slight degradation between an upgraded workstation and current version server, if the upgrade also includes server software that will be shortly deployed.

   - It will usually be acceptable to have a slight degradation between a current version workstation and an upgraded server, if the upgrade also includes workstation software that will be deployed. This will last only until all workstations are upgraded.

   - It will *not* be acceptable to have a slight degradation between an upgraded workstation and current version server, if the upgrade does not include server software. This means that application response time has degraded.

3. If there are performance-specific enhancements included in the upgrade, comparable response times should not be measured for cross-platform access. Improvements should be measured for the upgraded configuration, but may vary for cross-platform testing:

   - It will usually be acceptable to have the same performance or slightly degraded performance between an upgraded workstation and current version server, if the upgrade also includes server software that will be deployed.

   - It will usually be acceptable to have the same or slightly degraded performance between a current version workstation and an upgraded server, if the upgrade also includes workstation software that will be deployed. This will last only until all workstations are upgraded.

   - It will *not* be acceptable to have the same or slightly degraded performance between an upgraded workstation and current version server, if the upgrade does not include server software. This means that response time has not improved, which was an objective of the upgrade.

For cross platform response time testing, don't try to replicate the same number of load points used in a standard response time test; it is too time-consuming. Experience has shown that taking two measurements will suffice. Measure response time for the equivalent user production load and the equivalent user production load, plus 10 percent. This will provide data on which to base the preceding conclusions.

Throughput

If the upgrade only modifies workstation application software, response time regression testing effectively covers the upgrade. Throughput testing, which is

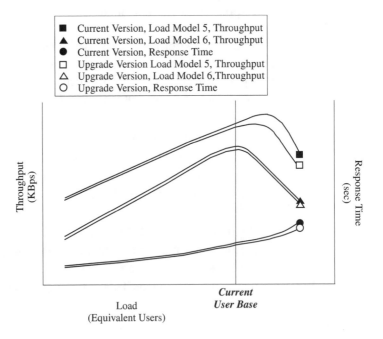

Figure 26.7   Throughput as a measure of server capacity using different load models.

mainly server focused, is not required. But, if the upgrade changed workstation software below the application (that is, OS, protocol stack, or adapter driver) or hardware, Load Models 4 or 5 can be used to determine whether workstation -to-server throughput was affected by the change. If the upgrade changed server or database software or hardware, Load Models 4, 5, 6, 7, and 8 can measure how the changes impact server throughput.

Throughput results are used to guarantee that the upgrade provides performance equivalent to the current release. But be aware that equivalent performance may not mean equivalent throughput. Response time tests can indicate that the upgrade provides the same performance for the users, but throughput tests show a decrease in maximum throughput between the server and workstations. This illustrates that excess system capacity has decreased, but that effective throughput is still sufficient to maintain system responsiveness to the users. Figure 26.7 illustrates these conclusions. If there is no immediate plan to add more users, and if the upgrade provides significant new features, the upgrade can be deployed with lower excess throughput capacity than the current version.

It is not advisable to deploy upgrades that provide lower system throughput without plans for future throughput improvement, as such upgrades will result in degraded system performance over its life cycle. Such a decision should be considered as a one-time only option.

Used in a different way, throughput results can help isolate bottlenecks that may be causing degraded response, or modify configuration sizing to improve upgrade response time. While response time tests measure only system-level performance, the different throughput load models can isolate the performance of various server components. Analyzing throughput test results can determine if performance is degraded by:

- hard disk or cached I/O

- specific transactions

- a server CPU bottleneck

- network I/O congestion

Chapter 21, Data Interpretation, explains how to analyze throughput data to determine server bottlenecks.

Experience indicates that performance impacts are often indirectly caused by a seemingly unrelated change in the application or other software. Regression testing both response time and throughput provides results that can be evaluated for anomalies that point to problems that need to be fixed.

Regression Test Conclusions

Interpreting regression test results isn't always clearcut, and reliability and throughput results are often open to interpretation. There is, however, a clear point at which the test results indicate a failing grade. Experience indicates that this point is reached when conclusions on two or more of the test cases must be made based on "judgment calls." When this is the case, results indicate that the upgrade has several problems relative to the current release, and going ahead with deployment is only asking for trouble on the production network.

TEST CASE 2: NETWORK PLATFORM TESTING

Network platform regression testing can verify that a hardware or software upgrade does not impact the performance, reliability, or functionality of the

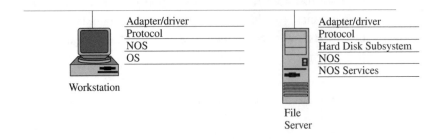

Figure 26.8   Regression testing the components of the network platform.

network system. It indirectly measures impact on the upgrade by other nodes on the network and internetwork based on the test configuration. Regression testing does not, however, measure new features or capabilities. Such tests fall under functional testing, as discussed in Chapter 25. For a network platform, regression testing is used to verify upgrades to network-level components, as illustrated in Figure 26.8.

Test Measurements

Regression test measurements depend on which capabilities are defined as critical to the production network, and which corresponding tests are included in the regression test plan. As a minimum, throughput (Chapter 21) and reliability (Chapter 24) should be verified for a new release of software and selected hardware upgrades. Functional testing, explained in Chapter 25, can be performed to verify critical functions of the NOS for new software releases.

Use test data from the individual test objectives or a past regression test project as the baseline for the current regression test. If no current data exists, first run tests against the current network platform before testing the upgrade. Without a baseline against which to compare the upgrade, it cannot be determined that the network has improved or regressed. The key to successful regression testing is establishing pass/fail criteria as discussed in the upcoming Data Interpretation section.

Test Configurations

All test configurations are emulated. If all workstations and servers on the production system will be upgraded at one time, use the same test configuration as for throughput testing. If the upgrade will be deployed across workstations and servers over several weeks to months, start with the test configuration used for throughput testing, then add additional hardware and software to allow cross-platform testing between the current revision and the upgrade, as shown in Figure 26.9.

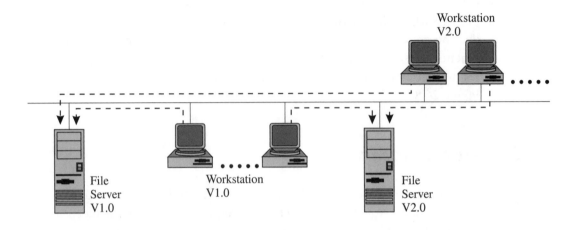

Figure 26.9   Regression test configuration when the upgrade is not deployed across all nodes concurrently.

Cross-platform testing ensures that workstations and servers with the current release can interoperate with workstations and servers with the upgrade without lose of functionality, reliability, or performance.

Before starting the test project, begin a test journal and document the test configuration hardware and software, as described in Chapter 6. Also establish pass/fail criteria for each test as discussed under Data Interpretation.

Load Model

The load model and test scripts for regression testing can be leveraged from the other test objectives. Details on creating these are discussed in Chapters 18, 19, and in the appropriate test objective chapters. For network platform testing, Load Models 9 and 10 are used. Individual functional test scripts are required if specific NOS features are to be tested. New features should be tested in QA or acceptance prior to the regression test.

It is very important that the load model used is the exact one used in the previous test against which the regression test results will be compared. If the test methodology outlined in Chapter 6 for documenting and archiving test project information has been followed, it should be easy to reuse the load scripts from the previous tests.

Test Execution and Data Collection

For each of the test objectives included in the regression test plan, follow the basic instructions contained in that test objective's chapter for test execution and data collection. If the test configuration only includes the upgrade, run one pass of each test case against the configuration with the upgraded software or hardware.

If the test configuration includes both the current release and the upgrade, as shown in Figure 26.9, run two passes against the test configuration, similar to client-server application regression testing, as shown in Figure 26.5. Run one pass of each test case against the portion of the configuration containing the upgraded software or hardware. This will provide a measurement of how the upgrade compares to the current version. Next, run the same test with cross-platform access to provide a measurement of interoperability between the current revision and the upgrade.

Use the following data interpretation procedures rather than the procedures included in the test objective chapters. The order in which you conduct regression tests is important because some results will influence subsequent tests, as discussed under Data Interpretation. The preferred order of testing is reliability, functional, response time, and throughput. Reliability testing is done before functional testing to verify that the upgrade is sufficiently stable to conduct the other tests. If the upgrade isn't reliable, this approach saves time and effort.

Data Interpretation

Typically, throughput and reliability are the primary regression tests for the network platform. These are discussed in the following subsections.

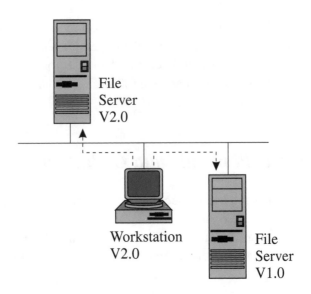

Figure 26.10   Regression testing workstation side changes.

Throughput

If the upgrade changed workstation NOS software or hardware, the tests will determine whether workstation-to-server throughput was affected by the change. This test is best run using one workstation, as illustrated in Figure 26.10. This will ensure that the server is not the bottleneck. Pay attention to throughput by file, record size, and read versus write. Sometimes, changes that improve one size data I/O impact another. Read versus write performance is often a function of workstation buffering and caching.

If the upgrade changed server software or hardware, the tests must measure how the changes impact file server performance. The simplest method of validating the upgrade's throughput is to compare a single user and maximum equivalent user load points for the current version and the upgrade:

- If the upgrade has higher throughput or is within 4 percent of the current release, the test has passed.

- If the upgrade's single user throughput is less than the current version, the test has failed.

- If the upgrade's maximum user throughput is less than the current version, the test results indicate that the upgrade provides lower performance and capacity than the current version. The tester will have to make a judgment call as to whether this will impact performance, based on the current network baseline loading. If the server is close to capacity, this will impact performance and the test has failed. Otherwise, the upgrade may be acceptable if other value (functional or reliability) overshadows the performance degradation. Note that such a decision is rare to nonexistent for today's networks.

Used in a different way, throughput results can help isolate bottlenecks that may be causing degraded performance, or modify configuration sizing to improve upgrade response time. The two throughput load models can isolate the performance of various server components. Analyzing throughput test results can determine whether performance degradation is caused by:

- hard disk or cached I/O

- a server CPU bottleneck

- network I/O congestion

Chapter 21, Data Interpretation, explains how to analyze throughput data to determine server bottlenecks.

Reliability

For regression testing, the system approach is recommended because it measures the system as the user sees it, and it provides the highest return in the shortest time and for the least amount of effort. If problems are encountered that indicate server problems, a second test can be run to isolate the server. Chapter 24 explains reliability testing for an individual file server.

A test failure has occurred when one or more of the following conditions manifests:

1. Throughput degrades significantly, greater than 20 percent.

2. An error causes the file server to fail.

3. An error causes the workstation(s) to fail.

4. An error causes the link(s) between the server and workstation(s) to be dropped.

Either significant degradation or a failed server flunks the reliability test. Failure conditions 3 and 4 have a degree of latitude in their interpretation. The tester can be strict or lenient in determining the criteria for stopping or continuing the test. If the upgrade was to the server, failure of one workstation is rarely sufficient grounds for failing the test. But, if the upgrade was to the workstation, a single workstation failure is cause for failing the test.

In evaluating test duration, the first consideration is to determine whether the upgrade ran as long as the current system. Assume that the current system failed the 72-hour test. All test cases ran between 62 and 65 hours before failure. If this is causing no problems in the production network, then the upgrade pass/fail criteria should be based on a 65-hour test. If, on the other hand, reliability has been a problem, or the upgrade specifically includes improved reliability features, a 65-hour pass/fail criteria is not sufficient. Seventy-two hours should be the target.

Regression Test Conclusions

Interpreting regression test results isn't always clearcut. Reliability and throughput results are often open to interpretation, but the basic premise of upgrading the network platform is to improve network system performance, reliability, and capacity. Therefore, a decrease in either test is sufficient grounds for failing the test. Reality is that NOS upgrades are often made for reasons other than purely technical reasons. NetWare 3.x to 4.0 is an excellent case in point.

Test results can provide guidance because they are hard facts on which to base decisions. But, there are no hard and fast rules for using test data; it is just one more piece to the puzzle of how to keep the network up and running.

Application: Acceptance Testing

TEST MATRIX

Like regression testing, acceptance testing is not one objective, but a combination of one or more test objectives. For client-server applications, acceptance test objectives generally include feature set and response time (Chapter 20) verification. If there are specific business requirements for server throughput, growth capacity, or uptime (reliability), these test objectives should be part of the final acceptance test plan.

Since most client-server applications are deployed on existing networks, it is generally not possible to conduct the final acceptance test on the target network. If the opportunity presents itself for testing on the real-world target network, follow the control group process guidelines discussed in the Chapter 20 section, Test Case 2: Response Time Testing on Real-World Configurations.

Acceptance testing of client-server application systems is usually conducted using an emulated test configuration and load. Acceptance testing for a network platform is identical to testing for an internetwork configuration, which is discussed in Chapter 15. Also see Chapter 5, Acceptance Testing, for more information on test configuration criteria.

CLIENT-SERVER ACCEPTANCE TESTING

Client-server acceptance testing should be performed on the complete and final application software just prior to deployment. Feature or functional testing starts with verification of the application feature set. This can be accomplished using

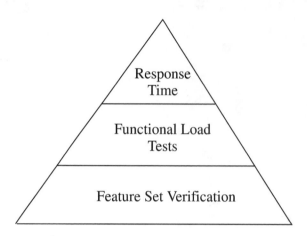

Figure 27.1   Three primary levels of final client-server acceptance testing.

a set of QA test scripts that are modified to measure the applications' ability to perform specific business-oriented sequences.

Next, run one or two load-sensitive functional tests, such as discussed in Chapter 25, to verify that the application works properly under load. The final test measures application performance. Figure 27.1 illustrates the three levels of

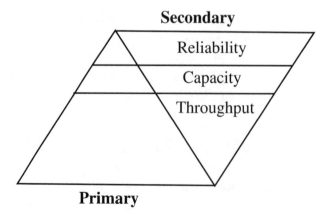

Figure 27.2   Three secondary levels of final client-server acceptance testing.

final client-server acceptance tests. Figure 27.2 illustrates the typical secondary levels of final client-server acceptance tests—reliability, capacity, and throughput.

Test Measurements

The test objective is not to isolate specific errors, but to verify that, under the defined load conditions, the client-server application performs as expected. The key to successful acceptance testing is defining meaningful test cases and establishing pass/fail criteria for the testing, as discussed in Chapter 5 and in the following Data Interpretation section.

Test Configurations

Since the acceptance tests are focused on the client-server application and database server software, the emulated test configuration does not have to model the target network. For the three primary levels of final client-server acceptance

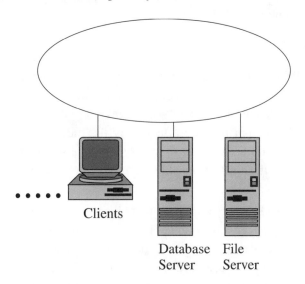

Figure 27.3   Single segment client-server acceptance test configuration.

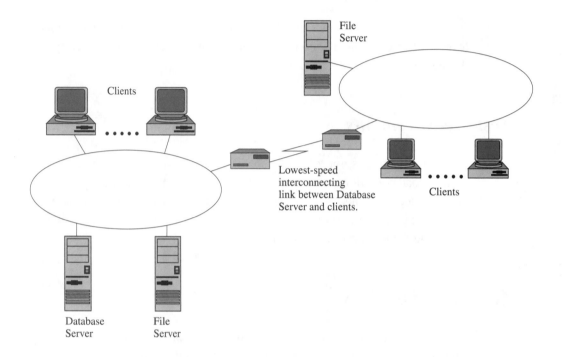

Figure 27.4   Two segment client-server acceptance test configuration with slow-speed intermediate link.

testing, only response time may be influenced by the test configuration media, and only if the database server and workstations are located on segments interconnected by slow-speed links. For the three secondary test objectives, only throughput may be affected by the media. Therefore, the test configuration should mimic either Figure 27.3, single segment, or Figure 27.4, two segments with the appropriate slow-speed interconnecting link.

It is very important that all software be the version that will be included in the final client-server application system. Often, a vendor releases a new version of software, but because development and testing has been conducted on the current version, it is decided to deploy the application using the older version and upgrade later. This is a very sound and conservative strategy. Make sure that software versions are correct across the test configuration.

Before starting the test project, prepare a test journal, document the test configuration hardware and software, and establish pass/fail criteria for each test as discussed under Data Interpretation.

Load Model

Application/presentation layer acceptance test scripts can usually be modified versions of scripts created during the development cycle. Once developed, these scripts can also be used for regression testing application upgrades. Details on creating these are discussed in Chapters 18 and 19. Remember to adhere to the rules discussed in Chapter 5 when developing the load model:

1. Base the criteria on business or technical requirements.

2. Be selective in defining the criteria.

3. State the criteria in measurable terms.

Based on the complexity of the acceptance test plan, there may be up to six load models required. These are:

- **Feature load model:** Derived from QA test scripts to measure business-oriented operational sequences. Do not attempt to verify all application commands. Select two or three command sequences that are the most critical application functions. A test script could exercise a command sequence based on customer requests to debook a back order, return merchandise, and place a new order; or it could run critical end-of-day inventory summary reports.

- **Network functional load model:** Measure load-sensitive multiuser activity, such as discussed in Chapter 25. This could be an expanded feature test where several users must work with common records; or a key background test, such as database synchronization, that must be completed every day without interference from other network activity.

- **Response time:** Verifies response as the user will see the application using Load Model 2, Chapter 20. The number of equivalent users must represent the planned user base. The feature test scripts from the feature load model, item 1, can be used as the Load Model 2 test scripts for this test.

- **Throughput:** Verifies sustained throughput capacity of the database server using Load Model 5, Chapter 21. Response time is the key performance acceptance test, but server throughput may also be used. Since the test configuration is rarely the target network, as discussed, and throughput requirements can rarely be defined accurately, it is recommended that capacity, rather than throughput, be used as the next best acceptance criteria.

- **Capacity:** Verifies excess system-level capacity as described in Chapter 23, Test Case 1. Use the results from response time tests for the planned user base. Rerun the test with a higher load and measure degradation. For example, valid acceptance criteria is that response time be X seconds for the initial user load of Y users, and be no worse that 1.2 times X for up to 1.5 times Y users.

- **Reliability:** Verifies the reliability of the client-server application system, excluding hardware as explained in Test Case 2, Chapter 24. Since the test configuration is rarely the target network, this test measures only application and database software reliability, and its results can be influenced by unstable or faulty hardware. While this is a good test to run during development, it does not provide relevant results on which to base final acceptance. If this test is part of the test plan, use the operational load level discussed in Chapter 24, Test Case 2, and run the application for 72 hours.

Test Execution and Data Collection

For each of the test objectives included in the acceptance test plan, follow the instructions in the respective test objective chapter. The preferred order of testing, as shown in Figure 27.5, is the same as the order of the load models just listed:

1. feature verification, required

2. functional verification, recommended

3. response time, required

4. throughput, not recommended

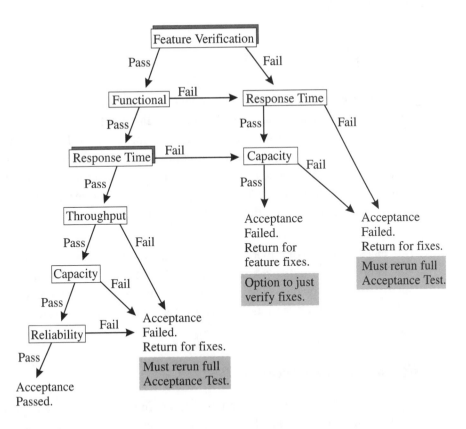

Figure 27.5　Client-server acceptance test flowchart.

5. capacity, recommended

6. reliability, not recommended

For response time, throughput, and capacity, select test loads based on the initial user load and estimated growth over one year. This reduces the number of test points to two per test objective and the overall time for acceptance testing.

Test only the function under test. Do not verify the converse operation, as discussed in Chapter 25. Acceptance testing is designed to be a quick confirmation of the tests conducted during development and QA. Keep it simple, quick, and focused.

Data Interpretation

The initial step of data interpretation occurs before the first acceptance test is run. The best way to ensure that an acceptance test has a better than average chance of succeeding is to verify its objectives during the development stage, as discussed in Chapter 5. The next best approach is to review development and QA test result summaries covering the same areas planned for acceptance testing. Figure 27.6 depicts trends to look for in preacceptance test results that indicate a high probability of passing final acceptance tests.

Get summaries of previous test results, including a list of all features tested, outstanding problems, response and throughput numbers, and reliability data. Determine when and on which version of software the tests were run. Test results that are old or on back versions of software may not reflect current status, whether negative or positive.

Feature and Functional Tests

Verify that the feature or function under test completed as expected. Feature or function failures at any level should not be tolerated during a final acceptance test. Make sure that if a failure occurs, the application is retested in QA prior to being retested for acceptance. The QA retest should exercise a sufficiently broad

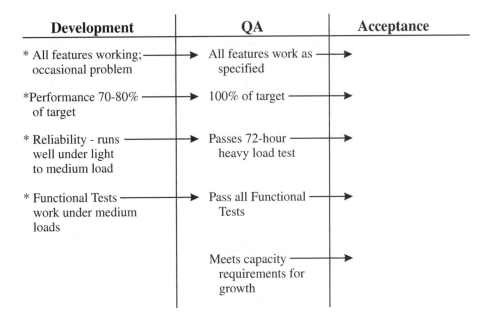

Figure 27.6   Preacceptance test result trends for forecasting acceptance results.

set of features to include all related or complementary features to those that were fixed. The QA testing must be done, because an acceptance retest to verify that the feature was fixed, is not sufficient to ensure that other problems were not introduced by the fix.

Response Time

Load Model 2 represents what a typical user will experience with application response. If the measured response does not meet the target, the test fails.

Generally, functionality, reliability, and performance are achieved in that order. And, it is possible to determine progress by reviewing development and QA results and trends before running the final acceptance test. Performance is often achieved near the end of many product development cycles. However, if performance is low or marginal throughput development, it is rare that it can be achieved by the end of the cycle. If performance is above average or good, then it is often possible to "tweak" the right things to make it acceptable or great. Usually, performance begins to improve in the last quarter of the project and continues improving through QA testing. If test results don't indicate this trend, but acceptance test results pass, be cautious of the system having been tuned for specific operations. The results may not be representative of overall system performance. If this occurs, choose several other operations randomly and test their response time to double-check the application.

Throughput

If throughput is used as an acceptance criterion, there are two methods of defining the pass/fail criteria. The first approach is to define a specific sequence(s) of transactions and the required server throughput for the acceptance test. Usually, it is difficult to define what is the right level of throughput for a transaction mix.

A simpler approach is to take two throughput measurements, which is effectively taking a capacity measurement, and verify that the server is capable of sustaining a load higher than the initial equivalent user loading. This test determines only that the database server will not be at capacity when it is deployed. There are no additional criteria for pass/fail. If the second throughput measurement at a higher equivalent user load is equal to or less than the first, the test fails; otherwise, it passes.

The second throughput measurement should be lower than the first because the additional load impacts server resource, or the overhead of managing the load actually decreases the effective capacity of the server. This is the same type of degradation seen in routers. A higher packet rate often causes more packets to be dropped, which results in more retransmissions, which results in more load, which results in more dropped packets, and, finally, degraded throughput. A file or database server can experience similar degradation as load increases. Often, a primary symptom is dropped sessions. When the server is too busy to respond to all clients, some workstations time-out because they don't hear back from the server.

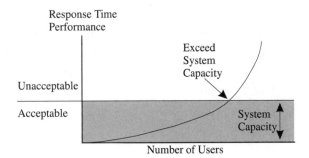

Figure 27.7   Capacity versus performance.

Capacity

The difference between the second type of throughput test and a capacity test is that the capacity test has a defined requirement for excess capacity. If the capacity test results indicate that the server cannot support additional users without degrading to an unacceptable level, the test fails. Figure 27.7 illustrates performance versus excess capacity measurements.

Reliability

If the test completes without critical errors, the client-server application passes the acceptance test. If the test completes the time duration and noncritical errors are recorded, the system passes, but the cause of the noncritical errors should be investigated and resolved before the system is deployed into production.

If critical errors are encountered or portions of the network fail, the difficulty lies in determining whether the failures are hardware- or software-based. Since the test configuration is not the target hardware, hardware failures do not reflect application stability. This is the main reason that reliability testing is not a good criterion for final acceptance testing. Any failure requires research to determine whether it is hardware or software, and this impacts the intent and effectiveness of the testing.

Since reliability is always a key concern, it is better to review results of reliability tests conducted during development and QA, where failures were fully investigated and isolated to hardware or software problems. Read Chapter 5, If the Acceptance Test Fails, for further actions that should be taken if failures occur in any of these categories.

Application: Product Evaluation

INTRODUCTION

Product evaluation testing can encompass features, performance, reliability, error recovery, support, ease of installation, configuration, use, and management. A successful project is one that measures the most critical system components, focuses on a few key measurements, and uncovers information previously unknown about the products.

Application/presentation layer product evaluation (primarily software-oriented) is much more difficult to conduct than hardware product evaluation discussed in Chapter 16 because:

- Hardware specifications are usually easier to verify than software specifications.

- Software tends to have more permutations to test than hardware.

- Since there are no interface standards across database products or NOSs, specific tests have to be developed for each software package, whereas hardware tests can be reused across multiple platforms and vendors with minor changes.

- Each software package takes time to learn in order to properly evaluate it.

- Feature evaluation is person-intensive and time-consuming.

- For new client-server applications, it is hard to determine representative load models before application development has even begun.

Further, experience with software product evaluations has shown:

- They tend to be less conclusive than hardware evaluations.

- They take longer.

- They miss more key points.

- They focus more on software performance than other aspects.

- Often, they simply are not done.

A brief review of client-server testing tools on the market finds that most of these tools are focused on GUI/front-end testing, and require the application to be in development (past the point of product selection) before they are useful. Additionally, these tools do not address the complete database environment,

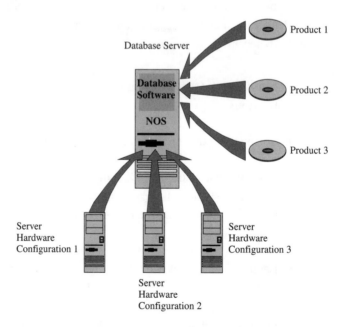

Figure 28.1   Traditional method of product evaluation—product swapping.

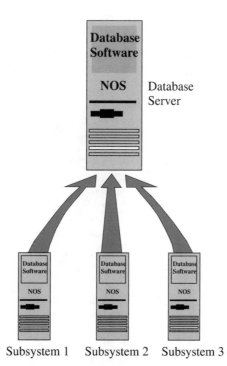

Subsystem 1   Subsystem 2   Subsystem 3

Figure 28.2   Subsystem approach for database server product evaluation.

including the database server software, server hardware, and the network platform.

Product evaluation can be conducted in the traditional fashion, in which all components, except one, are held fixed. This test configuration is shown in Figure 28.1. But, based on experience, it is often better to evaluate the database server as a subsystem, as shown in Figure 28.2. If one or two of the products are already in place, such as the NOS and server platform, it is still possible to consider different configurations for evaluation that complement the existing system. Some examples are shown in Figure 28.3.

All that said, when is application/presentation layer product evaluation important? For client-server applications, the critical component is the server. Product evaluation testing, therefore, should be used in selecting the:

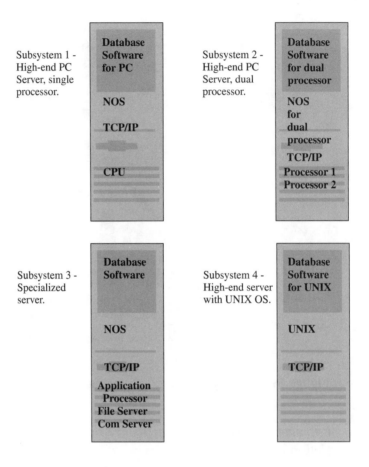

Figure 28.3   Examples of valid database subsystem comparisons.

database software

NOS

server platform

These three products are tightly coupled and complementary, therefore it is difficult to evaluate one independently of the others. For example, a server platform may support dual processors, but without software support in the NOS, the second processor cannot be used. Likewise, database software may support distribution of functions across a multiprocessor architecture, but this option is not available if the server hardware or NOS support only a single processor.

The objective of product evaluation, as the name implies, is to compare existing products to determine their relative ability to meet specific goals. While many test labs and trade publications like product comparisons because they produce a quick winner and subsequent losers, the real value to end-users is the technical information the test generates.

DATABASE EVALUATION TESTING

The following sections address product evaluation testing from a network perspective only, where the test objectives focus on throughput, load-sensitive functionality, and reliability. Testing individual features of the product or subsystem can provide valuable information, but feature testing is not typically a network-intensive test. Often, such testing is manual, time-intensive, and done with one or two workstations. Since each database subsystem combination provides a different feature set, the number of test permutations is very large. In fact, a complete book would be required to discuss all the possible test permutations. In test planning, a common set of features supported across all subsystems, such as record access, record updates, sorting, report formatting, and so on must be chosen. And, because there are no standards across database products, different test scripts will be required for each test.

Creating a product evaluation test is tantamount to creating a regression test. In a product evaluation test, two or more different products are compared. In a regression test, the same product is compared to an earlier version. Many times, the criteria used in selecting a product is also valid for ensuring that future product upgrades work correctly. This is an excellent way of leveraging the testing done in the planning and design phase. The initial product evaluation test suites can be refined in the deployment stage for acceptance testing, then used in the evolution phase for regression testing.

Test Measurements

Consult the Part III chapters on throughput, functional, and reliability testing for specifics on the different test objective measurements. Collect the same basic information for product evaluation.

Test Configurations

All test configurations are emulated. The test configuration does not have to represent a typical production network configuration for product comparison. Any valid, unbiased configuration should provide an accurate relative ranking of the tested products. Nevertheless, the more closely the test configuration and load model represent the real world, the more accurately the test results will predict the operation on your network of the units under test.

There are two procedures in installing and configuring the test network that should be strictly adhered to:

1. Make sure that the latest versions of all test components are included in the configuration. If you use a prerelease version from one vendor, solicit from other vendors comparable levels of hardware and software. Make the test as fair and consistent as possible to achieve best results. Be cautious in testing prereleases, since, often, release dates slip and making a decision on prerelease results could delay the project. Also, prerelease products often "change" by the time they reach production, and therefore test results may differ from released product tests.

2. Be consistent in comparing "out-of-the-box" or "tuned" versions of the products. They can make a significant difference in test results and create an apples-to-oranges comparison. If the products are tuned, be sure to document all configuration settings in the test journal.

Before starting the test project, begin a test journal and document the test configuration hardware and software. Be very specific about any configuration settings.

Load Model

The load model and test scripts for product evaluation testing can be constructed to measure best case engineering results or real-world differences in the products or subsystems under test. Each approach provides a unique and important measurement, but the most important point is that the tester understand the test result differences.

Engineering measurements are best case differences between the products or technologies, which often do not illustrate the difference that will be seen in the production environment. Although, real-world measurements provide better insight to production network differences, they do not provide insight into product growth capacity; so, if time allows, run tests with both loads. Generally, however, testers only have time to do one test series and choose a best case comparison. Most publications and independent test reports also provide best case comparisons. Based on the measured results, the upcoming Data Interpretation section discusses how to evaluate price and performance numbers relative to production system needs.

Refer to Chapters 18, 19, 21, 24, and 25 for information on how to create load models for the respective tests. Since client-server database evaluations are typically done prior to developing the application, it is not possible to use the same approach for baselining real-world loads as for infrastructure testing. The following sections discuss creating maximum and real-world load scripts.

Maximum Load Scripts

A maximum load script does not exist at the start of the testing, but is developed through the effort of product evaluation testing. The maximum load script is determined by increasing the load on the product or subsystem-under-test until it shows marked degradation; that is, the knee in the throughput curve is determined, or failures occur in the reliability or functional tests.

For throughput testing, use Load Models 5 and 6. For reliability testing, use Chapter 24, Test Case 1, Server Reliability Testing load models. For functional testing, use Chapter 25, Test Case 1, Client-Server Functional Testing load models. This basically entails using Load Model 5 or 6 for throughput and reliability testing, and tailored load models to test specific functional aspects of the product or subsystem.

Real-world Load Scripts

Because there is generally no existing application environment to baseline, two approaches are possible:

- Estimate the anticipated TPS and transaction mix that will be applied against the production database by the initial number of users. Use this to create a load script for the transaction load generator program. This is the best method of determining how the products compare in the anticipated production environment. It is difficult to estimate the transaction mix, therefore, create three or four different mixes and compare test results as discussed under Data Interpretation.

- Use one of the transaction tests available from organizations such as the Transaction Performance Council. Doing so will provide an unbiased comparison, but be aware that assumptions made concerning transaction rates and sizes may not equate to your application environment. This type of testing is more like a maximum load test; therefore, it is recommended when taking this approach, to run only one test case, namely this one. This saves time and effort. Running both this test and a maximum load script won't provide significantly different conclusions.

Test Execution and Data Collection

For each of the test objectives included in the product evaluation test plan, follow the instructions contained in that test objective's chapter for basic test execution, data collection, and data interpretation steps. For maximum load tests, make sure that the load is increased until the knee in the curve is found or failures occur. For real-world tests, run the test at the estimated load point and then increase the load by 20 to 50 percent to determine degradation.

The order of conducting tests is not important in product evaluation testing, because typically this is not a one-pass sequence, but an iterative process. As tests generate new information, previous tests are rerun to confirm earlier data, or with slight differences to evaluate another facet of the product. Vendors often provide new product releases or prereleases during evaluation against which various tests must be rerun. Be sure to maintain a good test journal and problem log to avoid confusion during the project.

Data Interpretation

As noted, software evaluation is inherently more complex than hardware evaluation. Software testing requires more critical resources, time, and people, but because these are limited, it is often constrained, and test coverage is never enough. Consequently, discern as much as possible from the test data collected. The following sections discuss four aspects of data interpretation that experience shows are particularly important:

performance analysis

failures and problem symptoms

interoperability and compatibility

price/performance

Performance Analysis

Figure 28.4 illustrates the results of four database software tests, which provide raw performance comparison across the products. Since the NOS and server hardware also are major contributors to throughput results, the differences between database software comparisons may not be as significant on the same server platform.

Figure 28.5 focuses the analysis on product number 1. Comparing the different throughput results concludes that product 1 works well in a high-

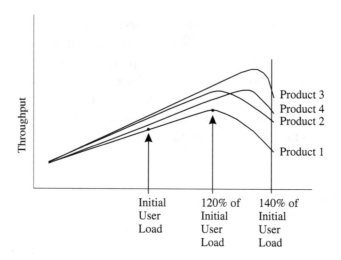

Figure 28.4   Comparing maximum throughput of four products under test.

transaction environment (Load Model 4), and is relatively slower on CPU-intensive operations (Load Model 6) than the other products. It also shows that, at 120 percent of the anticipated production load, throughput begins to degrade, while the average across the tests does not show the same level of

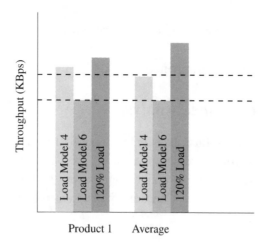

Figure 28.5   Comparing Product 1 throughput to average test results.

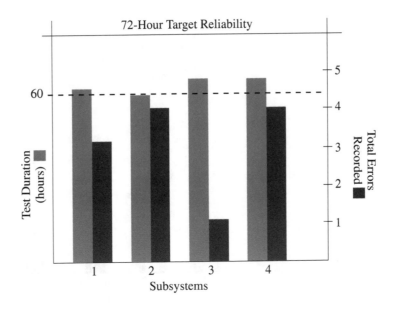

Figure 28.6   Comparing first-level reliability test results of four subsystems under test.

degradation. Using the same method for subsystem comparisons, you will usually notice that the differences between subsystems tend to be more substantial than between products. This reflects the basic fact that when more parts of the puzzle can be changed, the end result is usually better than when the system is constrained and only minimal changes are made. Similar comparisons can be made for other load models used in the testing.

Failures and Problem Symptoms

Figure 28.6 shows first-level reliability test results of four subsystems. Each had intermediate errors and failed during the test at approximately the same test duration. Figure 28.7 shows the failure mode of each subsystem. Although the tests ran for about the same duration, the failure modes were significantly different. The subsystem that appeared the worst in Figure 28.6 (subsystem 2 ran for the shortest duration) is actually the winner of the test based on the severity of the failures. Although subsystem 2 ran for a slightly shorter duration,

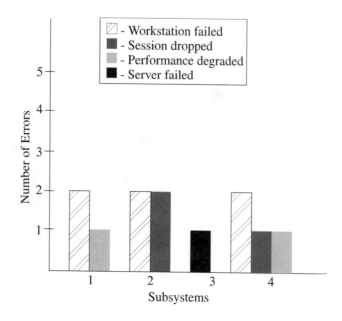

Figure 28.7   Comparing detailed reliability test results of four subsystems under test.

subsystems 1 and 4 showed performance degradation, and subsystem 3 experienced a server failure, as shown in Figure 28.7.

Interoperability and compatibility

Most database software is platform-dependent. There are generally specific versions of the product for individual NOSs and often for specific server hardware platforms. If the database under evaluation may be run on different platforms, subsystem tests can be used to compare how interoperable and compatible the product is across the various platforms. Normalized database tests results can be compared to normalized network platform throughput results to determine how the different product versions compare.

Relative to the volume and type of test errors in Figure 28.7, product reliability can be compared on a weighted basis by calculating total error severity during the test. In this example, server failure is weighted 10, performance degradation is weighted 5, dropped sessions are weighted 2, and a workstation crash is weighted 1, since this is a server test.

Price/Performance

Comparable to the traditional price/performance (P/P) metric, price/reliability (P/R) or errors/dollars spent, as shown in Figure 28.8, is an interesting comparison. Reliability can be either the duration of the test, the total number of errors encountered, or the error severity, which is the preferred metric.

Assuming all four subsystems have a $20,000 price tag, throughput as shown in Figure 28.4, and weighted errors are used in the calculations. Figure 28.8 shows P/P and P/R results plotted on the same graph. The subsystem with the lowest values, subsystem 2, is the best alternative.

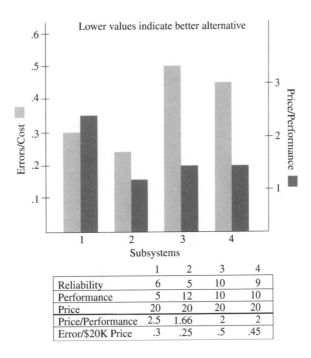

	1	2	3	4
Reliability	6	5	10	9
Performance	5	12	10	10
Price	20	20	20	20
Price/Performance	2.5	1.66	2	2
Error/$20K Price	.3	.25	.5	.45

Figure 28.8 Comparing systems on price/performance and reliability.

Application: Problem Identification

INTRODUCTION

Identification and resolution of application/presentation layer problems can be improved using testing techniques. Debugging, as it is commonly called, is much less procedural than the other test objectives, and guidelines and suggestions that have worked for other companies are presented here.

Most debugging is done using network analyzers. This approach works well if the condition that causes the fault can be trapped and decoded using the analyzer, which is often the hardest part of the debugging process. For applications, this is more difficult because analyzers do not trap application-centric data, but rather individual packets that have to be "reconstructed" to provide application-specific information. Using testing techniques in conjunction with a network analyzer can improve the process by:

1. Verifying that a suspected failing component or node can or cannot perform basic required functions. This can be done simply by running known test cases against the node and determining whether its behavior has changed from previous tests. This may either confirm what is working, thereby eliminating certain areas to investigate, or point to the cause of the problem.

2. Reproducing the problem off-line so it can be isolated, debugged, and corrected.

A major securities firm runs daily tests across its network to verify that the system has not changed over the last 24 hours. These tests are run during off-hours using a client-server testing tool as the load generator. The test scripts replicate application commands and functions that are widely used across the network. Any day-to-day changes measured by the testing are immediately investigated. The firm's objective is to avoid problems by detecting symptoms early and addressing them before a problem arises.

Today's testing tools for the application/presentation layer and client-server applications are not well-suited for problem debugging or execution on the production network. The reasons for this are twofold:

- *On a production network, loading, monitoring, and test feedback must be iterative and automated so that the system can automatically control the impact of the test on the production system.* For example, if a database server is suspected of having a load-related problem, an optimal real-world test would automatically supplement the existing production load with higher loads or lower loads to maintain the load that is suspected of causing failure. It could then be run for several hours or days until the real-world condition that caused the error is reproduced. It would also provide immediate test feedback on transaction completion's or failures. In this way, conditions can be re-created that cause the problem, based on the real-world loads being used as background loading. To duplicate this in a test lab is virtually impossible, which is why it is difficult to re-create problems in the lab.

- *It is difficult to determine which transaction request(s) resulted in error conditions, response time issues, or capacity problems.* Most client-server applications include complex GUI front ends. Often, an individual GUI selection or request results in multiple transaction requests being sent to the database server or to multiple database servers. A problem is easy to detect, but pinpointing the cause is difficult. Today's client-server testing tools do not provide features to assist the tester in isolating individual problem causes, and most do not address network-related problems that can impact the client-server application. These tools can, however, assist in problem debugging on emulated test configurations by following the flow diagram shown in Figure 29.1.

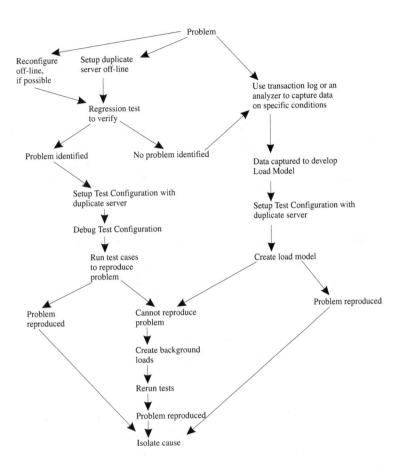

Figure 29.1   Flow diagram for problem debugging using client-server testing tools.

Debugging is simply the application of existing test scripts from reliability, throughput, and functional testing for the reproduction and isolation of problems.

DEBUG TESTING

In response time, throughput, reliability, and functional testing, the test measurements are designed to collect data on how well the unit under test is running. When these same tests are used in debugging, the measurement emphasis switches focus, and the objective becomes to create and trap problems or symptoms that point to an underlying problem. For example, if users report that application response time degrades when certain commands are run in a specific sequence, test scripts can re-create the transaction sequence. Unfortunately, things are usually not that simple. What is probably happening is that some users are experiencing degradation, while other users are performing tasks that, when coupled with the suspected transactions, actually cause the system degradation. By creating test scripts of other user scenarios, testing can try to re-create the combined transaction flow that is causing problems.

Similarly, reliability testing can be used to accelerate the time domain and attempt to re-create a problem in the lab that is seen "every so often" on the production network. For debugging, the time the test runs is not nearly as important as failures or problems trapped along the way. These are often reproductions, perhaps in another form, of the suspected problem. If problems on the network occur often during month-end closing when activity is high, accelerated tests can be run to emulate the higher loads with the intent of re-creating the problems in a shorter timeframe. If a problem can be reproduced on a repetitive basis, it can usually be fixed.

Feature and functional testing can be used to confirm that the product works properly, thereby eliminating possible areas for debugging. Feature and functional tests can also be modified to create forced error conditions that are suspected of causing a problem. This can help determine whether the unit under test correctly handles a particular error condition.

Error handling/recovery testing is an often-overlooked element of functional testing. Many times, it is as important how the system acts when an error condition arises as when a capability functions properly. Errors that are apparently handled effectively often leave lingering "gotchas," which don't cause an immediate problem, but lead to a problem further down the line. If a client, in the process of adding a new record and key to the database, loses contact through a dropped session, the database software is designed to roll back any portion of the in-process transaction. But, if the transaction spans two servers and the first server fails before it notifies the second server, how does the software handle rolling back the second server's partial transaction when the first server recovers? The best way to determine this is to test it by causing the session and server failures, then measuring how well the software recovers.

Test Configurations

All test configurations are emulated and should represent as closely as possible the production network configuration on which the problem exists.

Load Model

The load model and test scripts for debugging can be modeled from the conditions on the production system when the problem occurred, or scripts can be used from other test objectives. The former modeling is the best, but often it is hard to impossible to trap and re-create the conditions just prior to a failure or problem. Data collected at the transport level, where analyzers work, isn't easily converted to individual client-server transactions. If the database software provides a monitoring or logging function for transaction tracking, this is a good source for test script input.

Often, a perceived problem on one segment is caused by conditions in the database subsystem due to load or problems on other attached segments. Therefore, it may be required to capture data from multiple segments to re-create the background traffic that is actually causing the problem. This can be very difficult and time-consuming, which is one reason that it is often easier, more timely, and just as effective to use or modify existing test scripts to attempt to reproduce problems.

Test Execution And Data Collection

Referring to the flow diagram outlined in Figure 29.1, the following provides additional detail on the steps and test execution for problem debugging:

1. For a suspected or detected problem, a transaction log can be used to attempt to trap the specific conditions prior to the problem. If possible, the server can be tested off-line during off-hours to verify its integrity. Existing regression test script(s) can be used for the integrity testing.

2. If a hardware problem is identified through the testing, the unit can be swapped out and debugged later. If the problem identified is a suspected software bug, a duplicate server test configuration is required for debugging.

3. If no problem is detected in item 2, use transaction logs and an analyzer to attempt to trap the error conditions.

4. If production network conditions are not recorded, existing test scripts can be used to attempt to reproduce and isolate the problem. If some information is collected that indicates certain conditions are causing the problem, test scripts can be modified or created to model conditions prior to the problem.

5. If testing cannot reproduce the problem, it may indicate that other factors, such as background traffic on that segment or load on the subsystem from other segments, contribute to the cause of the problem. This would require expanding the test configuration to more accurately model the production system.

6. Once the problem can be reproduced on a repetitive basis, cause isolation and resolution can be achieved.

Part

IV

Testing Tools

INTRODUCTION

The proceeding product listings are not a comprehensive collection of the products available for network testing (monitoring and load generation). Instead, the following product categories are the key ones you should consider when developing your test toolkit. In each category, I have included a few representative products that are being used by companies described in the book. You can use this as a guideline, but remember that new products and product enhancements are being introduced constantly, so be sure to get the latest information before making a selection.

PACKET GENERATORS

Novell's LANalyzer: LANalyzer for Windows is a software analyzer that provides packet and frame generation and monitoring capability. For more information, the company can be reached at 800.638.9273.

Sniffer from Network General: Sniffer provides packet and frame generation and monitoring for most network media. For more information, the company can be reached at 703.448.6606.

Hewlett Packard Analyzers: Hewlett Packard provides a range of network analyzers for LAN and WAN topologies which provide both monitoring and packet generation capability. For more information, the company can be reached at 800.452.4844.

Wandel & Golterman DA-30:   The DA-30 network analyzer provides simultaneous packet generation and capture across most network media. For more information, the company can be reached at 800.346.6332.

PowerBits from Alantec: PowerBits is a dedicated hardware box for packet generation and monitoring that supports Ethernet and FDDI networks. For more information, the company can be reached at 800.ALANTEC.

LANQuest's FrameThrower: FrameThrower is a family of packet, frame, and ATM cell generators that run on standard PCs and support Ethernet, Token Ring, FDDI, and ATM (types OC3SC, DS-3, and TAXI) media types. For more information, the company can be reached at 800.487.7779.

CLIENT-SERVER APPLICATION TESTING TOOLS

Mercury Interactive's "Runner" product series: Mercury provides a family of products that provide automated scripting and testing of network applications for Windows and UNIX.   It also provides extensive GUI testing capabilities. For more information, the company can be reached at 800.TEST.911.

MS-Test from Microsoft: This product runs under Windows and allows scripting and playback of operating system level and application commands. It can be used to test the Windows desktop, applications, and other operating system levels. For more information, the company can be reached at 206.882.8080.

Performix's EMPOWER: EMPOWER includes a family of products for scripting and SQL transaction capture and playback for load testing client-server and simple character based applications. For more information, the company can be reached at 703.448.6606.

AutoTester by AutoTester: Provides automatic test script generation and replay of scripts for DOS, Windows and OS/2 applications.   For more information, the company can be reached at 214.368.1196.

Ziff-Davis' ServerBench and NetBench: These testing tools are primarily for network benchmarking of NetWare, Windows NT, and SCO UNIX, but can be used for other test objectives. They are available at no cost through PC Week and PC Magazine Labs. For more information, the company can be reached at 415.578.7300.

Segue's QA Partner: QA partner and their latest product, Go, support automated application testing on Windows, NT, and UNIX platforms. For more information, the company can be reached at 617.969.3771.

MONITORING SOFTWARE

Saber's Server and LAN Workstation Managers: This family of products provides information for baselining network and server usage. For more information, the company can be reached at 800.338.8754.

Intrak's ServerTrak: This Windows-based monitor for NetWare servers provides server, network, and file statistics for baselining the system. For more information, the company can be reached at 800.695.1900.

CoroNet's Management System (CMS): The CoroNet Management System includes several products that automatically detect and track application layer conversations between clients and servers. This provides information which is useful in baselining the network from an application perspective. CoroNet was recently acquired by CompuWare and the product has been renamed EcoNet. For more information, the company can be reached at 415.960.3255.

Intel's LANDesk: LANDesk provides analyzer and monitoring facilities, including the ability to monitor client application usage across the network, which is valuable in baselining the network. For more information, the company can be reached at 800.538.3373.

SIMULATION TOOLS

CACI COMNET III: This simulation tool provides an object-oriented approach to building a network model. It allows topology, workload, and protocols to be modeled using input from various analyzers and network management systems. For more information, the company can be reached at 619.457.9681.

Systems & Networks BONeS: BONeS includes a library of network devices, protocols, and traffic modes that can be used in developing your specific network topology for both LAN and WAN configurations. For more information, the company can be reached at 800.9-BONES-3.

FILE I/O

Novell's Perform3: This test utility is useful for testing network layers and file servers. It is available free-of-charge through Novell bulletin boards.

Glossary

A

Accelerated loading: Form of load model that attempts to compress into a few hours the type and levels of loads a system may experience over many months in the field.

Acceptance testing: A "shakedown" of the system prior to deploying it into production. It is an excellent method of ensuring that the new system will be stable and provide acceptable performance in its initial release.

Actual user loading: On the test network each node generates the load of one user, and the test network must contain the same number of nodes as the production network it is modeling.

Aggregate sustained throughput for the device: This is the rate at which all packets sent on *all* source segments are forwarded to *all* destination segments.

Aggregate throughput for the device: This is the maximum packet forwarding rate from *all* source to *all* destination segments without regard to the number of dropped packets.

Application layer: For testing purposes, this includes the applications, GUI interfaces, and database software on the network.

Application/presentation layers: These include the software layers above the NOS, namely, the applications, client-server software, graphical user interfaces (GUI), and multitasking workstation operating systems.

Application response time: This test measures how long it takes an application to complete a series of tasks, and best represents the user's perception of the network system (application, NOS, and network components).

B

Background load: Additional load placed on key test network components to more accurately emulate the load they experience on the production network.

Baseline: Characterization of the production network as input for developing a load model. Networks can be baselined for packet, file, and transaction activity.

Baseline reliability: Tests run on a network platform or internetwork test configuration that confirm the hardware and software is sufficiently stable for application layer testing.

Bottleneck identification: Identifies which network components are limiting response time and throughput.

Bursty traffic pattern: A flow of packets or I/O requests whose type and rate vary over time during the test duration. This represents the typical clustering of data transmissions across a network.

C

Capacity planning: This test measures how much excess capacity exists on the network. It determines at what point network resources need to be increased to support additional demand before significant degradation in performance or throughput occurs.

Client-server testing tool: Software designed to test the application GUI and to generate transaction loads to exercise the database server. These tools are also called automated software quality (ASQ) and GUI automated development tools.

Clog: Condition in which a device does not forward packets, frames, or cells between network segments.

Configuration sizing: Used to size network components to achieve improved performance, or meet specific response time or throughput requirements.

Control group: Test scripts run on production network workstations to measure the degradation in production network throughput during real-world testing of new network applications.

Cumulative errors: Errors caused by repeating an operation multiple times. Usually detected in reliability testing.

D

Daily activity log: Provides a centralized, chronological history of the test project.

Data interpretation: Analyzing raw test measurements to determine subsequent load points, reproducibility of test data, and to develop conclusions and actions to be taken.

Deployment (Phase III): The effort of installing new hardware, software, and services. This phase should also include an acceptance test, which is a formal procedure for verifying that the system is ready for production use.

Development (Phase II): The time during which an application or other network service is coded, constructed, and tested.

Downtime: Term used to describe the time when a system or network is not operational because of a failure that interrupts its operation.

E

Emulation: "To imitate with effort to equal or surpass." The objective in emulation is to get as close as possible to real-world test results, while achieving the benefits of emulation that make the testing practical. Both the test configuration and the network load can be emulated.

Equivalent user loading: On the test network each node generates the load of more than one actual user. The test network usually contains less nodes than the production network it is emulating.

Evolution (Phase V): This phase represents network change and expansion or, more accurately, the realization that modification and expansion is required.

F

Fairness of throughput across segments: This determines how fairly the subsystem handles throughput across all ports.

Feature testing: This testing verifies individual commands and capabilities of the application. It is usually conducted with minimal to light loads. It is focused on the user interface and application operations or transactions invoked by the user. Feature testing is typically done by the developer on his or her workbench and in QA on a small network configuration.

Functional testing: Functional testing is network-oriented. It verifies that the application's multiuser characteristics and background functions work correctly under heavy loads. It focuses on the network and file system or database server interaction when multiple users are running the application. Functional testing requires a network configuration and loads that closely model the production environment.

L

Legacy systems: Term used to describes the large installed base of mainframes and minicomputers.

Life cycle of a network: The five phases of planning and design, development, deployment, production, and evolution that can be used to describe the current state of a network installation and applications.

Load distribution: Determines whether the loads will be emulated (equivalent user load or accelerated load) or real-world (actual user load). It defines the amount of each type of load required for the test.

Load generator: The software that creates the network load. This can be an application, test utility, hardware, or a batch file.

Load generator script, or script for short: The keyboard macro file, parameters, or commands that are input to the load generator and describe the output to be generated.

Load model: Defines how much and what types of load need to be created to achieve the test objective.

Load versus response time curve: Method of representing the performance of an application by graphing load on the horizontal axis and response time on the vertical axis.

Load versus throughput curve: Method of representing the performance of the network by graphing load on the horizontal axis and throughput on the vertical axis.

M

Margin of error: The difference in test measurements between identical test runs on the same hardware and software configuration. If the difference is less than or equal to 4 percent, the test results are considered to be reproducible.

Maximum sustained throughput per segment: This is the rate at which *all* packets sent on the source segment are forwarded to the destination segment.

Maximum throughput across the internetwork: This measures the point-to-point (requester-to-responder) throughput across the internetwork.

Maximum throughput per segment: This is the maximum packet forwarding rate from the source to destination segment without regard to the number of dropped packets.

N

Network infrastructure: The network hardware, transport layer protocols, network operating system (NOS), media, communication links, and nodes, such as routers, switches, and hubs.

Network management: The effort and tools used to monitor and troubleshoot network systems.

Network platform: For testing purposes, includes the NOS, file server, and workstations on the network.

Network test management (NTM): NTM defines the testing process by which network, product, and application quality is verified before deployment, measured in production, and maintained during upgrades.

Network traffic pattern: The combination of packet types, sizes, and rates that represent the activity across the network.

O

Operational reliability: Tests conducted using typical case production network loads to verify that the network is stable and reliable under normal loading.

P

Packet generator: Category of software or hardware testing tools that generate packets, frames, or cells (ATM) for loading the network.

Packet stream: Sequence of individual packet formats combined to create a specific traffic pattern for testing network infrastructure subsystems.

Planning and design (Phase I): Activities such as defining requirement specifications, evaluating new products, designing the network topology, and simulation studies are included in this phase.

Problem isolation: Tests for and analyzes failures to isolate which component is causing the problem.

Problem resolution log: This log contains problem reports that document each problem and resolution encountered during the test project. At the end of the project, the log should be archived with other logs to create a database of problems and resolutions for referencing in other test projects and by network support.

Product evaluation: Includes comparing products, technologies, and subsystem configurations for performance, functionality, reliability, and ease of use.

Production (Phase IV):   This is when the benefits of the network and its services are realized by the users. This is the network phase around which most network management and troubleshooting tools are oriented.

R

Real-world testing: Real-world testing refers either to using the production network or an exact replica; or to a load model that includes user typing and think time, or both.

Reduce test data: The process by which basic test measurements are correlated, consolidated, and analyzed to provide results and conclusions.

Regression testing: Compares the performance, reliability, and functionality of a new release of hardware or software to the current release.

Reliability testing: Used to measure the stability of network components, internetworks, and applications under heavy loads.

Reproducible results: Identical test runs on the same hardware and software configuration culminate in reproducible results when the measurements differ by less than the test margin of error, usually 4 percent.

Requester: File I/O load generator that creates load for internetwork testing; typically an application or test utility running on a workstation.

Requirements specification: Document that describes the needs and features of a product or service.

Responder: Node that replies to requester I/O for internetwork testing; typically a file server.

Rip: Condition in which a device incorrectly forwards all packets, frames, or cells between network segments. Generally associated with a filtering problem wherein the process forwards packets or frames that should be filtered.

Runt packets: Ethernet packets that are smaller than the minimum packet size allowed, but have a valid CRC value. These are less than 64-bytes in length.

S

Scripting: Creating a sequence of application commands that are executed to create network loads for application/presentation layer testing.

Simulation: Simulation attempts to replicate production network performance through computer-aided modeling

Slowdown: Term used to describe the degradation in response time or throughput of a system. It can be caused be increasing loads or system problems.

Statistical errors: Errors caused by two or more random operations occurring in a manner that result in a fault. Usually detected in reliability testing.

Stressed reliability: Tests conducted using worse case or maximum loads to verify that the network is stable and reliable under peak load conditions.

T

Test configuration: This defines the hardware, media, and topology on which tests will be conducted. Testing can be conducted in one of three places: on a test network, on a production network at off-hours, or on a production network during normal hours.

Test configuration log: This log contains information covering the hardware and software configuration of the test environment in either hard copy or electronic form. The test configuration log documents: test bed equipment, software and applications, and configuration information.

Test data: Hard copy or electronic file of all test data, data reduction programs, spreadsheets, and graphs pertaining to measurements collected during the test project.

Test lab: Dedicated physical location including network hardware and software used for testing.

Test methodology: Defines the process and procedures for testing.

Test objective: Defines the type of test and test measurements.

Test philosophy: Establishes what should be tested and why.

Test plan: Blueprint for the test project. Contains project test objectives; identifies personnel and other resources; details test configuration, load model, and load points; identifies milestones and task time line; and outlines deliverables (reports, etc.).

Test report: The basic deliverable from the test project. Includes the test objective, consolidated test data, conclusions, test configuration, and other pertinent information.

Test script: Defines the implementation details for the load model. The test script lists which load generator and script will be run on each node during the test.

Throughput testing: Measures kilobytes per second (KBps) or packets per second (PPS) of data transferred. This test is used to measure servers, disk subsystems, adapter/driver combinations, bridges, routers, hubs, switches, and communication links.

Timing errors: Errors caused by two or more time-dependent operations that occur out of sequence or without the proper delay. Usually detected in reliability testing.

Typical case load: The combination of packet sizes and rate that produce a load that represents the general level of activity the subsystem under test will experience on the production network.

V

Variance across test configuration: This measures how test results change as configuration parameters are changed, while the test configuration hardware and software are held constant.

W

Worse case load: The combination of packet sizes and rate that produce the heaviest load the subsystem under test will experience on the production network.

 # Bibliography

Corrigan, Peter and Mark Gurny. *Oracle Performance Tuning,* O'Reilly and Associates, Inc.: 1994.

Schnaidt, Patricia. *Enterprise Wide Networking,* SAMS Professional Reference Series: Indianapolis, IN, 1992.

Stallings, William. *SNMP, SNMP v2 and CMIP. The Practical Guide to Network Management Standards*, Addison-Wesley Publishing Co: Reading, MA, 1993.

Terplan, Kornel. *Benchmarking for Effective Network Management,* McGraw Hill Series on Computer Communication: 1995.

Terplan, Kornel. *Communication Network Management*, Prentice-Hall: Englewood Cliffs, NJ, 1992.

Index

A

acceptance test, 71-72, 79, 100, 315
    client-server, 509-520
    criteria, 83-84
    failure of, 86-87
    final, 85
    internetwork, 315-324
    measurable terms, 84
    milestone, 85
    nonperformance, 86

application (subsystem), 103

application development tool, 36, 40

application feature/functional test, 68-69

application layers, 345

application load modeling:
    application commands, 371
    client-server, 372
    equivalent-user load, 364

    key features, 361
    key functions, 361
    mouse point-and-click sequences, 371
    network centric, 361
    QA test script, 362
    real-world, 361
    workstation/GUI centric, 362

application/presentation layers, 63, 345

application response time test, 66-67, 72, 78

B

baseline, 191-201, 269
    network, 85

bottleneck, 76, 94
    identification, 76-78
    isolation, 99

C

capacity, 78, 443
>   planning, 75-76, 443-452

client-server testing, 359, 372

clog, 250

communication:
>   gateway, 28
>   server, 28

configuration sizing, 72-73, 429-442

critical internetwork nodes, 105

D

data:
>   collection, 124
>   forecasting, 128
>   intermediate verification, 128
>   interpretation, 126
>   presentation, 129
>   reduction, 127

database software, 34

debugging, 335-338, 535

debug testing, 537-540

downtime, 14-15, 19

E

electronic journal, 107-108

emulation, 135-136

F

fatal error, 84

file I/O load generation:
>   C or BASIC program, 233, 383
>   DOS batch file, 227, 380
>   Perform3, 230, 382
>   ZD server benchmarks, 231, 383

file server, 101

forecasting, 128

functionality testing, 473-484

G

GUI testing, 31

W